The Corpus Christi Play
of the English Middle Ages

The Corpus Christi Play

OF THE ENGLISH MIDDLE AGES

an edition
with introduction and notes by
R. T. DAVIES

Reginald

ROWMAN AND LITTLEFIELD
Totowa, New Jersey

First published in the United States 1972
by Rowman and Littlefield, Totowa, New Jersey

ISBN 0-87471-124-X

Printed in Great Britain by
Butler & Tanner Ltd Frome

For Kenneth and Miriam Allott

CONTENTS

PREFACE

It would have been impossible for me to make this book without the expert work of those scholars some of whose achievements are included in the list beginning on page 441. My debt to them is immeasurable. I have made some special acknowledgements on page 68, and in addition I should like to express my gratitude for their generous and ready help to Dr. W. O'Sullivan, Keeper of Manuscripts at Trinity College, Dublin, Dr. H. C. Schulz, Curator of Manuscripts at the Huntington Library, California, and to Miss Jean F. Preston, the Assistant Curator there. Professor S. J. Kahrl, Director of the Center for Medieval and Renaissance Studies at Ohio State, and Professor N. Davis, of Merton College, Oxford, have been most readily informative and encouraging. Professor Davis was also constructively critical and my warm gratitude to him increases with each book I tackle. I am also grateful to a number of my colleagues in the University of Liverpool with whom I have discussed this book in general or in detail, particularly Dr. R. A. Markus and Dr. J. Margetts. I am specially indebted to four of them whose generous gift of time and learning has immensely improved my work. They are Miss Joyce Bazire, who helped with my glosses and my modernization of the spelling, Mr. J. C. B. Foster, who put right my countless abuses of the Latin, and Dr. A. D. Mills and Mr. B. F. Nellist whose advice I sought at many stages in the planning of the book and who read and criticized most of it in its making. The staff of the Library of the University of Liverpool have been invariably helpful and I wish to thank in particular Mr. T. S. Broadhurst, Mr. A. N. Ricketts, Miss Anne M. Fishburn and Miss J. Bullen. Miss

11

Margaret Burton, Mrs. M. Thompson, and Mrs. P. Deane, secretaries in our Department of English, have disentangled my manuscript, typed it and re-typed. My publishers have been, as always, patient, efficient, helpful and enthusiastic for things medieval.

To the following bodies I am indebted for their permission to print from manuscripts in their keeping: the Board of Trinity College, Dublin, the Trustees of the British Museum, and the authorities of the Henry E. Huntington Library and of the Library of Yale University. I am also grateful for permission to quote short passages as follows: to Edward Arnold (Publishers) Ltd. and V. A. Kolve, from *The play called Corpus Christi*; to the University of Chicago Press and J. B. Severs, from *Modern philology*; to the University of Toronto Press and F. M. Salter, from *Mediaeval drama in Chester*; to the Johns Hopkins Press and M. J. Benkovitz, from *Modern language notes*; to the Clarendon Press and E. K. Chambers, from *The mediaeval stage*.

I should like, finally, to thank Mr. P. F. McDonald of the University of Salford whose excellent work on the Chester Corpus Christi play for the M.A. degree of the University of Liverpool in 1967 focussed and helped to reorientate my thinking.

ABBREVIATIONS

With regard to abbreviations, n. 1 or n. 10 in the introduction and glosses, for example, when not associated with any book or article, means 'see note 1' or 'see note 10' at the back of this book, n(n). = note(s), p(p). = page(s), l(l). = line(s), pl. = plate, fol. = folio, MS = the base manuscript from which the text is derived, ms(s) other manuscript(s), P.B. = English Prayer-book, and A.V. = Authorized version of the Bible. Abbreviations of the books of the Bible should be obvious. Details of books and articles referred to will be found in the alphabetical list beginning on page 441: thus, a reference to 'Chambers, ii, 268' can be expanded by turning to page 441 and looking for 'Chambers' when the reference will be found to be to E. K. Chambers, *The mediaeval stage*, volume two, page 268; in the same way, a reference to 'Chambers, *Eng. lit. at close middle ages*, 61' = E. K. Chambers, 'Medieval drama' in *English literature at the close of the middle ages*, page 61; '*Cornish drama*' = *The ancient Cornish drama*, ed. and trans. E. Norris, etc.

INTRODUCTION

This book has two main parts. In the first there is the text of
one Corpus Christi play from which I have omitted only the
episodes of the Baptism and Temptation of Christ, the
episode of Mary's Assumption, and those episodes involving
Mary which are not found in the other cycles. In this part,
then, will be found, to all intents and purposes, a cycle that
can be enjoyed as a whole and that is more or less repre-
sentative of all those we know that flourished in England in
the two centuries or so from Chaucer's time to Shakespeare's.
(A table on page 446 compares the episodes of all these
cycles up to the Passion.) In Part Two there are the texts of
all the extant versions of one episode found in all the known
cycles, that of Abraham and Isaac. In this part, then, there
can be enjoyed a sample of the diversity of the religious
drama. Section 6 of this introduction is particularly concerned with the cycle in Part One, and Section 7 with the
plays in Part Two. Further examples of the religious drama
can conveniently be read in Professor A. C. Cawley's
excellent *Everyman and medieval miracle plays* in Everyman's
Library, while the version of *The York cycle of mystery plays*
by Canon J. S. Purvis (S.P.C.K.: London, 1957) will enable
the reader to appreciate some of the respects in which the
cycle in Part One of this book differs from others.

I

It was for mixed reasons that the audience came to see a
religious play at Beverley one summer's day in the thirteenth
century. The performance was a representation of the
Resurrection of the Lord outside the church as was the

custom, and before a great crowd. Finding it difficult to see, because they were short or squashed together, some went into the church to pray or look at pictures or 'through some sort of recreation and solace' escape boredom. Some had come to see the play for pleasure, some out of curiosity, and some with the holy intention of stirring up their devotion. The recorder of these varied motives was the writer of the life of St. John of Beverley,[1] whose working of a miracle on this occasion he then went on to describe.

But it is for a single-minded purpose that religious plays were referred to in a story of 1526.[2] In a village in Warwickshire, so the story goes, 'there was a parish priest, and though he were no great clerk nor graduate of the university, yet he' taught his parishioners every Sunday the articles of the Creed. If you do not believe them, he used to say, because you doubt my authority and want a surer one, go to Coventry 'and there you shall see them all played in Corpus Christi Play'. That, he implied, should convince anyone, for there you will see played out before your very eyes the facts of our Faith.

But there were churchmen who disagreed fundamentally with this simple preacher and argued that, on the contrary, going to see religious plays had the opposite effect. One[3] such in Chaucer's time began to make his case by listing what might appear to be the excellent arguments in favour of the playing of 'miracles' (that is, the dramatic representation of 'the marvellous works of God' in English): they are done in worship of God, they convert men and move their hearts, they reach those who can be reached only by 'play and game', men must have recreation, and better this than any other, and, finally, since pictorial images are acceptable, why not dramatic? Then he replied: first, the purpose of those who act is not to worship God but 'more to be seen of the world

---

1 Extract quoted Young, ii, 539–40.
2 *A hundred merry tales*, ed. P. M. Zall (Lincoln (U.S.A.), 1963), 115–16.
3 *Reliquiae antiquae*, ed. T. Wright and J. O. Halliwell (London, 1845), ii, 42 ff.

and to please the world than be seen of God or please him' (and can we doubt that such was one of the motives of some whose disposition drew them into acting?). Secondly, the plays take the name of God in vain so that they are contrary to God's command and pervert rather than convert. Thirdly, hearts are stirred at the plays by the moving story rather than by sorrow for sin: and if men are not reached by the word of God and the sacraments they will not be reached by plays. True recreation is good, but dramatic recreation is worldly and false; and, finally, pictures have religious value when they tell the plain truth, like a book, but plays are not so much books for the ignorant as 'to delight men bodily'.

The manifold argument is important because it shows that some men thought strenuously and percipiently about religious drama in the early days of the Corpus Christi play. And occasionally, throughout the middle ages, sometimes in this European country, sometimes in that, local Church authorities made distinctions between playing that was permitted and playing that was not.[1] In general, what was approved was edifying drama inside the church, performed with propriety, free from coarseness, and attended reverently, whereas what was condemned were the folk rites the people played, secular entertainers, unseemly clergy and disorderly spectators.

Of edifying drama inside the church, that about which most is known is what may be called liturgical drama.[2] From at least as early as the tenth century and—though they were fully developed by the time the plays in this book began—continuing in some instances, though perhaps in a modified form, throughout the period of the Corpus Christi drama, some churches of Western Europe included in their annual observance of particular festivals relatively short and appropriate plays. For example, at Christmas, keyed into one of

[1] Young, ii, 410–21; Craig, 89–90; Owst, 480–5.
[2] Young and Hardison: the latter has radically controverted the arguments of the former about the growth of liturgical drama.

the services of that Feast, probably Matins, might be a play of the Shepherds and their visit to the Holy Manger, or, at the Epiphany, a play of the Magi or the Three Kings. The play of the Resurrection at Easter was the most important of all these dramas but Passion plays were rare and none survives from before the thirteenth century. Liturgical plays were generally in Latin, that is in the language of the liturgy and the clergy. In prose or in verse, they were sung or chanted by solo voices and the choir, sometimes by a larger congregation, and, being stylized like the liturgy itself, they were more like an opera than a play. The actors were usually the clergy of almost any rank but the highest, young or old, except that in monasteries other members might act, and, in convents of women, the nuns. They were dressed for the most part in the ordinary vestments of church services, albs, for example, amices and copes, and helped by a few symbolic or realistic objects such as a flask to represent anointing balm, a crown for a king or a star in the form of clustered candles.[1]

Liturgical plays probably belonged to the religious houses and the greater churches, but, in the two centuries or so during which the plays in this book were performed, medieval towns and villages knew quite a wealth of other religious drama.[2] Our detailed knowledge is slight though references, in church account-books, for example, are many. There were plays inside church and in the market-place, plays organized by church wardens and parish clergy, by the Corporations of towns or by religious guilds, and even some performed, in later years, by professional companies. There were plays about Noah, for example, as at Hull in the fifteenth and earlier part of the sixteenth century, or the Three Kings, as at Shrewsbury in 1518, or the Harrowing of Hell with which King Henry VII was entertained in 1486 by the

---

[1] Young, 400–3; Marshall.

[2] Harbage; Chambers, ii, App. W and 109–23, 128–35; Craig, 142–4, esp. 144, n. 1, 152; Loomis; *Digby plays; Non-cycle plays*; Wilson, 212 ff.

boys of two abbeys as he dined at Winchester. The Brome and Dublin plays of Abraham and Isaac may be examples of such isolated works. There were also groups of plays such as a sequence from the late fifteenth century for performance on St. Anne's day in honour of 'Our Lady and St. Anne', her mother, of which there survives one part comprising a combination of a Massacre of the Innocents with a Purification and Presentation. From this extant part we learn that, on the same day in the previous year, this company, whoever they were, had acted a Shepherds and a Three Kings and promised, next year, a Christ and the Doctors. Meanwhile, to conclude their present proceedings, they asked the minstrels, 'Before our departing give us a dance'.

What the plays were like that were acted inside the great churches of England while the Corpus Christi plays were flourishing outside, we do not know, for the little evidence we have, for example, in the records of Lincoln cathedral,[1] does not tell us how much they were like the liturgical drama described above, or something more ambitious, whether they were in Latin or the vernacular. Details of their performance are infrequent, but, when given, mention choir or nave as the place and the clergy as performers. It is possible that examples of such plays are to be found in what are known as the Shrewsbury Fragments (page 51 below) or a mid-fifteenth-century play of Christ's Burial and Resurrection which was performed in English on Good Friday and Easter Day.[2] At Lincoln cathedral there was, in the fourteenth century, a play of the Three Kings, for the Feast of the Epiphany, one of St. Thomas, presumably about his incredulity and, on the one occasion when it is dated, done on Easter Monday, and a play of the Resurrection, which could, conceivably, be the same play. From 1390 until at least 1465 and perhaps well into the sixteenth century there was an Annunciation done on Christmas mornings, and, from the

---

[1] V. Shull, *Pub. Mdn. Lang. Ass.*, lii (1937), 946–66; Loomis; Craig 268–9.
[2] *Digby plays*, 169 ff.

later fifteenth century, an Assumption which, as we shall see on page 44, must, from 1483 at least, have been in English.

'A great play from the beginning of the world . . . that lasted seven days continually' and that showed 'how God created Heaven and earth out of nothing and how he created Adam and so on to the Day of Judgement' was recorded in 1409 and 1411 at Skinners' Well or Clerkenwell in London.[1] As early as 1300 the Abbess of Clerkenwell had had reason to complain to the king of damage done to her fields and crops by crowds attending the miracles and wrestling bouts, but these few records of this 'great play' are perhaps the most tantalizing of all in a field with which time has anyway dealt most unkindly: there are no extant texts and only these few words describing its subject. It seems to have been attached to no special feast, and is never called a Corpus Christi play. But such descriptions as we have of it could readily be applied to the cycle of plays in Part One of this book, which could well have taken seven days to perform 'continually'. A play in Cornish, however, known from the middle of the fourteenth century and still extant,[2] though it covers much the same range of subject matter as the Corpus Christi play, is in three parts for performance on three days. But it has no Nativity episodes at all, and it ends with the Ascension. Since, in these respects, it resembles rather the Passion plays of the Continent, H. Craig has suggested that it may have derived from that other Celtic area, Brittany.

On a lesser scale, there were Saints plays, especially about St. George. The earliest that is mentioned, however, is about St. Katherine:[3] it is of the early twelfth century. Another kind of play, the Morality,[4] enjoyed particular popularity in the fifteenth century: in the *Castle of Perseverance* and *Everyman*, for example, good and evil powers

---

[1] Chambers, ii, 380–2; W. O. Hassall, *Mdn. lang. rev.* xxxiii (1938), 564–7, xxxiv (1939), 79.

[2] *Cornish drama;* Craig, 73.   [3] Craig, 89.

[4] *Macro plays; Everyman; Non-cycle plays.*

battle allegorically for the soul of man. Both plays survive and have been produced with conspicuous success. Like the Moralities, in all probability, and about the Seven Deadly Sins, were the Pater Noster plays recorded throughout our period in Beverley, York and Lincoln,[1] while Creed plays,[2] one of which was acted in York every ten years from 1446 in the Common Hall, probably taught the Apostles' Creed through the representation in turn of the apostles and prophets who, it was believed, were responsible for each clause.

In the more expressly secular field,[3] impersonation and imitation, mime and dialogue must have been as common as in modern shows, so much evidence is there of professional entertainers and their troupes. Among secular plays there were some probably to be understood as dramatizations of themes from the two genres of romance and fabliau. At Chester and Lincoln, in the fifteenth and early sixteenth centuries, the play of *King Robert of Sicily* was a likely example of the first, while the texts that survive of *Interludium de Clerico et Puella*, from the late thirteenth century, and of what goes by the name of 'Dux Moraud', from the first half of the fifteenth century, are likely examples of the second.[4] What survives of this latter play of incest and murder is the part for the character of that name.

In the streets[5] of medieval towns formal pageantry abounded. Tableaux and spectacles, both processional and stationary, celebrated both secular and religious occasions, the coming of the King, or, at Corpus Christi, the passage of the Sacred Host.

In so far as folk lore and tale, folk dance and rite were a major component of medieval culture, they, too, must have

---

[1] Chambers, ii, 341 (Beverley), 403 f. (York), 378 (Lincoln).
[2] cf. Fairford church (p. 30 below): stained glass windows opposite each other in north and south aisles represent prophets, on one side, and apostles, on the other, with clauses of creed.   [3] Chambers, i, chap. iv.
[4] Chambers, ii, 324–6; *Non-cycle plays*; Chambers, *Eng. lit. at close middle ages*, 65.
[5] Chambers, ii, 166–76; Wickham.

their place in this brief account of the diversity of medieval 'drama'.[1] But we must bear in mind how much their importance must have varied with the strength, locally and personally, of such other components, for example, as Christian learning and piety, courtly sophistication, or that increasing individualism, related to both of these, that separates each man from the group. It is disputed whether there existed in the middle ages a folk play of the mummers' kind such as is found in Thomas Hardy's *Return of the Native*, set in Wessex in the nineteenth century, and the argument for it turns chiefly on extrapolation from the abundant evidence of later times, consistent as it would be with a few indications in the religious drama itself. It is a speculation that the underlying mythical dynamic in such folk drama, of death and rebirth, of conflict and suffering issuing in a satisfying resolution, contributed to the emotional depth and significance of the religious drama; but that very mythical pattern is precisely that of Christian belief, so that it is quite impossible to infer simply from its presence in medieval literature the influence and existence of pagan folk cults.

One kind of drama that can, to all intents and purposes, be excluded, until early Tudor times, from a description of the diversity found in medieval England is that of ancient Greece and Rome and imitations of it.[2] Classical drama was largely unknown and, as drama, dead. Knowledge of Terence was exceptional and through his school use as a rhetorical and moral text book. Comedy and tragedy were not conceived of as dramatic but as narrative forms, as is clear from their use in Chaucer and Dante,[3] and, so far as I know, these

---

[1] Chambers, i, chaps. vi-viii; ii, 276–9; Mill, 10, 14–16; Chambers, *Eng. folk-play*; Brown, 'Folk-lore elements'; R. C. Cosbey, *Speculum*, xx (1945), 310–17.

[2] Chambers, ii, 206–15; Frank, 5–16. There is no reason to believe that the example of the extraordinary Saxon nun of 10 c., Hrotsvitha, who wrote six prose plays, claiming Terence as her model, was known in England. There is a likeness between the bragging soldiers at the tomb (p. 323 below) and the *milites gloriosi* (cf. Frank, 27).

[3] *Prol. Monk's tale; La divina commedia.*

words were never applied in England to any of the plays we have been considering.

2

In this diverse range of drama, most important was what were called the play or plays of Corpus Christi. From the variety of evidence it is more or less clear that this particular kind of drama was performed in Beverley, Chester, Coventry, Ipswich, Kendal, Lincoln, Newcastle-on-Tyne, Norwich, Wakefield, Worcester, York and probably Canterbury, Lancaster, Louth and Preston, and in one or two Scottish towns, though here the evidence is less conclusive.[1] There have survived, relatively complete, the texts of four cycles of Corpus Christi plays and of one or two of the component plays from several others.

They were known as Corpus Christi plays, in the first instance, because of their association with that ecclesiastical Feast.[2] Its annual celebration on the second Thursday after Pentecost, in the high summer season of later May or the first three weeks of June, was extended to the whole Church by the Pope in 1264 and confirmed in 1311. It was declared a principal Feast of Canterbury in 1317 and in that same year the Pope ordered that, on this day, the Blessed Sacrament should be borne through the streets in procession. It was left to local devotion to invent what was then done, but it is difficult to believe that plays were ever performed as part of the procession. To say the least, this would have entailed the halting of the Host which, for any length of time, would have been dishonourable and precarious. In Dublin in the later fifteenth and sixteenth centuries, as in some other places in these islands,[3] there were in the procession what are most likely to have been tableaux or, perhaps, dumb-shows, of episodes from sacred history. In Dublin there were

---

[1] Chambers, ii, App. W; Mill.   [2] Craig, 127 ff.
[3] Chambers, ii, App. W: Bungay, Newcastle (?), Hereford.

also represented in the procession such famous men and events from more secular history as King Arthur and the Nine Worthies. We do not know whether the drama of other towns grew out of such processional set pieces, as it seems to have done, by the end of the fifteenth century, in Barcelona and Valencia.[1] There is some evidence that in some places plays were performed separately on the same day as their silent actors were drawn along in the procession on their wagons. In the state of the evidence, it is just as likely that such dumb representations grew from plays as plays from them. In York, procession and plays seem to have become rivals, for a friar called William Melton[2] complained that the plays diverted popular attention from the services of the day and from the procession, and sought to have the former acted on another day. But it would appear that, in the outcome, it was the plays that won, for in 1426 it was the procession that was displaced.

The fact that so much of the celebrations of Corpus Christi day were out of doors may have been significant, for Corpus Christi drama seems to have been essentially an out-of-doors affair. Perhaps it was a response to the potentialities thus afforded in terms of space, elaborateness and public occasion.

The purpose of the Feast and of the services of the day may also have been both stimulating and formative. They were to celebrate the sacrament of the Lord's Supper, which commemorates the redeeming Passion of the Lord, and it was officially explained[3] in 1264 that a separate feast, more capable of appropriate observance, was now instituted for this purpose because Maundy Thursday, the day of the institution of the Last Supper, was, in the crowded business of Holy Week, too occupied with other important matters. Now it is clear from sermons and homiletic literature which have the Corpus Christi Feast as their subject, that, inasmuch

[1] Shergold, chaps. iii and iv.
[2] Chambers, ii, 400–1.   [3] Kolve, 44–9.

as Jesus was believed to be really present in the Sacrament, it was the miraculous power of the Holy Eucharist, or, more specifically, of the consecrated Host, that engaged most devotional attention. This was why the Host was carried in procession on this day. Thus, among the wide range of medieval plays, it might rather have been one such as that known as the Croxton play[1] of the Sacrament which became the natural drama of Corpus Christi, because it enacted miracles worked by the Host.

But it did not, and we must look elsewhere for clues to any deeper relationship between the nature and the name of Corpus Christi plays. One fact of outstanding importance is that the name is frequently applied to an entire cycle: the cycle is conceived of as a whole. Thus in 1476 at York there is official reference to 'Corpus Christi play', comprising a number of 'plays' and 'pageants', and in 1500 at Canterbury, likewise, to 'a play called Corpus Christi play . . . maintained and played at the costs of the Crafts and Mysteries'.[2] If we examine the four known cycles, Chester, York, Towneley and *Ludus Coventriae*, together with the list of plays performed at Beverley, we find that common to them all are the plays shown in the table on page 446 together with the plays of the Passion, Resurrection, Ascension and Doomsday, so that their subject, it is clear, was sacred history from its beginning in eternity to its ending there, too, Creation to Doomsday, the basic and ineluctable facts of human destiny, created, cherished, redeemed and eternally judged by God.

Now V. A. Kolve and O. B. Hardison, in books of quite outstanding importance, have argued that, since this is its subject, the association of the play with the Feast was entirely appropriate, for in the Holy Eucharist there is celebrated man's redemption in Christ which implies the whole of sacred history. Moreover, it is argued, since this is the history of God's faithful people, the association with the Feast is doubly appropriate for they are the Corpus Christi

---

[1] *Non-cycle plays.*   [2] Chambers, ii, 344, 401.

in another sense, that of the Mystical Body of Christ. But the later middle ages have left us very little evidence in specific support of these contentions and neither author quotes much from commentators contemporary with Corpus Christi plays. H. Craig[1] has suggested that the play and the Feast are connected through 'the service of the day', but he does not support his contention with an analysis of the content of the service, particularly of its readings and responses. We cannot, therefore, say to our complete satisfaction why the play with the name of Corpus Christi has this nature.

Cycles comparable in at least some major aspects existed in two or more parts of the Continent,[2] the first cycle having no recorded association with the Feast, the second going by the same name as in England. The first, at Cividale, in north-eastern Italy, is heard of on only two occasions and there are no extant texts. In 1298, at Whitsuntide, clergy enacted before local dignitaries the Passion, Resurrection, Ascension, Pentecost and Christ in Judgement, and, in 1304, added to these at least a Creation of Adam and Eve, an Annunciation and a Nativity. The second, in southern Germany, were Corpus Christi plays (Fronleichnamsspiele) whose content was the entire chronological range of sacred history. Neither these nor the plays of Cividale can be shown to have had any influence in England. To all intents and purposes the full achievement of the religious drama of these islands in the Corpus Christi play is original if not unique.

This achievement may have been, however, the continuation of a process which all authorities agree was apparent in the earliest religious drama throughout Europe and both inside and outside the church. This was the apparently

---

[1] pp. 133–4.

[2] Young, ii, 540–1; Craig, 107–8; Dr. J. Margetts of the University of Liverpool also kindly draws my attention to articles on Fronleichnamsspiele in *Die deutsche Literatur des Mittelalters. Verfasserlexikon.* Ed. W. Stammler. Vol. i (Berlin–Leipzig, 1933), 698–773; vol. v (Berlin, 1955), 239.

natural accumulation of single episodes in groups, such as a Christmas play or an Easter play, or the *Mystère d'Adam*, a twelfth-century play which comprised at least a Fall of Adam and Eve, a Cain and Abel, and a Prophets. One monastery may have followed the example of another, inspired by the talk of a visiting cleric, one town may have learned from another by making a deliberate visit to see how people did it elsewhere, and neither need have had a theory to work on nor have been able to say exactly why each undertook the larger grouping. Perhaps the catalyst provided by the institution of the Feast of Corpus Christi might have proved unnecessary for the ultimate achievement of the plays that took its name. Perhaps small groups of plays already formed constituted nuclei about which bigger works were shaped by artists with a sense of quite another dimension. But we can only speculate: we do not know how the cycles began.

What kind of unity and coherence they have also requires thought. It is a question which faces, in much the same way, the critic of what has been known as Malory's *Morte Darthur*. Here, too, is a large and conglomerative work, called 'the whole book of King Arthur and of his noble knights of the Round Table',[1] but more loosely knit than modern taste might be thought to enjoy. Among the factors responsible for this is the relative disconnection of Malory's major sections. They were derived from separate sources and still seem so separate to some that E. Vinaver, editor of the standard text, believes that they ought to be treated as independent tales. Therefore he refers no longer to the *Morte Darthur*, nor uses the title of the 'whole book' but instead edits what he calls Malory's 'Works'. In something of the same way, individual plays of a Corpus Christi cycle may have an identity and sufficiency of their own, and it is not by any means always made clear through explicit links

---

[1] *The works of Sir Thomas Malory*, ed. E. Vinaver, 2nd. edn. (Oxford, 1967), iii, 1260.

and obvious evolution how much and in what way they cohere. This makes it not at all unlikely that the Brome and Dublin Abraham and Isaac plays, so apparently self-contained, may, at one time, have belonged to a cycle.

The various sources and models used by the authors of these plays do not always help their unity and coherence. How much liturgical drama was an influence is difficult to assess. Although no clear line of development can be seen between liturgical plays and the plays in this book, what is certain is that some form of liturgical drama continued contemporaneously with them, and the fact that, in particular instances, the one derived ultimately from the other becomes clear when some of the characteristic elements of the liturgical 'Quem Quaeritis' play, for example, are observed in the Resurrection plays[1] of the Towneley, York and Chester cycles, and when it is appreciated that these are elements not to be found in any one gospel, nor in a conflation or harmony of them all. A second and major influence on the vernacular drama was due to the appearance in the fourteenth century, at much the same time as that drama was forming, of various works in English which were intended to help laymen to understand their religion, if at second hand by helping clergy to preach and pray better. One of them ordered history in Seven Ages from the Creation to the End; some of them retold bible stories, and especially Christ's life, in a historical sequence, harmonizing the often divergent gospels; some of them were more theological, some more devotional: but the use of *Cursor Mundi*, the *Northern Passion*, the *Mirror of the Blessed Life of Jesus Christ*, the *Stanzaic Life of Christ* as sources of the drama is clear.[2] The apocryphal *Gospel of Nicodemus* could have been known to our authors in English and in Latin and from it came, ultimately, for example, the Harrowing of Hell, while from other apocryphal gospels

---

[1] Towneley, 317–18, ll. 382 ff.; York, 408–9, ll. 235 ff.; Chester, 344, ll. 345 ff.
[2] *Ludus Coventriae*, xliii–l; Craig, 196–8; Prosser, 21, 39–42; Seven Ages in *Cursor Mundi*, see pp. 31–2 below.

came, ultimately, for example, the subject of the Joseph play. It was, however, more immediately from the later *Legenda Aurea* that the drama probably derived much of the Conception of Mary and her Assumption. Various Latin gospel harmonies and exegetical commentaries such as a cleric might know may have contributed at one stage or another to the development of this play or that. And in general, and always to be borne in mind, is that the background of these plays was the general tradition of medieval Christian learning and of the daily services of the Church filled with readings from the Fathers, lives of the saints, legends and lessons from the Scriptures.

Incidental enrichments, then, from this source or that, partial rewriting in the light of a newly interesting authority, limited borrowing from another cycle, the division of one pageant into two because a further company wanted to take part, the combination of two plays into one because a second company could no longer afford to go on, all and more were constantly occurring and constantly modifying the effect of the whole cycle.[1] How much this was ever a matter of concern to anyone involved it would be hard to say. After all, the cycle at Chester took three days to perform which could scarcely fail to affect what sense one had of the whole. And the second part of the Passion play in *Ludus Coventriae* was played a year after the first and with only the briefest summary of what had gone before. Certainly, where there was any sense of unity, much of the evidence suggests it was different from ours. An image used by C. S. Lewis in connection with Malory may be helpful. The Corpus Christi play is like a cathedral from the Gothic age of the plays themselves, in which the choir and the nave, built a century apart, may be strikingly different in style and even, partly, in materials, in which the transept may be obviously far less happily reconstituted after the steeple fell on it than the north aisle

---

[1] Chambers, ii, 145–7, 340, 412; Craig, 163–4; *Coventry plays*, xxiii, xxxv–xxxviii.

of which the window tracery is some of the most elegant, and in which a little scrap of a north-western tower always spoils to every eye the grandeur of the great west front. And yet the building is clearly one building, and, more or less, most of its parts contribute to its splendid look and purpose.

The particular purpose of the Corpus Christi play has already occupied us a little and to it we must now return. Its individual components, Noah, Prophets, the angel of the Annunciation, Jesus on the cross, the three Marys at the tomb, all are used, and countless others besides, in other artefacts of medieval religion, in the decoration of church buildings, in the liturgy, homilies, or devotional poems. It is with a common European tradition of Christian lore that we are concerned: it may vary locally in this or that respect, depending, say, on the teaching of a particular cleric or the availability of a particular text, and it may well be more a matter of memory than of record in writing or glass. It is the selection and organization of these components in the Corpus Christi play that is important. In the stained glass of Fairford Church, made in the fifteenth century in the heyday of these plays, there are many of the same dramatic episodes that portray the Redemption of Man, from the meeting at the Golden Gate of the parents of Mary through to Doomsday, and, with two major exceptions, they are arranged in chronological order. But there is a great deal else in addition which never occurs in the plays, and, moreover, the four Old Testament scenes differ from those with which the plays begin. They have been chosen because they are 'antitypes' of various aspects of the Incarnation: Eve (who is represented alone with the serpent) is the antitype of Mary, who is the second Eve; the burning bush of Moses and the fleece of Gideon represent Mary who bore Jesus but remained a virgin; and the Queen of Sheba visiting Solomon is an antitype of the visit of the Three Kings to the infant King. It so happens that the designer of these windows chose these particular Old Testament episodes for this particular purpose: he could have chosen many others that might have done as well. The writer of a moral treatise on the other hand, having a very different intention, might have chosen Eve as an example of the weakness of women or their danger to men.

Two principles of selection and organization can be observed in the extant Corpus Christi plays. The first is that the arrangement is predominantly chronological, Adam coming before Noah, Pentecost coming after the Resurrection; the second is that the material is relatively comprehensive, not in the sense that everything a Christian ever believed is there, but that the story of man's destiny begins at the beginning and goes on to the end. There is one major exception to this second principle and it is the cycle at Coventry itself.[1] Such evidence as we have of what happened there totally lacks Old Testament episodes. On the other hand it is likely that Coventry had four more plays whose subjects are unknown to us and it would be no bad guess that one of these was a Creation.

These two principles, alone, however, cannot account for the Old Testament selection. Other principles are needed, but nothing entirely adequate has yet been found, and we lack any contemporary comment on the plays that could give us a clue. V. A. Kolve and O. B. Hardison[2] have proposed that this choice was influenced by the concept of the Seven Ages of Man in the form most commonly found, that is the ages beginning in turn with Adam, Noah, Abraham, Moses, David, the return from captivity and Christ. But there are, plainly, in the plays one or two of these ages that are not represented at all; and even if one is concerned only with the five ages of St. Gregory, which exclude those of David and the return from captivity, there is, to the best of my knowledge, only one reference to any scheme of this

---

[1] *Coventry plays*, xvii–xix.
[2] Kolve, 88 ff.; Hardison, 88, n. 6; see p. 28 above, and cf. e.g. Augustine, *Patrologia Latina*, xxxiv, 190–4, Gregory, *ibid*, lxxvi, 1155.

kind in any of the plays and it is at note ten on page 92. It could be, however, that, while the selection persisted traditionally, the original reason for it became insignificant over the years. The same might be said with regard to another theory, which is typological. We have already seen how typology might determine a choice in the stained glass at Fairford, and it may well be that it was a factor at some stage in the selection for these plays of, say, Abel, Noah and Isaac, all of whom prefigured Christ (page 64). A further possibility to which we must give more attention in relation to the Abraham and Isaac plays is that choice and treatment were (if only to a degree) determined by general aesthetic or kindred considerations. For example, that Cain and Abel are the first children of man's first parents makes it natural for their story to follow that of Adam and Eve, while that they enact the first murder in the world makes their story, like the wonder and horror of the Deluge, potentially most enthralling. But on these grounds, of course, other things being equal, many another Old Testament story might also have been chosen. The theory of longest standing is that pattern and content were determined by the particular references of certain services, for example, those of the seventy days before Easter,[1] while one of the latest is that a cycle can be conceived of as 'one vast sermon on repentance': but it is acknowledged[2] that such an interpretation involves a selection from the regular corpus of episodes, so that Abraham and Isaac has scarcely any place at all. As good as any of these and ultimately as inadequate, not least because it does not cover Noah's Flood, is the theory that the choice turned on the medieval belief that all the other Old Testament episodes took place on the same day, namely that also of the Annunciation and the Crucifixion![3]

Further speculation is, however, prompted by the par-

---

[1] e.g. Kolve, 43 f.; Hardison, 284.   [2] Prosser, 17–18, 23–5.
[3] e.g. *South English Legendary*, ed. C. D'Evelyn and A. J. Mill, E.E.T.S. 235 (1956 for 1951), i, pp. 127–8.

ticularly provocative analogue of pictorial narrative which we have already mentioned in relation to stained glass. Representations of episodes from the Christian story in Psalters[1] of the twelfth century or in the Holkham Bible Picture-book, so called, of the fourteenth century, have been convincingly argued to derive from either the liturgical drama or the Corpus Christi play, in so far as what is happening in some of the pictures in the first can only be explained by what happens in the plays, and in so far as the pictures in the second are characteristically like dramatic scenes. Like that of the drama, too, are their chronological sequence and comprehensiveness. But in Holkham there is no Abraham and Isaac episode and no raising of Lazarus, while there are many of the apocryphal Infancy stories and many episodes from Christ's Ministry, neither of which are characteristic of any of the plays we know. It could be that the early date of this manuscript is all-important, for there is no sound evidence that by 1325–30 the Corpus Christi play had yet begun and it may be either that the influence was the other way round, or that both grew in a complex and interacting tradition, the precise rationale of which was not always apparent and in which also the Psalters grew at a much earlier date.

Within such a tradition—or whatever theory is adopted to account for the principal form of the Corpus Christi play— due weight would have to be given to the effects of local circumstances and, particularly, to the personal predilections of the writers. Although we have been looking rather at those elements of form and content which the cycles had in common, there are major differences between them. Thus it has been possible to maintain that the extended modification of Pilate's character in the Towneley cycle, so that he becomes a 'dramatic contrast to the suffering Christ', is the work of a unique artist, though not an entirely original one, and that the *Ludus Coventriae*, in Part One of this book, is

[1] Pächt, 44–52.

distinctively the responsibility of 'one major compiler-reviser, a man of true dramatic genius'.[1]

3

We have seen so far that what is special about the Corpus Christi play is its particular choice of episodes, its particular organization of them, and its magnificent scope. There are further respects in which we may distinguish Corpus Christi plays as an important phenomenon in our cultural history.

First, they flourished for some two hundred years, beginning, in all likelihood, in the time of Chaucer and ending in that of Shakespeare. That they may have begun some fifty years earlier is possible for they are related, at least in name, as we have seen, to the Feast of Corpus Christi, first accepted in England in 1317. There is also a confused tradition of no earlier than the sixteenth century about the origins of the Chester cycle;[2] if it is correct, then that cycle began as early as 1328. The fourteenth century affords us few records of the kind that prove informative later, and so casual and incidental are the first references to Corpus Christi plays in the later part of the fourteenth century that they can scarcely be taken to concern their inauguration. The plays have their first mention at York in 1376 and Beverley in 1377.[3] It so happens, also, that, at both these places, the plays are said to be 'old-established' quite soon afterwards, at Beverley in 1390 and York in 1394, and this might possibly provide a fourth reason for belief in their earlier beginnings. But it is the conclusion of F. M. Salter,[4] in the most thorough-going study of a particular cycle yet made, that the Chester play began about 1375. It is not heard of there again in performance after 1575, nor at York after 1569, nor at Coventry after 1579. In their latter years the plays suffered many

[1] Prosser, 205; Williams, 14–16.
[2] Craig, 168–70; Chambers, ii, 348 ff.
[3] A. Brown, in *Early English and Norse studies* (London, 1963), 1–5; Craig, 130.
[4] p. 45.

vicissitudes not least because of political and religious developments under the Tudors. There were thoughts of a revival in Wakefield in 1576 and in Coventry as late as 1591, but they came to nothing.[1]

However, whether the plays began earlier or later in the fourteenth century, they evince that growing use of English for artistic and religious purposes, which burgeoned in the poetry of Chaucer, Langland and the Gawain poet. Their success may well have been related to this linguistic phenomenon. They began to flourish, also, as English town life grew, at a time when all kinds of townsmen were increasingly organized in various guilds, fraternities and misteries which were as much a mixture, as may appear to the modern eye, of the religious and the secular as the plays themselves. The plays are conspicuously celebrations of civic communities.[2] In most of the towns about which evidence survives, they were the responsibility of the occupations or crafts, the bakers, for example, or the makers of parchment, under the direction of the Corporation. There were local variations, but, in general, each craft provided a play in all the aspects of its production and performance, maintained the wagon, for example, on which the pageant was to be played, together with the costumes and props, and provided the actors and rehearsed them. All this was a most expensive operation. F. M. Salter[3] notes that, at Chester, the total cost to the Smiths of a new wagon and the use of it in 1561 was 38/4$\frac{1}{4}$, 'a goodly sum of money in days when it could buy a man's labour for a full year and a half', and, at Coventry, in 1490, the total cost of the Smiths' pageant was £3.7.5$\frac{1}{2}$d. I know of only two instances when any part of the audience paid to watch.[4] The allocation of plays to particular crafts was often done with an eye to convenience, for

[1] Gardiner and Gwynn.
[2] Chambers, ii, 113 ff.; M. McKisack, *The fourteenth century. Oxf. Hist. Eng. V* (Oxford 1959), 373 ff.; E. F. Jacob, *The fifteenth century. Oxf. Hist. Eng. VI* (Oxford, 1961), 385 ff.
[3] p. 63.   [4] Chambers, ii, 117.

the Shipwrights played Noah at York and Newcastle, the Bakers the Last Supper at Beverley, York and Chester, and at the first and last, the Cooks the Harrowing of Hell.

What evidence there is shows that, sometimes more, sometimes less, the role of the Corporation was to organize the project, to see to the keeping of order, to preserve standards and distribute responsibilities. For example, at York in 1476 the Council ordered auditions:[1] 'in the time of Lent there shall be called before the mayor . . . four of the most cunning, discreet and able players within this city to search, hear and examine all the players and plays and pageants throughout all the artificers belonging to Corpus Christi Play'. To fulfil their responsibilities more readily the Smiths at Coventry in 1453 appointed a pageant-master[2] for twelve years, a Thomas Colclow (or Colchow?) who was a skinner. For an annual salary he was to 'find the players and all that longeth thereto'. Such appointments were also made at York and are well evidenced in France. In the later years the actors were sometimes paid,[3] and paid quite handsomely. This might suggest that then, if not earlier, the best men were chosen for the job whether they belonged to the craft or not. It is possible that such men were professionals. Although there is no evidence of payments to clerics, such a one as Chaucer's Absolon[4] might well have been the kind of born actor who would readily have played Herod on a scaffold high for any company who wanted him. At York[5] there was a special prohibition of playing more than twice in a day which can only mean, in the circumstances, that there were some actors so good or so willing that they were prepared to take three parts or more.

It is not known whether men, boys or women customarily played the female parts. In Chester, certainly, the 'worshipful wives' appropriately played the Assumption (and one

---

[1] *Coventry plays*, 72 ff.; Craig 203–4.
[2] Craig 145–6; Frank, 170; *Coventry plays*, 83; *York plays*, xxxviii, xli.
[3] e.g. *Coventry plays*, 83, 89–90, 91 etc. Salter, 74–5, 76–7.
[4] *Miller's tale*, A 3384.   [5] Chambers, ii, 401.

wonders if this means that they played the men's parts too).
Indeed there seems to have been a strong sense that all citizens should be involved. For example, at Beverley, about
1520, we find that the Emmaus play is listed as performed
by the 'Gentlemen' and the Coronation of our Lady by
the 'Priests',[1] and at Lincoln it was agreed in the early
sixteenth century that everyone in the town was to pay
towards the activities of the two guilds concerned. The
Corpus Christi play was a corporate venture. It was popular
art in the best sense of the word, but with this reservation,
that its relationship with the learned clerical traditions of
Europe was integral, since it was almost certainly written
and compiled by clerics. Moreover, to say the least, it is
scarcely likely so to have flourished contrary to the will of
the Church authorities in an age of such ecclesiastical power.

My account so far of these religious plays in their
characteristic performance as a civic and corporate celebration can be little better, for lack of evidence, than the painting of the blackest night punctured by a very few glittering
stars, or than a restoration, in what may often be the wrong
pattern, of the few remaining pieces of a shattered mosaic.
And so it is, too, when we turn to the staging and the way
of producing the Corpus Christi play: evidence is poor.
But two recent scholars have made the utmost of it that
sensitivity and sound imagination can.[2] And some of the
best evidence is in the stage directions of the *Ludus Coventriae*
in this book, and in the inferences that can be safely drawn
from the text of that play.

Three principal points can be made about staging and
production. They apply to all medieval religious drama,
inside church or out, processional or stationary. The first is
that the staging was of the kind called multiple or simultaneous: it represented different locations together at the
same time. In this it differed from the kind of staging

[1] Chambers, ii, 340–1; *Coventry plays*, 75–6; p. 43 below.
[2] Wickham, Southern; see also Frank.

appropriate in the more realistic theatre, but it has become increasingly popular again with playwrights and producers of the last fifty years. The second is that there was no proscenium arch with box-like stage beyond, and no division by a curtain of the areas for actors and audience. Instead, subject to convenience (as, for example, that the action should not be impeded by spectators) and to the particular circumstances (as, for example, that there might be only limited space inside a church or in a narrow street), the audience could see the playing space all the time and from many, if not all, sides of it. The third is that in or about this basic playing space there might be disposed what were sometimes called stations or mansions, scaffolds or tents. These represented some, though not necessarily all, of the locations involved: the rest might be represented in the other parts of the playing space by a minimum of what was probably movable stage furniture, or by the presence of the actors themselves or by some verbal reference.

These three characteristics are found in the staging of Corpus Christi plays, whether their performance was stationary, in a static playing space, or processional, on mobile pageant wagons. The York, Chester, and, in all probability, Towneley plays were performed processionally. At suitable intervals the pageant wagons started from an assembly point through the streets of the town on this high holiday and religious feast. They stopped at appointed places and the players acted their pageants[1] one after the other before an audience that remained there, perhaps from dawn to dusk, enjoying each play as it arrived in its turn. There is some reason to believe that the playing space afforded by each principal wagon might be supplemented by adding a second wagon drawn up beside it, and, in all likelihood, on occasion, by using the street itself and involving the audience. In one of the two Coventry plays Herod 'rages in the pageant

---

[1] Name used for both the representation (cf. pp. 148(?), 391) and the (mobile) stage (see below).

and in the street also', and the Three Kings speak 'in the street', just as in the Anglo-Norman *Mystère d'Adam*, wherever and however that was performed, Satan made sallies among the people as he went on his way to tempt Eve.[1]

Such evidence as we have of what the wagons were like points to their expensiveness and sturdiness. An inventory of the property of the Grocers' company of Norwich in 1565 includes[2] 'a pageant, that is to say, a house of wainscot, painted and builded on a cart with four wheels; a square-top to set over the said house'; and 'a griffon . . . to set on the said top'. 'Three painted cloths' are also listed, 'to hang about the pageant', as they are, also, in the inventory of the Cordwainers' company[3] at Lincoln. Two interpretations of their use are possible, one, that they formed the three closed sides of a kind of punch-and-judy show, the audience watching the play through the open fourth side, and the other, that they were chest-high and surrounded the stage on its three open sides, the fourth being entirely closed with a back of wainscot or some such more substantial material. Though the first seems more likely, the second is supported, at least for the Norwich Adam and Eve, by the stage directions of the *Mystère d'Adam* mentioned on page 40. Six horse-cloths are also included in the Norwich inventory and so we can probably picture this pageant drawn by horses, although, in some cases, pageants were drawn by men. Their storage is so often mentioned that it is likely that they were purpose-built for playing and used for nothing else.[4] At Chester, where the whole cycle was divided into three and performed on successive days, it was possible for the same wagon to be used by the Painters, Coopers and Skinners.[5]

[1] *Coventry plays*, 19, 27; *Adam*, 11: 'discursum faciet per populum'.
[2] Chambers, ii, 388.
[3] H. Craig, *Pub. Mdn. Lang. Ass.* xxxii (1917), 606.
[4] At Lincoln: Craig, 272; at York: Chambers, ii, 403; *Coventry plays*, 98, 99.
[5] Salter, 74–5.

How it was ever possible to get all the York plays performed in a day at what were, at one time, sixteen appointed stations, I cannot conceive, not least because the actors must have played the same play sixteen times over between dawn and dusk. What may often have happened, however, is suggested by a report at Coventry, in 1457, that since the Queen had come specially to see the plays, each of them was played first this year at Richard Woods, the Grocer's in Earl Street, where she was staying: but Doomsday could not be played at all 'for lack of day'.[1]

It cannot have been every year that royalty attended the plays, but all the evidence points to the comprehensiveness of the audience as much as of the subject-matter. High and low were there, the learned and the unlettered (to both of whom Contemplatio refers on page 120 and Doctor on page 390) and the richer with the poorer, for at York some paid and some did not.[2]

An occasional window opens on what props and scenery were used: for example, the Norwich Grocers[3] record in the inventory for their play of the Creation of Adam and Eve, 'a rib coloured red', costumes for Adam, Eve and the serpent, and a mask for God, and the stage-directions of the *Mystère d'Adam*[4] prescribe that Paradise shall have placed about it curtains at such a height that the actors within can be seen from the shoulders upward, and that there shall be sweet-smelling flowers and foliage and fruit upon the trees, God wearing a dalmatic, Adam red and Eve white. H. Craig[5] suggests that a prop for the Assumption play may be that which he says remained at St. Swithin's Church in Lincoln, 'a firmament with a fiery cloud and a double cloud'. There can be little doubt that costume would be chiefly

---

[1] York: Chambers, ii, 401 and A. H. Nelson, *Mod. Phil.* lxvii (1969–70), 303–20; *Coventry plays*, 74.

[2] Chambers, ii, 401; p. 37 above.   [3] Chambers, ii, 388; nn. 87 and 22.

[4] *Adam*, 1; 'circumponantur cortinae et panni serici, ea altitudine, ut personae, quae in paradiso erunt, possint videri sursum ad humeros'.

[5] p. 279.

that of the players' own day, for this is what the same characters are wearing when represented in contemporary paintings and glass, except that there would have to be special modifications in particular cases such as those of the High Priests described carefully in the stage directions of *Ludus Coventriae* on page 241. Apparatus could be elaborate and included hoists, for example, to raise Christ and his mother, or at least their effigies, at their several ascensions.[1]

What has so far been said about the audience, props, scenery, costumes and apparatus of the first way in which the Corpus Christi play was performed can also be said of the second, which was in one prepared place and not on wagons. It is in this way that at least the Passion part of the *Ludus Coventriae* was done and it is with the help of the exceptionally full stage-directions [2] that the reader may imagine for himself what happened. The scaffolds or stages referred to must have been large and substantial, in so much as one, for example, housed all the disciples and a supper table. They had curtains to enclose players not at that time acting and to prevent distraction away from the scene in hand. Constructions, similar in function, are found in the Cornish play and are there called 'tents'. We are fortunate in that there are simple diagrams in the Cornish manuscript recording their basic arrangement. There is also a rather more elaborate diagram in the Folger manuscript of the stage plan for the morality play, *The Castle of Perseverance*. In it, again, there are 'scaffolds', and it is clear that these 'stations' were distributed in a circle at the perimeter of the playing space[3] and, as in the Passion play of *Ludus Coventriae*, allocated to particular characters or locations, Heaven, say, or Abraham, Herod or Pilate. Between them and the playing space, characters ascended and descended. There is more evidence for such arrangements in relation to plays

---

[1] pp. 273–4 and nn. 82 and 87.
[2] pp. 241, 245, 255, 264, 279, 282, 288, 296, 298, 311.
[3] Called *platea* or *place*, cf. pp. 142, 147, 244 245, 248.

done on the Continent, and, in particular, in a manuscript
illustration by J. Fouquet which represents the martyrdom
of St. Apollonia and depicts a play in performance.[1] In the
light of this it is not unlikely that the scaffolds of *Ludus
Coventriae* were distributed not around the entire circum-
ference of a circle but about one half of it, with the audience
round the other half, or, possibly, in a straight line across a
broad front, with the audience facing them across the playing
space.

How those parts of *Ludus Coventriae* were played which
are on either side of the Passion plays is almost entirely a
matter for speculation. They may have been staged like the
York or Chester plays on wagons, at least before their
inclusion in this cycle. If they were played as part of this
cycle, perhaps each came into the playing space on its wagon,
played and went off, or lined up with the others already
there, or was stationed there from the beginning. Perhaps
wagons were not involved at all, and the players walked on
and off. Certainly little apparatus is required for the Old
Testament plays and might be carried. Moreover, full
provision is made for the management of the chief piece of
apparatus which is Noah's ark, and the implications are, as I
read it, that the ark is a unique carriage and that there are no
wagons besides. But from all we are led to expect by other
plays and illustrations of any episode in which Heaven
occurs, there would be required some means of providing a
raised platform to represent it, and for the Assumption or
Ascension plays a hoist would have to be arranged. Both of
these could be provided for by a wagon or a scaffold.

There are reasons for believing that the *Ludus Coventriae*
cycle may have been connected with Lincoln. What little
evidence we have for the organization of religious drama in
that town is not easy to interpret but it suggests a special

[1] Photograph in Southern and G. Cohen's *Histoire de la mise-en-scène dans le
théâtre religieux français du moyen âge* (Paris, 1926, rev. 1951), pl. 3; see also pl. 1
(Valenciennes Passion of 1547).

situation.[1] In the last three decades of the fifteenth and in
the earlier part of the sixteenth century such evidence as
there is in the minute books of the Corporation, in the
accounts of the Cordwainers' company and in those of the
Cathedral Chapter, points to the existence of two distinct
guilds, each associated with processions or plays or both
(the evidence of this is not always clear), one that of St. Anne
and the other that of Corpus Christi. These were not craft
guilds and it was agreed by the Common Council in 1519 and
1530, respectively, that every person in the city was to support them with money. Moreover, in regard to St. Anne's
Guild, every occupation in the city was assigned a pageant
that they must regularly bring forth, and there are almost
yearly references to the sights (*visus*) of St. Anne's day
(26 July). In regard to the play of Corpus Christi, the records[2]
of a number of years in the later fifteenth century reveal the
cathedral clergy at dinner on that Feast when they had come
together to see the Corpus Christi play. On two such
occasions they saw a Pater Noster play which, presumably,
took the place of the Corpus Christi in those years, but, of
course, the St. Anne's day procession went on unaffected.
The Cordwainers' company provided every year a 'Pageant
of Bethlehem' for the St. Anne's day procession, and there
is no evidence of the kind in guild accounts in other towns
that this was a play: for example, there is no mention of
rehearsals, or of a text. Presumably the pageant of Bethlehem
was a tableau and perhaps carried on men's shoulders. There
were also Corpus Christi Guilds, one of the Tilers and one of
the Sailors, who took part in a procession (and also of a
Corpus Christi Guild of Tailors but with no mention of a
procession). The processions of both St. Anne's day and
Corpus Christi went to the Cathedral and H. Craig is right
in saying that it is hard to conceive of the performance of

---

[1] Loomis; Craig, 268 ff., and *Publ. Mdn. Lang. Ass.* xxxii (1917), 605–15; Kahrl
and Cameron.

[2] 'ad videndum ludum Corporis Christi' . . . 'videntes ludum de la Pater Noster
play'.

plays on the way up the staggeringly steep hill which they would be forced to climb. Moreover, there are no records, such as exist in other towns, of the appointment by the Corporation of stations for playing. And yet there were plays done on both days: on St. Anne's day, in the last two decades of the fifteenth and the early decades of the sixteenth century, they played the Assumption in the Cathedral, and on Corpus Christi, in the later part of the fifteenth century, they played either the Corpus Christi play or the Pater Noster. Although there was one occasion, in 1483, when it was said that the Assumption was to be played and shown in the procession, there is no record of any such occasion for the play of Corpus Christi. Perhaps it was performed in the cathedral close where there is ample room at both the west and east ends.[1]

There is one final piece of evidence[2] from 1554 which could be taken to imply that by this very late date St. Anne's Guild and the Corpus Christi play were related; but, especially in the light of the other evidence, it seems to me more likely that it refers to two separate activities and organizations. It is the decree from that time when, Mary being on the throne, in many places the old customs were revived: 'St. Anne's Guild with Corpus Christi Play shall be brought forth and played this year, and every craft shall bring forth their pageants as it has been accustomed, and all occupations shall be contributory as shall be assessed.' And that provoking instruction is the last we hear of these plays in Lincoln.

4

The didactic function of medieval religious drama is one of its aspects that least needs pointing out. It is typified in the

[1] See p. 20; Assumption 'ad ludificatum et ostensum in processione': V. Shull, *Pub. Mdn. Lang. Ass.*, lii (1937), 946–66.
[2] Craig, 142.

instructional roles played by Contemplatio and Expositor of the *Ludus Coventriae* and Chester cycles, in the sermon preached at us by Moses in *Ludus Coventriae*, or, more subtly, in the sermon form[1] of the play of the Woman taken in adultery. The Corpus Christi play uses many of the characteristic methods of the sermon and homiletic literature as G. R. Owst has shown. Chief among them for our present consideration is realism.[2] Sacred history is treated as contemporary, sublime mysteries are presented through the immediate. God creates man or ponders the Redemption here and now. The Incarnate Son is crucified, rises and ascends in York or Lincoln, and, moreover, gives the impression of speaking the language of ordinary men. That this is his language is, of course, consistent with Scriptural practice, and in the localization of the mystery there is evinced that philosophical understanding, found, for example, in Boethius, of God's 'time' as an eternal present in which yesterday is as much today as tomorrow, for He is outside time and knows all always. Doubtless there is here, also, a great deal of that obliviousness to anachronism so characteristic of medieval story-tellers, who, with the exception of Chaucer, at least in England, make little demand on our historical imagination. But this is also a mode of the Friars[3] and their preaching. Theirs, too, was a popular art, they, too, belonged to the open-air and brought the sublime events of man's Redemption into the medieval market-place as they strove to open men's hearts to the immediate presence of God. Moreover, quite apart from whatever other theological and rhetorical theory there is behind this realism, it shows excellent teaching technique. So, too, does the practice of always illustrating what you affirm, technically using *exempla* to demonstrate *moralitas* or *sentence*. In one way, this is exactly what the religious drama is doing. Again, the medieval preacher knew how important it was to sweeten the pill,

---

[1] n. 46; Contemplatio: p. 60, n. 100. [2] Auerbach; Pächt, 42.
[3] Craddock.

and, in order to drive home his point, to disarm his listener in advance with matter arresting or entertaining. This is at least part of the reason for including devils and their devices, Herod and his raging, or, in the Towneley Shepherd's play II, Mak the sheep-stealer and the comic nativity.

In all these ways the realism of plays and sermons has the same functions and, in pursuit of it, the playwrights show a grasp of day-to-day life and a capacity to imitate it. Thus the Woman taken in adultery and her truculent visitor are presented frankly as prostitute and client, and he issues convincingly from her house still half undressed (p. 215). Thus, too, the speech of particular characters can be appropriately racy, or, at least, patently aim at vigour and rawness. The reservation is important, for these plays are quite often more interesting for what one senses they intend than for their achievement of it, and the strong colours and bold strokes with which the enthusiastic critic may paint their peculiar virtues can disappoint on actual reading or seeing.

The Corpus Christi plays have also an affective function. It is, of course, one that cannot in reality be distinguished properly from the didactic since religious teaching must be largely a schooling of what we might call the heart. Their intention is to orientate the will and convert the soul, to draw tears of penitence and to warm the audience into love. This intention they share with meditations and lyrics, devotions and pictures in a profoundly important tradition of European Christianity,[1] which, though its roots are far older, was increasingly conspicuous from the eleventh century. To this tradition belongs the representation of the excruciating agony of the crucified Lord, and of the impotent suffering of his virgin Mother. Characteristic of it is that scene in *Ludus Coventriae* in which Mary pathetically holds her son dead in her arms after his taking down from the cross. What

---

[1] e.g. A. Wilmart, *Auteurs spirituels et textes dévots du moyen âge latin* (Paris, 1932); chap. 5 of R. W. Southern's *The making of the middle ages* (London, 1953).

son and what mother watching would not be moved and, being so, find their faith strengthened?

A third function of the Corpus Christi play is one it shared with liturgical drama, with the liturgy itself, and with individual miracle plays, but which it was potentially capable of fulfilling more ambitiously. In so doing, it could give more satisfaction than they. It is what can be called its celebratory function. Again, it is not, in reality, possible to separate this properly from its didactic and affective functions, but by its celebratory function I mean that, as a species of both worship and self-realization, it acted out the destiny of mankind under God. Inherently the Christian Faith is a great drama and the Corpus Christi play, in giving it expression, assisted its achievement, while—to turn the coat inside out— what was potential in the subject became the making of the play. The conception was vast. Vast, too, as a consequence, was the length of the drama and vast, as we have seen, the complexity of its annual production. It was in the nature of a civic ritual, and although there is good reason to think that the compiler of *Ludus Coventriae* and the recorder of the Brome Abraham and Isaac had in mind the reader, too, and that the Anglo-Norman *Seinte Resureccion* play was meant for reading[1] as well as playing, yet, even more than most plays, that of Corpus Christi needs production for its fulfilment. So often the poetry and the characterization are too thin for solitary enjoyment: the reader lacks the body and colour of spectacle, for one thing, but also the involvement in an entire community's many-sided and diversely satisfying activity on a public holiday, inextricably religious and secular at once, in an age when recreation was less passive than we know it and when, despite the popularity of pilgrimage, it was not by escaping away that men achieved refreshment.

We examined earlier what some of its contemporaries

---

[1] cf. genealogies in Block, 36, 37, 63 etc., and details of Noah's ark, 41; the use of the past tense in the stage direction on p. 385; Frank, 89. Dr. A. D. Mills points out that this is probably true also of the Chester mss.

said about religious drama. There is one work which is more generous than some. V. A. Kolve[1] has rightly made much of it. In the following extract from what is known as *Dives et Pauper* the initial reservation is notable, but it is the main part of the statement that is immediately important: provided that they do not keep men 'from God's service, nor from God's Word-hearing and that there be no error meddled in such miracles and plays against the Faith of Holy Church, nor against good living', then, on a holiday when joy and ease are the order of the day, anticipating their full enjoyment in Heaven, religious plays may be performed 'for devotion, honesty and mirth, to teach men to love God the more'. But for most of us today that devotion is non-existent and our mirth is, in so many ways, of a different kind, so that this celebratory function is one we can never fully apprehend. We are used to celebrating our authors, but our ignorance of who were the authors of these plays suggests that medieval men were not. This fact is, of course, in no way excepttional in an age to which belong countless poems and romances, buildings, paintings and tunes whose creators no one felt the need to record. A further difference between us and the men of the middle ages is that, since the subject of these plays was generally so well known, even allowing for local variations in content and interpretation and emphasis, they must have enjoyed in their repeated performance a reassuring satisfaction which we who crave novelty, originality and stimulation can hardly appreciate. Moreover, it was oneself and one's friends who were retelling the tale, whether by watching or taking part, and in so doing bringing within compass and making manageable in one's own town and in one's own being the whole mysterious and eternal process of God's marvellous dealings with men.

The extent and kind of identification made by the audience with these plays as with much other drama in previous ages must have been affected by their performance in broad

[1] pp. 131 ff.

daylight. Moreover, spectators were compelled by moralizing commentators to stand back from their experience and to consider their relationship to it. In processional performances, at least, one character appearing in several pageants, Jesus, say, or his mother, would be played by several different characters. But in real life, medieval folk were more used than we are to responding to the role a man was performing as distinct from responding to the man himself, more used than we are to responding to priest or king than to Robert or Richard. This and these other factors must have modified the possibility of illusion. And, according to their particular skills and gifts and the part they were playing, I have no doubt that some actors were able to win their audiences to complete, though temporary belief by a compelling performance, just as Chaucer's Pardoner does, in his preaching, and some actors, too, must have been utterly caught up in their performances as the player is in *Hamlet*.[1]

Such compulsive and compelling playing is, I think, matched by occasions in these plays when our recourse to the rational conventions of sermon technique, or to the justification afforded by doctrine, or to the effects of long-standing tradition do not account fully for what we find and when we may wonder whether what has taken over is not, at its best, the shaping spirit of imagination, or at its worst, emotional indulgence. For example, for all that can be said about the full and fascinating propriety of the episode, I think A. C. Cawley[2] is right in seeing in the first part of the Towneley Shepherds play II an ebullient sense of fun which is exceptionally compelling and which, I suggest, being so successful in its own right, disrupts the play. On a much lower level of imaginative achievement than in the Towneley play, the Shepherds play of the *Ludus Coventriae* affords

[1] 'Alienation' in Woman taken in adultery: n. 46; Pardoner: *Canterbury tales*, C. 427 ff.; *Hamlet*, II, ii.
[2] *Wakefield Pageants*, xxiv.

another instance of this incongruity when the peasants crudely misrepresent the angelic Latin,[1] making ridiculous nonsense out of heavenly worship. The conjunction, in these Shepherds plays, of the comic and the sublime, the grotesque and the beautiful, is, of course, characteristic of much medieval sensibility. It seems then to have been possible, on other terms than those to which we are used, to accept, in the same context, what would be to us the contrary and incompatible. It may be simply that the taste of different ages varies.

V. A. Kolve has pointed out, however, that we are never, in medieval religious plays, invited to laugh at God, at Christ or at Mary, the mother of God, and this fact is particularly notable in the Trial of Joseph and Mary (pages 147 ff.), a play of which the subject is, otherwise, extraordinarily crude as well as superstitious. Our laughter is directed where it is deserved. The passionate anger of tyrannical Herod[2] had its seed in Matthew ii, 16, was consonant with the values of medieval political thought, and, moreover, had its place in the liturgical drama: Herod's ridiculous raging (e.g. page 194) and his pompous inanities are consistent with his valuation as an evil man made foolish by his sin. But sometimes it may well have been against the extravagant playing of this part in church that ecclesiastical authorities inveighed (page 17 above) when they deplored dramatic unseemliness, and it is clear from the references made to the acting of Herod by Chaucer and Shakespeare[3] that it was popularly felt that here was something dramatically exceptional. A sculptured boss in Norwich cathedral may well represent what a Corpus Christi actor looked like playing it, tearing his beard, kicking with rage and scarcely to be restrained by

[1] p. 172; R. C. Cosbey, Speculum, xx (1945), 310–7; M. M. Morgan, in Spec. xxxix (1964), 676–89, develops a theory of a 'double-plot' affording a 'false imitation or burlesque'.

[2] Kolve, 138–44, 172–4; S. S. Hussey, Neophilologus, xlviii (1964), 252–9; R. E. Parker, Speculum, viii (1933), 59–67 and xxv (1950), 237–44; Young, ii, 406–7; McNeir, 612–19; cf. F. T. Wood, Neophilologus, xxv (1939–40).

[3] Canterbury Tales, A 3384; Hamlet, III, ii; Anderson, pl. 11b.

his attendants. Is there not likely to have been here on the part of actor and audience pleasure in the outrageous passion for its own sake?

When the messenger comes running on in the *Ludus Coventriae* Passion play (p. 282), as he does in no other cycle, shouting as he circles the playing space, 'Jesus is taken, Jesus is taken!' the excitement we feel is appropriate because the taking of Jesus is essential to our Redemption. The exceptional genius of this particular artist has caused our disarmed implication, through the startling of our instinctual being, in the reliving of the very process by which God has reconciled to himself once again such creatures as ourselves, who, in any age, are stirred more by the sensational than by goodness. But there is here, one may feel, a sensational element, dramatically significant for its own sake. What dramatist or producer having thought of it could deny himself its use? On the other hand, the *Ludus Coventriae* cycle presents the crucifixion with characteristic restraint, whereas York, for example, exploits all its traditional possibilities of violence and torture, blood and pain. May there not have been in what was done at York something of that attraction that the horror film has for modern audiences and may not dramatist and actors have been caught up in it, in part if no more, for its own sake?[1]

5

Administering and producing the Corpus Christi Play might well have required several kinds of copy. There survive examples of, first, a part for a particular actor, with cues, secondly, an entire text of a pageant for producer or prompter, and, thirdly, a record of the entire town-cycle, kept in a central office.

An actor's part is found in what are known as the Shrewsbury Fragments, part of an early fifteenth-century manuscript

[1] cf. mixed motives and contemporary criticism, pp. 15 ff.

of Latin anthems perhaps belonging to a church in Lichfield town or diocese. The part is in English and Latin with music, and is that of the man who played the third shepherd in a Shepherds play, the third Mary in a Resurrection play, and one of the pilgrims in an Emmaus play. All these plays might be better referred to by their Latin names, *Pastores*, *Visitatio Sepulchri* or *Quem Quaeritis*, and *Peregrini*, for they are doubtless liturgical dramas, connected with particular services, and sung. (One incidental point is that elements in this *Pastores* resemble some in the corresponding York play so that it is the opinion of the latest[1] editor, N. Davis, that both the liturgical play and the cyclic play derive from a common original.)

This actor's copy is not, however, well thumbed and torn as we might have expected a working part to be, and, in this, our other manuscripts are like it except for parts of the *Ludus Coventriae* where stains and marginal scribblings suggest that they may have been used in actual production. According to G. Frank[2] a few French producers' or prompters' copies survive; and, in England, there survive[3] what may have been two prompt-books, or at least company copies—the second category of copy mentioned above—by way of separate versions of individual pageants which are found also in the chief copies of the Chester and York cycles. They are, from the first, the Antichrist play (of about 1500), and, from the second, that of Thomas, performed by the Scriveners.

The manuscript of the York plays is generally accepted to be a register,[4] or official copy, compiled for the Corporation in the first half of the fifteenth century from the texts of individual plays in the hands of the companies who played

---

[1] *Non-cycle plays*, especially p. xviii; see pp. 17–18.

[2] p. 174.

[3] ed. A. C. Cawley, 'The Sykes manuscript of the York Scriveners' play' in *Leeds studies in English*, nos. 7 and 8 (1952); ed. W. W. Greg, *The play of Antichrist from the Chester cycle* (Oxford, 1935).

[4] Greg, 23–4; Craig, 147–8.

them. The register is incomplete and there are blank pages left, presumably, in some cases, for the later entry of plays not available at the time. The manuscript of the Towneley plays may be of the same kind. They are known by the name of Towneley because the manuscript belonged at one time to the Towneley family of Lancashire. There is little doubt, however, that it contains the Corpus Christi play of Wakefield, and A. C. Cawley[1] has given good reasons for believing it may well have been the official register of that town, compiled in the second half of the fifteenth century.

In the case of both York and Towneley plays, only one manuscript of the cycle survives. But, in the case of the Chester plays, we have five manuscripts of the cycle, all much later than York and Towneley for they are of the late sixteenth and early seventeenth centuries. Both W. W. Greg and F. M. Salter have argued that there was in the hands of the Chester Corporation an official copy of the whole cycle, W. W. Greg proposing that it differed from that of York in that from it individual plays were copied. But H. Craig has suggested that the five manuscripts derived from plays still in the hands of individual guilds in the late sixteenth century and that two independent collections were made of them, perhaps for antiquarian reasons.

One conclusion certainly emerges from textual evidence of this kind and from a literary scrutiny, and it is that these plays were constantly changing. One play borrowed from another, or two plays grew from one original. The Brome and the Chester Abraham and Isaac plays are clearly related, and so, too, are the cycles of York and Towneley. H. Craig and E. K. Chambers[2] agree that at least five of the Towneley plays were originally borrowed from York—the Exodus or Pharaoh, Christ before the Doctors, Harrowing of Hell, Resurrection and Last Judgement. A. C. Cawley is, however,

---

[1] *Wakefield pageants*, xii–xvii.
[2] Craig, 214–15; Chambers, *Eng. lit. at close middle ages*, 35–6; *Wakefield pageants*, xxii, n. 2.

53

much less sure. The differences between the two cycles afford ample scope for disputing the theory, but they could be, rather, further evidence of how revisers were continually changing these plays. An artist of outstanding distinction rewrote at least five of the Towneley plays,[1] together with at least parts of Cain and Abel, and these were substituted for the existing ones. Indeed, generously inventive as he was, he wrote two versions of the Shepherds play, presumably for alternative production. The other plays of his are Noah, Herod and the Innocents and the Buffeting of Christ.

6

Compilation and revision are again plainly apparent in the last of the cycles that it remains to discuss, the *Ludus Coventriae*. I do not think it likely that this corpus of plays was ever played straight through from the beginning to the end,[2] but I think that its compilation is one of the surest testimonies we have to the existence of an inspiring and formative concept of the Corpus Christi play as we have understood it. That this is so is confirmed by the writing at the front of the manuscript in an early Elizabethan hand (much later, that is, than that of the manuscript itself) of the words, 'The play called Corpus Christi'.

Another inscription, written on the fly-leaf, makes three gross mistakes. It is, apparently, in the hand of Richard James, the librarian of Sir Robert Cotton. Cotton acquired the manuscript from a Robert Hegge of Durham who died in 1629. James wrote that its contents were from the New Testament, that it was monks or mendicant friars who were the actors, and that the 'book was popularly called *Ludus Coventriae*, or the Play of Corpus Christi'.[3] It is now every-

[1] *Wakefield pageants.*

[2] Passion plays in successive years: p. 279; cf. p. 47: meant for reading?; but cf. p. 20: the London 'great play'.

[3] Block, xxxvii–xxxviii: 'vulgo dicitur hic liber Ludus Coventriae sive ludus Corporis Christi'.

where agreed that this manuscript has nothing whatsoever to do with Coventry (its dialect is of the East Midlands) and that he was wrong in thinking that it was monks or friars who acted the cycle there. Moreover, to any eye, there is more in the manuscript than New Testament episodes.

On the other hand, we do not know where the manuscript came from or where any of the plays in this corpus were performed. There are no topical references in the text which could indicate its provenance as there are in the Towneley manuscript where they point clearly to Wakefield as its source. The Banns, or formal announcement of the plays, promises to perform them on 'Sunday next' in 'N. town'. This could mean that the Banns at least were used in conjunction with plays done at a town beginning with 'N': Norwich (which would scan) and Northampton have been guessed at. We have, however, no record of plays at Northampton, and there is little to connect *Ludus Coventriae* with the Guild plays of Norwich. But there is evidence that these were not the only plays done there. 'N' could also be the first letter of 'Nomen', and it could be intended that here there should be filled in whatever name was appropriate: the announcement would then refer to whatever town a travelling company intended to play in. This would imply a use of a Corpus Christi play for which there is no other evidence.

Though not beginning with 'N' Lincoln has been proposed as the original town on several counts. First of all, *Ludus Coventriae* is more concerned with Mary, the Mother of God, than any other known cycle. It is true that Chester, for example, had a play of Mary's Assumption, though it is no longer extant, and it is true that Mary has an important part in all the cycles in relation to the plays of the Nativity, Purification and Doctors, and the Crucifixion and Resurrection. But only in *Ludus Coventriae* do we find plays about her provenance, childhood, and betrothal as well as the play of her Assumption. Now Lincoln Cathedral was dedicated to Mary, an Assumption play was performed in the nave regularly, and the Guild of St. Anne appears to have been just as important in the town's affairs as any Corpus Christi Guild. St. Anne was the mother of Mary and this could account for the exceptional prominence, in this cycle, of plays about her life in relation to Mary's. Whatever may be the provenance of these plays which I have grouped together under the title 'Mother of Mercy', the character called Contemplatio clearly links them together and intends that we should enjoy them as a group. This kind of division is also exceptional in a Corpus Christi play.

Secondly, this particular corpus contains a pair of Passion plays whose staging, as we have seen, is not that of the processional towns but static. We have seen that there is no evidence at Lincoln of processional playing though there were processions to the Cathedral where, both inside and out, there is vast space for stationary performance. We have also seen that Corpus Christi plays were certainly performed in that town and seen by the Cathedral canons.

There would be a third reason for connecting *Ludus Coventriae* with Lincoln if it could be proved that the morality play, *The Castle of Perseverance*, was connected with Lincoln, too, as is suggested by a topical reference at l. 2421 in that play to the 'gallows of Canwick': Canwick lies just a little south of Lincoln. The Corpus Christi cycle and the morality have in common their stanza forms, their mode of staging, their use of the motif of the Four Daughters of God, and their apparently flexible provision for the announcement of their forthcoming performance. (In the morality a space is left in l. 134: 'At . . . on the green in royal array.') It is also notable that there is more use in *Ludus Coventriae* than in any other cycle of personified abstractions such as abound in the morality—Death, Contemplatio, Backbiter.

But it is the view of the editor of the standard edition of *The Castle of Perseverance* that its manuscript 'could not have been written by a scribe from Lincolnshire but it may very well have been written by a scribe from Norfolk'.

It is also the conclusion of the most authoritative of the students of the dialect in which *Ludus Coventriae* is recorded that the 'hypothesis of a Lincoln origin is untenable'.[1] Since the dialect is probably that of Norfolk it is only possible to argue that the plays once belonged to Lincoln if it is also acceptable that their only record should have been made by a Norfolk man. Perhaps their compilation was by a Norfolk man living in Lincoln who had a special concern for drama there, or by a Norfolk man who copied the Lincoln plays for performance in his own home area (where there is abundant evidence of dramatic activity) either in one place, perhaps Norwich, or on tour.[2]

This problem of the provenance of *Ludus Coventriae* is rivalled by that of the process and nature of its compilation. This problem also remains unresolved, but study of the different kinds of paper used in the manuscript and of the different handwriting on it may contribute to its solution. Three sections of the corpus are exceptional in that, in these, *Ludus Coventriae* differs from the other cycles: they are the early Mary plays, the Passion plays and the Assumption play. It is notable that the last two are written on different paper from the rest, and the Assumption play, moreover, is in a different hand. The paper also changes in the middle of one of the early Mary plays, that of her Conception, but I do not see the significance of this. Such is the stained state of the page at the beginning of the second Passion play that K. S. Block has concluded that it was once an outside leaf. This play, therefore, may have had use separate from the rest of the corpus, and, indeed, there is good reason to think that these copies of both Passion plays and the Assumption play had independent life before being brought together. With some few comparatively small exceptions, however, the entire manuscript, other than the Assumption play, is written by

---

[1] *Macro plays*, xi; E. J. Dobson, *Medium Aevum*, ix (1940), 153.
[2] cf. H. Whitehall quoted Loomis, 246, and M. Eccles, *Medium Aevum*, xl (1971), 135–41.

one man, probably in the third quarter of the fifteenth century, and all, again with some few small exceptions, has been rubricated by one man, including the Assumption play. It is probable, therefore, that the rubricator was the compiler himself or the scribe working closely under his direction. Moreover, the compiler has tried to impose on his material a division into numbered plays (see my notes) such as might have constituted a processional cycle. This he did not find easy, since the Passion plays are obviously conceived continuously and directed to be so staged, while several of the other[1] episodes, whatever may have been the case otherwise at any time in their history, are so written in the manuscript, without signs of separation or with signs of connection, that division is patently forced. I have omitted from the text the Banns with which this compilation begins since the complications that their consideration would introduce in relation to the body of the play would divert attention from the primary purpose of this book. But no attention can be properly given to the meaning of the numbering in the body of the text, or to the significance of the compilation generally, without referring to the numbering and content of the pageants announced in the Banns, and, in the notes, I have occasionally done this.

In any analysis of the stages by which Corpus Christi plays developed, much attention has often been given to stanza forms as evidence of different layers of work.[2] The crude rhythm of the long lines at some points in *Ludus Coventriae* does, in all likelihood, represent later composition than the complex stanzas in which much of the cycle is written. These are chiefly three. The first is the characteristic stanza of the Chester cycle the plays of which are commonly believed to have preserved their ancient form better than the others, and its shape is a a a^4 b^3 a a a^4 b^3, or a a a^4 b^3 c c c^4 b^3. The second is of thirteen lines rhyming a b a b

[1] e.g. nn. 5 and 8.
[2] e.g. Craig, 158–63; instances below, pp. 73 f., 96 f., 120 f., 171 f.

a b a b c d d d c (with some variations) and the fact that it is in this form that the Banns are written has sometimes been taken to corroborate the antiquity of both. The third is a double quatrain (often together with single quatrains), linked by the last line of the first to the first of the second. There are also other forms such as the ten-line stanza rhyming a a b a a b b c b c. Complex stanza forms are common in the English lyrics of the late thirteenth and early fourteenth centuries as they are in the French and Latin lyrics that were their models, but the use of such stanzas is not confined to those early days, and I see little reason why any later poet should not have written them in revising a Corpus Christi play, as the Wakefield Master did in the first half of the fifteenth century when he used, with greater accomplishment than any of these other dramatic writers, a form strongly resembling the second chief stanza form of the *Ludus Coventriae*.

It is a remarkable fact that miracle plays should ever have been composed in such a difficult metrical medium. Romances, too, probably orally delivered, were also often written in complex stanzas, but the exigencies of dramatic dialogue in such a medium must have been peculiarly demanding, especially when colloquial vigour rather than hieratic dignity is often the author's intention. Again, this intention he shares with the authors of verse romances and it is notable that the ability to accomplish verisimilar dialogue is a strength of much non-dramatic medieval English writing, most especially, of course, that of Chaucer in verse or of Malory in prose. Their use of rhyme and in such complex patterns meant that writers of these plays could never achieve the sustained and infinitely modulated dramatic poetry of the age of Shakespeare, had they been capable of it anyway, but that they were feeling their way a little towards it is suggested by the ambitious speech of Demon (pages 237–9) or that of Herod or Mors (pages 197–9), where there are some signs of copiousness both of idea and

59

word, and some signs of largeness of feeling, all managed in a metrical medium that seems able to expand to take them.

The diversity of tone, character and action within the Corpus Christi cycle and within some of its individual pageants is something also shared with the later and greater drama, as is the variety of accomplishment apparent when one play is compared with another. The *Ludus Coventriae* cycle, for example, differs from the others in that Mrs. Noah is here represented[1] as an example of wifely and creaturely virtue, consistent with and reinforcing the simple, unambiguous purpose of this Noah play, though humanly and dramatically much less interesting than her satirical representation in the other cycles as an example of that disobedient womanhood that causes the turbulence in any man's marriage.

The Lamech episode in this Noah play is found in no other, and one might have thought it a clear instance of the dramatist's inventiveness when faced with the need to engage the audience while Noah goes off to build his ark and actually to bring it on, were it not that in the Holkham Bible Picture-book this episode is also represented in conjunction with that of Noah suggesting (unless, of course, Holkham is derived from *Ludus Coventriae*) some other association independent of dramatic convenience.[2] The episodes of Jesse, Veronica and the miracle of the cherry tree in *Ludus Coventriae* are not found in other English cycles, while the role of Contemplatio,[3] though in some respects paralleled elsewhere, is here unique. So, too, are the Parliament of Heaven pageant and Demon's prologue to the Passion play. Both are doubtless to be related to the doctrinal slant which this cycle elsewhere evinces. To

[1] K. Garvin, *Mdn. lang. notes*, xlix (1934), 88–90; A. J. Mill, *Pub. Mdn. Lang. Ass.*, lvi (1941), 613–26.

[2] Mr. B. Nellist suggests this may be found in that the readings at three successive services of Matins in the Roman Breviary mention, first, Lamech, associated with Cain, then Lamech, father of Noah, and, lastly, Noah and the flood (Friday and Saturday in Septuagesima and Sexagesima Sunday; n. 10).

[3] pp. 115 ff., 120, 123, 142, 146–7, 161–2, 306.

explain why Demon, or the Devil, appears at this point M. J. Benkovitz quotes a passage from the *Mirror of the Blessed Life of Jesus Christ*:

> After the raising of Lazarus beforesaid, when the time nighed in the which our Lord Jesu disposed to work our redemption through the shedding of his precious blood, the Devil, father of envy, armed his knights and his ministers and whetted their hearts against our Lord Jesu finally into his death. And specially by occasion of his good and virtuous workings, but sovereignly for the raising of Lazarus, envy kindled in their hearts more and more in so much that they might no longer bear their woodness [frenzy] without execution thereof against Jesu. Wherefore the princes and the pharisees gathered a council against him.

In this action of his against Jesus, Lucifer does not know that he is God as well as man[1] The importance of this is that while Lucifer has power over all men because of the fall of Adam and Eve, their first parents, he has no power, of course, over God. As the play continues, then, he abuses his power and ultimately in the Harrowing of Hell episode realizes his fatal mistake. It was, according to this theory, because man was under Satan's dominion that he could not possibly redeem himself. But a second theory of the Redemption is also apparent in *Ludus Coventriae*: it is that God had to intervene because man's sin was against an infinite God, so that it was beyond his power, since he is far from infinite, to make satisfaction. Thus it is particularly apt that the deity of Jesus should be exceptionally emphasized in this cycle (it may appear, paradoxically) by the peculiar place given to Mary, the virgin Mother of God, for it was no mere man that was born of such immaculate flesh.

[1] pp. 209, 236 and n. 50. It was sometimes said that Christ's humanity was the bait to catch Satan on the hook of Christ's deity: e.g. *Stanzaic life Christ*, E.E.T.S. 166 (1926 for 1924), ll. 6345–6368. (M. J. Benkovitz, *Mdn. lang. notes*, lx (1945) 79.)

Such a doctrinal slant as this is typical of this cycle which has a more theological bent, perhaps because it was more closely connected with the Church than most and less a civic affair. It is also an exceptional means of unifying the compilation and for this reason, if for no other, it might be thought that both the prologue of Demon and the Parliament of Heaven were composed by the compiler himself. This would be a speculation modest in comparison with those of T. Fry who overplays his hand in arguing that this doctrinal slant is found throughout, so that the *Ludus Coventriae* is 'a closely unified cycle of plays worked out according to a definite pattern'.

7

The variety of accomplishment among the Corpus Christi plays, referred to a little earlier, is conspicuous in the plays of Abraham and Isaac comprising Part Two of this book. Here are six versions of the same topic, the sacrifice of Isaac, related in Genesis xxii, 1–19, four belonging to cycles and two preserved without any sign of connection with a cycle whatsoever. In none is the treatment uniform. No one can, however, mistake that one of these, the Brome play, is substantially related to the Chester play. Much attention has been given to the relationship of lines 10 on page 380 to 18 on page 386 of Brome and lines 24 on page 399 to 30 on page 404 of Chester, but the final answer seems yet to find, for in 1945 a very close study by J. B. Severs (which surveys all previous work) concluded 'that the central part of the Chester play is derived in some fashion from the central part of the original Brome play' (not, that is, the version we have today, but an earlier), and yet H. Craig (page 309) wrote in 1955, though without arguing his case, 'The Brome Abraham and Isaac is obviously a skilfully developed version of the Chester.' N. Davis in his new edition of Brome considers that Severs's arguments 'appear to be decisive' (page lxiv) and Severs's case is that Chester is manifestly and repeatedly corrupt, the deterioration beginning in transmission from the earlier Brome play perhaps through 'attempted but faulty memorial reconstruction of the original'—that is to say, a pirate from Chester may have stolen someone else's play in performance.

In the same book[1] H. Craig maintains a theory of the derivation of the Chester plays from a French source. One of his arguments is that, whereas the Melchizedek episode in the Chester play is unique in English, it occurs in connection with the story of Abraham and Lot in one French Old Testament play. Whatever its source, this Melchizedek part of the Chester Abraham and Isaac play, though in itself quite impressive in performance, makes an odd combination with the sacrifice of Isaac despite a connecting passage. In this passage, God promises to help Abraham, because he is pleased with what he has done, and Abraham then asks for a son. Perhaps it is in order to occupy symbolically the time for Isaac to be born and grow that there then follows a confusing section about the race that will descend from Abraham and culminate in Jesus and about the need for Abraham's people to be circumcised. But, disjointed though this play is, the prophecy about the progeny of Abraham joins this part of the Corpus Christi play to the later parts by looking forward to the Incarnation.

At three points Expositor tries to explain the significance of what is going on and the last of his expositions is perhaps the most interesting (page 406; the first, page 395, n. 8). He calls the play just finished a 'deed of devotion' (though it is possible that in those words he refers to the sacrifice itself) and says that, properly understood, it will edify the audience. He then interprets Abraham and Isaac as allegorical figures representing God the Father and Jesus. In so doing he is practising a mode of biblical exegesis that was of first importance in the middle ages. Jesus is recorded as having

[1] pp. 113, 138–9, 171–8, 189–91; Brown, 'Study Eng. med. drama'.

63

connected his own coming crucifixion and resurrection with two Old Testament episodes, the lifting up of the bronze serpent by Moses and the release of Jonah after three days in the belly of the whale (Matthew xii, 39, and John iii, 14). The wives of Abraham and their sons, in the Old Testament, are explained in Galatians iv, 24 ff. as an allegory of the old and the new covenants. Thus, on the basis of such Scriptural practice, there developed the theory that the historical events of the Old Testament prefigure those of the New, and Expositor's particular identification of Abraham with the Father and Isaac with the Son is one of the best-known instances of this theory in practice.

It has been argued that the reason for the inclusion of the Abraham and Isaac play in the Corpus Christi cycle is just this, that it presents one of the crucial 'types' or 'prefigurations' of the Redemption. This may have been a reason in the initial development of that body of plays which later became, perhaps, an expected repertoire for which the original justification was forgotten. It may well be that this signification is still implicit in the play and is suggested by the possible reflection in some of Isaac's speeches of the sayings of Christ on the cross: for example, Brome's 'receive me into thy hand' may reflect Luke xxiii, 46, 'into thy hands I commend my spirit', and York's 'shall not grudge/To work his will well paid' may reflect Matthew xxvi, 39, 'not as I will, but as thou wilt'. But the fact that Expositor is here made to draw out this particular signification, whereas none is so drawn out in any of the other plays, suggests that, despite what must have been general knowledge of this most common figure, the typological meaning has ceased to be important in the other[1] cycles. That this is so is confirmed when we observe that the lesson drawn from the Brome play by Doctor and from the Dublin play by Abraham himself at the end is in moral terms. Such an exposition is just as typical in the processes of medieval allegory. It need not,

[1] n. 11.

of itself, however, exclude the typological interpretation for it was not uncommon to crack the nut and expose the kernel in what were found to be its several significations. But in these plays no typological significance is mentioned when their nut is cracked.

Isaac's age clearly differs in two representations from that in one other. In both Brome and Chester versions he is 'but a child' (e.g. page 382) whereas in York he is thirty years old (page 431). There was authority[1] for both interpretations and neither is an invention of the dramatist. The difference of age, however, alters the situation as each dramatist develops it, which demonstrates that some of these writers were concerned, even if at no very ambitious level, with consistent character creation and with verisimilitude. That Isaac is a child, in the Brome play, makes more pathetic the varied devices by which this play plucks at the heart and exploits the sentimental potentialities of the situation more than any other does. This movement of the heart has both a moral and a typological justification: children should be obedient as Isaac, whatever their painful difficulties, and the obedient suffering of Christ on behalf of man was no less tragically human for being that of God the Son. But the play is singularly plangent and the invention of verisimilar dialogue and realistic psychology outstandingly ample and confident (e.g. pages 381 f., 384 f.). Here, as we have seen earlier (pages 49 etc.), there is good reason to believe that the development of those dramatic characteristics for themselves has been a major component in the dramatist's motivation: art has here, to a degree at least, been followed for art's sake.

The mature Isaac of the York play expresses only one such plangent sentiment when he confesses how sweet life is (page 437). For the rest, he is a model of calm acceptance of God's will, advising his father to kill him and, to that end, to bind him so that his greater and youthful strength will

---

[1] M. E. Wells, *Mdn. lang. notes*, liv (1939), 579–82; Kolve, n. 59, p. 259; Woolf, 'Effect of typology'.

not be able, in the stress of the moment of sacrifice, to impede the duty of his weaker and older father. Among all these plays, however, it is that in the *Ludus Coventriae* that presents this conception of Isaac and his father with most success. This is the most simple and dignified of the versions, emphasizing, without any extravagance, Abraham's anguish at what he must do; and, although the poetry is of no great significance, it decently supports this total effect. Whereas, on the one hand, the play is not thin and bare, on the other there are none of the sentimental developments we have seen in Brome.

Nor are there any of the ironic developments found in the Dublin version. On two occasions in the Dublin play dialogue is sharpened and the dramatic tension heightened by a play of ideas focussed in repeated words. In the case I shall illustrate it is led up to by Abraham's question, but, in the second, it arises more immediately (page 417, lines 26–27):

Abraham. Wife, I went for to sacrify—
But how, trow you? Tell me verily.
Sara. Forsooth, sovereign, I wot not I.
Peraventure some quick [living] beast?
Abraham. Quick? Yea! forsooth, quick it was! (p. 417.)

A second distinguishing feature of the Dublin version is the inclusion of Isaac's mother. In both Brome and Chester she is referred to and is one of the means by which pathos is achieved (what will my mother feel when I die?), but only in Dublin does she appear. Dublin, York and Towneley are distinguished from the other three by including two servants and their treatment in all three again varies. But one final and major instance of diversity is in Towneley which in this differs from all others. The dialogue between Abraham and Isaac on page 424, line 9, to page 425 (bottom) runs through five octaves in which the exigencies of rhyming four times on the same word might daunt the most accomplished poet, but are here managed at the same time as lines are broken, sometimes each into three parts, among the two characters, who conduct through them a conversation of varying pace, sometimes peremptory, sometimes agonized, sometimes pleading. There is more such distinguished dramatic inventiveness in what follows when Abraham goes aside, making a poor excuse for doing so, at page 425 (bottom) and soliloquizes at no mean length, and when attention is turned to God and the angel as he breaks off in the middle. He ends with his decision to overcome the anguish that inhibits him by suddenly rushing at Isaac and killing him impetuously, when at this moment of crisis, unexpectedly the angel intrudes and prevents the fulfilment of his hard-won power to act. In frustration Abraham strikes out against him, and the angel causes him to fall to the ground.

It is not my point, however, that the particular achievement of Towneley is altogether unprecedented. Such dialogue, for example, in a demanding stanza form also occurs, though less extensively, in the *Mystère d'Adam*[1] where, in dialogue between two characters, there is a similar breaking into two or three of lines rhyming in couplets and quatrains. In the *Mystère d'Adam*, also, there are psychological developments (consistent with the theology of the Fall) of such a kind as occur also in the later English plays, and an ambitious sense of staging that is like some of theirs. Written in Anglo-Norman and for performance outside a church, there is every likelihood that this play belongs to England and to a period in which we know very little otherwise about the drama of this country. Its associations with the liturgy are obvious since, in the play, a choir sings responses from it, but its originality and accomplishment could indicate that a tradition of popular, outdoor religious drama was substantially established in England in the twelfth century and was already a development far beyond what had been achieved inside church.

But these are speculations and about a period in which we

[1] *Adam*, ll. 81–4, 113–22.

all move in the dark; whereas the English Corpus Christi play of the two hundred years and more before the greatest flowering of our drama in the days of Shakespeare was an achievement of the human spirit clear for all to see and, as many successful performances of the last twenty years have proved, still to enjoy.

8

The text of the *Ludus Coventriae*[1] is that of K. S. Block (E.E.T.S. E.S. 120, 1922 for 1917, repr. 1960) which I use with the permission of the Oxford University Press and the Early English Text Society. It has been checked in countless places against a microfilm of the original and, in a number of places, against the manuscript, and has proved itself, if not impeccable, exceptionally reliable. The text of the Abraham and Isaac[2] plays I have taken from microfilm or photostat copies of the originals. I should like to acknowledge the help I have had in doing this from the work of previous editors and, with regard to the Brome and Dublin plays, from the editorial practice of Professor N. Davis in his *Non-cycle plays and fragments.*

I have silently expanded contractions but I have tried to indicate my very few emendations by the use of square brackets in the text (which always mean 'supplied by the editor'), or by comment in the footnotes, unless they are of obvious mistakes or repetitions, or the kind that would anyway be covered by my silent alterations in spelling. I have, of course, supplied the running titles. I have divided the text of the *Ludus Coventriae* into sections, with titles which are supplied by me unless their origin is explained in the notes. In most cases these divisions correspond with

[1] British Museum MS Cotton Vespasian D VIII.
[2] Brome: Book of Brome in Yale University Library; Chester: British Museum MS Harleian 2124; Dublin: Trinity College MS 432; Towneley: Henry E. Huntington Library MS HM1; York: British Museum MS Additional 35290.

those made in the manuscript (page 58 above), but, unlike the scribe, I have not begun new sections on a new page.

I have indicated the beginning of a new stanza by indentation or by an extra space after the character heading. Only the manuscript of the Chester play leaves a space between stanzas, but that of *Ludus Coventriae* marks a new stanza by a paragraph sign in the left margin. All the manuscripts, at some point or other, indicate rhymes by brackets which link them in the right margin, but I do not, personally, find it helpful to have rhyming lines indented, and not to indent makes the page of a play altogether more tidy.

Punctuation is mine. With regard to spelling, I tried at first to do no more than regularize by substituting 'i' for manuscript 'y', for example, or 'th' for 'þ', and by choosing those variants that happen to have the spelling of modern English and assimilating all the others to them. There proved, however, to be so many of these, and it brought me so near to complete modernization, that it seemed best to go all the way. Spelling, therefore, has been modernized as far as is possible in so much as the plays are in rhymed verse. I have gone further in the stage directions because they are prose. One of the difficulties faced by the modernizer is the apparent spoiling of rhymes. Thus in line 7 on page 73 *mind* represents *mend(e)* which, in the manuscript, rhymes perfectly. But this disadvantage has seemed tolerable provided an echo has remained, as it has in this instance. (If it has not, then the spelling has not been altered.) After all, on page 165, the spelling of *good, food, mood,* and *stood* is exactly as it is in the manuscript as well as being that of today: but changes in sound since the plays were written mean that these are for us echo rhymes only. A second disadvantage of modernizing the spelling is that indications may thereby be removed that the stress did not fall as in modern English. Thus on page 75 *dungeon* is spelt *donjoon* in the original so that there the reader is more likely to stress the final syllable. But now that he has been alerted to this difficulty the reader will be prepared to make such adjustments as he goes along. With regard to inflexional syllables, however, I have thought it best in this major respect not to deprive the reader of such evidence of rhythm as can be fairly left; in some cases, also, they are necessary for rhyme (page 90, *tithis*, *it is*). In general, therefore, they remain but, in some cases, with adjustments to reduce their strange appearance and archaic effect. Thus, for manuscript *knowyn* (= 'known', page 73, line 2) I have printed *knowen*, for *sterrys* (= 'stars', page 76) *starres*, for *hath* (page 77), *has*, for *knowe* (page 242), *known*. In a few limited instances I have substituted a modern English word for that in the manuscript. Thus for original *mote* on page 102 I have printed *may*, for *hem* on page 93, *them*, for *ben* on page 167, *are*. The standard editions listed on pages 441–44 will provide the linguistically competent with all the evidence that they can interpret.

With regard to the spelling of the Latin, I have made such adjustments as may make it more readily understood by those used to Classical or Church Latin. Biblical names in English are, in general, as in the Authorized Version.

The title which I have used for the cycle of plays in Part One is that by which it is known in the standard edition. I have explained on pages 54 and 55 how inappropriate this title is. The reader will not, therefore, be surprised to find this cycle referred to by others as the Hegge plays, the N-town plays, or the Lincoln plays.

PART ONE

Ludus Coventriae

Creation and Fall[1]

Deus. Ego sum Alpha et O, principium et finis.[2]
    My name is knowen, God and King!
My work for to make now will I wend.
In myself resteth my reigning:
It has no ginning nor no end;
And all that ever shall have being
It is closed in my mind.
When it is made, at my liking
I may it save, I may it shend,[3]
After my pleasance.
So great of might is my pousty[4]
All thing shall be wrought by me.
I am one God in Persones three,[5]
Knit in one substance.
    I am the true Trinity
Here walking in this wone.[6]
Three Persones myself I see
Locken[7] in me, God alone:[7]
I am the Father of pousty,
My Son with[8] me ginneth gone,[8]
My Ghost is grace[9] in majesty,
Wieldeth[10] wealth[10] up in heaven throne.

---

[1] *n. 1. The Creation and Fall of Lucifer begins all the English cycles. Though not in Gen. it depends on other Scriptural authority.*   [2] *Rev. i, 8 (and 11) (A.V.):* 'I am Alpha and Omega, the beginning and the ending, saith the Lord.' *All the extant English cycles begin with God saying much these same words.*   [3] *destroy.*   [4] *power.*
[5] *cf. Athanasian Creed (P.B.): The Catholic faith is this, that we worship one God in Trinity, and Trinity in Unity, neither confounding the Persons nor dividing the substance, etc.*   [6] *place.*   [7] *Bound up in me, the only God.*   [8] *goes along with me, cf. Athanasian Creed (P.B.): The Son is of the Father alone, not made, nor created, but begotten ... And in this Trinity there is no before or after.*   [9] *(supernatural) grace.*   [10] *enjoys felicity.*

One God three I call:
I am Father of might,
My Son keepeth[1] right,[1]
My Ghost has light
And grace withal.
   Myself beginning never did take,
And endless I am through my owen might.
Now will I begin my work to make.
First I make heaven with starres of light,
In mirth and joy evermore to wake.
In heaven I build[2] angel full bright
My servantes to be, and for my sake
With mirth and melody worship my might
I build them in my bliss.
Angel in heaven evermore shall be
In light full clear, bright as[3] ble,[4]
With mirth and song to worship me:
Of joy they may not miss.
Hic cantent angeli in caelo:[5] Tibi omnes angeli, tibi caeli et universae potestates, tibi cherubim et seraphim incessabili voce proclamant: Sanctus, Sanctus, Sanctus, Dominus Deus Sabaoth.

Lucifer.   To whose worship sing you this song?
To worship God or reverence me?
But[6] you me worship you do me wrong,
For I am the worthiest that ever may be.

Angeli boni.[7] We worship God of might most strong
Which has formed both us and thee.
We may never worship him too long,
For he is most worthy of majesty.
On knees to God we fall,
Our Lord God worship we,

---

[1] *maintains justice.*   [2] *fashion.*   [3] as (?), *emend* of (?).   [4] *hue, face, appearance.*   [5] *Here let the angels sing in heaven. (Verses from 'Te Deum' (P.B.))* 'To thee all angels cry aloud, the heavens and all the Powers therein, to thee Cherubin and Seraphin continually do cry, "Holy, holy, holy, Lord God of Sabaoth".'   [6] *Unless.*   [7] *Good angels.*

And in no wise honour we thee.
A greater lord may never none be
Than he that made us all.
Lucifer.   A worthier lord, forsooth, am I,
And worthier than he ever will I be.
In evidence that I am more worthy
I will go sitten in Godes see.[1]
Above sun and moon and starres on sky
I am now set as you may see.
Now worship me for most mighty,
And for your lord honour now me,
Sitting in my seat.
Angeli mali.[2] Godes might we forsake,
And for more worthy we thee take:
Thee to worship honour we make,
And fall down at thy feet.
Deus.   Thou, Lucifer, for thy mickle pride,
I bid thee fall from heaven to hell,
And all those that holden on thy side,
In my bliss never more to dwell.
At my commandment anon down thou slide,
With mirth and joy never more to mell.[3]
In mischief[4] and menace[4] ever shalt thou abide,
In bitter burning and fire so fell,[5]
In pain ever to be pight.[6]
Lucifer. At thy bidding thy will I work,
And pass from joy to pain smart.[7]
Now I am a devil full dark
That was an angel bright.
    Now to hell the way I take,
In endless pain there to be pight.
For fear of fire a fart I crack:
In hell dungeon my den is dight.[8]

[1] seat.   [2] Evil angels.   [3] mix.   [4] adversity and danger.   [5] fierce.
[6] fixed.   [7] severe, biting.   [8] arranged.

Deus.[1] Now heaven is made for angel sake,
   The first day and the first night.
   The second day water I make,
   The welkin[2] also full fair and bright.
   The third day I part water from earth;
   Tree and every growing thing,
   Both herb and flower of sweet smelling,
   The third day is made by my working.
   Now make I the day that shall be the fourth.
     Sun and moon and starres also,
   The fourth day I make in same,
   The fifth day, worm[3] and fish that swim and go,
   Birdes and beastes, both wild and tame.
   The sixth day my work I do
   And make thee, man, Adam by name:
   In earthly paradise withouten woe
   I grant thee biding less[4] thou do blame.[4]
     Flesh of thy flesh and bone of thy bone,
   Adam, here is thy wife and make.[5]
   Both fish and fowles that swim and gone
   To everich[6] of them a name thou take;[7]
   Both tree and fruit and beastes each one,
   Red and white, both blue and black,
   Thou give them name by thyself alone,
   Herbes and grass, both beetes and brake;[8]
   Thy wife thou give name also.
   Look that you not cease
   Your fruit to increase
   That there may be press[9]
   Me worship for to do.
     Now come forth, Adam, to paradise.
   There shalt thou have all manner thing:
   Both flesh and fish and fruit of price,
   All shall be buxom[10] at thy bidding.

---

[1] *n. 2.*   [2] *firmament.*   [3] *creeping things.*   [4] *unless. . . wrong.*   [5] *mate.*
[6] *each one.*   [7] *give.*   [8] *bracken.*   [9] *throng.*   [10] *obedient.*

Here is pepper, pyan[1] and sweet liquorice—
Take them all at thy liking—
Both apple and pear and gentle rice.[2]
But touch not this tree that is of cunning—[3]
All thing save this for thee is wrought.
Here is all thing that thee should please,
All ready made unto thy ease:
Eat not this fruit nor me displease,
For then thou diest—thou scapest not.

    Now have I made all thing of nought,
Heaven and earth, fowl and beast.
To all thing that my hand has wrought
I grant my blessing that ever shall last.
My way to heaven is ready[4] sought.[4]
Of working I will the seventh day rest,
And all my creatures that are about
My blessing you have both east and west.
Of working the seventh day you cease;
And all those that cease of labouring here
The seventh day withouten dwere,[5]
And worship me in good manner,
They shall in heaven have endless peace.

    Adam, go forth and be prince in place,
For to heaven I speed my way.
Thy wittes[6] well look thou chase[7]
And ghostly[8] govern thee as I say.

Adam.   Holy Father, blessed thou be,
For I may walk in wealth enough:[9]
I find dates great plenty,
And many fele[10] fruites full every bough.
All this weal[11] is given to me
And to my wife that on me laugh.[12]
I have no need to touch yon tree,

[1] *peony seeds (for spicing).*   [2] *young shoots (?), rice (?).*   [3] *knowledge.*
[4] *found right here (?).*   [5] *doubt.*   [6] *senses.*   [7] (=) *chaste (?), chasten, disci-*
pline.   [8] *spiritually.*   [9] *abundant.*   [10] *excellent.*   [11] *wealth, happiness.*
[12] *smiled.*

Against my Lordes will to work now.
I am a good gardener:
Every fruit of right name
I may gatheren with glee[1] and game;[1]
To break that bond I were to blame
That my Lord bade me keepen here.

Eva.   We may both be blithe and glad
Our Lordes commandment to fulfil:
With fele[2] fruites are we fair fed,
Wonder dulcet and never one ill.
Every tree with fruit is spread,
Of them to take as pleaseth[3] us till.[3]
Our wit were rakil[4] and over-done[5] bad
To forfeit[6] against our Lordes will
In any wise.
In this garden I will go see
All the flowers of fair beauty
And tasten the fruites of great plenty
That are in paradise.

Serpens.   Hail! fair wife and comely dame,
This fruit to eat I thee counsel.
Take this apple and eat this same:
This fruit is best as I thee tell.

Eva. That apple to eat I were to blame!
From joy our Lord would us expel:
We should die and be put out with shame,
In joy of paradise never more to dwell—
God himself thus said—
What day of that fruit we eat.
With these wordes God did us threat,
That we should die, our life to let.[7]
Therefore I am afraid.

Serpens.   Of this apple if you will bite,
Even as God is, so shall you be,

<hr>

[1] *light-hearted pleasure.*   [2] *many.*   [3] *it gives pleasure to us.*   [4] *rash.*
[5] *exceedingly.*   [6] *transgress.*   [7] *lose.*

Wise of cunning,[1] as I you plight,[2]
Like unto God in all degree.
Sun and moon and starres bright,
Fish and fowl, both sand and sea,
At your bidding both day and night,
All thing shall be in your pousty:[3]
You shall be Godes peer.
Take this apple in thy hand,
And to bite thereof thou fond.[4]
Take another to thy husband—
Thereof have thou no dwere.[5]

Eva. So wise as God is, in his great main,[6]
And fellow in cunning[1] fain would I be.
Serpens. Eat this apple and in certain
That I am true soon shalt thou see.
Eva. To my husband with heart full fain
This apple I bear as thou biddest me.
This fruit to eat I shall assayn
So wise as God is if we may be,
And Godes peer of might.
To my husband I walk my way,
And of this apple I shall assay
To make him to eat if that I may,
And of this fruit to bite.
Hic Eva reveniet Adae viro suo.[7]

My seemly spouse and good husband,
Listeneth to me, sir, I you pray.
Take this fair apple all in your hand:
Thereof a morsel bite and assay.
To eat this apple look that you fond,[8]
Godes fellow to be alway,
All his wisdom to understand,
And Godes peer to be for ay,
All thing for to make,

---

[1] *knowledge.* [2] *promise.* [3] *power.* [4] *try.* [5] *fear.* [6] *strength.*
[7] *Here Eve will return to Adam, her husband.* [8] *try.*

Both fish and fowl, sea and sand,
Bird and beast, water and land.
This apple thou take out of my hand,
A bite thereof thou take!

Adam.   I dare not touch thy hand for dread
Of our Lord God omnipotent.
If I should work after thy reed[1]
Of God our maker I should be shent.[2]
If that we do this sinful deed
We shall be dead by Godes judgement.
Out of thy hand with hasty speed
Cast out that apple anon[3] present,[3]
For fear of Godes threat.

Eva. Of this apple if thou wilt bite
Godes peer thou shalt be pight,[4]
So wise of cunning, I thee plight,
This fruit if thou wilt eat.

Adam.   If we it eat ourself we kill,
As God us told we should be dead.
To eat that fruit and my life to spill,[5]
I dare not do after thy reed.

Eva. A fair angel thus said me[6] till:[6]
'To eat that apple take never no dread.
So cunning as God in heaven hill[7]
Thou shalt soon be within[8] a stead.'[8]
Therefore this fruit thou eat.

Adam. Of Godes wisdom for to lere,[9]
And in cunning to be his peer,
Of[10] thy hand I take it here,
And shall soon taste this meat.[11]

    Alas! alas! for this false deed
My fleshly friend my foe I find.
Shameful sin does us unhide:[12]

[1] *advice.*   [2] *destroyed.*   [3] *this very moment.*   [4] *placed.*   [5] *destroy.*
[6] *to me.*   [7] *heaven is variously, in these plays, a hill, tower, hall, as in other contemporary literature (n. 3).*   [8] *on the spot.*   [9] *learn.*   [10] *From.*   [11] *food.*
[12] *uncover, expose.*

I see us naked before and behind.
Our Lordes word would we not dread,
Therefore we are now caitiffes unkind.[1]
Our poor privities for to hide
Some fig leaves fain would I find
For to hide our shame.
Woman, lay this leaf on thy privity,
And with this leaf I shall hide me.
Great shame it is us naked to see,
Our Lord God thus to grame.[2]

Eva.   Alas! that ever that speech was spoken
That the false angel said unto me.
Alas! our makers bidding is broken,
For I have touched his owen dear tree:
Our fleshly eyes are all unlocken,[3]
Naked for sin ourself we see.
That sorry apple that we have sucken
To death has brought my spouse and me.
Right grievous is our sin.
Of mickle shame now do we know.
Alas! that ever this apple was grow.
To dreadful death now are we throw,
In pain us ever to pin.[4]

Deus.   Adam, that with my handes I made,
Where art thou now? What hast thou wrought?

Adam. Ah! Lord, for sin our flowers do fade.
I hear thy voice but I see thee not.

Deus.   Adam, why hast thou sinned so soon?
Thus hastily to break my boon,[5]
And I made thee master under[6] moon[6]
Truly of every tree.
One tree I kept for my owe:[7]
Life and death therein I know.
Thy sin from life now thee has throw,

---

[1] *unnatural, wicked.*   [2] *anger, grieve.*   [3] *opened.*   [4] *fix, confine.*
[5] *command.*   [6] *in this world.*   [7] *own.*

From death thou mayst not flee.

Adam.   Lord, I have wrought against thy will.
I spared not myself to spill.[1]
The woman that[2] thou took me till[2]
She brought me thereto.
It was her counsel and her reed:[3]
She bade me do the same deed.
I walk as worm[4] withouten weed,[4]
Away[5] is shroud[5] and shoe.

Deus.   Woman, that art this mannes wife,
Why hast thou stirred your[6] bothers strife?[6]
Now you are from your fair life
And are deemed for to die.
Unwise woman, say me why
That thou hast done this foul folly?
And I made thee a great lady
In paradise for to play.

Eva.   Lord, when thou wentest from this place
A worm with an angeles face[7]
He hight[8] us to be full of grace,
The fruit if that we eat.
I did his bidding, alas! alas!
Now we are bounden in deathes lace.[9]
I suppose it was Sathanas,
To[10] pain he gan us put.[10]

Deus.   Thou worm with thy wiles wick,[11]
Thy false fables they are full thick.
Why hast thou put deathes prick
In Adam and his wife?
Though they bothen my bidding have broken,
Out of woe yet art[12] not wroken:[12]

---

[1] *ruin, destroy.*   [2] *whom you gave to me.*   [3] *advice.*   [4] *crawling creature with no covering.*   [5] *Lacking clothes.*   [6] *violence for you both.*   [7] *Presumably a handsome actor has his body dressed like a snake but his face exposed, and hands and feet free so that he can walk on and can offer Eve an apple. Later he falls to the floor and wriggles out as if he is a snake (n. 4).*   [8] *promised.*   [9] *cord, snare.*   [10] *He drove us into torment.*   [11] *wicked.*   [12] *you are not rescued.*

In hell lodge thou shalt be locken,
And never more latch[1] life.

Diabolus.   I shall thee say wherefore and why
I did them all this villainy:
For I am full of great envy,
Of wrath and wicked hate,
That man should live above the sky,
Whereas sometime dwelled I,
And now I am cast to hell sty,
Straight out at heaven gate.

Deus.   Adam, for thou that apple bit
Against my bidding, well I woot,[2]
Go! till[3] thy meat with swink[3] and sweat,
Unto thy lifes end.
Go! naked, hungry and barefoot,
Eat both herbes, grass and root:
Thy bale[4] has no other boot,[5]
As wretch in world thou wend.

Woman, thou soughtest this sinning,
And bade him break my bidding:
Therefore thou shalt be underling,
To mannes bidding bend.
What he biddeth thee, do thou that thing,
And bear thy childeren with great groaning,
In danger and in death dreading,
Unto thy lifes end.

Thou wicked worm, full of pride,
Foul envy sit by thy side.
Upon thy gut thou shalt glide
As worm, wicked in kind,[6]
Till a maiden in middle-earth[7] be born.
Thou fiend, I warn thee beforn,
Through her thy head shall be to-torn.[8]

---

[1] *have.*   [2] *know.*   [3] *get your food with toil.*   [4] *misery.*   [5] *cure.*
[6] *nature.*   [7] *earth (the middle of the geocentric universe). The maiden will be Mary, the mother of Jesus, the Redeemer.*   [8] *torn to pieces.*

On womb[1] away thou wend!

Diabolus. At thy bidding foul I fall,
I creep home to my stinking stall.
Hell pit and heaven hall
Shall do thy bidding[2] boon.[2]
I fall down here, a foul freke:[3]
For this fall I gin to quake,
With a fart my breech I break,
My sorrow cometh full soon.

Deus. For your sin that you have do
Out of this bliss soon shall you go,
In earthly labour to liven in woe,
And sorrow you shall ataste.
For your sin and misdoing
An angel with a sword burning
Out of this joy he shall you ding:[4]
Your wealth[5] away is past.

*Hic recedit Deus et angelus seraphicus cum gladio flammeo
verberat Adam et Evam extra paradisum.*[6]

Seraphim. You wretches unkind[7] and right unwise,
Out of this joy hie you in haste!
With flaming sword from paradise
To pain I beat you, of care to taste.
Your mirth is turned to careful sighs,
Your wealth with sin away is waste.
For your false deed of sinful guise
This bliss I spar[8] from you right fast.
Herein come you no more,
Till a child of a maid be born,
And upon the rood[9] rent and torn,
To save all that you have forlorn,[10]
Your wealth for to restore.

Eva. Alas! alas! and welaway!

---

[1] *belly.* [2] *bidden command.* [3] *creature.* [4] *strike.* [5] *well-being.* [6] *Here
God withdraws, and an angel of the seraphic order* (n. 21) *with a flaming sword
beats Adam and Eve out of paradise.* [7] *ungrateful, undutiful.* [8] *shut.*
[9] *cross.* [10] *utterly lost.*

That ever touched I the tree!
I wend as wretch in welsom[1] way.
In black bushes my bower shall be.
In paradise is plenty of play,[2]
Fair fruites right great plenty:
The gates be shut with Godes key.
My husband is lost because of me—
Lief[3] spouse, now thou[4] fand.[4]
Now stumble we on stalk and stone.
My wit away is from me gone—
Writhe in two my neck bone
With hardness of thy hand!

Adam.   Wife, thy[5] wit is not worth a rush![5]
Lief woman, turn thy thought!
I will not slay fleshly of my flesh,
For of my flesh thy flesh was wrought.
Our hap[6] was hard, our[7] wit was nesh,[7]
To paradise when we were brought.
My weeping shall be long fresh,
Short liking shall be long bought.
No more tell thou that tale!
For, if I should slay my wife,
I slew myself withouten knife—
In hell lodge to lead my life,
With woe in weeping[8] dale.[8]

But let us walk forth into the land,
With right great labour our food to find,
With delving and digging with my hand,
Our bliss to[9] bale and care to pind.[9]
And, wife, to spin now must thou fand,[10]
Our naked bodies in cloth to wind,
Till some comfort of Godes sand[11]
With grace relieve our careful mind.

---

[1] *dreary.*   [2] *delight.*   [3] *Dear.*   [4] *thou mayest find, experience (it to be so).*
[5] *you've not an ounce of sense.*   [6] *lot.*   [7] *we were weak in the head.*   [8] *vale of tears.*   [9] *(?) to torment into misery and grief (?). (Might to-pind = utterly tormented?).*   [10] *strive.*   [11] *sending.*

Now come! Go we hence, wife!
Eva. Alas! that ever we wrought this sin
  Our bodily sustenance for to win:
  You must delve and I shall spin,
  In care to leaden our life.

Cain and Abel[1]

Abel.[1]   I would fain know how I should do
  To serve my Lord God to his pleasing.
  Therefore, Cain brother, let us now go
  Unto our father without letting,[2]
  Suing[3] him in virtue and in nurture,[4]
  To come to the high joy celestial,
  Remembering to be clean and pure,
  For in misrule we might lightly fall
  Against heaven king.
  Let us now do our diligence
  To come to our fatheres presence.
  Good brother, pass we hence
  To know[5] for our living.[5]
Cain.   As to my father let us now tee[6]
  To know what shall be his talking.
  And yet[7] I hold it but vanity[7]
  To go to him for any speaking,
  To learn of his law:[8]
  For if I have good enough plenty
  I can be merry, so[9] may I the,[9]
  Though my father I never see—
  I[10] give not thereof an haw.[10]
Abel.   Right sovereign father, seemly,[11] sad[11] and sure,

---

[1] *n. 5.*   [2] *delay.*   [3] *following.*   [4] *moral discipline (?).*   [5] *learn how we
should live.*   [6] *go.*   [7] *yet, MS* y^t *or* þ^t; *. . . pointless.*   [8] *rule of life.*   [9] *upon my life.*
[10] *It doesn't matter to me one bit.*   [11] *fair, firm.*

Ever we thank you in heart, body and thought,
And always shall while our life may endure,
As inwardly in heart it can be sought,
Both my brother and I,[1]
Father, I fall unto your knee
To know how we shall ruled be,
For[2] goodes that falleth[2] both him and me,
I would fain wit[3] truly.[3]

Adam.   Sones, you are, to[4] speaken naturally,[4]
The first-fruit of kindly[5] engendrure,[5]
Before whom, save your mother and I,
Were never none of mannes nature.
And yet were we all of another portraiture[6]
As you have me often heard said soothly.
Wherefore, sones, if you will live sad and sure,
First I you counsel most singularly
God for to love and dread,
And such good as God has you sent
The first fruit offer to him in sacrifice burnt,
Him ever beseeching with meek intent
In all your workes to save and speed.

Abel.   Gramercy, father, for your good doctrine,
For as you us teachen, so shall we do.
And, as for me, through[7] Godes grace divine
I will forthwith apply me thereto.

Cain. And though me be loth, I will now also
Unto your counsel, father, me incline.
And yet I say now to you both two,
I had liefer go home well for to dine.

Adam. Now God grant good sacrifice to you both two!
He vouchsafe to accepten you and all mine,
And give you now grace to pleasen him so,
That you may come to that bliss that himself is in,

---

[1] *Difficult to punctuate next five lines which are written small in MS.*   [2] *With regard to the good things that belong to.*   [3] *know for sure.*   [4] *with reference to the natural order.*   [5] *natural procreation.*   [6] *likeness, image (that of God, see Gen. i, 26).*   [7] *MS* þō.

With ghostly[1] grace,
That all your here-living
May be to his pleasing,
And at your hence-parting
To come to good place.

Abel.   Almighty God, and God full of might,
By whom all thing is made of nought,
To[2] thee my heart is ready dight.[3]
For upon thee is all my thought.

Oh![4] sovereign Lord, reigning in eternity,
With all the meekness that I can or may,
This lamb shall I offer it up to thee.
Accept it, blessed Lord, I thee pray.
My gift is but simple, this[5] is no nay,[5]
But my will is good, and ever shall be,
Thee to serven and worshipen both night and day!
And thereto thy grace grant thou me,
Through thy great mercy,
Which in a lambes likeness[6]
Thou shalt, for mannes wickedness,
Ones[7] be offered in painfulness,
And die full[8] dolefully. [8]

For truly, Lord, thou art most worthy
The best to have in each degree.
Both best and worst, full certainly.
All is had through grace of thee.
The best sheep, full heartily,
Amongst my flock that I can see
I tithe[9] it to God of great mercy,
And better would if better might be.
Even here is my offering

---

[1] *spiritual.*   [2] *For.*   [3] *made.*   [4] *New stanza? (n. 6).*   [5] *there's no denying.*
[6] *Abel looks forward to the sacrifice of God the Son, the Lamb of God, on the cross (cf. John i, 29). The mass, in which this sacrifice is pleaded, refers to the offering of Abel (n. 91).*   [7] *once.*   [8] *in great suffering.*   [9] *Part of the Mosaic law to tithe, or give a tenth of a man's increase to God (Lev. xxvii, 30–34). Also the law of the medieval church.*

I tithe to thee with right good will,
Of the best thou sentest me[1] till.[1]
Now, gracious God on heaven hill,[2]
Accept now my tithing!

Cain.   Amongst all fooles that go on ground
I hold that thou be one of the most!
To tithe the best—that is not sound!—
And keep the worst that is near lost.
But I more wisely shall work this[3] stound.[3]
To tithe the worst, and make[4] no boast,[4]
Of all my cornes that may be found,
In all my fieldes, both croft[5] and coast,[5]
I shall looken[6] on every side.
Here I tithe this unthende[7] sheaf—
Let God take it, or elles leave,[8]
Though it be to me great reproof,
I[9] give no force this tide![9]

Abel.   Now Cain, brother, thou dost full ill,
For God thee sent both best and worst.
Therefore thou show to him good will,
And tithe to God ever of the best.

Cain. In faith thou showest[10] now a feeble skill:[10]
It would me hinder and do me grief.
What[11] were God the better, thou say me till,[11]
To given him away my best sheaf
And keep myself the worse?
He will neither eat nor drink,
For he does neither sweat nor swink.[12]
Thou showest a feeble reason, me[13] think—[13]
What! thou[14] fonnest[14] as a beast, I guess!

Abel.   Yet me thinketh my wit is good
To God evermore some love to show,

---

[1] *to me.*   [2] *n. 3.*   [3] *(at) this time.*   [4] *not talk about it.*   [5] *inside the enclosed ground and on its fringe.*   [6] *see to it.*   [7] *poor.*   [8] *leave (it).*   [9] *At this moment I couldn't care less.*   [10] *put up a weak argument.*   [11] *How much better-off would God be, you tell me.*   [12] *labour.*   [13] *it seems to me.*   [14] *you're as stupid.*

Of whom we have our daily food,
And elles we had but little drew.[1]

Cain. Yet me thinketh thy wit is wood,[2]
For of thy lore[3] I find but few.
I will never the more change my mood[4]
For no wordes that thou dost show.
I say I will tithe the worst.

Abel. Now God that sits in heaven above,
On whom is set all my whole love,
This wicked will from thee he shove,
As it pleaseth him best.

Hic ardent decimum Abel et Cain.[5]

Cain.   Hark! Abel, brother, what[6] array is this?[6]
Thy tithing burneth as fire full bright.
It is to me great wonder, iwis:[7]
I trow this is now a strange sight.

Abel. Godes will forsooth it is
That my tithing with fire is light,
For of the best were my tithis,
And of the worst thou didest him[8] dight.[8]
Bad thing thou him bade:[9]
Of the best was my tithing,
And of the worst was thy offering.
Therefore God Almighty, heaven king,
Alloweth right nought thy deed.

Cain.   What! thou stinking losel![10] and is it so?
Does God thee love and hateth me?
Thou shalt be dead—I shall thee slay!
Thy Lord, thy God, thou shalt never see!
Tithing more shalt thou never do:
With this chavil-bone[11] I shall slay thee.
Thy death is dight![12] Thy days are go!
Out of my handes shalt thou not flee!
With this stroke I thee kill.

[1] *morsel.*   [2] *mad.*   [3] *doctrine.*   [4] *mind.*   [5] *Here Abel and Cain burn the tithe.*   [6] *what is happening here.*   [7] *indeed.*   [8] *give to, appoint for, him.*   [9] *offered.*   [10] *rascal.*   [11] *jaw-bone: n. 7.*   [12] *fixed.*

Now this boy[1] is slain and dead
Of him I shall never more have dread:
He shall hereafter never eat bread.
With this grass I shall him hill.[2]

Deus.   Cain! come forth and answer me!
Absolve[3] my question anon right![3]
Thy brother, Abel, where is now he?
Have done! and answer me as[4] tight.[4]

Cain. My brothers keeper, who made me?
Since when was I his keeping-knight?[5]
I cannot tell where that he be.
To keep him was I never dight.[6]
I know not where he is.

Deus. Ah! cursed Cain! thou art untrue,
And for thy deed thou shalt sore rue.
Thy brothers blood, that thou slew,
Asketh vengeance of thy miss.[7]
   Thou shalt be cursed on the ground,
Unprofitable whereso thou wend,
Both vain[8] and naughty and nothing sound,
With what thing thou meddle thou shalt it shend.[9]

Cain. Alas! in woe now am I wound,
Accursed of God as man unkind.[10]
Of any man if I be found
He shall me slay—I have no friend.
Alas! and welaway!

Deus. Of what man that thou be slain
He shall have sevenfold more pain:
Him[11] were better[11] to be seen
  Alive by night nor day.

Cain.   Alas! alas! whither may I go?
I dare never see[12] man in the visage.[13]
I am wounden as a wretch in woe,

[1] *fellow.*   [2] *cover-up : n. 7.*   [3] *Resolve . . . straightway.*   [4] *immediately.*
[5] *security man?*   [6] *appointed.*   [7] *misdeed.*   [8] *worthless.*   [9] *spoil, ruin.*
[10] *alien, unnatural.*   [11] *It would be better for him (not?).*   [12] *look.*   [13] *face.*

And cursed of God for my falsage.[1]
Unprofitable and vain also,
In field and town, in[2] street and stage,[2]
I may never make mirthes mo.[3]
I wot never whither to take passage:
I dare not here abide.
Now will I go wend my way,
With sore sighing and welaway,
To look where that I best may
From mannes sight me hide.
Introitus 'Noë'.[4]

Noah[5]

Noë.   God of his goodness and of grace ground,
By whose glorious power all thing is wrought,
In whom all virtue plenteously is found,
Withouten whose will may be right nought,
Thy servantes save, Lord, from sinful sound,[6]
In will, in work, in deed and in thought—
Our[7] wealth in woe let never be found,[7]
Us help, Lord, from sin that we are in brought,
Lord God, full of might.
[*To audience.*] Noah, sires, my name is know,
My wife and my childeren here on[8] row.[8]
To God we pray with heart full low[9]
To please him in his sight.
    In me, Noah, the second age[10]
In deed beginneth as I you say.
After Adam, withouten[11] language,[11]

---

[1] *wickedness.*   [2] *on highway and in inn (?) = travelling or resting, (or?) in the
street or on the stand, scaffold (of the playing-place?).*   [3] *more.*   [4] *Enter 'Noah'
(n. 8).*   [5] *nn. 8 and 9.*   [6] *sleep, torpor.*   [7] *Never let our well-being be con-
founded (?) in misery.*   [8] *in order.*   [9] *lowly.*   [10] *p. 31.*   [11] *to put it briefly.*

The second father am I, in[1] fay,[1]
But men of[2] living are so outrage,[2]
Both by night and eke by day,
That less[3] than sin the sooner swage[3]
God will be venged on us some way
In deed.
There may no man go thereout,
But sin reigneth in every route;
In every place round about
Cursedness does spring and spread.

Uxor Noë.[4]   Almighty God of his great grace
Inspire men with heartly will
For to cease of their trespass,
For sinful living our soul shall spill.[5]
Sin offendeth God in his face,
And aggrieveth our Lord full ill.
It causeth to man right great menace[6]
And scrapeth him out of lifes bill,[7]
That blessed book.
What man in sin does always sleep
He shall go to hell full deep.
Then shall he never after creep
Out of that burning brook.
    I am your wife, your childeren these be.
Unto[8] us twain it doth long[8]
Them to teach in[9] all degree[9]
Sin to forsaken and workes wrong.
Therefore, fere,[10] for love of me,
Inform them well ever among
Sin to forsake and vanity,
And virtue to follow that they fong,[11]
Our Lord God to please.

Noë. I warn you, childeren, one and all,

---

[1] *believe me.*   [2] *are so outrageous in their living.*   [3] *unless sin quickly abate.*
[4] *Wife of Noah.*   [5] *kill.*   [6] *danger.*   [7] *cf. Rev. iii, 5, 'blot his name out of
the book of life', Psalm lxix, 28 etc.*   [8] *It is the iob of us two.*   [9] *in every respect.*   [10] *(my) mate.*   [11] *endeavour.*

Dread our Lord God in heaven hall,[1]
And in no forfeit[2] that we not fall
Our Lord for to displease.

Shem.   Ah! dear father! God forbid
That we should do in any wise
Any work of sinful deed
Our Lord God that should agrise.[3]
My name is Shem, your son[4] of price:[4]
I shall work after your rede.[5]
And also, wife, thee[6] well advise[6]
Wicked workes that thou[7] none breed[7]
Never in no degree.

Uxor Shem. Forsooth, sir, by Godes grace,
I shall me keep from all trespass
That should offend Godes face,
By help of the Trinity.

Cham.   I am Cham, your second son,
And purpose me by Godes might
Never such a deed for to don
That should aggrieve God in sight.

Uxor Cham. I pray to God me[8] grant this boon[9]
That he me keep in such a plight,
Morning, evening, midday and noon,
I to offenden him day nor night.
Lord God, I thee pray,
Both waking and eke in sleep,
Gracious God, thou me keep
That I never in danger creep
On dreadful Doomesday.[10]

Japhet.   Japhet, thy third son, is my name.
I pray to God, whereso we be,
That he us borrow[11] from sinful shame,
And in virtuous living evermore keep me.

[1] *n. 3.*   [2] *offence.*   [3] *offend.*   [4] *worthy son.*   [5] *counsel.*   [6] *consider carefully.*   [7] *you are not responsible for.*   [8] *(to) me.*   [9] *prayer.*   [10] *pp. 368 ff.*
[11] *protect.*

Uxor Japhet. I am your wife and pray the same,
  That God us save on sand and sea,
  With no grievance that we him grame.[1]
  He grant us grace sin to flee.
  Lord God, now hear our boon.
Noë. Gracious God, that[2] best may,[2]
  With hearty will to thee we pray,
  Thou save us secure both night and day,
  Sin that we none done.
Deus.   How? What meaneth this misliving man,
  Which my hand made and builded[3] in bliss?
  Sin so sore grieveth me, yea, in certain,
  I will be venged of this great miss.[4]
  My angel dear, thou shalt gon
  To Noah, that my servant is,
  A ship to make on hand to tan[5]
  Thou bid him, swith,[6] for him and his,
  From drenching[7] them to save.
  For as I am God of might
  I shall destroy this world down right:
  Their sin so sore grieveth me in sight
  They shall no mercy have.
    Fecisse[8] hominem nunc paenitet me.[8]
  That I made man sore does me rue.
  My handwork to slay sore grieveth me,
  But that their sin their death does brew.[9]
  Go! say to Noah, as I bid thee,
  Himself, his wife, his childeren true,
  Those eight soules in ship to be.
  They shall not dread the floodes flow:
  The flood shall harm them nought.
  Of all fowles and beastes they take a pair
  In ship to save both foul and fair

---

[1] *anger.*   [2] *who may bring about the best.*   [3] *established.*   [4] *wrong.*
[5] *take.*   [6] *instantly.*   [7] *drowning.*   [8] *It now repents me that I made man.*
[9] *bring about.*

From all doubtes[1] and great despair,
This vengeance ere it be wrought.

Angelus.   Noah! Noah! a ship look thou make,
And many a chamber thou shalt have therein.
Of every kindes[2] beast a couple thou take
Within the ship-board, their lives to win.
For God is sore grieved with man for his sin,
That all this wide world shall be drenched[3] with flood,
Save thou and thy wife shall be kept from this gin,[4]
And also thy childeren with their virtues good.

Noë.   How should I have wit a ship for to make?
I am of right great age, five hundred year old.
It is not for me this work to undertake:
For faintness[5] of age my legges gin[6] fold.[6]

Angelus. This deed for to do be both blithe and bold.
God shall inform thee and rule thee full right.
Of bird and of beast take as I thee told
A pair into the ship and God shall thee quight.[7]

Noë.   I am full ready, as God does me bid,
A ship for to make by might of his grace.
Alas! that for sin it shall be so betid[8]
That vengeance of flood shall work this menace.[8]
God is sore grieved with our great trespass
That with wild water the world shall be dreint,[9]
A ship for to make now let us hence pass,
That God against us of sin have no complaint.

Hic transit Noë cum familia sua pro navi, quo exeunte locum interludii sub intret statim Lamech conductus ab adolescente.[10]

Lamech. Great mourning I make and great cause I have,
Alas! now I see not, for age I am blind.

---

[1] *terrors.*   [2] *sort of.*   [3] *drowned.*   [4] *scheme.*   [5] *(?) (see Block)* = *feebleness(?).*   [6] *grow weak.*   [7] *deliver.*   [8] *brought about that vengeance shall bring this threat of flood to pass.*   [9] *drowned.*   [10] *Here Noah crosses [the playing-place] with his family to get the ship, and on his exit from the playing-place let Lamech take his place at once, led by a youth. (The Lamech episode is not found in the other English cycles—n. 10—in which the ark is made on stage and not off, as here.)*

Blindness does make me of wit for to rave;
Wanting of eyesight in pain does me bind.
While I had sight there might never man find
My peer of archery in all this world about,
For yet shot I never at hart, hare nor hind
But[1] if that he died,[1] of this no man have doubt.
    Lamech, the good archer, my name was over all,
For the best archer my name did ever spread.
Record of my boy here, witness this he shall,
What mark[2] that were set me, to death it should bleed.

Adolescens. It is true, master, that you say indeed,
For that time you had your bow bent in hand
If that your prick[3] had been half a mile in brede[4]
You would the prick have hit, if you nigh had stand.

Lamech.   I should never have failed, what mark that
    ever were set,
While that I might look and had my clear sight.
And yet, as me[5] thinketh,[5] no man should shoot bet[6]
Than I should do now, if my hand were set aright.
Espy some mark, boy, my bow shall I bend wight,[7]
And set my hand even[8] to shoot at some beast,
And I dare lay a wager, his death for to dight,[9]
The mark shall I hit, my life do I hest.[10]

Adolescens.   Under yon great bush, master, a beast do I
    see!
Take[11] me thy hand, swith,[12] and hold it full still.
Now is thy hand even as ever it may be!
Draw up thy tackle yon beast for to kill.

Lamech. My bow shall I draw right with hearty will,
This broad arrow I shoot that beast for to sail.[13]
Now have at that bush, yon beast for to spill![14]
A sharp shot I shot, thereof I shall not fail.

---

[1] *Without its dying.*   [2] *target.*   [3] *target.*   [4] *breadth. Lamech's boy is impertinently sarcastic to his master (perhaps to represent further unnatural wickedness, for those who are older and who are masters should be respected).*   [5] *it seems to me.*   [6] *better.*   [7] *swiftly.*   [8] *directly, straight.*   [9] *fix.*   [10] *pledge.*   [11] *Give.*   [12] *quickly.*   [13] *assail.*   [14] *kill.*

Cain.   Out! out! and alas! My heart is asunder!
With a broad arrow I am dead and slain.
I die here on ground. My heart is all to tunder:[1]
With this broad arrow it is cloven in twain.
Lamech. Hark! boy, come! Tell me the truth in certain!
What man is he that this cry does thus make?
Adolescens. Cain thou hast killed, I tell thee full plain!
With thy sharp shooting his death has he take.
Lamech.   Have I slain Cain? Alas! what have I done?
Thou stinking lurdein![2] What hast thou wrought?
Thou art the why[3] I slay him so soon:[3]
Therefore shall I kill thee here—thou scapest not!

Hic Lamech cum arcu suo verberat adolescentem ad mortem.[4]

Adolescens. Out! out! I die here. My death is now sought.
This thief with his bow has broke my brain.
There may none help be! My death is me brought.
Dead here I sink down, as man that is slain.
Lamech.   Alas! what shall I do, wretch, wicked on
wold?[5]
God will be venged full[6] sadly[6] on me.
For death of Cain I shall have sevenfold
More pain than he had, that Abel did slay.
These two mennes death full sore bought shall be.
Upon all my blood God will venge this deed.
Wherefore sore weeping hence will I flee
And look where I may best my head soon hide.

Hic recedat Lamech et statim intrat Noë cum navi cantantes.[7]

Noë.   With doleful heart, sighing sad and sore,
Great mourning I make for this dreadful flood.
Of man and of beast is drenched[8] many a score.
All this world to spill[9] these floodes are full wood,[10]
And all is for sin of mannes wild mood[11]
That God has ordained this dreadful vengeance.

---

[1] *tinder(?).*   [2] *loafer.*   [3] *cause of my slaying him just like that.*   [4] *Here Lamech beats the youth to death with his bow.*   [5] *earth.*   [6] *most surely.*   [7] *Here let Lamech withdraw and Noah enters immediately with his boat, singing.*   [8] *drowned.*   [9] *destroy.*   [10] *wild.*   [11] *heart, disposition.*

In this flood spilt is many a mannes blood:
For sinful living of man we have great grievance.[1]
   All this hundred year right here have I wrought
This ship for to make, as God did bid me.
Of all manner[2] beastes a couple is in brought,
Within my ship-board, alive for to be.
Right long God has suffered,[3] amending to see:[3]
All this hundred year God has showed grace.
Alas! from great sin man will not flee,
God does this vengeance for our great trespass.

Uxor Noë.   Alas![4] for great ruth of this great vengeance![4]
Great dole it is to see this water so wide!
But yet, thanked be God of[5] this ordinance,[5]
That we are now saved alive to abide.

Shem. For great sin of lechery all this does betide.
Alas! that ever such sin should be wrought!
This flood is so great on every aside
That all this wide world to care is now brought.

Uxor Shem.   Because of childeren of God, that weren
    good,
Did forfeit[6] right sore, what time that they were
Sinfully[7] compelled to Caines blood,[7]
Therefore are we now cast in right great care.

Cham. For sinful living this world does forfare:[8]
So grievous vengeance might never man see.
Over all this world wide there is no plot bare,
With water and with flood God venged will be.

Uxor Cham.   Rustiness[9] of sin is cause of these wawes.[10]
Alas! in this flood this world shall be lorn.[11]
For offence to God, breaking his lawes,
On rockes right sharp is many a man torn.

Japhet. So grievous floodes were never yet beforn.

---

[1] *suffering.*   [2] *kinds of.*   [3] *been patient, looking for amendment.*   [4] *How sad the most pitiful sight of this massive retribution!*   [5] *for . . . provision.*   [6] *transgress.*
[7] *Compelled to be sinful because they were of the family of Cain(?) (typical descendant of Adam and Eve from whose disobedience derived Man's 'original sin').*
[8] *perish.*   [9] *The corrosion, corruption of sin.*   [10] *waves.*   [11] *lost.*

Alas! that lechery this vengeance does gin.[1]
It were well better ever to be unborn
Than for to forfeiten evermore in that sin.

Uxor Japhet.   Our Lord God I thank of his great grace,
That he does us save from this dreadful pain.
Him for to worship in every stead and place
We are greatly bound, with might and with main.

Noë. Forty days and nightes has lasted this rain,
And forty days this great flood beginneth to slake.
This crow shall I send out to seek some plain,
Good tidinges to bring this message[2] I make.

Hic emittat corvum et parvum[3] expectans iterum dicat:

   This crow on some carrion is fall for to eat,
Therefore a new messanger I will forth now send.
Fly forth! thou fair dove, over these wateres wet,
And espy after some dry land our mourning to amend.

Hic evolet columba qua redeunte[4] cum ramo viridi olivae.

Joy now may we make of mirth that[5] that were friend.[5]
A great olive bush this dove does us bring.
For joy of this token right heartily we tend[6]
Our Lord God to worship, a song let us sing.

Hic decantent hos versus:[7] Mare vidit et fugit; Jordanis
conversus est retrorsum. Non nobis, domine, non nobis,
sed nomini tuo da gloriam.

Et sic recedant cum navi. Introitus Abrahae etc.

---

[1] *begin.*   [2] *messenger.*   [3] parvum, *MS.* parum; *Here let him send forth a
raven and, after waiting a little, let him say again. (Eating of carrion by the raven
or crow unscriptural: n. 11).*   [4] redeunte, *MS.* redeinte (?) redemte (?); *Here let
the dove fly away and when it returns with a green olive-branch (let Noah say).*
[5] *that that dove (?) act (?) was a friend (?) favourable (to us).*   [6] *intend (?)
attend (?).*   [7] *Here let them sing these verses. The sea saw it and fled; Jordan was
driven back. Not unto us, O Lord, not unto us, but unto thy name give glory (Psalms
cxiv, 3, and cxv, 1 (A.V.)). And so let them withdraw with the ship. Enter Abraham
etc. (n. 12).*

Abraham and Isaac[1]

[*Abraham.*]   Most mighty maker of sun and of moon,
  King of kinges and Lord over all,
  Almighty God in heaven throne,
  I thee honour and evermore shall.
  My Lord! my God! to thee I call,
  With hearty will, Lord, I thee pray,
  In sinful life let me never fall,
  But let me live ever to thy pay.[2]
     Abraham, my name is kidde,[3]
  And patriarch of age full old.
  And yet by the grace of God is bred
  In my old age a child full bold.
  Isaac, lo! here his name is told,
  My sweet son that standeth me by.
  Amongst all childeren that walken on wold[4]
  A lovelier child is none truly.
     I thank God with heart well mild
  Of his great mercy and of his high grace,
  And principally for my sweet child
  That shall to me do great solace.
  Now sweet son, fair fare thy face!
  Full heartily do I love thee.
  For true hearty love now, in this place,
  My sweet child, come kiss now me.
Isaac.   At your bidding your mouth I kiss.
  With lowly heart I you pray,
  Your fatherly love let me never miss,
  But bless me your child both night and day.
Abraham. Almighty God that best may,

[1] *n. 12.*   [2] *liking.*   [3] *renowned.*   [4] *earth.*

His dear blessing he grant thee,
And my blessing thou have alway
In what place that ever thou be.
   Now Isaac, my son so sweet,
Almighty God look thou honour,
Which that made both dry and wet,
Shining sun and sharp shower.
Thou art my sweet child and paramour,[1]
Full well in heart do I thee love.
Look that thy heart in heaven tower
Be set to serve our Lord God above.
   In thy youth[2] learn God to please,
And God shall quite thee well thy meed.
Now, sweet son, of wordes these
With all thy heart thou take good heed.
Now farewell, son—God be thy speed!
Even here at home thou me abide.
I must go walken for I have need—
I come again within a tide.[3]

Isaac.   I pray to God, Father of might,
That he you speed in all your way.
From shame and shenship,[4] day and night,
God[5] may you keep[5] in your journey.

Abraham. Now farewell, son, I thee pray,
Ever in thy heart look God thou wind;
Him to serve, both night and day,
I pray to God send thee good mind.
   There may no man love better his child
Than Isaac is loved of me.
Almighty God, merciful and mild,
For my sweet son I worship thee.
I thank thee, Lord, with heart full free,
For this fair fruit thou hast me sent.
Now gracious God, whereso he be,

---

[1] *loved one.*   [2] *MS* ʒou(?n)ge.   [3] *little while.*   [4] *disgrace.*   [5] *may God keep you.*

To save my son evermore be bent.[1]
 Dear Lord, I pray to thee, also,
Me to save for thy servant,
And send me grace never for to do
Thing that should be to thy displeasant.
Both for me and for my infant
I pray thee, Lord God, us to help:
Thy gracious goodness thou us grant,
And save thy servant from hell whelp.[2]

Angelus. Abraham! how! Abraham!
List and hark well unto me!

Abraham. All ready, sir, here I am.
Tell me your will what that it be.

Angelus. Almighty God thus does bid thee
Isaac, thy son, anon thou take,
And look him thou slay, anon, let see,
And sacrifice to God him make.
 Thy well-beloved child thou must now kill.
To God thou offer him, as I say,
Even upon yon high hill
That I thee show here in the way.
Tarry not by night nor day
But smartly thy gate[3] thou go:
Upon yon hill thou kneel, and pray
To God, and kill the child there and sloo.[4]

Abraham. Now Godes commandment must needes be
  done:
All his will is worthy to be wrought.
But yet, the father to slay the son,
Great care it causeth in my thought.
In bitter bale[5] now am I brought,
My sweet child with knife to kill.
But yet my sorrow availeth right nought,
For needes I must work Godes will.

---

[1] *intent.* [2] *Mr. Nellist suggests cf. Psalm xxii, 20.* [3] *way.* [4] *slay (him).*
[5] *grief.*

With heavy heart I walk and wend
My childes death now for to be.
Now must the father his sweet son shend—[1]
Alas![2] for ruth, it is pity![2]
My sweet son, come hither to me!
How! Isaac, my son dear,
Come to thy father, my child so free,[3]
For we must wend together in fere.[4]

Isaac.   All ready, father, even[5] at your will,[5]
And at your bidding I am you by;
With you to walk over dale and hill
At your calling I am ready.
To the father, ever most comely,
It hoveth[6] the child ever buxom[7] to be:
I will obey full heartily
To all thing that you bid me.

Abraham.   Now, son, on thy neck this fagot thou take,
And this fire bear in thy hand,
For we must now sacrifice go make,
Even after the will of Godes sand.[8]
Take this burning brand,
My sweet child, and let us go.
There may no man that[9] liveth in land[9]
Have more sorrow than I have woe.

Isaac.   Fair father, you go right still!
I pray you, father, speak unto me.

Abraham. My good child, what is thy will?
Tell me thy heart I pray to thee.

Isaac. Father! fire and wood here is plenty,
But I can see no sacrifice.
What you should offer fain would I see,
That it were done at the best advice.

Abraham.   God shall that ordain, that sits in heaven,

---

[1] *harm, destroy.*   [2] *What a shame and tragedy it is!*   [3] *noble, excellent.*
[4] *company.*   [5] *just as you wish.*   [6] *behoves.*   [7] *obedient.*   [8] *sending, envoy.*
[9] *= alive.*

My sweet son, for this offering.
A dearer sacrifice may no man nemmen[1]
Than this shall be, my dear darling.
Isaac. Let be, good father, your sad weeping!
Your heavy cheer aggrieveth me sore.
Tell me, father, your great mourning,
And I shall seek some help therefore.
Abraham.   Alas! dear son, for needes must me
Even here thee kill as God has sent.
Thy owen father thy death must be—
Alas! that ever this bow was bent.[2]
With this fire bright thou must be burnt:
An angel said to me right so.
Alas! my child, thou shalt be shent:[3]
Thy careful father must be thy foe.
Isaac.   Almighty God, of his great mercy,
Full heartily I thank thee certain.
At Godes bidding here for to die
I obey me here for to be slain.
I pray you, father, be glad and fain
Truly to work Godes will.
Take good comfort to you again,
And have no doubt[4] your child to kill,
    For Godes bidding, forsooth it is,
That I of you my death should take.
Against God you do amiss
His bidding if you should forsake.
Your owen damnation should you bake
If you me keep from this reed.[5]
With your sword my death you make
And work evermore the will of God.
Abraham.   The will of God must needes be done:
To work his will I said never nay.
But yet the father to slay the son

---

[1] *name.*   [2] *drawn: thus = Alas! that this business was ever begun.*   [3] *destroyed.*
[4] *fear.*   [5] *resolution, counsel.*

My[1] heart does cling and cleave as clay.[1]

Isaac. Yet work Godes will, father, I you pray,
And slay me here anon forthright,
And turn from me your face away,
My head when that you shall off smight.

Abraham. Alas! dear child, I may not choose:
I must needes my sweet son kill.
My dear darling now must me lose,
My owen sibb[2] blood now shall I spill.
Yet this deed ere I fulfil,
My sweet son, thy mouth I kiss.

Isaac. All ready, father, even at your will,
I do your bidding as reason is.

Abraham. Alas! dear son, here is no grace,
But needes dead now must thou be.
With this kerchief I cover thy face
In the time that I slay thee.
Thy lovely visage would I not see,
Not for all this worldes good.
With this sword that sore grieveth me
My child I slay and spill his blood.

Angelus. Abraham! Abraham! thou father free![3]

Abraham. I am here, ready. What is your will?

Angelus. Extend thy hand in no degree!
I bid thou him not kill.
Here do I see by right good skill[4]
Almighty God that thou dost dread.
For thou sparest not thy son to spill
God will acquit thee well thy meed.

Abraham. I thank my God in heaven above.
And him honour for this great grace.
And that my Lord me thus does prove
I will him worship in every place.
My childes life is my solace:

---

[1] *Causes my heart to cling and stick like clay.*   [2] *kin's.*   [3] *noble, excellent.*
[4] *demonstration.*

I thank my God ever for his life.
In sacrifice here, ere I hence pass,
I slay this sheep with this same knife.
    Now this sheep is dead and slain
With this fire it shall be burnt.
Of Isaac, my son, I am full fain
That my sweet child shall not be shent.[1]
This place I name, with good intent,
The hill of Godes visitation,
For hither God has to us sent
His comfort after great tribulation.

Angelus.   Hark! Abraham, and take good heed!
By himself God has thus sworn,
For that thou wouldest have done this deed
He will thee bless both even and morn.
For thy dear child thou wouldest have lorn,
At Godes bidding, as I thee tell,
God has sent thee word beforn
Thy seed shall multiply whereso thou dwell.

    As starres in heaven are many and fele,[2]
So shall thy seed increase and grow.
Thou shalt overcome[3] in wealth and weal[4]
All thy foemen[5] reckoned by[6] row.[6]
As sand in the sea does ebb and flow,
Has cheseles[7] many innumerable,
So shall thy seed—thou mayst me trow[8]—
Increase and be ever profitable.

    For to my speech thou didest obey
Thy enemies portes[9] thou shalt possede,[10]
And all men on earth, as I thee say,
They shall be blessed in thy seed.
Almighty God thus thee will meed[11]
For that good will that thou hast done.
Therefore thank God in word and deed,

---

[1] *harmed.*   [2] *numerous.*   [3] *surpass.*   [4] *well-being.*   [5] *enemies.*   [6] *in order.*
[7] *pebbles.*   [8] *believe.*   [9] *gates.*   [10] *possess.*   [11] *reward.*

Both thou thyself and Isaac thy son.

Abraham. Ah! my Lord God, to worship on knee now I
 fall,
I thank thee, Lord, of thy mercy.
Now my sweet child, to God thou call,
And thank we that Lord now heartily.

Isaac. With lowly heart to God I cry,
I am his servant both day and night.
I thank thee, Lord, in heaven so high,
With heart, with thought, with main, with might.

Abraham. Gramercy! Lord and King of grace,
Gramercy! Lord over lordes all.
Now my joy returneth[1] his trace,[1]
I thank thee, Lord, in heaven thy hall.

Isaac. Over all kinges, crowned King I thee call.
At thy bidding to die with knife
I was full buxom,[2] even as thy thrall.
Lord, now I thank thee thou grantest me life.

Abraham. Now we have worshipped our blessed Lord,
On ground kneeling upon our knee.
Now let us twain soon be of one accord
And go walk home into our country.

Isaac. Father, as you will, so shall it be.
I am ready with you to gon.
I shall you follow with heart full free,
All that you bid me soon shall be done.

Abraham. Now God, all thing of nought that made,
Ever worshipped he be on water and land.
His great honour may never more fade.
In field, nor town, sea, nor on sand.
As all thing, Lord, thou hast in hand,
So save us all, whereso we be,
Whether we sitten, walk or stand,
Ever on thy handwork thou have pity.

Explicit.[3]

1 *makes its way back.*   2 *obedient.*   3 *The end.*

Moses[1]

Introitus 'Moyses'.[2]
Moyses.   He[3] that made all thing of nought,
Heaven and earth, both sun and moon,
Save all that his hand has wrought,
Almighty God in heaven throne!
I am Moses that make this boon.[4]
I pray thee, Lord God, with all my mind,
To us incline thy mercy soon,
Thy gracious lordship let us find.

    Thee to pleasen in all degree,
Gracious God and Lord over all,
Thou grant us grace whereso we be,
And save us sound from sinful fall.
Thy will to work to us, thy thrall,
Inform and teach us all thy pleasance.
In pureness put us, that never[5] not fall,[5]
And ground us in grace from all grievance.
Hic Moyses videns rubum ardentem admirande dicit:[6]

    Ah! mercy, God, what meaneth yon sight?
A green bush as fire does flame,
And keepeth his colour fair and bright,
Fresh and green withouten blame.
It figureth[7] some thing of right great fame—
I cannot seyn[8] what it may be.
I will go near in Godes name
And wisely look this bush to see.
Deus.   Moses! how! Moses!

[1] *Title supplied: that it is correct is proved by 'Explicit' at end (p. 115 and n. 13).*   [2] *Enter 'Moses'.*   [3] *May he.*   [4] *prayer.*   [5] *will never fail.*   [6] *Here Moses, seeing the burning bush, says with wonder.*   [7] *is a figure for something (traditionally, the Incarnation: n. 14).*   [8] *see (say?).*

Hark to me, anon, this[1] stound![1]

Moyses. I am here, Lord, withouten[2] les,[2]
Your gracious will to do I am bound.

Deus. Thou take thy shoes anon full round
Off thy feet, in haste let see.
Full holy is that place and ground
There thou dost stand, I say to thee.

Moyses.   Barefoot now I do me make,
And pull off my shoes from my feet.
Now have I my shoes off take,
What is your will, Lord, fain would I wit.

Deus. Come near, Moses, with me to meet.
These tables I take[3] thee in thy hand.
With my finger in them is writ
All my lawes, thou understand.

Look that thou preach all about,
Whoso will have friendship of me
To my lawes look they lout,[4]
That they be kept in all degree.
Go forth and preach, anon, let see!
Look thou not cease night nor day.

Moyses. Your bidding, Lord, all wrought shall be.
Your will to work I walk my way.

Custodi praecepta Domini Dei tui (Deuteronomy vi.).[5]
The commandment of thy Lord God, man, look thou
keep,
Where that thou walk, wake or sleep,
Every man, take good heed,
And to my teaching take good intent,
For God has sent me now in deed
You for to inform his commandment.
You to teach God has me sent
His lawes of life that are full wise.

---

[1] *at this time.*   [2] *without lying = trust me.*   [3] *give.*   [4] *bow.*   [5] '*Keep the commandments of the Lord thy God*'. *Here begins a sermon, the text being pronounced first in Latin (which is extra-metrical) and then in English.*

Them to learn be diligent,
Your soules may they save at the last assize.[1]
    The preceptes that taught shall be
Are written in these tables twain.
In the first are written three
That touch[2] to God, this is certain.
In the second table are written full plain
The other seven that touch mankind.
Hark now well, man, what I shall sayn,
And print these lawes well in thy mind.
Primum mandatum: non habebis deos alienos.
    The first commandment of God, as I you say,
Of the first table, forsooth is this:
Thou shalt have neither night nor day
None other god but the King of Bliss.
Understand well what meaneth this,
Every man in his degree,
And set never your heart amiss
Upon this worldes vanity.
    For if thou set thy love so sore
Upon riches and worldly good,
Thy worldly riches thou takest evermore
Even for thy god, as man over-wood.[3]
Amend thee, man, and change thy mood.[4]
Lose not thy soul for worldes wealth.
Only him love, which bodily food
Does give all day, and ghostly[5] health.
Secundum mandatum: non assumes nomen Dei tui in vanum.
    The second precept of the first table:
The name of God take never in vain.
Swear no oathes by no false fable,
The name of God thou never distain.[6]
Beware of oathes, for doubt[7] of pain,
Amongst fellowship when thou dost sit.

---

[1] *judgement (p. 368).*   [2] *refer, pertain to.*   [3] *completely crazy.*   [4] *heart, disposition.*   [5] *spiritual.*   [6] *dishonour.*   [7] *fear.*

A little oath, this is certain,
May damn thy soul to hell pit.

Man, when thou art set[1] at the nale,[1]
And hast thy language as pleaseth thee,
Look thy oathes be none or small,
And yet always look true they be.
But swear not often, by rede[2] of me,
For if thou use oftentime to swear
It may gender custom in thee—
Beware of custom, for he will dere.[3]
Tertium mandatum: memento ut sabbatum sanctifices.

The third commandment of God, as I reed,[4]
Does bid thee hallow well thy Holy Day.
Keep thee well from sinful deed,
And care not greatly for rich array.
A right poor man, this[5] is no nay,[5]
Of simple estate in clothes rent,
May be better than rich with garmentes gay,
Oftentime does keep this commandment.

For rich men do show oftentime pomp and pride
On Holy Days, as often is seen.
When poor men pass and go beside,
At worthy feastes rich men will been.
Thy Holy Day thou keepest not clean
In gluttony to lead thy life.
In Godes house you should bedene[6]
Honour your God, both maiden and wife.
Quartum mandatum: honora patrem tuum et matrem tuam.

Of the second table the first commandment,
And in the order the fourth, I[7] say in fay:[7]
He biddeth thee evermore with heart bent[8]
Both father and mother to worship alway.
Though that thy father be poor of array,
And thou never so rich of gold and good,

---

[1] *sitting in the pub.*   [2] *advice.*   [3] *do harm.*   [4] *advise.*   [5] *it cannot be denied.*   [6] *entirely, indeed.*   [7] *believe me.*   [8] *submissive.*

Yet look thou worship him night and day
Of whom thou hast both flesh and blood.
   In this commandment included is
Thy bodily father and mother also.
Included, also, I find in this
Thy ghostly[1] father and mother thereto.
To thy ghostly father ever reverence do.
Thy ghostly mother is Holy Church.
These twain save thy soul from woe!
Ever them to worship look that thou work.

Quintum mandatum: non occides.

   The fifth commandment biddeth all us
Slay no man, no wight[2] that thou kill.
Understand this precept thus:
Slay no wight with word nor will.
Wicked word worketh oftentime great ill:
Beware therefore of wicked language.
Wicked speech many one does spill:[3]
Therefore of speech be not outrage.[4]

Sextum mandatum: non moechaberis.

   The sixth commandment biddeth every man
That no wight lead no lecherous lay.[5]
Forfeit[6] never by no woman,
Less[7] than[7] the law allow thy play.
Trespass never with wife nor may,[8]
With widow nor with none other wight.
Keep thee clean, as I thee say,
To whom thou hast thy troth plight.

Septimum mandatum: non furtum facies.

   Do no theft, no thing thou steal,
The seventh precept biddeth thee full sore.
While thou art in wealth and weal,
Evil-get[9] good[9] look thou restore.
Of handes and deed be true evermore,

---

[1] *spiritual.*   [2] *person.*   [3] *destroy.*   [4] *extravagant.*   [5] *way of life, custom.*
[6] *Transgress.*   [7] *Unless.*   [8] *maiden.*   [9] *Ill-gotten goods.*

For if thy handes limed[1] be
Thou art but shent,[2] thy name is lore[3]
In field and town and in all country.

Octavum mandatum: non loqueris contra proximum tuum
   falsum testimonium.

   The eighth precept thus does thee bid:
False witness look none thou bear.
The truth nevermore look that thou hide,
With false witness no man thou dere.[4]
Neither for love, nor dread, nor fear,
Say none other than truth is.
False witness if that thou rear
Against God thou dost greatly amiss.

Nonum mandatum: non desiderabis uxorem proximi tui etc.

   The ninth precept of law of life
Even thus does bid every man:
Desire not thy neighboures wife.
Though she be fair and white as swan,
And thy wife brown, yet not[5] for than[5]
Thy neighboures wife thou never rejoice.
Keep thee clean as ever thou can
To thy owen wife and thy owen choice.

Decimum mandatum: non concupisces domum proximi tui,
non servum, non ancillam, non bovem, non asinum, nec
omnia quae illius sunt etc.

   The tenth commandment of God, and last, is this:
Thy neighboures house desire thou not,
Maiden, nor servant, nor nought of his,
Desire them never in will nor thought,
Oxe, nor ass that he has bought,
Nor no thing that longeth him to.
Godes law must needes be wrought:
Desire no thing thy neighbour fro.[6]
   The sixth commandment of lechery

---

[1] *defiled.*   [2] *(nothing) but ruined.*   [3] *lost.*   [4] *harm.*   [5] *notwithstanding that.*   [6] *from.*

Does exclude the sinful deed.
But these twain last most straightly
Both deed and thought they do forbid.
In will nor thought no lechery thou lead:
Thy thought and will thou must refrain,
All thy desire, as I thee rede,
In cleanness of life thyself restrain.
    Friendes! these are the lawes that you must keep.
Therefore every man set well in mind,
Whether that thou do wake or sleep,
These lawes to learn thou hark full hend,[1]
And Godes grace shall be thy friend,
He succour and save you in wealth[2] from woe!
Farewell, good friendes, for hence will I wend:
My tale I have taught you, my way now I go.
Explicit[3] '*Moyses*'.

Jesse[4]

Isaias.   I am the prophet called Isaye,
    Replete with Godes great influence,
    And say plainly, by spirit of prophecye,
    That a clean maid, through meek obedience,
    Shall bear a child which shall do resistence
    Against foul Zabulon, the devil of hell.
    Mannes soul against him to defence,
    Open in the field, the fiend he shall fell.
        Wherefore I say quod[5] virgo concipiet,
    Et pariet filium, nomen Emanuel.[5]
    Our life for to save he shall suffer death,

---

[1] *courteously, readily.*   [2] *well-being.*   [3] *Here ends.*   [4] *For the title of this new pageant see* 'Explicit' *at its end* (*p. 119 and n. 15*).   [5] *that a virgin shall conceive and bear a son called Emmanuel* (*Isa. vii, 14*).

And buy us to his bliss in heaven for to dwell.
Of sacerdotal lineage,[1] the truth I you tell,
Flesh and blood to take God will be born.
Joy to man in earth, and in heaven angel,
At the childes birth joy shall make that morn.

Radix Jesse.   Egredietur[2] virga de radice Jesse,
Et flos de radice eius ascendet.[2]
A blessed branch shall spring of me
That shall be sweeter than balmes[3] breath.[3]
Out of that branch in Nazareth
A flower shall bloom of me, Jesse root,
The which by grace shall destroy death,
And bring mankind to bliss most sweet.

David Rex.   I am David of Jesse root,
The fresh[4] king by natural succession,
And of my blood shall spring our boot[5]
As God himself has made promission.[6]
Of regal life shall come such foison[7]
That a clean maid mother shall be,
Against the deviles false illusion
With regal power to make man free.

Jeremias Propheta.   I am the prophet, Jeremye,
And fully accord in all sentence[8]
With King David and with Isaye,
Affirming[9] plainly, before this audience,
That God, of his high benevolence,
Of priest and king will take lineage,
And buy us all from our offence,
In heaven to have his heritage.

Salamon Rex.   I am Solomon, the second king,
And that worthy Temple forsooth made I,
Which that is figure[10] of that maid young
That shall be mother of great Messy.[11]

[1] *n. 16.*   [2] *Translated in next two lines (Isa. xi, 1).*   [3] *the scent of balm (?).*
[4] *joyous.*   [5] *redemption, cure.*   [6] *promise.*   [7] *power.*   [8] *opinion, judgement.*
[9] *n. 17.*   [10] *the Temple (I Kings vi) prefigures Mary (cf. pp. 32 and 63–4 above,*
and M.E.L. no. 34, l. 31).   [11] *Messiah.*

Ezechiel Propheta. A vision of this full verily
   I, Ezekiel, have had also,
   Of a gate that sparred[1] was truly,
   And no man but a prince might therein go.
Roboas Rex.   The third king of the gentle Jesse,
   My name is known, King Roboas.
   Of our kindred yet men shall see
   A clean maid tread down foul Sathanas.
Micheas Propheta. And I am a prophet called Micheas.
   I tell[2] you plainly that thus it is:
   Even like as Eve mother of woe was
   So shall a maiden be mother of bliss.
Abias Rex.   I that am called King Abias
   Confirm for true that you have said,
   And say also as in this case
   That all our mirth cometh of a maid.
Daniel Propheta. I, Prophet Daniel, am well apayed:[3]
   In figure[4] of this I saw a tree—
   All the fiendes of hell shall be afraid
   When maidenes fruit thereon they see.
Asa Rex.   I, King Asa, believe all this,
   That God will of a maiden be born,
   And, us to bringen to endless bliss,
   Ruly[5] on rood[5] be rent and torn.
Jonas Propheta. I, Jonah, say that on the third morn
   From death he shall rise—this is a true tale—
   Figured[6] in me the which long beforn
   Lay three days buried within the whale.
Josaphat Rex.   And I, Josaphat, the sixth king certain
   Of Jesse root in the lineal succession,
   All that my progenitores have before me sayn
   Faithfully believe withouten all dubitation.
Abdias Propheta. I, Abdias,[7] prophet, make this protestation,

---

[1] *fastened: Ezekiel xliv, 2; as prefiguration of Mary cf.* M.E.L., *no. 34, ll. 49–52.*
[2] *cf. Mic. iv* (?); *n. 17.*   [3] *pleased.*   [4] *cf. Dan. iv, 10 ff.* (?)-*Nebuchadnezzar's dream. Jesus is the fruit of the Maiden on the tree of the cross (nn. 15 and 17).*
[5] *Pitifully on the cross.*   [6] *Matthew xii, 39–40, Jonah i, 17.*   [7] (?).

That, after he is risen to life ones again,
Death shall be driven to endless damnation,
And life shall be granted of paradise full plain.

Joram Rex.   And I, Joram, also, in the number of seven
Of Jesse root king, knowledge[1] that he
After his resurrection return shall to heaven,
Both God and very man there endless to be.

Habacuc Propheta. I, Habakkuk, prophet, hold[2] well with thee,
When he is risen he shall up stye,[3]
In heaven as judge sit in his see,[4]
Us for to deem[5] when we shall die.

Ozias Rex.   And I, Ozias, king of high degree,
Sprung of Jesse root, dare well say this:
When he is gone to his dignity
He shall send the spirit to his disciplis.

Joel Propheta. And I, Joel, know full true that is
God bade me write in prophecy,[6]
He would send down his spirit, iwis,[7]
On young and old full securely.[8]

Joatham Rex.   My name is known, King Joathan,
The ninth king, sprung of Jesse.
Of my kindred God will be man,
Mankind to save, and that joyth[9] me.

Aggaeus Propheta. With you I do hold,[10] that am Prophet Haggee,
Come of the same high and holy stock.
God of our kindred indeed born will be,
From the wolf to save all sheep of his flock.

Achaz Rex.   Of Jesse, King Achaz is my name,
That falsely worshipped idolatry,
Till Isaye put me in blame,
And said a maid should bear Messy.

Osee Propheta. Of that birth witness[11] bear I:

---

[1] *acknowledge.*   [2] *? : n. 17.*   [3] *ascend.*   [4] *seat.*   [5] *judge.*   [6] *Joel ii, 28.*
[7] *indeed.*   [8] *certainly.*   [9] *pleases.*   [10] *believe.*   [11] *(?): n. 17.*

A prophet, Hosea men me call,
And, after that tale of Isaye,
That maid shall bear Emmanuel.

Ezechias Rex. My name is knowen, King Ezekias,
The eleventh king of this genealogy,
And say forsooth as in that case
A maid by meekness shall bring mercy.

Sophonias Propheta. I, a prophet called Zephany,
Of this matter do bear witness,[1]
And for truth to certify
That maidens birth our wealth shall dress.[2]

Manasses Rex. Of this noble and worthy generation
The twelfth king am I, Manasses,
Witnessing here, by true testification,
That maidenes child shall be Prince of Peace.

Baruch Propheta. And I, Baruch, prophet, confirm[3] wordes
these:
Lord and Prince of Peace though that child be,
All his foemen[4] against him that press
Right a grim sire at Doomesday[5] shall he be.

Amon Rex. Amon, king, for the last conclusion,
All thing before said for truth do testify.
Praying that Lord of our sin remission,
At that dreadful day he us grant mercy.
Thus we all of this genealogy,
According[6] in one,[6] here in this place,
Pray that high Lord, when that we shall die,
Of his great goodness to grant us his grace.

Explicit[7] 'Jesse.'

---

[1] (?): n. 17.   [2] *prepare.*   [3] (?).   [4] *enemies.*   [5] *p. 368.*   [6] *Agreeing together.*   [7] *Here ends.*

Mother of Mercy[1]

Contemplatio.   Christ conserve this congregation
From perilles past, present and future,
And the persones here playing, that the pronunciation
Of their sentence[2] to be said may be sad[3] and sure,[3]
And that no oblocucion[4] make this matter obscure,
But it may profit and please each person present,
From the ginning to the ending so to endure
That Christ and every creature with the conceit[5] be content.
          This matter here made is of the Mother of Mercy:
How by Joachim and Anne was her conception;
Sithe[6] offered into the Temple—compiled briefly—
Then married to Joseph, and, so following, the salutation,
Meeting with Elizabeth and therewith a conclusion,
In few wordes talked, that it should not be tedious
To learned nor to lewd,[7] nor to no man of reason.
This is the process.[8] Now preserve you, Jesus!
          Therefore of peace I you pray, all that are here present,
And take heed to our talking, what we shall say.
I beteche[9] you[9] that Lord that is ever omnipotent,
To govern you in goodness as he best may,
In heaven we may him see.
Now God that is heaven king
Send us all his dear blessing,
And to his tower he[10] may[10] us bring—
Amen, for charity.

---

[1] *Titles from words used by Contemplatio (below and n. 18).*   [2] *meaning.*
[3] *strong, firm, and sure.*   [4] *abuse (bad delivery?).*   [5] *conception.*   [6] *Afterwards.*
[7] *the unlettered, laymen.*   [8] *gist of it, argument.*   [9] *commend you to.*   [10] *may he.*

[Joachim[1] and Anne are barren and promise to offer—to be Godes man—any child God may grant them. Ashamed, Joachim retreats to live with his shepherds, when an angel descends with a joyful song promising that Anne shall bear Mary:

And as she shall be born of a barreny body
So of her shall be born without[2] nature Jesus.

The angel then tells Anne to meet Joachim at the Golden Gate of Jerusalem as he returns,

And in great gladness return to your house
So by process thou shalt conceive and bear a child.

Contemplatio says:

Sovereignes, you have seen showed you before
Of Joachim and Anne their[3] botheres holy meeting.[3]
How our Lady was conceived and how she was bore
We pass over that, briefness of time considering.

Next, then, Mary is shown in the Temple, presented at three years old to God. After this, Contemplatio continues:

Now shall we proceed to her disponsation[4]
Which after this was fourteen year.
Time sufficeth not to make pausation.
Have patience with us, we beseech you here,
And in short space
The Parliament of Heaven soon shall you see,
And how Godes son come[5] man[5] shall be,
And how the salutation after shall be
By Godes holy grace.

Mary is then shown at fully fourteen, again in the Temple, unwilling, because of her dedication, to marry, though the law requires it. An angel bids all the kinsmen of David to bring white rods, and Mary to marry the man whose rod blossoms. Finding it is his that flowers, Joseph cries:

What! should I wed? God forbid!

---

[1] *There follows a series of episodes relating to Mary the first of which I summarize. For their continuity, n. 19.*   [2] *contrary to.*   [3] *the holy meeting of the two of them.*   [4] *betrothal.*   [5] *incarnate.*

I am an old man, so God me speed!
And with a wife now to liven in dread,
It were neither sport nor game!
. . . . . .
Ah! should I have her, you lose my life!
Alas! dear God, should I now rave?
An old man may never thrive
With a young wife,[1] so God me save!
Nay! nay! sir, let been!
Should I now in age begin to dote?
If I her chide she would clout[2] my coat,[2]
Blear[3] my eye and pick out a mote[3]—
And thus often times it is seen.
. . . . . .
Against my God not do I may:
Her warden and keeper will I ever be.
But fair maiden, I thee pray,
Keep thee clean as I shall me.
I am a man of age,
Therefore, sir bishop, I will that you wit
That in bed we shall never meet:
For, iwis,[4] maiden sweet,
An old man may not rage.[5]
For Joseph's good fame *the bishop recommends that three
women, Susanna, Rebecca and Sephor, stay with Mary
always. She rejoices that she is to be both a maid and a wife
and worships God while Joseph goes to a far country for nine
months to earn their living.*]

---

[1] *a medieval commonplace, cf. e.g. Chaucer's* Merchant's Tale *of old January
and young May.* [2] *beat me.* [3] *Utterly deceive me (Throw dust in my eyes) and
blame me for the slightest fault (?).* [4] *indeed.* [5] *be sexually excited.*

Mother of Mercy:
Parliament of Heaven and Annunciation[1]

Contemplatio.   Four thousand, six hundred, four year I
tell,
Man for his offence and foul folly
Has lain[2] yeares in the paines of hell,
And were worthy to lie therein endlessly,
But then should perish your great mercy.
Good Lord, have on man pity!
Have mind of the prayer[3] said by Isaye:
Let mercy meek[4] thy highest majesty.

     Would God thou wouldest break thy heaven mighty,
And come down here into earth,
And liven yeares three and thirty,
Thy famished folk with thy food to feed.
To staunch thy thirsty, let thy side bleed,
For erst[5] will not be made redemption.[5]
Come! visit us in this time of need.
Of thy careful creatures have compassion.

     Ah! woe to us wretches that[6] wretched[7] be,
For God has added sorrow to sorrow.
I pray thee, Lord, thy soules come see
How they lie and sob for sickness and sorrow.
With thy blessed blood from bales[8] them borrow,[9]
Thy careful[10] creatures, crying in captivity.
Ah! tarry not, gracious Lord, till it be tomorrow:
The devil has deceived them by his iniquity.

---

[1] *Supplied from Contemplatio's forecast on p. 121 (n. 20).*   [2] *MS* loin.   [3] *?: cf.
Daniel at p. 172, ll. 14–17.*   [4] *appease, make humble.*   [5] *there will be no redemption before that.*   [6] *MS* of *(crossed out,* that *in a different hand above).*
[7] *MS* wrecchis.   [8] *sufferings.*   [9] *save.*   [10] *full of care.*

'Ah!' quod Jeremy,[1] 'Who shall give welles to my
    eynes,
That I may weep both day and night
To see our brethren in so long paines?'
Their mischiefes amend may thy much[2] might.
As great as the sea, Lord, was Adames contrition[3] right.
From our head is fall the crown.[4]
Man is cumbered in sin, I cry to thy sight:
Gracious Lord! gracious Lord! gracious Lord, come
    down!

Virtutes.[5]   Lord! pleaseth it thy high Domination,
On man, that thou made, to have pity.
Patriarches and Prophetes have made supplication:
Our office is to present their prayeres to thee.
Angeles, Archangeles,[5] we three,
That are in the first hierarchy,
For man to thy high majesty,
Mercy! mercy! mercy! we cry.

    The angel, Lord, thou made so glorious,
Whose sin has made him a devil in hell,
He moved man to be so contrarious.
Man repented, and he in his obstinacy does dwell.
His great malice, good Lord, repel,
And take man unto thy grace.
Let thy mercy make him with Angeles dwell,
Of Lucifer to restore the place.

Pater.[6] *Propter*[7] *miseriam inopum*
et gemitum pauperum
nunc exsurgam.[7]

    For the wretchedness of the needy,
And the poores lamentation,
Now shall I rise that am Almighty:
Time is come of reconciliation.

---

[1] *Jer. ix, 1.*   [2] *great.*   [3] *pp. 81–6.*   [4] *(Man was made to reign in Paradise p. 77).*   [5] *n. 21.*   [6] *The Father.*   [7] *Extra-metrical. Translated in next three lines. No indication in MS that a new section begins here unless it be the big red capital of* Propter.

My prophetes with prayers have made supplication;
My contrite creatures cry all for comfort;
All my Angeles in heaven, without cessation,
They cry that grace to man might exort.[1]

Veritas.   Lord, I am thy daughter, Truth,
Thou wilt see I be not lore.[2]
Thy unkind[3] creatures to save were ruth:[4]
The offence of man has grieved thee sore.
When Adam had sinned thou saidest there
That he should die and go to hell,
And now to bliss him to restore—
Two contraries may not together dwell!

    Thy truth, Lord, shall last withouten end—
I may in no wise from thee go.
That wretch that was to thee so unkind,
He may not have too much woe.
He despised thee and pleased thy foe;
Thou art his creator and he is thy creature.
Thou hast loved truth, it is said, evermo,
Therefore in paines let him evermore endure.

Misericordia.   Oh! Father of Mercy and God of Com-
    fort,
That counsel us in each tribulation,
Let your daughter, Mercy, to you resort,
And on man that is mischiefed,[5] have compassion!
Him grieveth full greatly his transgression.
All heaven and earth cry for mercy.
Me seemeth there should be none exception
There[6] prayers are offered so specially.

    Truth says she has ever been, than[7]—
I grant it well she has been so.
And thou sayst endlessly that mercy thou hast kept for
    man—
Then, merciable Lord, keep us both two!

---

[1] *arise.*   [2] *lost.*   [3] *undutiful, unnatural.*   [4] *a calamity, pity.*   [5] *afflicted,*
brought to ruin.   [6] *where.*   [7] *then (?).*

Thou sayst, 'Veritas mea et misericordia mea cum ipso.'[1]
Suffer not thy soules, then, in sorrow to sleep.
That hell hound that hateth thee, biddeth him, 'Ho!'—
Thy[2] love, Man,[2] no longer let him keep.

Justitia.   Mercy, me[3] marveleth what you moveth![3]
You know well I am your sister, Righteousness.
God is rightful and rightfulness loveth.
Man offended him that is endless,
Therefore his endless punishment may never cease.
Also he forsook his maker that made him of clay,
And the devil to[4] his master he chose.
Should he be saved? Nay! nay! nay!
As wise as is God he would[5] have be[5]—
This was the abominable presumption.
It is said you know well this of me,
That the righteousness of God has no definition.[6]
Therefore let this be our conclusion:
He that sore sinned lie still in sorrow.
He may never make asseth[7] by reason:[7]
Who might then thence him borrow?[8]

Misericordia.   Sister Righteousness, you are too venge-
able!
Endless sin God, endless, may restore.
Above all his workes God is merciable:
Though he forsook God by sin, by faith he forsook him
never the more.
And though he presumed never so sore,
You must consider the frailness of mankind.
Learn, and[9] you list,[9] this is Godes lore:[10]
The mercy of God is withouten end.

Pax.   To spare your speeches, sisteres, it sit.[11]
It is not honest[12] in Virtues to be dissension.[13]
The Peace of God overcometh all wit.

---

1 '*My faithfulness and my mercy shall be with him (i.e. David)*' (*A.V.*), Psalm
lxxxix, 24.   2 *Man, whom you love.*   3 *your argument amazes me.*   4 *for.*
5 *wanted to be.*   6 *limit.*   7 *satisfaction in logic.*   8 *redeem.*   9 *if it pleases
you.*   10 *teaching.*   11 *is fitting.*   12 *decorous, appropriate.*   13 *contentious.*

Though Truth and Right say great reason,
Yet Mercy says best to my pleason,[1]
For, if mannes soul should abide in hell,
Between God and man ever should be division,
And then might not I, Peace, dwell.
    Therefore me seemeth best you thus accord:[2]
Then heaven and earth you shall queme.[3]
Put[4] both your sentence in our Lord,[4]
And in his high wisdom let him deem.[5]
This is most sitting,[6] me should seem,[6]
And let see how we four may all abide.
That mannes soul it should perish it were sweme,[7]
Or that any of us from other should divide.

Veritas.   In truth hereto I consent.
    I will pray our Lord it may so be.
Justitia. I, Righteousness, am well content,
    For in him is very[8] equity.
Misericordia.   And I, Mercy, from this counsel will not
    flee,
    Till wisdom has said I shall cease.
Pax. Here is God now! Here is unity!
    Heaven and earth is pleased with Peace.
Filius.[9]   I think the thoughtes of Peace and not of
    wickedness.
This I deem, to cease your controversy:
If Adam had not died, perished had Righteousness,
And also Truth had been lost thereby—
Truth and Right would chastise Folly.[10]
If[11] another death come not, Mercy should perish,
Then Peace were exiled finally,[11]
So twain deathes must be, you four to cherish.
    But he that shall die, you must know,
    That in him may be no iniquity,

---

[1] *pleasure (?).*   [2] *agree.*   [3] *gratify.*   [4] *Commit the opinions of both of you to our Lord.*   [5] *determine.*   [6] *fitting, it would seem to me.*   [7] *grief, pity.*   [8] *true.* [9] *The Son.*   [10] *evil.*   [11] *Unless there is a second (atoning) death, Mercy would be non-existent and there would be no chance of Peace ever.*

That hell may hold him by no law,
But that he may pass at his liberty.
Where such one is, previde[1] and see!
And his death for mannes death shall be redemption.
All heaven and earth seek now ye,
Pleaseth[2] it you this conclusion.[2]

Veritas.   I, Truth, have sought the earth, without and
within,
And in sooth there can none be found
That is of one day birth, without sin,
Nor[3] that to death will be bound.[3]

Misericordia. I, Mercy, have run the heavenly region round,
And there is none of that charity[4]
That for man will suffer a deadly wound.
I cannot wit[5] how this shall be.

Justitia.   Sure I can find none sufficient,
For servantes unprofitable we are each one.
His[6] love needeth to be full ardent
That for man to hell would gone.

Pax. That good may do is none but one,
Therefore this is Peaces advice!
He that gave this counsel, let him give the comfort alone,
For the conclusion in him of all these lies.

Filius.   It paineth me that man I made—
That is to say, pain I must suffer for.
A council of the Trinity must be had
Which of us shall man restore.

Pater. In your wisdom, Son, man was made there,
And in wisdom was his temptation.[7]
Therefore, Son, Sapience you must ordain herefore,
And see how of man may be salvation.

Filius.   Father, he that shall do this must be both God
and man.

---

[1] *look ahead.*   [2] *If you like this resolution of controversy.*   [3] *And that is not
destined for death* (?): *that to, MS to that.*   [4] *love.*   [5] *understand.*   [6] *MS* he
corrected by different hand.   [7] *p. 79.*

Let me see how I may wear that weed.[1]
And sith[2] in my wisdom he began
I am ready to do this deed.

Spiritus Sanctus. I, the Holy Ghost, of[3] you twain do proceed,
This charge I will take on me:
I, Love, to your lover shall you lead—
This is the assent of our unity.

Misericordia. Now is the Loveday[4] made of us four finally,
Now may we live in peace as we were wont.
Misericordia et Veritas obviaverunt sibi,
Justitia et Pax osculatae sunt.[5]
Hic osculabunt pariter omnes.[6]

Pater. From us, God, angel Gabriel, thou shalt be sent
Into the country of Galilee—
The name of the city, Nazareth is kend—[7]
To a maid, wedded to a man is she,
Of whom the name is Joseph, see,
Of the house of David bore;[8]
The name of the maid free[9]
Is Mary, that shall all restore.

Filius. Say that she is without woe and full of grace,
And that I, the Son of the Godhead, of her shall be bore.
Hie thee, thou[10] were there apace!
Elles we shall be there thee before—
I have so great haste to be man there,
In that meekest and purest virgin.
Say her she shall restore
Of you, angeles, the great ruin.[11]

Spiritus Sanctus. And if she ask thee how it might be,
Tell her I, the Holy Ghost, shall work all this.

---

[1] *dress.* [2] *since.* [3] *from.* [4] *Occasion (or, as here, agreement then made) for the settlement of legal disputes out of court.* [5] *Mercy and Truth are met together, Righteousness and Peace have kissed each other (Psalm lxxxv, 10 (A.V.)).* [6] *Here they will all kiss each other.* [7] *known.* [8] *born.* [9] *noble, excellent.* [10] *so that thou.* [11] *fall.*

She shall be saved through our unity.
In token, her barren cousin, Elizabeth, is
Quick with child in her great age, iwis.[1]
Say her, to us is nothing impossible.
Her body shall be so fulfilled with bliss
That she shall soon think[2] this sound credible.[2]

Gabriel.   In thy high ambassade,[3] Lord, I shall go.
It shall be done with a thought!
Behold now, Lord, I go hereto,
I take my flight and bide not.
Ave, gratia plena, Dominus tecum.[4]
Hail! full of grace, God is with thee,
Among all women, blessed art thou.
Here this name, Eva,[5] is turned 'Ave',[5]
That is to say, without sorrow are you now.
    Though sorrow in you has no place
Yet of joy, Lady, you need more.
Therefore I add and say, 'Full of grace',
For so full of grace was never none bore.
Yet, who has grace, he needeth[6] keeping sore,[6]
Therefore I say, 'God is with thee,'
Which shall keep you endlessly there,
So among all women blessed are ye.

Maria.   Ah! mercy, God! this is a marvellous hearing.
In the angeles wordes I am troubled here.
I think, how may be this greeting?
Angeles daily to me do appear,
But not in the likeness of man, that is my fere.[7]
And also thus highly to commended be,
And am most unworthy—I cannot answer;
Great shamefastness and great dread is in me.

---

1 *indeed.*   2 *believe what she hears.*   3 *ambassadorial mission.*   4 *extra-metrical, translated in next line. In MS after* Ave *is written* Maria, *crossed out, Block thinks, in different ink, but of the latter I am not certain.*   5 *an old medieval commonplace and characteristic play on words and images (cf. M.E.L. no. 5, ll. 19–25): the repair of the sin of Eva, the first woman, in disobedience, is begun by the messenger angel's greeting, 'Ave' (the converse of 'Eva'), to the Mother of Mercy, who is obedient.*   6 *greatly needs defending, maintaining.*   7 *equal.*

Gabriel.   Mary, in this take you no dread,
  For at[1] God grace found have ye.
  You shall conceive in your womb in deed
  A child, the Son of the Trinity.
  His name of you, Jesu, cleped[2] shall be.
  He shall be great, the Son of the Highest cleped, of
    kind.[3]
  And of his father, David, the Lord shall give him the see,[4]
  Reigning in the house of Jacob, of which reign shall be
    no end.

Maria.   Angel, I say to you,
  In what manner of wise shall this be?
  For knowing of man I have none now.
  I have evermore kept, and shall, my virginity.
  I doubt not the wordes you have said to me,
  But I ask how it shall be do?

Gabriel.   The Holy Ghost shall come from above to thee,
  And the virtue[5] of him highest[5] shall shadow thee so,
    Therefore that Holy Ghost of thee shall be bore:
  He shall be cleped the Son of God sage.[6]
  And see, Elizabeth, your cousin there,
  She has conceived a son in her age:
  This is the sixth month of her passage,[7]
  Of her that cleped was barren.
  Nothing is impossible to Godes usage—
  They[8] thinketh long[8] to hear what you will sayn.
  Here the angel makes a little resting, and Mary beholds him.
    Mary, come off and haste thee!
  And take heed in thy intent
  How the Holy Ghost—blessed he be!—
  Abideth thy answer and thy assent.
  Through wise work of Divinity,
  The Second Person,[9] verament,[9]

---

[1] *from.*   [2] *called.*   [3] *nature, birth.*   [4] *seat.*   [5] *power of him who is the highest.*   [6] *wise.*   [7] *pregnancy.*   [8] *The Three Persons of the Trinity eagerly wait (?).*   [9] *Person (of the Trinity), truly.*

131

Is made man by[1] fraternity[1]
Within thyself in place present.
    Furthermore, take heed this space,
How all the blessed spirites of virtue
That are in heaven before Godes face,
And all the good livers and true
That are here in this earthly place,
Thy owen kindred, the sooth[2] who knew,
And the chosen soules, this time of grace,
That are in hell and bide[3] rescue,
    As Adam, Abraham and David, in[4] fere,[4]
And many other of good reputation,
That thy answer desire to hear,
And thy assent to the Incarnation
In which thou standest as preserver
Of all mankind salvation—
Give me my answer, now, Lady dear,
To all these creatures comfortation.

Maria.   With all meekness I cline[5] to this accord,[6]
Bowing down my face with all benignity.
See here the handmaiden of our Lord,
After thy word be it done to me!

Gabriel. Gramercy! my Lady free,
Gramercy! of your answer on[7] height,[7]
Gramercy! of your great humility,
Gramercy! you lantern[8] of light.

*Here the Holy Ghost descends with three beams[9] to our Lady,
the Son of the Godhead next with three beams to the Holy
Ghost, the Father godly with three beams to the Son. And so
enter all three to her bosom.*

Maria. Ah! now I feel in my body be
Perfect God and perfect man,
Having[10] all shape of childly carnality,[10]

[1] *as a brother to other men and to his mother (cf. e.g.* M.E.L. *no. 62, ll. 49–56, 93).*
[2] *truth.*   [3] *wait for.*   [4] *together.*   [5] *incline.*   [6] *agreement.*   [7] *open, out-spoken.*   [8] *conventional image of Mary, cf.* M.E.L. *p. 374.*   [9] *n. 22.*   [10] *Having the entire form of a fleshly child.*

Even[1] all at ones,[1] thus God began,
  Not taking first one member and sithe[2] another,
But perfect childhood you have anon.
Of your handmaiden now you have made your mother,
Without pain in flesh and bone.
Thus conceived never woman none,
That ever was being in this life.
Oh! my highest Father on your throne,
It[3] is worthy your son—now, my son—have a prerogative.[3]
  I cannot tell what joy, what bliss,
Now I feel in my body.
Angel Gabriel, I thank you for this,
Most meekly recommend me to my Fathers mercy.
To have been the mother of God, full little weened[4] I.[4]
Now my cousin, Elizabeth, fain would I see,
How she has conceived as you did specify.
Now blessed be the high Trinity!
Gabriel.   Farewell, turtle,[5] Godes daughter dear,
Farewell, Godes mother, I thee honour.
Farewell, Godes sister, and his playing-fere,[6]
Farewell, Godes chamber and his bower.[5]
Maria. Farewell, Gabriel, specially,
Farewell, Godes messenger express.
I thank you for your travail[7] high,[7]
Gramercy of your great goodness,
      And namely[8] of[8] your comfortable message,
For I understand by inspiration
That you know by singular privilege
Most of my sones Incarnation.
I pray you, take[9] it into usage
By a custom occupation
To visit me oft by my passage:[9]
Your presence is my comfortation.

---

[1] *directly, all at once.*   [2] *afterwards.*   [3] *Your son, now my son, too, deserves to have such a prerogative (in being born thus).*   [4] *I expected.*   [5] *conventional images of Mary (n. 23).*   [6] *play-mate.*   [7] *lofty labour.*   [8] *especially for.*
[9] *make it a habit to visit me often during my pregnancy.*

133

Gabriel.   At your will, Lady, so shall it be,
You gentlest[1] of blood and highest of kindred
That reigneth in earth in any degree,
By principal incheson[2] of the Godhead.
    I commend me unto you, thou throne of the Trinity.
Oh! meekest maid, now the mother of Jesu,
Queen[3] of heaven, Lady of earth, and Empress of hell be
    ye,
Succour to all sinful,[3] that will to you sue.[4]
Your[5] body beareth the babe our bliss shall renew.
To you, Mother of Mercy, most meekly I recommend,
And as I began, I end with an 'Ave' new.
Enjoined[6] heaven and earth, with that I ascend!
Angeli[7] cantando istam sequentiam:
Ave! Maria, gratia plena,
Dominus tecum, Virgo serena.[7]

Mother of Mercy: Joseph[8]

Joseph.   How! dame, how! undo your door, undo!
Are you at home? Why speak you not?
Susanna. Who is there? Why cry you so?
Tell us your errand—will you ought?
Joseph. Undo your door! I say you to,
For to come in is all my thought.
Maria. It is my spouse that speaketh us to—
Undo the door, his[9] will were wrought.[9]
    Welcome home, my husband dear!
How have you fared in far country?

---

[1] *noblest.*   [2] *cause.*   [3] *conventional titles of Mary.*   [4] *appeal.*   [5] *MS* Thour your.   [6] *joined together (?): MS* enjonyd.   [7] *Angels singing this sequence: Hail, Mary, full of grace, the Lord is with thee, virgin pure; serena, probably so MS corrected from* sesena.   [8] *n. 24. Prosser examines this play, chap. v.*   [9] *so that his will might be done.*

Joseph. To get our living, withouten dwere,[1]
  I have sore laboured for thee and me.
Maria.   Husband, right graciously, now come be ye.
  It solaceth me sore soothly to see you in sight.
Joseph. Me[2] marvelleth,[2] wife, surely, your face I cannot
    see,
  But as the sun with his beames when he is most bright.
Maria.   Husband, it is as it pleaseth our Lord: that grace
    of him grew.
  Who that ever beholdeth me, verily,
  They shall be greatly stirred to virtue.
  For this gift and many more, good Lord, gramercy!
Joseph.   How hast thou fared, gentle maid,
  While I have been out of land?
Maria. Secure, sir, be nought dismayed!
  Right after the will of Godes sand.[3]
Joseph. That seemeth evil, I am afraid—
  Thy womb too high does stand.
  I dread me sore I am betrayed,
  Some other man thee had in hand,
  Hence[4] sithe that I went.[4]
  Thy womb is great, it ginneth to rise.
  Then hast thou begun a[5] sinful guise.[5]
  Tell me now in what wise
  Thyself thou hast thus shent.[6]
    How! dame, what thing meaneth this?
  With child thou ginnest right great to gone.
  Say me, Mary, this childes father who is.
  I pray thee, tell me, and that anon.
Maria. The Father of heaven and you it is—
  Other father has he none.
  I did never forfeit[7] with man, iwis,[8]
  Wherefore I pray you amend your moan.
  This child is Godes and your.

---

[1] *doubt.*   [2] *I'm filled with wonder.*   [3] *sending, dispensation.*   [4] *Since I went hence.*   [5] *sinful behaviour.*   [6] *ruined, injured.*   [7] *transgress.*   [8] *indeed.*

Joseph. Godes child! Thou liest in[1] fay![1]
God did never jape[2] so with may.[2]
And I came never there, I dare well say,
Yet so nigh thy bower.
     But[3] yet[3] I say, Mary, whose child is this?
Maria. Godes, and your, I say, iwis.[4]
Joseph.   Yea! yea! all old men to me take[5] tent,[5]
And weddeth no wife in no[6] kindes wise[6]
That is a young wench, by my assent,
For doubt[7] and dread and such service.[8]
Alas! alas! my name is shent.[9]
All men may me now despise,
And say, 'Old cuckold, thy[10] bow is bent
Newly now, after the French guise,[10]
Alas! and welaway!
Alas! dame, why didest thou so?
For this sin that thou hast do
I thee forsake and from thee go,
For ones, ever and ay!
Maria.   Alas! good spouse, why say you thus?
Alas! dear husband, amend your mood.[11]
It is no man but sweet Jesus:
He will be clad in flesh and blood,
And of your wife be born.
Sephor. Forsooth the angel, thus said he,
That Godes Son in Trinity
For mannes sake a man would be,
To save that is forlorn.[12]
Joseph.   An angel! Alas! alas! fie! for shame.
You sin now in that you do[13] say,
To putten an angel in so great blame.
Alas! alas! let be! do way!
It was some boy began this game

---

[1] *upon my word.*   [2] *play such games with a maiden.*   [3] *Again, Therefore.*
[4] *for sure.*   [5] *pay heed.*   [6] *any manner whatsoever.*   [7] *fear.*   [8] *treatment.*
[9] *ruined.*   [10] *here's a different experience for you, in the French style* (n. 25).
[11] *disposition, mind.*   [12] *utterly lost.*   [13] *MS to.*

That clothed was clean and gay,
And you give him now an angel name.
Alas! alas! and welaway!
That ever this game betid.[1]
Ah! dame, what thought haddest thou?
Here may all men this proverb trow,
That many a man does beat the bough—
Another man has the bird.

Maria.   Ah! gracious God in heaven throne,
Comfort my spouse in this hard case.
Merciful God, amend his moan,
As I did never so great trespass.

Joseph.   Lo! lo! sires, what told I you?—
That it was not for my prow[2]
A wife to take me to.
And that is well seen now,
For Mary, I make God avow,
Is great with child, lo!
Alas! why is it so?
To the Bishop I will it tell,
That he the law may here do
With stones her to quell.[3]
   Nay! nay! yet God forbid
That I should do that vengeable deed,
But[4] if[4] I wist well why.
I knew never with her, so God me speed,
Token of thing in word nor deed
That touched villainy.
Nevertheless, what forthy?[5]
Though she be meek and mild,
Without mannes company
She might not be with child.
   But I ensure, mine was it never!
Though that she has not[6] done her devoir,[6]
Rather than I should plainen[7] openly,

[1] *happened.*   [2] *good.*   [3] *kill.*   [4] *Unless.*   [5] *of that?*   [6] *been undutiful.*   [7] *complain.*

Certainly yet had I liefer
Forsake the country for ever,
And never come in her company.
For, and[1] men knew this villainy,
In reproof they would me hold.
And yet many better than I,
Yea, has been made cuckold.
   Now, alas! whither shall I gone?
I wot never whither, nor to what place.
For oftentime sorrow cometh soon,
And long it is ere it pass.
No comfort may I have here.
Iwis, wife, thou didest me wrong!
Alas! I tarried from thee too long.
All men have pity on me among,
For to my sorrow is no cheer.

Maria.   God, that[2] in my body art seized,[2]
Thou knowest my husband is displeased
To see me in this plight.
For[3] unknowledge he is diseased,[3]
And, therefore, help that he were eased,
That he might know the full[4] perfect,[4]
For I have[5] liefer abide respite,[5]
To keep thy son in privity,
Granted by the Holy Spirit,
Than that it should be opened by me.

Deus.   Descend, I say, my angel,
Unto Joseph for to tell
Such as my will is.
Bid him with Mary abide and dwell,
For it is my Son full snell[6]
That she is with,[7] iwis.

Angelus. Almighty God of Bliss,

---

[1] *if.*   [2] *(you) who are the legal possessor of my body.*   [3] *He is distressed because he doesn't know the truth.*   [4] *whole (truth) perfectly (?): MS* perfyght.   [5] *would rather suffer delay.*   [6] *good.*   [7] *(pregnant) with.*

I am ready for to wend
Whither as thy will is,
To go both far and hend.[1]
    Joseph! Joseph! thou weepest shrill!
From thy wife why comest thou out?
Joseph. Good sir! let me weep my fill.
Go forth thy way and let[2] me not.
Angelus. In thy weeping thou dost right ill.
Against God thou hast miswrought.
Go! cheer thy wife with hearty will,
And change thy cheer, amend thy thought.
She is a full clean may.[3]
I tell thee, God will of her be born,
And she clean maid as she was beforn,
To save mankind that is forlorn.
Go, cheer her, therefore, I say.
Joseph.   Ah! Lord God, benedicite![4]
Of thy great comfort I thank thee
That thou sent me this space.
I might well have wist, parde,[5]
So good a creature as she
Would never have done trespass,
For she is full of grace.
I know well I have miswrought.
I walk to my poor place,
And ask forgiveness I[6] have misthought.[6]
    Now is the time seen at[7] eye[7]
That the child is now to verify,[8]
Which shall save mankind,
As it was spoke by prophecy.
I thank thee, God, that sittes on high,
With heart, will and mind,
That ever thou wouldest me bind
To wed Mary to my wife,

---

[1] *near.*   [2] *hinder.*   [3] *maiden.*   [4] *bless you.*   [5] *by heavens.*   [6] *that I have thought ill.*   [7] *before our very eyes.*   [8] *prove true.*

Thy blissful son so near to find,
In his presence to lead my life.
   Alas! for joy I quiver and quake,
Alas! what hap now was this?
Ah! mercy, mercy, my gentle make![1]
Mercy!—I have said all amiss.
All that I have said here I forsake:
Your sweet feet now let me kiss.
Maria. Nay! let be my feet—not those you take!
My mouth you may kiss, iwis,
And welcome unto me!
Joseph. Gramercy! my owen sweet wife,
Gramercy! my heart, my love, my life.
Shall I nevermore make such strife
Betwixt me and thee.
   Ah! Mary, Mary, well thou be,
And blessed be the fruit in thee,
Godes Son of Might!
Now, good wife, full of pity,
As[2] be not evil paid[2] with me,
Though that thou have good right,
As for my wrong in sight
To wite[3] thee with any sin.
Had thou not been a virtuous wight,[4]
God would not have been thee within.
   I knowledge I have done amiss.
I was never worthy, iwis,
For to be thy husband.
I shall amend after this,
Right as thy owen will is,
To serve thee at foot and hand,
And thy child both to understand,
To worship him with good affection.
And therefore tell me, and nothing[5] whonde,[5]

---

[1] *match, mate.*   [2] *Please do not be displeased.*   [3] *blame.*   [4] *person.*   [5] *do not hesitate at all.*

The holy matter of your conception.

Maria.   At your owen will, as you bid me:
There came an aunge,[1] hight[1] Gabriel,
And greet me fair and said, 'Ave!'
And furthermore to me gan tell
God should be born of my body,
The fiendes pousty[2] for to fell,
Through the Holy Ghost, as I well see,
Thus God in me will bide and dwell.

Joseph.   Now I thank God with[3] speech and spell[3]
That ever, Mary, I was wedded to thee.

Maria. It was the work of God as I you tell.
Now blessed be that Lord, so[4] purveyed[4] for me.

Mother of Mercy : Salutation[5]

Maria.   But, husband, of one thing I pray you most
    meekly:
I have knowing that our cousin, Elizabeth, with child is—
That it please you to go to her hastily.
If ought we might comfort her it were to me bliss.

Joseph. A[6] Godes[6] sake! Is she with child? She?
Then will her husband, Zachary, be merry.
In Montana they dwell, far hence, so[7] may I the![7]
In the city of Juda, I know it verily.
It is hence, I trow, miles two and fifty:
We are like to be weary ere we come at that same.
I will with a good will, blessed wife, Mary:
Now go we forth, then in Godes name.

Maria.   Go, husband, though it be to you pain,

---

[1] *angel called.*   [2] *power.*   [3] *in speech after speech.*   [4] *(who) so provided.*
[5] *Supplied from Contemplatio's programme on p. 120 (n. 26).*   [6] *For God's.*   [7] *so help me!*

This journey, I pray you, let us go fast,
For I am shamefast[1] of[1] the people to be seen,
And namely[2] of men, thereof I am aghast.
Pilgrimages and helpinges[3] would be gone in haste:[3]
The more the body is pained the more is the meed!
Say you your devotiones and I shall mine icast.[4]
Now in this journey God[5] may us speed![5]

Joseph.   Amen! amen! and evermore.
Lo! wife, lo! how starkly[6] I go before.
Et sic transient circa plateam.[7]

Contemplatio.   Sovereignes, understandeth that King
   David[8] here
Ordained four and twenty priestes of great devotion,
In the Temple of God after their lot[9] appear.
They were[10] cleped[11] summi sacerdotes[11] for their
   ministration,
And one was prince of priestes, having domination.
Among which was an old priest cleped Zachary,
And he had an old woman to his wife, of holy conver-
   sation,
Which[12] hight[12] Elizabeth, that never had child verily.
   In his ministration, the hour of incense,
The angel Gabriel appeared him to.
That his wife should conceive he gave him intelligence.
His[13] judge, his unworthiness and age not believed so,[13]
The plague of dumbness his lippes lapped, lo!
They wenten home and his wife was conceiving.
This conception Gabriel told our Lady to,
And, in sooth, soon after, that sage she was seeking,
   And of their[14] twainers meeting[14]
Here ginneth[15] the process.[15]

---

[1] *ashamed by.*   [2] *especially.*   [3] *helpful errands require to be done speedily.*
[4] *utter: n. 27.*   [5] *may God help us.*   [6] *stoutly.*   [7] *And so they will go round
about the playing-space.*   [8] *I Chron. xxiv(?)*   [9] *MS let.*   [10] *MS weryd.*
[11] *called High Priests.*   [12] *Whose name was.*   [13] *(?) His age and his sense of
his unworthiness prevented his believing the angel's judgement (?).*   [14] *the meeting
of the two of them.*   [15] *begins the account, performance.*

Now God be our beginning!
And of my tongue I will cease.

Joseph. Ah! Ah! wife, in faith I am weary!
Therefore I will sit down and rest me right here.
Lo! wife, here is the house of Zachary.
Will you I clepe Elizabeth to you to appear?

Maria. Nay! husband, and[1] it please you,[1] I shall go near.
Now the blessed Trinity be in this house!
Ah! cousin Elizabeth, sweet mother, what cheer?
You grow great! Ah! my God, how you be gracious![2]

Elizabeth. Anon as I heard of you this holy greeting,
Meekest maiden and the Mother of God, Mary,
By your breath the Holy Ghost us was inspiring,
That the child in my body enjoyed[3] greatly,
And turned down on his knees[4] to our God reverently.
Whom you bear in your body, this verily I ken.
Fulfilled with the Holy Ghost thus loud I cry,
'Blessed be thou among all women!
 And blessed be the fruit of thy womb, also,
Thou worthiest virgin and wife that ever was wrought!'
How is it that the Mother of God me should come to,
That wretch of all wretches, a wight[5] worse than nought?
And thou art blessed that believed verily in thy thought
That the word of God should profit in thee.
But how this blessedness about was brought,
I cannot think nor say how it might be.

Maria. To the praising of God, cousin, this said must be:
When I sat in my little house, unto God praying,
Gabriel came and said to me, 'Ave!'
There I conceived God, at my consenting,
Perfect God and perfect man at ones being.
Then the angel said unto me
That it was six monthes since your conceiving:
This causeth my coming, cousin, you to comfort and see.

Elizabeth. Blessed be you, cousin, for your hither coming!

---

[1] *if you don't mind.* [2] *full of God's grace.* [3] *rejoiced.* [4] *n. 28.* [5] *person.*

How I conceived I shall to you say.
The angel appeared the hour of incensing,
Saying I should conceive, and him[1] thought nay![1]
Sethe[2] for his mistrust he has been dumb alway!
And thus of my conception I have told you some.

Maria. For this holy psalm I begin here this day:
    Magnificat anima mea Dominum,[3]
Et exultavit spiritus meus in Deo salutari meo.[4]

Elizabeth. By the Holy Ghost with joy Godes Son is in thee
    come,
That thy spirit so enjoyed the health of thy God so.

Maria.   Quia respexit humilitatem ancillae suae.[5]
Ecce enim ex hoc beatem me dicent omnes generationes.

Elizabeth. For he beheld the lowness of his handmaides,[5]
So farforth for that, all generationes bless you in peace.

Maria.   Quia fecit mihi magna qui potens est,
Et sanctum nomen eius.

Elizabeth. For great thinges he made and also mightiest,
And right holy is the name of him in us.

Maria.   Et misericordia eius a progenie in progenies
Timentibus eum.

Elizabeth. Yea! the mercy of him from that kind[6] into the
    kind[6] of peace,
For all that him dread now is he come.

Maria.   Fecit potentiam in bracchio suo,
Dispersit superbos mente cordis sui.

Elizabeth. The power in his right arm he has made so
The proud to despair and the thought of their heartes only.

Maria.   Deposuit potentes de sede,
Et exaltavit humiles.

---

[1] *it seemed to him (her husband) impossible.*   [2] *Since.*   [3] *This line appears to conclude the stanza beginning at* Blessed *on p. 143, and to begin a new one.*   [4] *My soul doth magnify the Lord, and my spirit hath rejoiced in God my Saviour (A.V.). See Luke i, 46 ff. (the Magnificat). The exigencies of riming (if not the ignorance of the translator) have made very odd the English renderings which follow the Latin verses in the mouth of Elizabeth and I have thought it, therefore, improper to emend where it might otherwise have seemed called for.*   [5] *Rime odd?* (MS, sue *and, in hand-maydeze, some sign of alteration: see Block).*   [6] *family, sort, species, nature.*

Elizabeth. The proud men from high seates put he,
  And the lowly upon height in the seat of peace.
Maria.   Esurientes implevit bonis,
  Et divites dimisit inanes.
Elizabeth. All the poor and the needy he fulfilleth with
  his goodes,
  And the rich he felleth to voidness.
Maria.   Suscepit Israel puerum suum,
  Recordatus est misericordiae suae.
Elizabeth. Israel for his child uptook he to come,
  On his mercy to think for his that be.
Maria.   Sicut locutus est ad patres nostros,
  Abraham et semini eius in saecula.
Elizabeth. As he spoke here to our forefatheres in[1] close,[1]
  Abraham and to all his seed of him in this world sa.[2]
Maria.   Gloria Patri et Filio
  Et Spiritui Sancto.
Elizabeth. Praising be to the Father in heaven, lo!
  The same to the Son here be so,
    The Holy Ghost also to ken.[3]
Maria. Sicut erat in principio, et nunc, et semper,
  Et in saecula saeculorum, amen.
Elizabeth. As it was in the beginning, and now is, and shall
    be for ever,
  And in this world in all good workes to abiden then.
Maria.   This psalm of prophecy said between us twain
  In heaven it is written with angeles hand,
  Ever to be sung, and also to be sayn,
  Every day among us at our Even-song.
    But, cousin Elizabeth, I shall you here keep,
  And these three monthes abide here now,
  Till you have child, to wash, scour and sweep,
  And in all that I may to comfort you.
Elizabeth. Ah! you, Mother of God, you show us here how
  We should be meek that wretches here be.

---

[1] *face to face(?) privately(?).*   [2] *so (? filler for rime).*   [3] *know, make known.*

All heaven and earth worship you mow,[1]
That are throne[2] and tabernacle[2] of the high Trinity.
Joseph.   Ah! how do you? how do you, father Zachary?
We fall fast in age, without[3] oath![3]
Why shake you so your head? Have you the palsy?
Why speak you not, sir? I trow you are not wroth.
Elizabeth. Nay! wise father, Joseph, thereto[4] he were full
    loth.[4]
It is the visitation of God, he may not speak, verily.
Let us thank God therefore both:
He shall remedy it when it pleaseth his mercy.
    Come,[5] I pray you specially.
Iwis, you are welcome, Mary!
For this comfortablest coming, good God, gramercy![5]
Contemplatio.   Listeneth, sovereignes! Here is conclusion.
How the 'Ave'[6] was made, here is learned us.[6]
The angel said, 'Ave! gratia plena, Dominus tecum,
Benedicta tu in mulieribus.'
Elizabeth said, 'Et benedictus
Fructus ventris tui.' Thus the Church added 'Maria' and
    'Jesus' here.
Who[7] says our Ladyes psalter daily for a year thus,
He has pardon ten thousand and eight hundred year.[7]
    Then further to our matter for to proceed:
Mary with Elizabeth abode there still
Three monthes fully as we read,
Thanking God with heartly will.
    Ah! Lord God, what house was this one,
That[8] these childeren and their motheres two,
As Mary and Elizabeth, Jesus and John,
And Joseph and Zachary, also.[8]
    And ever our Lady abode still thus,

---

[1] *may.*   [2] *Conventional figures or titles for Mary: n. 29.*   [3] *it speaks for itself.*
[4] *he would be most reluctant to lose his temper.*   [5] *n. 30.*   [6] *prayer, 'Ave!*
Maria' . . . taught to us.   [7] *Whosoever says these psalms of Mary (cf. 144, 'this*
holy psalm'), once a day for a year shall have remission of ten thousand and eight hun-
dred years otherwise to be spent in purgatory after death.   [8] *a verb is wanting here.*

Till John was of his mother born,
And then Zachary spake, iwus,[1]
That had been dumb and his speech lorn.[2]
He and Elizabeth prophesied as thus,
They made 'Benedictus'[3] them beforn
And so 'Magnificat'[3] and 'Benedictus'
First in that place there made worn.[4]
    When all was done, our Lady free[5]
Took her leave then after this
At[6] Elizabeth and at[6] Zachary,
And kissed John and gan[7] him bless.
    Now most meekly we thank you of your patience,
And beseech you of your good supportation.
If here has been said or done any inconvenience
We assign it to your good deliberation,
Beseeching to Christes precious Passion
Conserve and reward your hither coming.
With 'Ave'[8] we begun and 'Ave' is our conclusion:
'Ave Regina caelorum' to our Lady we sing.[8]

Trial of Joseph and Mary[9]

Den.[10] [*To audience.*[10]]   Avoid,[11] sires, and let my Lord
    the Bishop come
And sit in the court the lawes for to do.
And I shall go in this place[12] them for to summon;
Those that are in my book the court you must come to.
    I warn you here all about
That I summon you all[13] the rout.[13]
Look you fail for no doubt

[1] *indeed.*   [2] *lost.*   [3] Benedictus: *Luke i, 68 ff.;* Magnificat: *p. 144; cf. p. 143,*
'Blessed be thou', *etc.*   [4] *were.*   [5] *noble, excellent.*   [6] *Of.*   [7] *did.*
[8] *n. 31.*   [9] *Supplied from Latin on p. 148: n. 32.*   [10] *n. 32.*   [11] *Stand aside.*
[12] *(playing-) place.*   [13] *the whole crowd.*

At the court to pear,[1]
Both John Jordan and Geoffrey Gile,
Malkin Milk-Duck and fair Mabel,
Steven Sturdy and Jack-at-the-Stile,
And Sawdir Saddler.
   Tom Tinker and Beatrice Bell,
Piers Potter and Wat-at-the-Well,
Sim Small-Faith and Kate Kell,
And Bartholomew the butcher;
Kit Cackler and Colette Crane,
Jill Fetise[2] and fair Jane,
Paul Pewterer and Pernel Prane,
And Philip the good fletcher.
   Cock[3] Crane and Davy Dry-Dust,
Lucy Liar and Letice Little-Trust,
Miles the Miller and Coll Crake-Crust,
Both Bette the Baker,
And Robin Reed.
And look you ring well in your purse,
For elles your cause may speed the worse,
Though that you sling Godes curse
Even[4] at my head.
Fast come away,
Both Bouting the Brewster and Sibyly Sling,
Meg Merry-Weather and Sabin Spring,
Tiffany Twinkler, fail for nothing,
The court shall be this day.

Hic intrabit pagetum de purgatione Mariae et Joseph.[5]
Primus detractor.[6] [*To audience.*]   Ah! sires, God save
    you all!
Here is a fair people, in good fay.
Good sires, tell me what men me call—
I trow you cannot by this day!

---

[1] *appear.*   [2] *Elegant.*   [3] *I am uncertain how to arrange the lines of this stanza.*
[4] *Straight.*   [5] *Here will enter the pageant of the trial of Mary and Joseph* (n. 32).
[6] *The first and second 'detractors' are called Raise-Slander and Back-Biter: they are
often complained about in sermons, etc. (e.g. Owst, 450 ff.).*

Yet I walk wide and many way,
But yet there I come I do no good.
To raise slander is all my lay—[1]
Back-Biter is my brother of blood.
    Did[2] he ought come hither in all this day?[2]
Now would God that he were here!
And, by my troth, I dare well say
That, if we twain together appear,
More slander we two shall arear[3]
Within an hour, through-out this town,
Than ever there was this thousand year,
And elles I shrew[4] you both up and down.
    Now, by my troth, I have a sight
Even of my brother, lo! where he is.
Welcome, dear brother, my troth I plight,
Your gentle mouth let me now kiss.
Secundus detractor.[5] Gramercy! brother, so have[6] I[6] bliss!
I am full glad we met this day.
Primus detractor. Right so am I brother, iwis,
    Much gladder than I can say.
    But yet, good brother, I you pray,
Tell all these people what is your name,
For, if they knew it, my life I lay,[7]
They will you worship and speak great fame.
Secundus detractor. I am Back-Biter that[8] spilleth all game,[8]
Both kid[9] and knowen in many a place.
Primus detractor. By my troth, I said the same,
And yet[10] some saiden thou should have evil grace.[10]
Secundus Detractor.   Hark! Raise-Slander, canst thou
    ought tell
Of any new thing that wrought was late?
Primus detractor. Within a short while a thing befell.
    I trow thou wilt laugh right well thereat,

---

[1] *practice, custom.*   [2] *Did he come here at all today?*   [3] *arouse.*   [4] *curse*
[5] *See Note 6 on previous page.*   [6] *(may) I have.*   [7] *wager.*   [8] *who spoils all*
sport.   [9] *notorious.*   [10] *moreover some people said you would suffer misfortune.*

For, by troth, right[1] mickle[1] hate,
    If it be wist, thereof will grow.
Secundus detractor. If I may raise therewith debate,
    I shall not spare the seed to sow.
Primus detractor.   Sir, in the Temple a maid there was,
    Called Maid Mary, the truth to tell,
    She seemed so holy within that place,
    Men said she was fed with holy angel.
    She made a vow with man never to mell,[2]
    But to live chaste and clean virgin.
    However it be, her womb does swell,
    And is as great as thine or mine.
Secundus detractor.   Yea! That old shrew, Joseph, my
      troth I plight,
    Was so enamoured upon that maid
    That of her beauty, when he had sight,
    He ceased not till had her assayed!
Primus detractor. Ah! nay, nay! Well worse she has him paid!
    Some fresh young gallant she loveth well more
    That his[3] legges to her has laid,[3]
    And that does grieve the old man sore!
Secundus detractor.   By my troth! all may well be,
    For fresh and fair she is to sight,
    And such a morsel as seemeth me[4]
    Would cause a young man to have delight.
Primus detractor. Such a young damsel of beauty bright,
    And of shape so comely, also,
    Of[5] her tail oft-time be light,
    And right tickle under the toe.[5]
Secundus detractor.   That old cuckold was evil-beguiled
    To that fresh wench when he was wed,
    Now must he fatheren another mannes child,
    And with his swink[6] he[6] shall be fed.
Primus detractor. A young man may do more cheer in bed

---

[1] *very great.*   [2] *have to do.*   [3] *has had sexual intercourse with her.*   [4] *(to)
me.*   [5] *loose and easy to seduce.*   [6] *labour the child.*

To a young wench than may an old:
That is the cause such law[1] is led,
That many a man is a cuckold.

Hic sedet Episcopus Abiyachar inter duos legis doctores et,
audientes hanc defamationem, vocat ad se detractores[2]

Episcopus.   Hark! you fellowes, why speak you such
    shame
Of that good virgin, fair Maid Mary?
You are accursed so her for to defame,
She that is of life so good and holy.
Of her to speak such villainy
You make my heart full heavy of mood.
I charge you, cease of your false cry!
For she is sib[3] of my owen blood.

Secundus detractor.   Sib of thy kin though that she be,
All great with child her womb does swell.
Do call her hither, thyself shall see
That it is truth that I thee tell.

Primus detractor. Sir, for your sake I shall keep counsel,
You for to grieve I am right loth.
But list! sires, list! What says[4] the bell?[4]
Our fair maid now great with child goth.

Primus doctor legis.   Take good heed, sires, what you do
    say!
Advise you well what you present!
If this be found false another day
Full sore you shall your tale repent.

Secundus detractor. Sir, the maid forsooth is good and gent,[5]
Both comely and gay and a fair wench,
And feetly[6] with help she can[7] consent
To set[8] a cuckold on the high bench.[8]

Secundus doctor legis.   You[9] be too busy of your language![9]
I hope to God you false to prove.

---

[1] *way of life.*   [2] *Here Bishop Abiyachar sits between two doctors of law, and,*
when they have heard this defamation, he calls the detractors to him.   [3] *relation.*
[4] *is spread abroad, heard, everywhere.*   [5] *pretty, neat.*   [6] *trimly.*   [7] *did.*
[8] *put a cuckold on display (?).*   [9] *You talk far too much.*

It were great ruth[1] she should so[2] outrage,[2]
Or with such sin to mischieve.[3]
Episcopus. These heavy tales my heart do grieve,
Of her to hear such foul daliance.[4]
If she be founden in such reproof[5]
She shall sore rue her governance.[6]
    Sim Summoner, in haste wend thou thy way,
Bid Joseph and his wife by name
At the court to appear this day,
Here them[7] to purge of their defame.[7]
Say that I hear of them great shame,
And that does me great heaviness.
If they are clean, withouten blame,
Bid them come hither and show witness.
Den.   All ready, sir, I shall them call
Here at your court for to appear,
And, if I may them meet withal,
I hope right soon they shall be here.
    [*To audience.*][8] Away, sires, let me come near,
A man of worship here cometh to[9] place![9]
Of courtesy me[10] seemeth you be to lere,[10]
Do off your hoodes with[11] an evil grace![11]
    Do me some worship before my face—
Or by my troth I shall you make!
If that I roll you up in my race,[12]
For fear I shall do[13] your arse quake.
But[14] yet some meed and you me take,[14]
I will withdraw my great rough tooth:
Gold or silver I will not forsake,
But even as all summoners doth.
    [*To Joseph.*]   Ah! Joseph, good day, with thy fair
spouse!

---

[1] *shame.*   [2] *act so outrageously.*   [3] *do wrong.*   [4] *talk, sexual behaviour.*
[5] *sin.*   [6] *conduct.*   [7] *to clear themselves of these accusations.*   [8] *n. 32.*
[9] *into the (playing-?) place.*   [10] *it seems to me you need to be taught.*   [11] *damn you!*   [12] *onset, haste, course.*   [13] *make.*   [14] *But if, on the other hand, you give me a bribe.*

My lord, the Bishop, has for you sent.
It is him told that in thy house
A[1] cuckold his bow is each night bent.[1]
He that[2] shot the bolt is like to be shent.[2]
Fair maid, that tale you can best tell:
Now, by your troth, tell your intent—
Did not the archer please you right well?

Maria. Of God in heaven I take witness
That sinful work was never my thought.
I am a maid yet of pure cleanness,
Like as I was into this world brought.

Den. Other witness shall none be sought—
Thou art with child, each man may see.
I charge you both you tarry not,
But to the Bishop come forth with me.

Joseph. To the Bishop with you we wend,
Of[3] our purgation[3] have we no doubt.

Maria. Almighty God shall be our friend
When the truth is tried out.

Den. Yea! In this wise excuseth her every scowt[4]
When their owen sin them does defame.[5]
But lowly then they gin[6] to lout[6]
When they are guilty and founden in blame.
Therefore come forth, cuckold by name.
The Bishop shall your life appose.[7]
Come forth, also, you goodly dame,
A clean housewife as I suppose.
I shall you tellen, withouten[8] gloss,[8]
And[9] you were mine, withouten lack,[10]
I[11] would each day beshrew your nose
And you did bring me such a pack.[11]
My lord the Bishop, here have I brought

---

[1] *Each night you have the experience of being cuckolded (n. 25).*   [2] *who (shot the arrow) did the (sexual) deed is likely to suffer for it.*   [3] *That we shall clear ourselves.*   [4] *term of abuse.*   [5] *give a bad name.*   [6] *are submissive.*   [7] *examine.*   [8] *plainly, straight.*   [9] *If.*   [10] *fail.*   [11] *Not a day would pass but I'd let you know what's what, if you brought me such a packet.*

153

This goodly couple at your bidding.
And as me seemeth as by her[1] fraught[1]
'Fair[2] child, lullay', soon must she sing.[2]
Primus detractor. To her a cradle and[3] you would bring
   You might save money in her purse.
   Because she is your cousin[4] young,
   I pray you, sir, let her never fare the worse.
Episcopus.   Alas! Mary, what hast thou wrought?
   I am ashamed even for thy sake.
   How hast thou changed thy holy thought?
   Did old Joseph with strength thee take?
   Or hast thou chosen another make[5]
   By whom thou art thus brought in shame?
   Tell me who has wrought this wrake?[6]
   How hast thou lost thy holy name?
Maria.   My name, I hope, is safe and sound,
   God to witness, I am a maid.
   Of fleshly[7] lust and ghostly wound[7]
   In deed nor thought I never assayed.
Primus doctor legis. How[8] should thy womb thus be arrayed,[8]
   So greatly swollen as that it is?
   But[9] if[9] some man thee had over-laid
   Thy womb should never be so great, iwis.
Secundus doctor legis.   Hark! thou, Joseph, I am afraid
   That thou hast wrought this open sin.
   This woman thou hast thus betrayed
   With great flattering or some false gin.[10]
Secundus detractor. Now, by my troth, you hit the pin![11]
   With that purpose in faith I hold.
   Tell now how thou thus her didest win,
   Or knowledge[12] thyself for[12] a cuckold.
Joseph.   She is for[13] me a true, clean maid,
   And I for her am clean, also.

---

1 *what she's carrying.*   2 *i.e. sing a lullaby.*   3 *if.*   4 *relation.*   5 *mate.*
6 *harm.*   7 *bodily pleasure and spiritual injury.*   8 *How could your belly get into this condition.*   9 *Unless.*   10 *trick.*   11 *nail on the head.*   12 *acknowledge yourself to be.*   13 *with regard to.*

Of fleshly sin I never assayed
Sithin[1] that[1] she was wedded me to.
Episcopus. Thou shalt not scape from us yet so.
First thou shalt tellen[2] us another lay.[2]
Straight to the altar thou shalt go,
The drink of vengeance there to assay.
　　Here is the bottle of Godes vengeance.
This drink shall be now thy purgation.
This has such virtue by Godes ordinance
That what man drink of this potation,
And goes certain in procession,
Here in this place, this altar about,
If he be guilty some maculation[3]
Plain in his face shall show it out[3].
　　If thou be guilty, tell us, let see!
Over Godes might be not too bold.
If thou presume and guilty be,
God thou dost grieve many afold.[4]
Joseph. I am not guilty, as I first told—
Almighty God I[5] take[5] witness.
Episcopus. Then this drink in haste thou hold,
And on procession anon thee[6] dress.[6]
　　Hic Joseph bibit et septies circuivit altare.[7]
Joseph. 　　This drink I take with meek intent.
As I am guiltless, to God I pray:
Lord, as thou art omnipotent,
On me thou show the truth this day.
　　Modo bibit.[8]
About this altar I take the way.
Oh! gracious God, help thy servant.
As I am guiltless against yon may,[9]
Thy hand of mercy this time me grant.
Den. 　　This old shrew may not well gon,

---

[1] *since.*　　[2] *(?).*　　[3] *disfigurement will be bound to reveal it plainly in his face.*
[4] *times over.*　　[5] *is my.*　　[6] *get yourself ready.*　　[7] *Here Joseph drinks and goes
seven times round the altar.*　　[8] *Now he drinks.*　　[9] *maiden.*

Long he tarrieth to go about.
Lift up thy feet, set forth thy ton,[1]
Or by my troth thou gettest a clout!
Secundus detractor. Now, sir, evil[2] thedom come to thy
    snout![2]
What aileth thy legges now to be lame?
Thou didest them put right freshly out
When thou didest play with yon young dame!
Primus detractor.   I pray to God give him mischance!
His legges here do[3] fold for[3] age—
But with this damsel when he did dance
The old churl had right[4] great courage![4]
Den. The shrew was then set[5] in a dotage,[5]
And had good lust[6] that time to playn.[6]
Gave she not you[7] caudel to potage,[7]
When you had done, to comfort your brain?
Joseph.   Ah! gracious God, help me this tide,[8]
Against this people that me do fame;[9]
As I never more did touch her side,
This day help me from wordly shame.
About this altar, to keep my fame,
Seven times I have gone round about.
If I be worthy to suffer blame,
Oh! rightful God, my sin show out.
Episcopus.   Joseph, with heart thank God, thy Lord,
Whose high mercy does thee excuse.
For thy purgation we shall record,
With[10] her of sin thou didest never muse.[10]
But, Mary, thyself mayst not refuse:
All great with child we see thee stand.
What myster[11] man did thee misuse?
Why hast thou sinned against thy husband?
Maria.   I trespassed never with earthly wight.

[1] *toes.*   [2] *bad luck to you!*   [3] *give way with.*   [4] *plenty of spirit.*   [5] *completely infatuated (also = senile).*   [6] *desire (at) that time for (sexual) play.*   [7] *(to) you a warm, spiced drink as your beverage.*   [8] *time.*   [9] *defame.*   [10] *You never thought about sinning with her.*   [11] *kind of.*

Thereof I hope, through Godes sand,[1]
Here to be purged before your sight,
From all sin clean, like as my husband.
Take[2] me the bottle out of your hand.
Here shall I drink before your face:
About this altar then shall I fand[3]
Seven times to go by Godes grace.

Primus doctor legis.   See! This bold[4] bismare[4] would presume
Against God to prove his might.
Though Godes vengeance her should consume
She will not tell her false delight.
Thou art with child, we see in sight:
To us thy womb thee does accuse.
There was never woman yet in such plight,
That[5] from mankind her could excuse.[5]

Primus detractor.   In faith, I suppose that this woman slept
Withouten all covert[6] while that it did snow,
And a flake thereof into her mouth crept,
And thereof the child in her womb does grow.

Secundus detractor. Then beware, dame, for this is well iknow:
When it is born, if that the sun shine,
It will turn to water again, as I trow,
For snow unto water does evermore recline![7]

Secundus doctor legis.   With[8] Godes high might look thou not jape!
Of thy purgation well thee advise.[8]
If thou be guilty, thou mayst not scape.
Beware ever of God that rightful justice.
If God with vengeance set on thee his size,[9]
Not only thou, but all thy kin, is shamed.
Better it is to tell the true[10] devise[11]

---

[1] *dispensation.*   [2] *Give.*   [3] *try.*   [4] *shameful wretch.*   [5] *Who could exonerate herself from intimacy with a man.*   [6] *covering.*   [7] *tend to return.*
[8] *Take care you don't treat God Almighty lightly. Think carefully about your trial.*
[9] *assize.*   [10] *MS* trewth.   [11] *intent.*

Than God for to grieve and of[1] him be gramed.[1]

Maria.   I trusten in his grace I shall him never grieve:
His servant I am in word, deed and thought,
A maid undefiled I hope he shall me prove.
I pray you let[2] me not.

Episcopus. Now by that good Lord that all this world has
    wrought,
If God on thee show any manner[3] token,[3]
Purgation, I trow, was never so dear bought,
If I may on thee in any wise be wroken.[4]
    Hold here the bottle and take a large draught,
And about the altar go thy procession.

Maria. To God in this case my cause I have betaught.[5]
Lord, through thy help I drink of this potation.

Hic Beata Virgo bibit de potatione et postea circuivit altare.[6]

Maria. God, as I never knew[7] of mannes maculation,[7]
But ever have lived in true virginity,
Send me this day thy holy consolation,
That all this fair people my cleanness may see.
    Oh! gracious God, as thou hast chose me,
For to be thy mother, of me to be born,
Save thy tabernacle[8] that clean is kept for thee,
Which now am put at reproof and scorn.
Gabriel me told with wordes here[9]-beforn
That you of your goodness would become my child.
Help now of your highness my worship be not lorn.
Ah! dear son, I pray you, help your mother mild.

Episcopus.   Almighty God! what may this mean?
For[10] all the drink[10] of Godes potation,
This woman with child is fair and clean,
Withouten foul spot or maculation.
I cannot by no imagination
Prove her guilty and sinful of life.

---

[1] *by him be punished.*   [2] *hinder.*   [3] *kind of indication (of her sin).*   [4] *avenged.*
[5] *committed.*   [6] *Here the Blessed Virgin takes a draught of the drink and after that
goes round the altar.*   [7] *was defiled by sexual intercourse with a man.*   [8] *n. 29.*
[9] *MS he.*   [10] *Though she has drunk.*

It showeth openly by her purgation
She is clean maid, both mother and wife.
Primus detractor.　　By my father soul, here is great guile!
Because she is sib of your kindred
The drink is changed by some false wile,
That she no shame should have this[1] stead.[1]
Episcopus. Because thou deemest that we do falsehood,
And for thou didest them first defame,
Thou shalt right here, maugre[2] thine heed,[2]
Before all this people drink of the same.
Primus detractor.　　Sir, in good faith, one draught I pull,
If these two drinkeres have not all spent.
Hic bibit et sentiens dolorem in capite cadit.[3]
Out! out! alas! what aileth my skull?
Ah! my head with fire me thinketh is burnt.
Mercy! good Mary, I do me repent
Of my cursed and false language.
Maria. Now good Lord, in heaven omnipotent,
Of his great mercy your sickness assuage.
Episcopus.　　We all on knees fall here on ground,
Thou, Godes handmaid, praying for grace.
All cursed language and shame unsound[4]
Good Mary, forgive us here in this place.
Maria. Now God forgive you all your trespass,
And also forgive you all defamation
That you have said, both more and less,
To my hinderance[5] and maculation.[5]
Episcopus.　　Now, Blessed Virgin, we thank you all,
Of your good heart and great patience.
We will go with you home to your hall
To do you service with high reverence.
Maria. I thank you heartily of your benevolence.
Unto your owen house I pray you you go,
And take this people home with you hence:

---

[1] *(in) this place.*　　[2] *whether you like it or not.*　　[3] *Here he drinks and feeling
ill falls on his head.*　　[4] *ill-founded.*　　[5] *injury and defilement.*

I am not disposed to passen hence fro.
Episcopus.   Then farewell, maiden and pure virgin!
Farewell, true handmaid of God in bliss!
We all to you lowly incline,
And take our leave of you as worthy is.
Maria. Almighty God your ways wisse,[1]
For that high Lord is most of might.
He may you speed that you not miss
In heaven of him to have a sight.
Joseph.   Honoured in heaven be that high Lord
Whose endless grace is so abundant,
That he does show the true record
Of each wight[2] that is his true servant.
That Lord to worship with heart pleasant
We both are bound right in this place,
Which our purgation us did grant,
And proved us pure by high grace.
Maria.   Forsooth, good spouse, I thank him highly
Of his good grace for our purgation.
Our cleanness is knowen full openly
By virtue of his great consolation.

Birth of The Son[3]

Joseph.   Lord! what[4] travail to man is wrought![4]
Rest in this world behoveth him none!
Octavian, our Emperor, sadly[5] has besought[5]
Our tribute him[6] to bear folk must forth each one.
    It is cried in every borough and city by name.
I that am a poor timber-wright, born of the blood of David,
The Emperores commandment I must hold with,

---

¹ *direct.*   ² *person.*   ³ *n. 33.*   ⁴ *what a hard life is made for man.*
⁵ *has strongly requested.*   ⁶ *(to) him.*

And elles I were to blame.
   Now my wife, Mary, what say you to this?
For secure,[1] needes I must forth wend
Unto the city of Bethlehem far hence, iwis.[2]
Thus to labour I must my body bend.
Maria. My husband and my spouse, with you will I wend.
   A sight of that city fain would I see.
If I might of my ally[3] any there find
It would be great joy unto me.
Joseph.   My spouse, you are with child—I fear you to carry,
   For me seemeth it were workes wild.
But you to please right fain would I.
Yet women are ethe[4] to grieve when they are with child.
Now let us forth wend as fast as we may,
And almighty God speed us in our journey.
Maria.   Ah! my sweet husband, would you tell to me
What tree is yon standing upon yon hill?
Joseph. Forsooth, Mary, it is cleped[5] a cherry tree.
   In time[6] of year[6] you might feed you thereon your fill.
Maria.   Turn again, husband, and behold yon tree,
How that it bloometh now so sweetly.
Joseph. Come on, Mary, that we were at yon city,
   Or elles we may be blamed I tell you lightly.
Maria.   Now, my spouse, I pray you to behold
How the cherries growen upon yon tree.
For to have thereof right fain I would,
And it pleased you to labour so much for me.
Joseph.   Your desire to fulfil I shall assay securely.[7]
   How! to pluck you of these cherries, it is a work wild,
For the tree is so high it will not be lightly—
Therefore let him pluck you cherries begat[8] you with child!
Maria.   Now, good Lord, I pray thee, grant me this boon,

---

[1] *certain.*   [2] *indeed.*   [3] *kin.*   [4] *easy.*   [5] *called.*   [6] *season.*   [7] *for certain.*   [8] *(who) got.*

To have of these cherries, and[1] it be your will.
Now I thank it God, this tree boweth to me down.
I may now gatheren enough[2] and eaten my fill.
Joseph.   How! I know well I have offended my God in
     Trinity,
Speaking to my spouse these unkind wordis.
For now I believe well it may no other be
But that my spouse beareth the Kinges Son of Bliss.
He[3] help us now at our need.
Of the kindred of Jesse worthily were you bore,
Kinges and Patriarches you before,
All these worthy of your kindred were,
As clerkes[4] in story read.
Maria.   Now, gramercy! husband for your report.
In our ways wisely let us forth wend.
The Father Almighty, he be our comfort.
The Holy Ghost Glorious, he be our friend.
Joseph.   Hail! worshipful sir, and good day!
A citizen of this city you seem to be.
Of harbour for spouse and me I you pray,
For truly this woman is full weary,
And fain at rest, sir, would she be.
We would fulfil the bidding of our Emperor
For to pay tribute, as right is our,
And to keep ourself from dolour[5]
We are come to this city.
Cives.   Sir, hostage[6] in this town know I none
Thy wife and thou in for to sleep.
This city is beset with people every wone,[7]
And yet they lie without, full every street.
     Within no wall, man, comest thou not,
Be thou ones within the city gate.
Onethes[8] in the street a place may be sought,
Thereon to rest without debate![9]

---

[1] if.   [2] plenty.   [3] (May) he.   [4] men of learning.   [5] trouble.
[6] accommodation.   [7] place.   [8] Scarcely.   [9] fighting (for it).

Joseph.   Nay, sir, debate, that will I not!
All such thinges passen my power.
But yet my care and all my thought
Is for Mary my darling dear.
    Ah! sweet wife, what shall we do?
Where shall we lodge this night?
Unto the Father of Heaven pray we so
Us to keep from every wicked wight.
Cives.   Good man! one word I will thee say,
If thou wilt do by the counsel of me.
Yonder is an house[1] of aras[1] that stands by the way:
Among the beastes harboured may you be.
Maria.   Now the Father of Heaven he[2] may you yield![2]
His Son in my womb forsooth he is.
He[3] keep thee and thy good[4] by frith and field![4]
Go we hence, husband, for now time it is.
    But hark! now, good husband, a new relation,[5]
Which in myself I know right well:
Christ,[6] in me has take incarnation,
Soon will be born, the truth I feel.
    In this poor lodge my chamber I take,
Here for to abide the blessed birth
Of him that all this world did make.
Between my sides I feel he stirth.
Joseph.   God be thy help, spouse, it swemeth[7] me sore,
Thus feebly lodged and in so poor degree,
Godes Son among beastes to be bore.
His wonder workes fulfilled must be.
    In a house that is desolate without any wall,
Fire nor wood none here is.
Maria. Joseph, my husband, abiden here I shall,
For here will be born the Kinges Son of Bliss.
Joseph.   Now, gentle wife, be of good mirth,
And, if you will ought have, tell me what you think,

---

[1] *stable for horses.* [2] *may he reward you.* [3] *(May) he.* [4] *property everywhere.*
[5] *consideration.* [6] *Christ, (who).* [7] *grieves.*

I shall not spare, for[1] cheap nor dearth—[1]
Now tell me your lust[2] of meat and drink.
Maria.   For meat and drink lust I right nought:
Almighty God my food shall be.
Now that I am in chamber brought
I hope right well my child to see.
Therefore, husband, of[3] your honesty,[3]
Avoid you hence out of this place,
And I alone with humility
Here shall abide Godes high grace.
Joseph.   All ready, wife, you for to please,
I will go hence out of your way.
And seek some midwives you for to ease,
When that you travail of child this day.
Farewell, true wife and also clean may,[4]
God be your comfort in Trinity!
Maria. To God in heaven for you I pray,
He you preserve whereso you be.
    Hic dum Joseph est absens partit Maria Filium Unigenitum.[5]
Joseph.   Now God, of whom cometh all relief,
And as all grace in thee is ground,[6]
So save my wife from hurt and grief
Till I some midwives[7] for her have found.
Travailing women in care are bound
With great throwes[8] when they do groan.
God help my wife that she not swound:[9]
I am full sorry she is alone.
    It is not convenient a man to be
There women go in travailing,
Wherefore some midwife fain would I see
My wife to help that is so young.
Zelomy. Why makest thou, man, such mourning?
Tell me some deal[10] of your great moan.

---

1 *whether there's a lot of it or a little.*   2 *desire.*   3 *out of decency.*   4 *maiden.*
5 *Here while Joseph is away Mary bears the Only-Begotten Son.*   6 *grounded (?).*
7 *n. 34.*   8 *labour-pains.*   9 *swoon.*   10 *part.*

Joseph. My wife is now in great longing,
　　Travailing of child and is alone.
　　For Godes love that sits in throne,
　　As you midwives that[1] can your good,[1]
　　Help my young spouse in haste anon.
　　I[2] dread me sore of that fair food.[2]
Salome. Be of good cheer and of glad mood!
　　We two midwives with thee will go.
　　There was never woman in such plight stood
　　But we were ready her help to do.
　　　My name is Salome—all men me know
　　For a midwife of worthy fame.
　　When women travail grace does grow:
　　Thereas[3] I come[3] I had never shame.
Zelomy. And I am Zelomy—men know my name.
　　We twain with thee will go together
　　And help thy wife from hurt and grame.[4]
　　Come forth, Joseph, go we straight thither!
Joseph.　　I thank you, dames, you comfort my life.
　　Straight to my spouse walk we the way.
　　In this poor lodge lies Mary my wife.
　　Her for to comfort, good friendes, assay.
Salome. We dare not enter this lodge, in[5] fay,[5]
　　There is therein so great brightness.
　　Moon by night nor sun by day
　　Shone never so clear in their lightness.
Zelomy.　　Into this house dare I not gon,
　　The wonderful light does me affray.[6]
Joseph. Then will myself go in alone,
　　And cheer my wife if that I may.
　　All hail! maiden and wife I say,
　　How dost thou fare? Tell me thy cheer.
　　Thee for to comfort in gesine[7] this day
　　Twain good midwives I have brought here.

---

[1] *who know what to do.*　　[2] *I am terribly afraid for that fair girl.*　　[3] *In the cases
I have come to.*　　[4] *trouble.*　　[5] *believe me.*　　[6] *frighten.*　　[7] *child-bed.*

Thee for to help that art in hard[1] bond,[1]
Zelomy and Salome are come with me.
For doubt[2] of dread without they do stand,
And dare not come in for light that they see.
Maria. (Subridendo.)[3] The might of the Godhead in his
Majesty
Will not be hid now at this while.
The child that is born will prove his mother free[4]
A very clean maid, and therefore I smile.
Joseph.   Why do you laugh, wife, you are to blame!
I pray you, spouse, do no more so.
In[5] hap the midwives will take it to grame,[5]
And at your need help will none do.
If you have need of midwives, lo!
Peradventure they will go hence.
Therefore be sad,[6] and[6] you may so,
And winneth all the midwives good diligence.
Maria.   Husband, I pray you, displease you not,
Though that I laugh and great joy have.
Here is the child[7] this world has wrought,
Born now of me, that all thing shall save.
Joseph. I ask you grace for I did rave.
Oh! gracious child, I ask mercy.
As thou art Lord and I but knave,
Forgive me now my great folly.
Alas! midwives, what have I said?
I pray you come to us more near,
For here I find my wife a maid,
And in her arm a child has here.
Both maid and mother she is in[8] fere——[8]
That[9] God will have may nevermore fail.[9]
Mother on earth was never none clear
Without she had in birth travail.

---

[1] *distress.*   [2] *fear, danger.*   [3] *smiling.*   [4] *gracious.*   [5] *Perhaps the midwives
will be made angry by it.*   [6] *serious, if.*   [7] *child (who).*   [8] *together.*   [9] *What
God chooses to have cannot fail.*

Zelomy.   In birth travail must she needes have,
   Or elles no child of her is born.
Joseph. I pray you, dame, and you vouchsafe,
   Come see the child my wife beforn.
Salome.   Great God be in this place!
   Sweet sister, how fare ye?
Maria. I thank the Father of his high grace,
   His owen Son and my child here you may see.
Zelomy.   All hail! Mary, and right good morn!
   Who was midwife of this fair child?
Maria. He that nothing will have forlorn[1]
   Sent me this babe, and I maid mild.
Zelomy.   With hand let me now touch and feel
   If you have need of medicine.
   I shall you comfort and help right well
   As other women if you have[2] pine.[2]
Maria. Of this fair birth that here is mine
   Pain nor grieving feel I right none.
   I am clean maid and pure virgin—
   Taste with your hand yourself alone.
   Hic palpat Zelomy Beatam Mariam Virginem.[3]
Zelomy.   Oh! mightful God, have mercy on me!
   A marvel that never was heard beforn!
   Here openly I feel and see
   A fair child of a maiden is born,
   And needeth no washing as other don.
   Full clean and pure forsooth is he,
   Withouten spot or any pollution,
   His mother not hurt of virginity.
      Come near, good sister, Salome,
   Behold the breastes of this clean maid,
   Full of fair milk how that they be,
   And her child clean as I first said;
   As others are, not foul arrayed,

---

[1] *utterly lost.*   [2] *are suffering.*   [3] *Here Zelomy examines the Blessed Virgin Mary.*

But clean and pure both mother and child.
Of this matter I am dismayed,[1]
To see them both thus undefiled.
Salome.   It is not true! It may never be!
That both are clean I cannot believe!
A maid milk have never man did see,
Nor woman bear child without great grief.
I shall never trow it but[2] I it prove,
With hand touching, but[2] I assay,
In[3] my conscience it may never cleave[3]
That she has child and is a may.[4]
Maria.   You for to put clean out of doubt,
Touch with your hand and well assay,
Wisely ransack and try the truth out
Whether I be fouled or a clean may.
*Hic tangit Salome Mariam et cum arescerit manus eius
ululando et quasi flendo dicit.*[5]
Salome. Alas! alas! and welaway!
For my great doubt and false belief
My hand is dead and dry as clay.
My false untrust has wrought mischief.
    Alas! the time that I was born
Thus to offend against Godes might!
My handes power is now all lorn,[6]
Stiff as a stick and may not plight.[7]
For I did tempt[8] this maid so bright,
And held against her pure cleanness,
In[9] great mischief now am I pight—[9]
Alas! alas! for my lewdness.[10]
    Oh! Lord of might, thou knowest the truth,
That I have ever had dread of thee:
On every poor wight[11] ever I have ruth,

[1] *filled with fear.*   [2] *unless.*   [3] *In my mind the idea can never have a place.*
[4] *maiden.*   [5] *Here Salome touches Mary and, since her hand (n. 35) is dried up,
howling and, as it were, weeping she says.*   [6] *lost.*   [7] *close up, (fold).*   [8] *put to
the test.*   [9] *I am now stuck in great trouble.*   [10] *ignorance, foolishness, wickedness.*
[11] *creature.*

And gave them almes for love of thee.
Both wife and widow that asketh, for thee,
And friendless childeren that hadden great need,
I did them cure, and all for thee,
And took no reward of them nor meed.
 Now as a wretch for false belief,
That I showed in tempting this maid,
My hand is dead and does me grieve.
Alas! that ever I her assayed!

Angelus. Woman, thy sorrow to have delayed,[1]
Worship that child that there is born,
Touch the clothes there he is laid,
For he shall save all that is lorn.

Salome. Oh! glorious child and King of Bliss!
I ask you mercy for my trespass.
I knowledge[2] my sin, I deemed[3] amiss,[3]
Oh! blessed babe, grant me some grace.
Of you maid, also, here in this place,
I ask mercy, kneeling on knee.
Most holy maid, grant me solace:
Some word of comfort say now to me.

Maria. As Godes angel to you did tell,
My child is medicine for every sore.
Touch his clothes, by my counsel—
Your hand full soon he will restore.
 Hic Salome tangit fimbriam Christi.[4]

Salome. Ah! now, blessed be this child evermore.
The Son of God forsooth he is,
Has healed my hand that was forlore[5]
Through false belief and deeming amiss.
 In every place I shall tell this,
Of a clean maid that God is born,
And in our likeness God now clad is,
Mankind to save that was forlorn.[6]

---

[1] *taken away.* [2] *acknowledge.* [3] *thought wrongly.* [4] *Here Salome touches the hem of Christ's garment.* [5] *wasted.* [6] *damned.*

His mother a maid as she was beforn,
Not foul polluted as other women be,
But fair and fresh as rose on thorn,
Lily white, clean with pure virginity.
　　Of this blessed babe my leave now do I take,
And also of you, high Mother of Bliss.
Of this great miracle more knowledge to make,
I shall go tell it in each place, iwis.
Maria.　Farewell! good dame, and God your way wisse![1]
In all your journey, God be your speed!
And of his high mercy that Lord so you bless
That you never offend more in word, thought nor deed.
Zelomy.　　And I also do take my leave here
Of all this blessed, good company,
[*To Jesus.*] Praying your grace, both far and near,
On us to speed your endless mercy.
Joseph.　The blessing of that Lord that is most mighty
Mote[2] spread on you in every place;
Of[3] all your enemies to have the victory,
God, that[4] best may,[4] grant you his grace. Amen.

The Shepherds[5]

Angelus. [*Ad pastores.*][6]　　Joy to God that sits in heaven,
And peace to man on earth ground.
A child is born beneath the leven,[7]
Through him many folk shall be unbound.
Sacramentes[8] there shall be seven,
Wonnen[9] through that childes wound.[9]
Therefore I sing a joyful steven,[10]

[1] *direct.*　　[2] *Shall.*　　[3] *Over.*　　[4] *who is best able.*　　[5] *n. 36.*　　[6] [*To the Shepherds*].　　[7] *lightning.*　　[8] *Sacraments, i.e. of Baptism, the Eucharist, Absolution, Confirmation, Ordination, Marriage and Anointing.*　　[9] *(The grace given in which was) won by the atoning death of Christ.*　　[10] *sound.*

The flower of friendship now is found.
God that woneth[1] on high,
He is gloried, mannes ghost[2] to win.
He has sent salve to mannes sin,
Peace is comen to mannes kin,
Through Godes sleightes[3] sly.[3]

Primus pastor.   Maunfras! Maunfras! fellow mine,
I saw a great light with sheen shine,
Yet saw I never so selcouth[4] sign
Shapen upon the skies.
It is brighter than the sun beam,
It cometh right over all this realm,
Even above Bethlehem
I saw it burn thries.

Secundus pastor.   Thou art my brother, Boosras.
I have beholden the same pass.
I trow it is tokening of grace
That shining showeth beforn.
Balaam spoke in prophecy:[5]
A light should shine upon the sky
When a son of a maid, Mary,
In Bethlehem was iborn.

Tertius pastor.   Though I make little noise,
I am an herd[6] that hatteth[6] Mose.
I heard carping[7] of a cross,[8]
Of Moses in his law——[8]
Of a maid a bairn born,
On a tree he should be torn.
Deliver[9] folkes that are forlorn[9]
The child should be slaw.[10]

Primus pastor.   Balaam spoke in prophecy:
Out of Jacob should shine a sky——[11]
Many folk he should buy

---

[1] *dwells.*   [2] *soul.*   [3] *wise devices.*   [4] *wonderful (a).*   [5] *Numbers xxiv,*
17 (and Rev. xxii, 16).   [6] *shepherd called.*   [7] *talk.*   [8] *Numbers xxi, 8–9 and*
John iii, 14–15.   [9] *(To) deliver . . . damned.*   [10] *slain.*   [11] *scion (?).*

With his bright blood.
By that bright blood that he should bleed
He shall us bring from the deviles dread,
As a duke[1] most doughty in deed,
Through his death on rood.[2]

Secundus pastor.   Amos[3] spoke with mild meth,[4]
A[5] fruit sweeter than balmes[6] breath.[6]
His death should slay our soules death
And draw us all from hell.
Therefore such light goes beforn
In token that the child is born
Which shall save that is forlorn
As prophetes gonne[7] spell.[7]

        Tertius pastor. Daniel the prophet thus gan[8] speak:[8]
Wise God, from woe us wreak,[9]
Thy bright heaven thou[10] to-break,[10]
And meddle[11] thee[11] with a maid.
This prophecy is now sped:[12]
Christ in our kind[13] is clad,
Therefore mankind may be glad,
As prophetes before have said.
Cantent: Gloria in excelsis Deo.[14]

Primus pastor.   Eh! eh! this was a wonder note
That was now sungen above the sky.
I[15] have that voice full well I wote:[15]
They sang, 'gle glo glory.'[16]

Secundus pastor.   Nay! so[17] may I the,[17] so was it not!
I have that song full well inum:[18]
In my wit well it is wrought.
It was 'gle glo, glas, glum.'[16]

Tertius pastor.   The song me thought it was 'glory',

---

[1] duke, *commander: n. 37.*   [2] *cross.*   [3] *Amos viii, 1–2 (?); cf. p. 116, ll. 6–13 (?)*
[4] *gentleness.*   [5] *(Of) a.*   [6] *scent of balm (?).*   [7] *told.*   [8] *spoke; Daniel vii,*
13–14 (?), ix, 3 ff., 24 ff., and cf. p. 117, ll. 17 ff., 123. 9–10.   [9] *rescue.*   [10] *do thou*
break open.   [11] *have intercourse.*   [12] *fulfilled.*   [13] *(human) nature.*   [14] *Let (the*
angels) sing: Glory be to God on high.   [15] *I think I've got every bit that was said.*
[16] *p. 50 above; Holkham, fol. 13.*   [17] *upon my life.*   [18] *grasped.*

And afterward he said us to,
'There is a child born shall be a prince mighty.'
For to seek that child I rede[1] we go.
Primus pastor.   The prophecy of Boosdras is speedily
    sped.[2]
Now lake[3] we[3] hence as that light us led.
Might we see ones that bright[4] on bed
Our[5] bale it would unbind—[5]
We should shudder for no shower.[6]
Busk[7] we us hence to Bethlehem bower
To see that fair fresh flower,
The maid mild in mind.[8]
Secundus pastor.   Let us follow with all our might.
With song and mirth we shall us[9] dight,[9]
And worship with joy that worthy wight
That Lord is of mankin.
Let us go forth fast on[10] hie[10]
And honour that babe worthily
With mirth, song and melody.
Have done! This song begin!
*Tunc pastores cantabunt, 'Stella caeli extirpavit', quo facto
ibunt ad quaerendum Christum.*[11]
Primus pastor.   Hail! flower of flowers, fairest ifound.
Hail! pearl peerless, prime[12] rose of price.[12]
Hail! bloom on bed, we shall be unbound
With[13] thy bloody woundes and workes full wise.
Hail! God greatest, I greet thee on ground.
The greedy devil shall groan, grisly as a grise,[14]
When thou winnest this world with thy wide wound,
And puttest man to paradise with plenty[15] of price.[15]
To love thee is my delight.

---

[1] *advise.*   [2] *fulfilled.*   [3] *let us go quickly.*   [4] *bright (one, i.e. Jesus).*   [5] *It
would free us from our sufferings.*   [6] *shower (i.e. of misfortune).*   [7] *Hasten.*
[8] *disposition.*   [9] *make our way.*   [10] *speedily.*   [11] *Then shall the shepherds sing,
'The star of Heaven has rooted up the mortal pestilence which our first father planted'
(cf. Horae, Beatae Mariae Virginis, or Sarum and York Primers, ed. E. Hoskins
(London, 1901, 1969), 165, 169–70), whereupon they will go to seek Christ.*   [12] *first
and excellent rose.*   [13] *By.*   [14] *boar (?).*   [15] *precious abundance (?).*

Hail! flower fair and free,[1]
Light from the Trinity.
Hail! blessed[2] may thou be![2]
Hail! maiden fairest in sight.

Secundus pastor.   Hail! flower over[3] flowers founden in
    frith.[3]
Hail! Christ kind in[4] our kith.[4]
Hail! worker[5] of weal to wonen us with.[5]
Hail! winner,[6] iwis,[6]
Hail! former[7] and friend,
Hail! feller of the fiend.
Hail! clad in our kind,[8]
Hail! Prince of Paradise.

Tertius pastor.   Hail! Lord over lordes that liest full[9]
    low.[9]
Hail! King over kinges, thy kindred to know.[10]
Hail! comely knight,[11] the devil to overthrow.
Hail! flower of all.
Hail! worker to win
Bodies bounden in sin.
Hail! in a beastes bin,[12]
Bestad[13] in a stall.

Joseph.   Herdes on hill,
Be not still[14]
But say your will
To many a man:
How God is born
This merry morn—
That[15] is forlorn[15]
Finden he can.

Primus pastor.   We shall tell
    By dale and hill

---

[1] *noble.*   [2] *blessings upon you.*   [3] *superior to flowers in the meadow.*   [4] *in our country, come among us (?).*   [5] *Doer of good (come) to live with us.*   [6] *winner (of souls), indeed.*   [7] *creator.*   [8] *(human) nature.*   [9] *most lowly.*   [10] *acknowledge.*   [11] *n. 37.*   [12] *manger, stall.*   [13] *Placed.*   [14] *silent.*   [15] *What is damned (i.e. mankind).*

How harrower[1] of hell
Was born this night,
Mirthes[2] to mell[2]
And fiendes to quell,
That were so fell
Against his right.

Secundus pastor.   Farewell! babe and bairn of bliss.
Farewell! Lord, that lovely is.
Thee to worship thy feet I kiss,
On knees to thee I fall.
Thee to worship I fall on knee,
All this world may joy[3] of[3] thee.
Now farewell! Lord of great pousty,[4]
Yea! farewell! King of all.

Tertius pastor.   Though I be the last that take my leave,
Yet, fair[5] mulling, take it not at no grief.[5]
Now, fair babe, well[6] may thou chieve,[6]
Fair child, now have good day!
Farewell! my owen dear darling,
Iwis, thou art a right fair thing.
Farewell! my Lord and my sweeting.
Farewell! born in poor array.

Maria.   Now you herdmen, well[7] may you be![7]
For your homage and your singing
My son shall acquit[8] you in heaven see,[8]
And give you all right good ending.

                              Amen

---

[1] *p. 315.*   [2] *To add pleasure (?).*   [3] *rejoice in.*   [4] *might.*   [5] *pretty little one, don't be offended.*   [6] *good luck to you.*   [7] *I wish you well.*   [8] *requite . . . seat, throne.*

Herod and the Three Kings[1]

Herod.   As a lord in royalty, in no region so rich,
  And ruler of all realmes, I ride in royal array.
  There is no lord of land in lordship to me like,
  None lovelier, none lovesommer, everlasting is my lay.[2]
    Of beauty and of boldness I bear[3] evermore the bell.[3]
  Of main and of might I master every man.
  I ding with my doughtiness the devil down to hell,
  For both of heaven and of earth I am king certain.
    I am the comeliest king clad in glittering gold,
  Yea! and the seemliest sire that may bestride a steed.
  I wield at my will all wightes[4] upon mold,[4]
  Yea! and worthily I am wrapped in a worthy weed.
    You knightes so comely, both courteous and keen,
  To my palace will I pass, full prest,[5] I you plight.[5]
  You dukes so doughty, follow me bedene,[6]
  Unto my royal palace the way lies full right.
    Wightly[7] from my steed I skip down in haste.
  To my high halles I haste me in my way.
  You minstrel of mirth, blow up a good blast,
  While I go to chamber and change my array.
Primus rex.   Hail! be you, Kinges twain,
  Far riding out of your reign.
  Me[8] thinketh by your presentes seen[8]
  You seeken our saviour.
  From Saba have I followed far
  The gleaming of yon gay star:
  A childes blood shall buy us dear
  That there is born in beastes bower.

[1] n. 38.   [2] law.   [3] take the prize for ever.   [4] people on earth.   [5] quickly, I promise you.   [6] immediately, together.   [7] Nimbly.   [8] It seems to me it is obvious from your presents.

My name is King Baltazare.
Of prophetes speech I am ware.
Therefore a far way I fare,
A maidenes child to seek.
For[1] he made man of the mould,[2]
And is King of Heaven held,
I will him offer the red gold,
As reason will me teach.

Secundus rex.　　Melchizar, that my name is kid.[3]
In hot love my heart is hid,
To the blossom upon his bed,
Born by beastes bin.[4]
In Taris I am King with crown.
By bankes and brimmes[5] brown
I have travelled by many a town
My Lordes love to win.

I seek him with incense sweet:
Of all priestes he shall be root.
His bright blood shall be our boot,[6]
To bring us out of bond.
The child shall be chosen a priest,
In all virtues founden most:
Before his Fatheres fair breast
Incense he shall up send.

Tertius rex.　　In Ypotan and Archage
I am King knowen in cage.[7]
To seek a child of semblance sage
I have faren right far.
Jasper is my name knowen
In many countries that are my owen.
Through bitter blastes that gin[8] blowen[8]
I strike after the star.

I bring myrrh to[9] my present,
A bitter liquor verament,[10]

---

[1] *Because.*　　[2] *earth.*　　[3] *known.*　　[4] *stall.*　　[5] *rivers.*　　[6] *cure, remedy.*
[7] *in the scaffold of the playing-place (?).*　　[8] *blow.*　　[9] *as.*　　[10] *truly.*

For he shall[1] tholen bitter dent[1]
In a maidenes flesh is clad:
On bitter tree he shall be bent,
Man and God omnipotent,
With bitter beating his flesh be rent,
Till all his blood be bled.

Herod.   Now[2] I reign like a king, arrayed full rich,
Rolled in ringes and robes of array.
Dukes with dentes I drive into the ditch.
My deedes be full doughty deemed by day.
I shall marren those men that r . . . n on a miche[3]
And therein set their sacramentes sottes[4] . . . say
There is no lord in this world that looketh me like,
For to lame liveres of the lesse[5] lay[5]
I am jollier[6] than the jay.[6]
Strong thieves to stake[7]
That will our lawes break,
On those wretches I will be wreak,[8]
And hunt them under[9] hay.[9]

     In kirtle of cammaka[10] King am I clad,
Cruel[11] and curred[11] in my crown know.[12]
I sit in under Caesar in my se. . .e[13] sad[13]
Sorwen[14] to sottes such seed will I sow.[14]
Boys[15] now blabberen, boasting of a baron[16] bad,
In bed is born by beastes, such boast is blow.
I shall prune that paphawk[17] and proven[18] him as a pad.[19]
Shieldes and shaftes[20] sh. . .lh. . .y sowe.
My knightes shall riden on[21] row[21]
Knave[22] childeren for to quell.[22]
By Mahound, digne[23] Duke of hell!

---

[1] *(who) shall suffer bitter blow(s).*   [2] *from here on there has been much revision in MS (n. 39).*   [3] *loaf of bread, sacramental wafer (see Block).*   [4] *fools.*   [5] *lesser law (?).*   [6] *? = sweeter than honey, i.e. nice to 'lame livers' but not to 'thieves'? (n. 40).*   [7] *shut up.*   [8] *avenged.*   [9] *into the net.*   [10] *rich fabric.*   [11] *curred (?), emend cursed (?), savage, vicious (or ? = curly (-haired) and (well-) combed?).*   [12] *known.*   [13] *(?).*   [14] *I will give such cause for sorrow to fools (?).*   [15] *Knaves.*   [16] *child (?), rascal (?).*   [17] *suckling (?).*   [18] *treat.*   [19] *toad.*   [20] *spears.*   [21] *in order.*   [22] *boy . . . kill.*   [23] *worthy.*

Sour death his life shall sell,[1]
Such[2] threat would me throw.[2]
   Steward bold
Walk thou on wold
And wisely behold
All about;
If anything
Should grieve the King,
Bring me tiding
If there be any doubt.

Senescallus.[3]   Lord King in crown,
I go from town
By bankes brown.
I will abide,
And with eares list,
East and west,
If any jest[4]
On[5] ground ginneth glide.[5]
Tunc ibit Senescallus et obviabit tribus Regibus.[6]
   Kinges three,
Under this tree
In this country
Why will you abide?
Herod is King
Of this woning:[7]
Unto his dwelling
Now shall you glide.

Primus rex.   Now lead us all
To the Kinges hall.
How[8] it befall,
We pray to thee
Wittes to wete
He may us pete,

---

[1] *betray (?).*   [2] *(Who) would so threaten me.*   [3] *Steward.*   [4] *story.*   [5] *Runs round about.*   [6] *Then the steward shall go and meet the three kings.*   [7] *dwelling.*
[8] *(?) However it may turn out, we beg thee that he (the King) may put us so that our eyes may know (him who) in flesh is embodied* (O.E.D. *s.v.* glet (*?*)), *God's noble son (?).*

In flesh be glete,
Godes fruit free.[1]
Senescallus.   Followeth[2] in stound[2]
Upon this ground
To the castle round.
I shall you teach
Where[3] King ginny wide.[3]
Upon[4] this tide[4]
In pomp and pride
His might ginneth reach.
  Sir King in throne
Here cometh anon,
By street and stone,
Kinges three.
They bear present:
What they have meant,
Nor whither they are bent
I cannot see.
Herodes rex.   I shall them crave
What they have.
If they rave,
Or waxen wood,[5]
I shall them[6] reave,
Their wittes deave[6],
Their heades cleave,
And sheden their blood.
Primus rex.   Hail! be thou, King in cage[7] full high,
Hail we nigh thy hall right nigh.
Knowest thou ought that child sly?[8]
He is born here about.
He is born of a maid young.
He shall be King over every king.
We go to seek that lovely thing.
To him fain would I lout.[9]

---

[1] See Note 8 on previous page.   [2] Follow now.   [3] (?).   [4] At this time.
[5] crazy.   [6] rob them, stupefy their senses.   [7] on scaffold of playing-place (?).
[8] wise.   [9] do homage.

Secundus rex.   Balaam spoke in prophecy,
  A star should full lovely
  Lighten upon Maid Mary,
  Comen of Jacobes kin.[1]
  The child is born and lies here by,
  Bloomed[2] in a maidenes body.
  A star has streaken[3] upon[3] the sky,
  And led[4] us fair by fen.[4]
Tertius rex.   The star has led us out of the east
  To seek a bairn born best.
  He shall be King of mightes most,
  As prophecy ginneth[5] spell.[5]
  We are kinges in way weary.
  Sir King for thy courtesy,
  Tell[6] us to that child so lovely,
  In what town ginneth[7] he dwell.
Herodes rex.   You three kinges, reckoned by row,
  Lay now down your wordes low!
  Such a carping[8] is unknow,
  Unreckoned in my reign!
  I am a king of high degree:
  There shall none be above me.
  I have florins and frithes[9] free[9],
  Parkes and poundes[10] plain.[10]
    But go to find that you seek,
  And if you know such a leech,
  And[11] you him find, I you beseech,
  Cometh again by me,
  And I shall be both blithe and boune[12]
  That all worship to him be done.
  With reverence I shall seek him soon,
  And honour him on knee.

---

[1] *Matt. i, 2 ff. and Luke iii, 34.*   [2] *(Who) flowered.*   [3] *made its swift way across.*   [4] *been a good guide to us through difficult country (?).*   [5] *tells.*   [6] *direct.*   [7] *does.*   [8] *talking.*   [9] *fine meadows.*   [10] *open, clear ponds, enclosures (?).*   [11] *If.*   [12] *ready.*

And therefore kinges, I you pray,
When you have done your journey,
Come again this same way,
The truth to me to tell.
Come and tell me as you speed,
And I shall quite[1] right well your meed[1]
With gold and treasure and rich weed,[2]
With furres rich and worth[3] pell.[3]

Primus rex.   King, have good day!
I go my way
To seek
Lord of Might.
He shall be right
Our leech.

Secundus rex.   King full stern!
By[4] field and fern[4]
I go
To seeken a king.
He taketh[5] woning
In woe.[5]

Tertius rex.   If we him find,
Our King full kind,
By a may,[6]
From King and Queen
We comen again
This day.

Herodes rex.   Ah! fie! fie! on tales that I have been
told!
Here before my cruel knee
How should a bairn wax so bold
By beastes if he born be?
He is young and I am old,
An hardy King of high degree.
This day the kinges shall be cold.[7]

---

[1] *reward you abundantly.*   [2] *raiment.*   [3] *valuable skin(s).*   [4] *Everywhere.*
[5] *He makes his home with misery.*   [6] *maiden.*   [7] *i.e. not find what they are looking for.*

If they come again by me
My goddes I shall upraise:
A dark devil with falseness, I say,
Shall cast a mist in the kinges eye,
By bankes[1] and by dales dree,[1]
That by dark they shall come these wayes.

Primus rex.   Go we to seek our Lord and our leech.
Yon star will us teach the wayes full soon.
To save us from mischief, God I here beseech,
Unto his joyes that we may reach—
I pray him of[2] this boon.
Tunc ibunt reges cum muneribus ad Jesum.[3]

Primus rex.   Hail be thou King, cold[4] clad[4]!
Hail! with maidenes milk fed!
Hail! I come to thee with gold glad.
As wise writing bears it record,
Gold is the richest metal
And to[5] wearing most royal.
Gold I give thee in this hall,
And know[6] thee for my Lord.

Secundus rex.   Lord, I kneel upon my knee,
Sweet incense I offer to thee,
Thou shalt be the first of high degree
None so mickle of might.
In Godes house as men shall see
Thou shalt honour the Trinity,
Three persones in one God free,[7]
And all one Lord of might.

Tertius rex.   Lord, I kneel down by thy bed.
In maidens flesh thou art hid.
Thy name shall be wide read,
And King over all kinges.
Bitter myrrh to thee I bring,
For bitter dentes[8] on thee they shall ding,[8]

---

[1] *hills . . . wearisome, dreary valleys.* [2] *for.* [3] *Then the Kings shall go with gifts to Jesus.* [4] *without warm clothing.* [5] *for.* [6] *acknowledge.* [7] *gracious.* [8] *blows . . . rain.*

And bitter death shall be thy ending,
And therefore I make mourninges.

Maria.   Kinges kind,
From the fiend,
God you defend.
Homeward you wend,
And to your places you lend[1]
That you should tend.[2]

Primus rex.   Now have we the place found,
To Herod go we this stound.[3]
With our wordes we were bound
That we should come again.
Go we apace and say our speech,
For we have found our Lord and leech,
All the truth we will him teach,
How the King is born of a Queen.

Secundus rex.   My head is heavy as lump[4] of lead!
But[5] if[5] I sleep I am adread
My wit shall fare the worse.
I wax heavy in limb and flank,
Down I lay me upon this bank,
Under this bright star, iwis.

Tertius rex.   Brother, I must lie thee by.
I will go never over this sty[6]
Till I have a sleep.
The young King and his mother, Mary,
Save us all from every villainy.
Now Christ us save and keep!

Primus rex.   Such heaviness has us caught
I must drink with you a draught
To sleep a little while.
I am heavy, head and foot,
I should stumble at rush and root
And[7] I should go a mile.

Hic dormiunt reges et venit angelus.[8]

---

[1] *go.*   [2] *attend to (?).*   [3] *moment.*   [4] *MS* lympe.   [5] *Unless.*   [6] *path.*   [7] *If.*
[8] *Here the Kings go to sleep and there comes an angel.*

184

Angelus.   You kinges on this hill,
Work you not after Herodes will,
For if you do he will you kill
This day or night.
My Lord you sent this tiding
To rest you, kinges in rich clothing,
And, when you risen and go to your dwelling,
Take home the way full right.
    Whether that you be waken or sleep,
My Lord God shall you keep.
In good time you did down drop
To take your rest.
Herod to the devil he trust
To mar[1] you in a murk[1] mist.
My Lord God is full of lust[2]
To glad[3] you for[3] his guest.
    And therefore, kinges, when you rise,
Wendeth forth by ways wise
There[4] your hall be set in size[4]
In diverse land.
Father of God in all thing
Has you granted his sweet blessing.
He shall you save from all shending[5]
With his right hand.
Tunc surgant reges.[6]

Primus rex.   A bright star led us into Bethlehem!
A brighter thing I saw in dream,
Brighter than the sun beam,
An angel I saw right here.
The fair flower[7] that here gan fall[7]
From Herodes King he gan[8] us call.[8]
He taught[9] us home till[10] our hall
A way by another mere.[11]

[1] *confuse, lead you astray, in a dense.*   [2] *desire.*   [3] *give you pleasure as.*   [4] *(To)
where . . . is properly set (?), is seated in assize, doing justice (?).*   [5] *injury.*   [6] *Then
let the Kings get up.*   [7] *(i.e. the angel) who appeared here.*   [8] *called us.*   [9] *directed.*
[10] *to.*   [11] *road (?).*

Secundus rex.   I saw a sight,
  My heart is light:
  To wenden home,
  God full of might
  Has us dight
  From deviles doom.[1]
Tertius rex.   Our God I bless!
  He sent us, iwis,
  His angel bright.
  Now we wake,
  The way to take
  Home full right.

Presentation and Purification [2]

Simeon Justus.[2]   I have been priest in Jerusalem here
  And taught Godes law many a year,
  Desiring in all my mind
  That the time were[3] nighhand near
  In which Godes Son shall appear
  In earth to take mankind,[4]
  Ere I died that I might find
  My saviour with my eye to see.
  But that it is so long behind
  It is great discomfort unto me.
    For I wax old and want my might,
  And begin to fail my sight,
  The more I sorrow this tide,[5]
  Save only, as I tell you right,
  God of his grace has me hight[6]
  That blissful birth to bide.
  Wherefore now here beside

---

[1] *jurisdiction.*   [2] *n. 41.*   [3] MS *we.*   [4] *human nature.*   [5] *time.*   [6] *promised.*

To sancta[1] sanctorum[1] will I go
To pray God to be my guide,
To comfort me after my woe.
Here Simeon kneeleth.

Ah! good God in Trinity!
How long shall I abide thee
Till that thou thy son[2] dost send,
That I in earth might him see.
Good Lord, consider to me—
I draw fast to an end—
That, ere my strengthes from me wend,
Good Lord, send down thy Son,
That I with my full[3] mind[3]
Might worship him if I can.

Both with my feet and handes two
To go to him and handle also,
My eyes to see him in certain,
My tongue for to speak him to,
And all my limbes to work and do,
In his service to be bain.[4]
Send forth thy son, my Lord sovereign,
Hastily anon without tarrying,
For from this world I would be fain,
It is contrary to my living.

Angelus.   Simeon, leave[5] thy careful steven,[5]
For thy prayer is heard in heaven.
To Jerusalem fast now win,[6]
And there shalt see full[7] even[7]
He that is Godes son for to nemen[8]
In the Temple there thou dwellest in.
The darkness of original sin
He shall make light and clarify,
And now the deed shall begin
Which has been spoken by prophecy.

---

[1] *holy of holies, i.e. the sanctuary.*   [2] MS son *þ*[u].   [3] *whole heart.*   [4] *obedient.*
[5] *stop your anxious cry.*   [6] *go.*   [7] *right before you.*   [8] *name.*

Simeon.　　Ah! I thank thee, Lord of Grace,
That has granted me time and space
To live and bide this,
And I will walk now to the place
Where I may see thy Sones face,
Which is my joy and bliss.
I was never lighter, iwis,
To walk never here beforn,
For a merry time now is
When God, my Lord, is born.

Anna prophetissa.　　All hail! Simeon, what tidinges with you?
Why make you all this mirth now?
Tell me whither you fare.

Simeon.　　Anne prophetess, and[1] you wist how,
So should you, I make avow,
And all manner men that are.
For Godes Son, as I declare,
Is born to buy mankind.
Our saviour is come to ceasen our care,
Therefore have I great mirth to wend.
And that is the cause I haste me
Unto the Temple him to see,
And therefore let[2] me not, good friend.

Anna. Now blessed be God in Trinity!
Since that time is come to be.
And with you will I wend
To see my saviour hend[3]
And worship him, also,
With all my will and my full mind.
As I am bound now will I do.
Et tunc ibunt ambo ad Templum.[4]

Simeon.　　In the Temple of God, who[5] understood,[5]
This day shall be offered with mild mood
Which[6] that[6] is King of all,

---

[1] *if.*　　[2] *hinder.*　　[3] *fair; MS* ende.　　[4] *And then both will go to the Temple*
[5] *if the truth were known.*　　[6] *(Him) who.*

188

That shall be scourged and shed his blood,
And after dien on the rood[1]
Withouten cause to call.
For whose Passion there shall befall
Such a sorrow, both sharp and smart,
That as a sword pierce it shall
Even through his motheres heart.

Anna prophetissa.　　Yea! that shall be, as I well find
For redemption of all mankind,
That bliss for to restore
Which has been lost, from[2] out of mind,
As by our father of our owen kind,
Adam and Eve before.

Maria.　　Joseph, my husband, withouten miss,
You wot that fourty days near is
Sithe[3] my sonnes birth full right,
Wherefore we must to the Temple, iwis,
There for to offer our Son of Bliss
Up to his Father in height,
And I in Godes sight
Purified for to be
In clean soul with all my might,
In presence of the Trinity.

Joseph.　　To be purified have you no need,
Nor thy son to be offered, so God me speed,
For first thou art full clean,
Undefouled in thought and deed,
And, another, thy son, withouten dread,[4]
Is God and man to[5] mean.[5]
Wherefore it needed not to been,
But to keep the law, in Moses wise.
Wherefore we shall take us between
Doves and turtles for sacrifice.
Et ibunt ad Templum.[6]

---

[1] *cross.*　[2] *since time.*　[3] *Since.*　[4] *doubt.*　[5] *as mediator (?) in significa-tion (?).*　[6] *And they shall go to the Temple.*

Simeon.   All hail! my kindly comforter.
Anna prophetissa. All hail! mankindes creator.
Simeon. All hail! thou God of Might.
Anna prophetissa. All hail! mankindes saviour.
Simeon. All hail! both king and emperor.
Anna prophetissa. All hail! as it is right.
Simeon. All hail! also, Mary bright.
Anna prophetissa. All hail! salver[1] of sickness,
Simeon. All hail! lantern of light.
Anna prophetissa. All hail! thou mother of meekness.
Maria.   Simeon, I understand and see
    That bothen of my son and me
    You have knowing clear,
    And also in your company
    My son desireth for to be,
    And therefore have him here.
Simeon. (*Et accipiet Jesum.*[2])   Welcome, Prince without peer!
    Welcome, Godes owen Son!
    Welcome, my Lord so dear!
    Welcome, with me to wone![3]
    Suscepimus Deus misericordiam tuam.[4]
       Lord God, in majesty,
    We have received this day of thee
    In middes of thy Temple here
    Thy great mercy, as we may see.
    Therefore thy name of great degree
    Be worshipped in all manner
    Over all this world, both far and near,
    Even unto the unterest[5] end,
    For now is man out of danger,
    And rest and peace to all mankind.
    Nunc dimittis servum tuum, Domine, etc.[6] *The psalm
    sung every verse, and, therewhile, Simeon plays with the
    child. And when the psalm is ended, he says:*

---

[1] *healer.*   [2] *And he will welcome Jesus.*   [3] *live.*   [4] *extra-metrical, translated next four lines.*   [5] *MS* u(?)nterest, *utmost.*   [6] *Luke ii, 29 ff.*

Now let me die, Lord, and hence pass,
For I, thy servant, in this place
Have seen my saviour dear,
Which thou hast ordained before the face
Of all mankind, this time of grace,
Openly to appear.
Thy light is shining clear
To all mankindes salvation.
Mary, take your child now here,
And keep well this, mannes salvation.

Anna prophetissa.   Ne[1] I wroth nere to die, also,[1]
For[2] more than four score year and two
This time have bode to see.
And sithe[3] that it is come thereto,
What Godes will is with me to do,
Right even so may it be.

Joseph. Take here these candles three,
Mary, Simeon and Anne,
And I shall take the fourth to me,
To offer our child up then.

Maria.   Highest Father, God of power,
Your owen dear Son I offer you here,
As I to your law am sworn.
Receive thy child in glad manner,
For he is the first, this child so dear,
That of his mother is born.
But though I offer him you beforn,
Good Lord, yet give me him again,
For my comfort were fully lorn
If we should long asunder been.
Mary lays the child on the altar.

Joseph.   Sir priest of the Temple, now
Have here[4] five pence unto you:
Our child again to take
It is the law as you wot how.

---

[1] *I, also, have no regret at all at dying.*   [2] *(Who) for.*   [3] *since.*   [4] *MS* he.

Capellanus.[1] Joseph, yea! and do right enough,
 As for your childes sake,
 But other offering yet must you make.
 And therefore take your son, Mary.
 In much joy you may awake
 Whiles he is in your company.
Maria. Thereto I am full glad and fain
 For to receive my child again,
 Elles were I to blame,
 And afterward for to be bain[2]
 To offer to God in full certain,
 As in my sonnes name,
 With fowles both wild and tame,
 For in Godes service I shall never irk.
Joseph. Lo! Mary, have here those same,
 To do thy duties of Holy Kirk.
 And there Mary offers fowls onto the altar.
Maria. Almightiful Father, merciful King,
 Receiveth now this little offering,
 For it is the first in degree
 That your little child so young
 Presenteth today by my showing
 To your high majesty.
 Of his simple poverty,
 By his devotion and my good will,
 Upon your altar receive of me
 Your Sones offering, as it is skill.[3]

[1] *Chaplain.* [2] *ready.* [3] *appropriate, right.*

Slaughter of the Innocents[1]

Tunc respiciens Senescallus vadit ad Herodem.[1]
Senescallus.[1]   Lord, I have walked by dale and hill,
And waited[2] as it is your will.
The kinges three stealen away full still
Through Bethlehem land.
They will never, so[3] may I the,[3]
Come in the land of Galilee
For to see your fair city,
Nor deedes of your hand.
Herodes rex.   I ride[4] on my rowel, rich in my reign![4]
Ribbes full red with rape shall I rend!
Popetes[5] and paphawkes[5] I shall putten in pain,
With my spear[6] proven pichen and to pend.[6]
The gomes[7] with gold crownes ne get never again—[7]
To seek those sottes[8] sondes[8] shall I send.
Do[9] owlet hooten, hoberd and hein,[9]
When her bairnes bleed under[10] cradle-band.[10]
Sharply I shall them shend,[11]
The knave[12] childeren that be
In all Israel country:
They shall have bloody ble[13]
For[14] one I called unkind.[14]
    It is told in Gru[15]
His name should be Jesu
Ifound.

---

[1] (n. 42.) *Then, looking back, the Steward goes to Herod.*   [2] *kept good look out.*
[3] *upon my life.*   [4] *set spurs to my horse, mighty in my royal power.*   [5] *Baby darlings and suckling children.*   [6] *trusty spear to pierce and torment.*   [7] *men (i.e. three Kings) . . . shall not escape again (?).*   [8] *fools messengers.*   [9] *Make the she-owl hoot, the wretched clown (?).*   [10] *in their swaddling clothes.*   [11] *injure.*
[12] *male.*   [13] *looks.*   [14] *Because of one child I called unnatural.*   [15] *Greek.*

To have him you gone,
Hew the flesh with the bone,
And give him wound.

Now keen knightes, kith[1] your craftes,
And killeth knave[2] childeren and casteth them in clay!
Showeth on your shoulderes shieldes and shaftes,
Shapeth[3] among schel chownis a shrilling shray.[3]
Doth[4] rounces runnen with raking raftes[4]
Till ribbes be to-rent with a red ray.[5]
Let no bairn be left unbeat baftes[6]
Till a begger bleed by beastes bay.[7]
Mahound,[8] that best may![8]
I warn you, my knightes,
A bairn is born, I plightes,[9]
Would climben king and knightes,
And let[10] my lordly lay.[10]

Knightes wise,
Chosen full choice,
Arise! arise!
And take your tool,
And every page,[11]
Of two year age,
Ere ever you swage,[12]
Slayeth ilke[13] a[13] fool!

One of them all
Was born in stall—
Fooles him call
King in crown!
With bitter gall
He shall down fall:
My might in hall
Shall never go down.

Primus miles.   I shall slay churles,

[1] *make known.*   [2] *boy.*   [3] *(?).*   [4] *Make your horses run with dashing spears.*
[5] *array (?), display.*   [6] *behind.*   [7] *(at?) bay.*   [8] *(By) Mahound who has the*
power.   [9] *promise.*   [10] *interrupt my lordly way of life.*   [11] *boy.*   [12] *give over.*
[13] *each.*

And queenes[1] with therles,[1]
Their knave[2] girles,[2]
I shall stick.
Forth will I speed
To do[3] them bleed.
Though girles greet,[4]
We shall be wreak.[5]

Secundus miles.   For swordes sharp
As an harp
Queenes shall carp,[6]
And of sorrow sing.
Bairnes young,
They shall be stung:
Through liver and lung
We shall them sting.

Angelus.   Awake, Joseph, and take thy wife,
Thy child also—ride belife![7]
For King Herod, with sharp knife,
His knightes he does send.
The Father of Heaven has to thee sent
Into Egypt that thou be bent,
For cruel knightes thy child have meant
With sword to slay and shend.[8]

Joseph.   Awake, good wife, out of your sleep,
And of your child taketh good keep,[9]
While I your clothes lay on heap,
And truss them on the ass.
King Herod the child will slay,
Therefore to Egypt must we go:
An angel of God said me so,
And therefore let us pass.

Tunc ibunt milites ad pueros occidendos.[10]

Prima femina.[11]   Long lulling have I lorn.

---

[1] *coarse women with slaves.*   [2] *boy children.*   [3] *make.*   [4] *cry out.*   [5] *avenged.*
[6] *talk.*   [7] *at once.*   [8] *harm.*   [9] *care.*   [10] *Then the soldiers will go to kill the baby boys.*   [11] *First woman.*

Alas! why was my bairn born?
With swapping sword now is he shorn,
The head right from the neck.
Shank and shoulderen is all to-torn.
Sorrowen I see behinden and beforn,
Both midnight, midday and at morn—
Of my life I not reck.

Secunda femina.　　Certainly I say the same,
Gone is all my good game,
My little child lies all lame,
That lulled on my pappes.
My fourty weekes groaning
Have sent me seven year sorrowing:
Mickle is my mourning,
And right hard are my happes.[1]

Primus miles.　　Lord in throne,
Maketh no moan!
Queenes[2] gin groan[2]
In world about.
Upon my spear
A girl I bear,
I dare well swear.
Let motheres hoot!

Secundus miles.　　Lord, we have sped
As you bade.
Bairnes are bled
And lie in ditch.
Flesh and vein
Have tholed[3] pain,
And you shall reign
Evermore rich.

Herodes rex.　　You shall have steedes
To[4] your meedes,[4]
Landes and ledes,[5]

---

[1] *fortunes.*　　[2] *Women groan.*　　[3] *suffered.*　　[4] *For your rewards.*　　[5] *people.*

Frith[1] and fee.[1]
Well have you wrought:
My foe is sought,
To death is he brought.
Now come up to me!
　　In seat now am I set as King of mightes most,
All this world for their love to me shall they lout,[2]
Both of heaven and of earth and of hell coast.[3]
For digne[4] of my dignity they have of me doubt,[5]
There is no lord like alive to me worth a toast,
Neither king nor kaiser in all this world about.
If any briber do brag or blow against my boast
I shall rap[6] those ribaldes and rake them on rout
With my bright brand.[6]
There shall be neither kaiser nor king
But that I shall them down ding,
Less[7] than[7] he at my bidding
Be buxom[8] to my hand.
　　Now my gentle and courteous knightes, hark to me this[9]
　　　　stound.[9]
Good time soon me thinketh at dinner that we were.
Smartly, therefore, set a table anon here full sound,
Covered with a curious[10] cloth and with rich worthy fare,
Service for the loveliest lord that living is on ground,
Best meates and worthiest wines look that you none spare,
Though that a little pint should cost a thousand pound.
Bring always of the best, for cost take you no care—
Anon that it be done!
Senescallus. My lord, the table is ready dight,
　　Here is water, now wash forthright!
　　Now blow up minstrel with all your might,
　　The service[11] cometh in soon.
Herodes rex.　　　Now am I set at meat

---

[1] *Estates and goods.*　　[2] *make obeisance.*　　[3] *region.*　　[4] *worth.*　　[5] *fear.*
[6] *smite those rascals and rake them one after the other with my shining sword.*
[7] *Unless.*　　[8] *obedient.*　　[9] *(at) this time.*　　[10] *sumptuous.*　　[11] *i.e. of the meal.*

And worthily served at[1] my degree.[1]
Come forth knightes, sit down and eat,
And be as merry as you can be!
Primus miles. Lord, at your bidding we take our seat,
With hearty will obey we thee.
There is no lord, of might so great,
Through all this world in no country,
In worship to abide.
Herodes. I was never merrier here beforn,
Sithe[2] that I was first born,
Than I am now right in this morn.
In joy I gin to glide.
Mors.[3]   Ow! I heard a page[4] make praising of pride!
All princes he passeth,[5] he weeneth, of[6] pousty.[6]
He weeneth to be the worthiest of all this world wide,
King over all kinges, that page weeneth to be.
He sent into Bethlehem to seek on every side
Christ for to quell[7] if they might him see.
But of his wicked will, lurdein,[8] yet he lied!
Godes Son does live—there is no lord but he.
Over all lordes he is King!
I am Death, Godes messenger.
Almighty God has sent me here
Yon lurdein to slay, withouten[9] dwere,[9]
For his wicked working.
    I am sent from God—Death is my name.
All thing that is on ground[10] I wield[10] at my will,
Both man and beast and birdes, wild and tame.
When that I come them to with death I do them kill,
Herb, grass and trees strong, take them all in[11] same[11]—
Yea! the great, mighty oakes with my dent[12] I spill.[12]
What man that I wrestle with he shall right soon have
    shame—

---

[1] *according to my station.*   [2] *since.*   [3] *Death: n. 43.*   [4] *(mere) servant, churl.*   [5] *surpasses.*   [6] *in might.*   [7] *destroy.*   [8] *loafer.*   [9] *no two ways about it.*   [10] *earth I rule.*   [11] *together.*   [12] *blow I kill.*

I[1] give him such a tripett[1] he shall evermore lie still.
For Death can[2] no sport!
Where I smite there is no grace!
For after my stroke man has no space
To make amendes for his trespass,
But[3] God him grant comfort.
 Ow! see how proudly yon caitiff sits at meat!
Of death has he no doubt,[4] he weeneth to live evermore.
To him will I go and give him such an heat[5]
That all the leeches[6] of the land his life shall never
 restore.
Against my dreadful dentes it vaileth[7] never to plead.[7]
Ere I him part from, I shall him make full poor.
All the blood of his body I shall him[8] out sweat,[8]
For now I go to slay him with strokes sad[9] and sore,
This[10] tide;[10]
Both him and his knightes all,
I shall them make to me but thrall,
With my spear slay them I shall,
And so cast down his pride.
Herodes rex.   Now, kind[11] knightes, be merry and glad!
With all good diligence show now some mirth!
For, by gracious Mahound! more mirth never I had,
Nor never more joy was in from time of my birth.
For now my foe is dead and prended[12] as a pad![12]
Above me is no king, on ground nor on garth,[13]
Mirthes, therefore, make you and be right nothing sad!
Spare neither meat nor drink and spare for no dearth
Of wine nor of bread,
For now am I a king alone.
So worthy as I may there be none,
Therefore knightes be merry each one,
For now my foe is dead.

---

[1] *I so trip him up (in wrestling) that.*   [2] *knows.*   [3] *Unless.*   [4] *fear.*   [5] *fever.*
[6] *doctors.*   [7] *is never any use to appeal.*   [8] *squeeze out of him.*   [9] *heavy.*   [10] *At this
time.*   [11] *good.*   [12] *taken (?) as a toad.*   [13] ? *MS* gerth: *i.e. no king anywhere.*

Primus miles.   When the boys sprawled at my speares end,
　　By Sathanas, our sire, it was a goodly sight!
　　A good game it was that boy[1] for to shend,[1]
　　That would have been our king and put you from your
　　　right.
Secundus miles. Now truly, my lord the King, we had been
　　unhend[2]
　　And never none of us able for to be a knight,
　　If that any of us to them had been a friend
　　And had saved any life against thy mickle might,
　　From death them to flit.[3]
Herodes rex. Amongst all that great rout
　　He is dead, I have no doubt.
　　Therefore minstrel round about,
　　Blow up a merry fit!
　　Hic dum buccinant, Mors interficiat Herodem et duos milites
　　subito et Diabolus recipiat eos.[4]
Diabolus.   All ours! all ours! This chatell[5] is mine!
　　I shall them bring unto my cell,
　　I shall them teach plays[6] fine,
　　And show such mirth as is in hell.
　　It were more better amongst swine,
　　That evermore stinken, thereby to dwell,
　　For in our lodge is so great pain
　　That no earthly tongue can tell.
　　With you I go my way.
　　I shall you bear forth with me,
　　And show you sportes[7] of our glee.[7]
　　Of our mirthes now shall you see,
　　And ever sing welaway.
Mors.   Of King Herod all men beware,
　　That has rejoiced in pomp and pride.
　　For all his boast of bliss full bare

---

[1] *male child, man of low birth . . . harm.*   [2] *discourteous.*   [3] *deliver.*   [4] *Here,*
while they blow their trumpets, let Death kill Herod and the two soldiers suddenly
and let the Devil receive them.   [5] *property.*   [6] *amusements.*   [7] *games with*
which we entertain ourselves.

He lies now dead here on his side.
For when I come I cannot spare:
From me no wight may him hide.
Now is he dead and cast in care,
In hell pit ever to abide,
His lordship is all lorn.
Now is he as poor as I,
Wormes meat is his body,
His soul in hell, full painfully,
Of[1] deviles is all to-torn.

All men dwelling upon the ground
Beware of me, by my counsel,
For faint[2] fellowship in me is found.[2]
I[3] can no courtesy,[3] as I you tell,
For be a man never so sound,
Of health in heart never so well,
I come suddenly within a stound.[4]
Me withstand may no castel,
My journey will I speed.
Of my coming no man is ware,
For when men make most merry fare,
Then suddenly I cast them in care,
And slay them even[5] in deed.[5]

Though I be naked and poor of array,
And wormes gnaw me all about,
Yet look you dread me night and day,
For when Death cometh you stand in doubt.
Even like to me, as I you say,
Shall all you be here in this rout.[6]
When I you challenge, at my day,
I shall you make right low to lout,[7]
And naked for to be.
Amongst wormes, as I you tell,
Under the earth shall you dwell,

---

[1] *By.* [2] *I'm a very poor friend.* [3] *I don't stand on ceremony.* [4] *trice.*
[5] *right in the act.* [6] *crowd.* [7] *bow.*

And they shall eaten both flesh and fell,[1]
As they have done me.

Jesus and the Doctors[2]

Modo de doctoribus disputantibus cum Jesu in Templo.[3]
Primus doctor.   Scripturae sacrae esse dinoscimur doctos,[4]
We to[5] bear the bell of all manner clergise.[5]
Secundus doctor. Velud rosa omnium florum flos,[6]
Like unto us was never clerk[7] so wise.
Primus doctor. Look what science[8] you can devise,
Of reading, writing and true orthography,
Amongst all clerkes we bear the prize,
Of grammar, cadence[9] and of prosody.
Secundus doctor.   No clerk able to bear our book,
Of versifying nor of other science.
Of sweet music, whoso will look,
Seek no further but to our presence.
Of dialectic[10] we have the high excellence,
Of sophistry, logic and philosophy:
Against our argument is no resistence,
In metaphysic nor astronomy.
Primus doctor.   Of calculation[11] and necromancy,
Also of augrim[12] and of asmatrik,[13]
Of lineation that longeth to geometry,
Of dietes and doomes[14] that longeth to physic,[14]
In all this science is none us like.

[1] *skin.*   [2] *n. 44.*   [3] *Now for the Doctors disputing with Jesus in the Temple.*
[4] *In Sacred Scripture we are recognised to be distinguished experts.*   [5] *to be the best in all kinds of learning.*   [6] *Like the rose of all the flowers the flower.*   [7] *man of learning.*   [8] *branch of learning.*   [9] *rhetorical use of rhythm.*   [10] *art of arguing.*
[11] *calculation, art of reckoning (? or, more likely here since necromancy follows) astrological computation, making a horoscope.*   [12] *computing (with Arabic numerals).*
[13] *the art of measuring and calculating.*   [14] *judgements that are part of medicine.*

In Caton,[1] Griscism[2] nor Doctrinal,[3]
And for inditing[4] with rhetoric,[4]
The highest degree is ours be[5] call.[5]
Secundus doctor.   In great canon and in civil law,
　　Also in science[6] of policy,[6]
　　Is none to[7] us worth an haw.[7]
　　Of[8] all cunning we bear the mastery.[8]
　　Therefore in this Temple we sit on high,
　　And of most worship keep the sovereignty,
　　There is on earth no man so worthy
　　The high state to holden as we twain be.
Jesus.   Omnis scientia a Domino Deo est.[9]
　　All wit and wisdom of God it is lent.
　　Of all your learning within your breast
　　Thank highly that Lord that has you sent.
　　Through boast and pride your soules may be shent.[10]
　　Of wit and wisdom you have not so much
　　But God may make at his intent
　　Of[11] all your cunning[11] many men you like.
Primus doctor.   Go home! little babe, and sit on thy
　　　　motheres lap,
　　And put a mokador[12] aforn thy breast,
　　And pray thy mother to feed thee with the pap!
　　Of thee for to learn we desire not to list![13]
Secundus doctor. Go to thy dinner! for that behoveth thee
　　best.
　　When thou art athirst then take thee a suck,
　　After go to cradle therein to take thy rest.
　　For that canst thou do better than for to look on book.
Jesus.   Standing[14] that you are so witty and wise,
　　Can you ought tellen how this world was wrought?

---

[1] *a work on ethics attributed to Cato and used as a school text-book in Latin.*   [2] *a Latin Grammatical treatise.*   [3] *book of basic principles.*   [4] *rhetorical writing.*
[5] *at call?: in MS crossed out and over all written in another hand suggesting the original not understood.*   [6] *art of managing public affairs.*   [7] *compared with us worth a penny.*   [8] *In all knowledge we have supremacy.*   [9] *Translated next line.*   [10] *injured.*
[11] *In . . . your cleverness, knowledge.*   [12] *bib.*   [13] *listen.*   [14] *Understanding.*

How long shall it last, can you devise,
With all the cunning that you have sought?
Primus doctor. Nay! all earthly clerkes that[1] tell cannot![1]
It passeth our wit that for to contrive.
It is not possible about to be brought—
The worldes ending no man can descrive.[2]
Jesus. How it was wrought and how long it shall endure
That I tell by good deliberation:
Not only thereof, but of every creature,
How it is wrought I know the plasmation.[3]
Secundus doctor. Of thy wordes I have scorn and derision!
How should a child, that never letter did lere,[4]
Come to the wit[5] of so high cognition[6]
Of those great workes that so wonderful were?
Jesus. All thing is brought to information
By three persones, one God in Trinity.
And one of those three has take incarnation,
Both flesh and blood, of a maid free.[7]
And by that might of those persones three
Heaven and earth and all thing is wrought,
And as it pleaseth that high majesty
All thing shall last—and longer nought.
Primus doctor. I grant[8] well all thing that God did make,[8]
And withouten him nothing may be.
But one thing thou saidest, and that I forsake,
That one God alone was persones three.
Right impossible that is to me,
That one is three I cannot think.
If thou canst prove it anon let see,
For in our heartes it may never sink.
Jesus. In the sun consider you thinges three—
The splendour, the heat and the light.
As those three partes but one sun be,
Right so three persones are one God of Might.

---

[1] *cannot tell that.*   [2] *discern.*   [3] *formation.*   [4] *learn.*   [5] *knowledge.*
[6] *apprehension.*   [7] *gracious.*   [8] *I allow fully that God made everything.*

Secundus doctor. In very faith this reason is right!
But yet, fair babe, one thing we pray you:
What[1] do all those three persones hight?[1]
Us to inform you say to me now.

Jesus.　　The first is called the Father of Might,
The second, the Son of Wisdom and Wit,
The Holy Ghost, the third, of Grace he is hight,
And in one substance all these three are knit.

Primus doctor. Another question I ask you yet:
You said one of these three took flesh and blood,
And she a clean maid—I cannot believe it!
Clean maid and mother never yet in one person stood.

Jesus.　　Like as the sun does pierce the glass,
The glass not hurt of his nature,
Right so the Godhead entered has
The Virgines womb, and she maid pure,
That maidenes child shall do[2] great cure.[2]
Convict the devil in the open field,
And with his bold breast fetch home his creature,
Mankind to save, his breast shall be the shield.

Secundus doctor.　　This childes doctrine does pass our
　　wit!
Some angel of heaven I trow that he be.
But blessed babe of one doubt yet
We pray you inform us for charity:
Which took flesh of the persones three,
Against the fiend to hold such battail?

Jesus. The second person forsooth is he
Shall fray[3] the fiend without fail.

Primus doctor.　　Why rather he than any of that other?
The first or the third, why come they not?

Jesus. This is the cause why, certes, and none other:
Against the second the trespass was wrought.
When the serpent Adam to sin brought
He tempted him not by the Fatheres might;

[1] *What are all . . . called.*　　[2] *take great pains.*　　[3] *attack.*

Of the Ghostes goodness spoke he right nought;
But in cunning[1] he tempted[1] him right.

    Might is the Fatheres owen property;
To[2] the Ghost appeared[3] is[3] goodness:
In none of these twain tempted he,
Mankind to sin when he did[4] dress.[4]
To the Son cunning does[5] long express:[5]
Therewith the serpent did Adam assay.
Eat of this apple, he said, no less,
And thou shalt have cunning as God[6] verray.[6]

    Thus the second person attribute
Was only touched by temptation,
Wherefore himself will hold[7] the suit.[7]
And keep his property from maculation.[8]

Secundus doctor. This is an heavenly declaration:
Our natural wit it does exceed.
So young a child of such information!
In all this world never[9] ere none yede.[9]

Primus doctor.   We are not worthy to keep this seat
While that our master is in presence.
The mastery of us this child does get:
We must him worship with high reverence.
Come forth, sweet babe, of great excellence!
The wisest clerk that ever yet was born!
To you we give the high residence
Us more to teach as you have done beforn.

*Hic adducunt Jesum inter ipsos et in scamno altiori ipsum
sedere faciunt, ipsis in inferioribis scamnis sedentibus.*[10]

Secundus doctor.   So young a child such[11] clergy to reach,[11]
And so sadly[12] to say it, we wonder sore
Who was your master? Who did you teach?
Of what man had you this worthy lore?

---

[1] *wisdom, knowledge: p. 79.*   [2] *By (?).*   [3] *is symbolized (?).*   [4] *got ready.*
[5] *belongs manifestly.*   [6] *the true God (?), God, for certain (?).*   [7] *defend the
action.*   [8] *defilement.*   [9] *none ever went before.*   [10] *Here they lead Jesus
between them and cause him to sit in a higher seat, themselves sitting on lower seats.*
[11] *to achieve such learning.*   [12] *profoundly, weightily.*

Jesus. My wit and my learning is no young[1] store.[1]
    Ere this world was wrought all thing did I know.
    First, ere you were born, yeares many score,
    Through the might of my Father my wit in me did flow.
Primus doctor.   Ere that we weren born? Nay that may
        not be!
    The youngest of us twain is three score year of age,
    And thyself art but a child, all men may well see,
    Late[2] camst[2] out of cradle, as it seemeth by thy visage.
Jesus. I am of double birth and of double lineage.
    First by my Father I am without ginning,
    And like as he is endless in his high stage,[3]
    So shall I also nevermore have ending.
      For by my Father, King celestial,
    Without beginning I am endless,
    But by my mother, that is carnal,
    I am but twelve year of age, that is express.
    My body of youth does show witness,
    Which of my mother here I did take.
    But[4] my high Godhead—this is no[5] less[5]—
    All thing in this world forsooth did I make.
Secundus doctor.   By your Father that endless is,
    Who is your mother? Tell us we pray.
Jesus. By my Father, the high King of Bliss,
    A motherless child I am verray.
Primus doctor. Who was your father, to us then say,
    By your mother, a woman that was?
Jesus. I am fatherless, as for that may:[6]
    Of fleshly lust she did never trespass.
Secundus doctor.   Tell us, I pray you, what is your name?
    What hight your mother, tell us also.
Jesus. Jesu of Nazareth, I am the same.
    Born of a clean maid, prophetes said so.
    Isaye said thus: Ecce virgo![7]

---

[1] *recent acquisition.*   [2] *Who came recently.*   [3] *station (?), scaffold, p. 41.*
[4] *But (in).*   [5] *(no lie), for certain (?).*   [6] *maiden.*   [7] *Behold a virgin.*

A maid shall conceive in cleanness a child,
Yet, against[1] nature and all kind,[1] lo!
From all wem[2] of sin, pure and undefiled.
    Mary, the child of Joachim and Anne,
Is that clean maid, and her child am I.
The fruit of her womb shall save every man
From the great doubt[3] of the fiendes tormentry.

Primus doctor. All the clerkes of this world truly
    Cannot bring this to declaration,
    Less[4] than[4] they have of God Almighty
    Some influence[5] of information.

Secundus doctor.   No! Gentle Jesu, we you pray,
    While that we study, a while to dwell,
    In case mo[6] doubtes that we find may
    The truth of them you may us tell.

Jesus. Go! take your study, and advise you well,
    And all your leisure I shall abide.
    If any doubtes to me you mell[7]
    The truth thereof I shall unhide.

Maria.   Alas! alas! my heart is woe!
    My blessed babe away is went.
    I wot never whither that he is go.
    Alas! for sorrow my heart is rent.
    Gentle husband, have you[8] him sent
    Out on errand to any place?
    But[9] if[9] you know where he is bent
    My heart for woe asunder will race.[10]

Joseph.   On my message I him not sent,
    Forsooth, good wife, in no degree,
    How long is it that he hence went?
    What time did you your child last see?

Maria. Truly, good spouse, not these days three.
    Therefore my heart is cast in care.

---

[1] *contrary to all nature.*   [2] *spot.*   [3] *terror.*   [4] *Unless.*   [5] *flowing in.*   [6] *more.*
[7] *utter.*   [8] *added in later hand.*   [9] *Unless.*   [10] *tear.*

Him for to seek, whereso he be,
  In haste, good husband, let us forth fare.
Joseph.   Then to Jerusalem let us straight wend,
  For kindred gladly together will gon.
  I hope he is[1] there with some good friend—
  There he has cousines[2] right many one.
Maria. I am afraid that he has fon,[3]
  For his great wittes and workes good:
  Like him of wit forsooth is none,
  Every child with him is wroth and wood.[4]
    Alas! my babe, my bliss, my blood,
  Whither art thou thus gone from me?
  My soul, my sweeting, my fruit, my food,[5]
  Send me some word where that thou be.
  Tell me, good sires, for charity,
  Jesu, my child, that babe of bliss,
  Among this company did you him see?
  For Godes high love, tell where he is.
Primus doctor.   Of one question I am be-thought
  All of your mother, that blessed may,
  In what governance is she brought?
  How is she ruled by night and day?
Jesus. An old man, Joseph, as I you say,
  Her wedded by miracle unto his wife,
  Her for to feed and keep alway,
  And bothen in[6] cleanness be maidenes of life.[6]
Secundus doctor.   What need was it her to be wed
  Unto a man of so great age?
  Less[7] than[7] they might both ago to bed,
  And kept the law of marriage?
Jesus. To blind the devil of his knowledge,
  And my birth from him to hide,
  That holy wedlock was great stoppage,[8]
  The devil in doubt to do[9] abide.

---

[1] *added in later hand.*   [2] *relatives.*   [3] *foes.*   [4] *mad.*   [5] *baby.*   [6] *to remain virgins in purity of life.*   [7] *Unless.*   [8] *barrier.*   [9] *cause (to); p. 61.*

Also, when she should to Egypt gone,
And flee from Herod for doubt[1] of me,
Because she should not go alone,
Joseph was ordained her make[2] to be,
My Father, of his high majesty,
Her for to comfort in the way.
These are the causes, as you may see,
Why Joseph wedded that holy may.[3]

Maria.   Ah! dear child, dear child, why hast thou thus
    done?
For thee we have had great sorrow and care.
Thy father and I three days have gone
Wide thee to seek, of bliss full bare.

Jesus. Why have you sought me with heavy fare?
Wit you not well I must been
Among them that is my Fatheres ware,[4]
His ghostly[5] chatell for to overseen?[5]

Maria.   Your Fatheres will must needes be wrought:
It is most worthy that it so be.
Yet on your mother have you some thought,
And be nevermore so long from me!
As to my thinking, these days three,
That you absent have been away,
Are more longer in their degree
Than all the[6] space of twelve year day.[6]

Jesus.   Now for to please my mother mild
I shall you follow with obedience.
I am your son and subject child,
And ought to do you high reverence.
Home with you I will go hence.
Of you clerkes my leave I take.
Every child should with good diligence,
His mother to please, his owen will forsake.

Primus doctor.   Oh! blessed Jesu, with you we wend,

---

[1] *fear.*   [2] *companion.*   [3] *maiden.*   [4] *people (?) stock (?).*   [5] *spiritual property to supervise.*   [6] *i.e. your life so far.*

Of you to have more information.
Full blessed is your mother hend,[1]
Of whom you took your incarnation.
We pray you, Jesu, of[2] consolation,
At our most need of you to have.
All that have heard this consummation[3]
Of this pageant, your grace them save!
Amen.

Johannes Baptista (the Baptism of Jesus) and the Temptation[4]

omitted

Woman taken in Adultery[5]

Hic de muliere in adulterio deprehensa[6]
Jesus.   Nolo mortem peccatoris:[7]
Man for thy sin take repentance!
If thou amend that is amiss
Then heaven shall be thy heritance.
Though thou have done against God grievance,
Yet mercy to ask look thou be bold.
His mercy does pass,[8] in true balance,[8]
All cruel judgement by many fold.
    Though that your sinnes be never so great,

---

[1] *gracious.*   [2] *for.*   [3] *performance.*   [4] *n. 45.*   [5] *n. 46; Prosser examines this play, chap. vi.*   [6] *And now concerning the woman taken in adultery.*   [7] *I do not wish the death of a sinner. (Part of antiphon in Prime during Lent:* Sarum Breviary, II, *col.* dlxxxix; *Ezekiel xviii, 23, xxxiii, 11; n. 46.)*   [8] *exceed, when truly weighed.*

For them be sad and ask mercy.
Soon of my Father grace you may get,
With the least tear weeping out of your eye.
My Father me sent thee, man, to buy,
All thy ransom myself must pay.
For love of thee myself will die—
If thou ask mercy I say never nay.

Into the earth from heaven above,
Thy sorrow to cease and joy to restore,
Man, I came down all for thy love:
Love me again[1]—I ask no more.
Though thou mishap and sin full sore,
Yet turn again and mercy crave:
It is thy fault and[2] thou be lore[2]—
Ask thou mercy and thou shalt have.

Upon thy neighbour be not vengeable,
Against the law if he offend!
Like as he is, thou art unstable,
Thy[3] owen frailty ever thou attend.
Evermore thy neighbour help to amend,
Even as thou wouldest he should thee.
Against him wrath if thou accend[4]
The same in[5] hap[5] will fall on thee.

Each man to other be merciable,
And mercy he shall have at need.
What man of mercy is not treatable,[6]
When he asketh mercy he shall not speed.
Mercy to grant I come in deed—
Whoso asks mercy he shall have grace.
Let no man doubt[7] for his misdeed,
But ever ask mercy while he has space.

Scriba.   Alas! alas! our law is lorn![8]
A false hypocrite, Jesu by name,
That of a shepherdes daughter was born,

---

[1] *in return.*   [2] *if . . . lost.*   [3] *(To) thy.*   [4] *kindle.*   [5] *perhaps; or*
(?) = unhap = *mishap.*   [6] *yielding.*   [7] *fear.*   [8] *done for.*

Will break our law and make it lame.
He will us work right mickle shame
His false purpose if he uphold.
All our lawes he does defame—
That stinking beggar is wonder bold!

Phariseus.   Sir Scribe, in faith, that hypocrite
Will turn this land all to his lore.[1]
Therefore I counsel him[2] to indict,[2]
And chastise him right well therefore.

Scriba. On him believe many a score:
In his preaching he is so gay.[3]
Each man him followeth ever more and more:
Against that he says no man says nay.

Phariseus.   A false quarrel if we could feign,
That hypocrite to putten in blame,
All his preaching should[4] soon distein,[4]
And then his worship should turn to shame.
With some falsehood to spillen[5] his name
Let us assay his lore to spill.
The people with him if we could grame,[6]
Then should we soon have all our will.

Accusator.[7]   Hark! Sir Pharisee and Sir Scribe,
A right good sport I can you tell.
I undertake that right a good bribe
We all shall have to keep counsel!
A fair young quean[8] hereby does dwell,
Both fresh and gay upon to look,
And a tall[9] man with her does[10] mell[10]—
The way into her chamber right[11] even[11] he took.

   Let us three now go straight thither,
The way full[12] even[12] I shall you lead,
And we shall take them both together
While that they do that sinful deed.

---

[1] *teaching.*   [2] *to indict him.*   [3] *brilliant, plausible (?).*   [4] *would soon be put in the shade, vanish.*   [5] *destroy.*   [6] *anger.*   [7] *Informer.*   [8] *prostitute.*   [9] *lusty.*   [10] *is having intercourse.*   [11] *just this moment.*   [12] *straight there.*

Scriba. Art thou secure[1] that we shall speed?[2]
  Shall we him find when we come there?
Accusator. By my troth! I have no dread,
  The hare from the form[3] we shall arear![4]
Phariseus. We shall have game and[5] this be true.
  Let us three work by[6] one assent[6].
  We will her bring even before Jesu,
  And of her life the truth present,
  How in[7] adultery her life is lent.[8]
  Then him before when she is brought
  We shall him ask the true judgement,
  What lawful death to her is wrought.
    Of grace and mercy ever he does preach,
  And that no man should be vengeable.
  Against the woman if he say[9] wrech[9],
  Then of his preaching he is unstable.[10]
  And if we find him variable,
  Of his preaching that he has taught,
  Then have we cause, both just and able,
  For a false man that he be caught.
Scriba. Now by great God! you say full well.
  If we him finden in variance
  We have good reason, as you do tell,
  Him for to bring to foul mischance.
  If he hold[11] still his dalliance,[11]
  And preach of mercy her for to save,
  Then have we matter of great substance
  Him for to kill and put in grave.
    Great reason why I shall you tell,
  For Moses does bid in our law
  That every adulterer we should quell,[12]
  And yet with stones they should be slaw.[13]
  Against Moses, if that he draw,

---

[1] *certain.*   [2] *have success.*   [3] *lair.*   [4] *rouse.*   [5] *if.*   [6] *with one mind.*
[7] *to.*   [8] *given.*   [9] *speak contemptuously (?), call for punishment (?).*   [10] *inconsistent.*
[11] *still maintain his talk.*   [12] *destroy.*   [13] *slain.*

That sinful woman with grace[1] to help,
He shall never scape out of our awe,[2]
But he shall die like a dog whelp.
Accusator.   You tarry over long, sires I say you.
They will soon part, as that I guess.
Therefore if you will have your prey now,
Let us go take them in their wantonness.
Phariseus. Go thou before, the way to dress.[3]
We shall thee follow within short while.
If that we may that quean distress,
I hope we shall Jesu beguile.
Scriba.   Break up the door and go we in!
Set to the shoulder with all thy might.
We shall them take even in their sin,
Their owen trespass shall them indict.
*Hic juvenis quidam extra currit in deploido calligis non legatis
et braccas in manu tenens.*[4]
Accusator. Stow[5] that harlot! some earthly wight,[5]
That in adultery here is found.
Juvenis. If any man stow me this night,
I shall him give a deadly wound!
    If[6] any man my way does stop,
Ere[7] we depart[8] dead shall I[9] be!
I shall this dagger put in his crop!
I shall him kill or[10] he shall me!
Phariseus.   Great Godes[11] curse may[11] go with thee!
With such a shrew will I not mell.[12]
Juvenis. That same blessing I give you three,
And queath[13] you all to the devil of hell!
[*He escapes away.*]
    In faith, I was so sore afraid
Of yon three shrewes, the sooth to say,

---

[1] *mercy.*   [2] *awful power.*   [3] *prepare.*   [4] *Here a certain young man runs
out in his doublet with his shoes unlaced and holding his trousers in his hand (or?)
holding up . . . with (?): cf. fifteen ll. later.*   [5] *arrest that rascal, somebody.*   [6] *If,
MS I.*   [7] *Ere, MS or.*   [8] *part.*   [9] *so MS.*   [10] *or, before (?), or (?).*   [11] *may
God's curse.*   [12] *associate.*   [13] *bequeath.*

My breech be not yet well up-tied—
I had such haste to run away.
They shall never catch me in such affray.[1]
I am full glad that I am gone.
Adieu! adieu! a twenty devil way!
And Godes curse have you everyone!   [*Exit.*]

Scriba.   Come forth! thou stot,[2] come forth! thou scout,[2]
Come forth! thou bismare[3] and brothel[3] bold.
Come forth! thou whore and stinking bitch[4] clout,[4]
How long hast thou such harlotry hold?[5]

Phariseus. Come forth! thou quean, come forth! thou scold,
Come forth! thou sloven, come forth! thou slut,
We shall thee teach with[6] cares cold
A little better to keep thy cut.[6]

Mulier.   Ah! mercy! mercy! sires, I you pray,
For Godes love, have mercy on me!
Of[7] my misliving me[8] not bewray![8]
Have mercy on me, for charity!

Accusator. Ask us no mercy—it shall not be!
We shall so ordain for thy lot
That thou shalt die for thy adultery.
Therefore come forth, thou stinking stot.

Mulier.   Sires, my worship[9] if you will save,
And help I[10] have no open[10] shame,
Both gold and silver you shall have,
So[11] that in cleanness you keep my name.

Scriba. Meed[12] for to take we were to blame,
To save such stottes, it shall not be.
We shall bring thee to such a game
That all adultereres shall learn by thee.

Mulier.   Standing[13] you will not grant me grace,
But for my sin that I shall die,
I pray you kill me here in this place

[1] *an attack.*   [2] *(terms of abuse).*   [3] *wretch and harlot.*   [4] *clod (?) rag (?) of a bitch.*   [E] *maintained.*   [6] *through suffering to keep your distance rather better.*   [7] *With regard to.*   [8] *don't inform against me.*   [9] *honour.*   [10] *(so that) I have no public*   [11] *Provided.*   [12] *Bribe(s).*   [13] *Understanding.*

And let not the people upon me cry.
If I be slandered openly
To all my friendes it shall be shame.
I pray you kill me privily!
Let not the people know my defame.[1]

Phariseus.   Fie on thee, scout, the devil thee quell![2]
Against the law shall we thee kill?
First shall hang thee the devil of hell
Ere we such follies should fulfil!
Though it like[3] thee never so ill,
Before the prophet thou shalt have law.
Like as Moses does charge it[4] till[5]
With great stones thou shalt be slaw.[6]

Accusator.   Come forth apace, thou stinking scout!
Before the prophet thou[7] were[7] this day,
Or I shall give thee such a clout
That thou shalt fall down even in the way.

Scriba. Now, by great God! and[8] I thee pay,
Such a buffet I shall thee take[9]
That all the teeth, I dare well say,
Within thy head for woe shall shake.

Phariseus.   Hark! sir prophet, we all you pray
To give true doom[10] and just sentence
Upon this woman which this same day
In sinful adultery has done offence.
*Hic Jesus dum isti accusant mulierem continue debet digito
suo scribere in terra.*[11]

Accusator. See! we have brought her to your presence,
Because you are a wise prophet,
That you shall tell by conscience
What death to her you think most meet.

Scriba.   In Moses law right thus we find,
That such false lovers shall be slain:
Straight to a stake we shall them bind,

[1] *infamy.*   [2] *destroy.*   [3] *please.*   [4] it (*or* us), *MS* ut.   [5] *to.*   [6] *slain.*
[7] (*do*) *you defend* (*yourself*) (?).   [8] *if.*   [9] *give.*   [10] *judgement.*   [11] *Here, while
those folk accuse the woman, Jesus ought to go on writing with his finger in the earth.*

And with great stones burst out their brain.
Of your conscience tell us the plain,[1]
With this woman what shall be wrought?
Shall we let her go quite[2] again?
Or to her death shall she be brought?
Jesus nihil respondit sed semper scribit in terra.[3]

Mulier.   Now, holy prophet, be merciable!
Upon me wretch take no vengeance!
For my sinnes abominable
In heart I have great repentance.
I am well worthy to have mischance,
Both bodily death and worldly shame,
But, gracious prophet, of[4] succourance[4]
This time pray[5] you for Godes name.

Phariseus.   Against the law thou didst offence,
Therefore of grace speak thou no more.
As Moses[6] giveth in law sentence
Thou shalt be stoned to death therefore.

Accusator. Have done! sir prophet, tell us your lore!
Shall we this woman with stones kill?
Or to her house her home restore?
In this matter tell us your will.

Scriba.   In a cold[7] study me thinketh you sit.
Good sir, awake, tell us your thought.
Shall she be stoned?—tell us your wit—[8]
Or in[9] what rule[9] shall she be brought?

Jesus. Look! which of you that never sin wrought,
But is of life cleaner than she,
Cast at her stones and spare her nought,
Clean[10] out of[10] sin if that you be.

Hic Jesus iterum se inclinans scribet in terra et omnes accusatores
quasi confusi separatim in tribus locis se disiungent.[11]

---

[1] open (judgement).   [2] free.   [3] Jesus makes no reply but keeps on writing in
the earth.   [4] for help.   [5] (I) pray.   [6] Lev. xx, 10.   [7] brown.   [8] mind.
[9] to what disciplinary action.   [10] Entirely free from.   [11] Here Jesus, again
bending down, will write in the earth, and all the accusers, as if confused, will go
off separately in three directions.

Phariseus.   Alas! alas! I am ashamed.
   I am afraid that I shall die.
   All my sinnes even properly named
   Yon prophet did write before my eye.
   If that my fellowes that[1] did espy[1]
   They will tell it both far and wide.
   My sinful living if they out cry
   I wot never where my head to hide.
Accusator.   Alas! for sorrow my heart does bleed.
   All my sinnes yon man did write.
   If that my fellowes to them took heed
   I cannot me from death acquit.
   I would I were hid somewhere out of sight,
   That men should me nowhere see nor know.
   If I be take I am aflight[2]
   In mickle shame I shall be throw.
Scriba.   Alas! the time that this betid![3]
   Right bitter care does me embrace.
   All my sinnes be now unhid:
   Yon man before me them all does trace.
   If I were ones out of this place
   To[4] suffer death great and vengeance able,
   I will never come before his face
   Though[5] I should die in a stable.[5]
Mulier.   Though I am worthy for my trespass
   To suffer death abominable,
   Yet, holy prophet, of your high grace,
   In your judgement be merciable.
   I will nevermore be so unstable:
   Oh! holy prophet, grant me mercy!
   Of my sinnes unreasonable
   With all my heart I am sorry!
Jesus.   Where are thy foemen[6] that did thee accuse?
   Why have they left us two alone?

---

[1] *observed it.*   [2] *afraid.*   [3] *happened.*   [4] *Where I am liable to (?).*   [5] *i.e.*
never mind how wretched the alternative.   [6] *enemies.*

Mulier. Because they could not themself excuse
    With shame they fled hence everyone.
    But, gracious prophet, list to my moan,
    Of my sorrow take compassion!
    Now all my enemies hence are gone,
    Say me some word of consolation.
Jesus.   For those sinnes that thou hast wrought
    Has any man condemned thee?
Mulier. Nay, forsooth, that has there not!
    But in your grace I put me.
Jesus. For[1] me[1] thou shalt not condemned be.
    Go home again and walk at large!
    Look that thou live in honesty,
    And will[2] no more[2] to sin, I thee charge.
Mulier.   I thank you highly, holy prophet,
    Of this great grace you have me grant.
    All my lewd[3] life I shall down[4] let,[4]
    And fond[5] to be Godes true servant.
Jesus.[6] What man of sin be repentant,
    Of God if he will mercy crave,
    God of mercy is so abundant
    That, what man ask it, he shall it have.
      When man is contrite and has won grace,
    God will not keep old wrath in mind.
    But better love to them he has,
    Very contrite when he them find.
    Now God, that died for all mankind,
    Save all these people both night and day,
    And of our sinnes he us unbind,
    High Lord of Heaven, that[7] best may.[7]

                              Amen.

---

[1] *For my part.*   [2] *do not will any more.*   [3] *wicked.*   [4] *leave behind.*   [5] *try.*
[6] *n. 47.*   [7] *who is best able to.*

Raising of Lazarus[1]

Hic incipit de suscitatione Lazari[2]
Lazarus. God that all thing did make of nought,
And puttest each creature to his fenance,[3]
Save thy handwork that thou hast wrought,
As thou art Lord of high substance.
Oh! gracious God, at thy pleasance,
Of my disease now comfort me,
Which[4] through sickness has such penance,
Onethes[5] for head-ache may I now see.
  Sister Martha and Magdalen eke,[6]
With haste help me in bed to dress,[7]
For truly I am so wonderly sick
I may never scape this great sickness.
My death is come now I guess—
Help into chamber that I be led.
My great disease I hope shall less,[8]
If I were laid upon a bed.
Martha. Lazarus, brother, be of good cheer!
I hope your sickness right well shall slake.
Upon this bed rest you right here,
And a good sleep essay to take.
Magdalen. Now, gentle brother, for Godes sake,
Lift up your heart and be not faint.
An heavy household with us you make
If deadly sickness have you ataint.[9]
Lazarus. Forsooth, dear sisteren, I may not sleep,
My sickness so sore does ever increase.

---

[1] n. 48.   [2] *Here begins the raising of Lazarus.*   [3] *divine purpose.*   [4] *Who.*
[5] *Scarcely.*   [6] *also.*   [7] *get (ready).*   [8] *abate, grow less.*   [9] *infected, overcome.*

Of me I pray you take right good keep,
Till that my pain begin release.
Martha. God grant grace that it may cease!
Of sickness God make you sound,
Or elles our joy will soon decrease
In so great paines if you lie bound.
Magdalen. Ah! brother, brother, lift up your heart!
Your heavy cheer does us grievance.
If death from us you should depart[1]
Then were we brought in cumberance.[2]
You are our brother, sib[3] of alliance:[3]
If you were dead then had we none.
You do us bring[4] in distemperance[4]
When you us tell you shall hence gone.
Primus consolator. Dame Martha and Magdalen
How fareth your brother? Let us him see.
Martha. He is right sick and has great pine.[5]
I am afraid dead he shall be.
Magdalen. A man may have right great pity
The fervent heat of him to feel.
Secundus consolator. Take[6] you no thought in no degree:[6]
I hope that he shall fare full well.
Martha. He may not live! His colour does change!
Come to his bed, you shall him see.
Magdalen. If he long live it will be strange.
But as God will so may it be!
Cheer him, good friendes, for charity!
Comfort of him we can none get.
Alas! alas! what aileth me?
My heart for woe is[7] wonder great![7]
Tertius consolator. All hail! sir Lazarus, how do you fare?
How do you feel you in your heart?
Lazarus. I am with sickness all wounden in care,
And look[8] when death me should depart.[8]

---

[1] *separate.*   [2] *deep distress.*   [3] *our closest kinsman.*   [4] *deeply disturb.*   [5] *suffering.*
[6] *Don't be in the least anxious.*   [7] *will burst.*   [8] *look for death to dismiss me.*

Quartus consolator et nuntius.[1] You shall have heal[2] and live
    in quart,[2]
  If you will take to you good cheer.
Lazarus. When death on me has shot his dart,
  I shall have heal and lie on bier.
Primus consolator.   Be of good comfort and think not so.
  Put out of heart that idle thought!
  Your owen misdeeming[3] may work you woe,
  And cause you sooner to death be brought.
Secundus consolator. With great sickness though you be
    sought,[4]
  Upon[5] yourself have no mistrust.[5]
  If that you have, I wonder right not
  Though you be dead and cast in dust!
Tertius consolator.   Many one has had right great sickness,
  And after has had his heal again.
  And many a man, this is no[6] less,[6]
  With his wantrust[7] himself has slain.
  You are a man of right sad brain:
  Though that your sickness grieve you right ill,
  Pluck up your heart, with might and main,
  And cheer yourself with all your will.
Lazarus.   Against my sickness there is no ease
  But Jesu Christ, my master dear.
  If that he wist of my disease
  Right soon I trust he would be here.
Quartus consolator. I shall go to him withouten[8] dwere,[8]
  And of your sickness tell him certain.
  Look that you be of right good cheer
  While that I go and come again.
Martha.   Now, gentle friend, tell him right thus:
  He that he loveth has great sickness.
  Hither to come and comfort us,
  Say that we prayed him, of his goodness.

---

[1] *messenger.*   [2] *health and be alive and well.*   [3] *false judgement.*   [4] *afflicted.*
[5] *Don't lack confidence in yourself.*   [6] *the truth.*   [7] *lack of faith.*   [8] *have no fear.*

Magdalen. Recommend us unto his Highness,
  And tell him all our heartes woe.
  But[1] he comfort our heaviness,
  Our worldly joy away will go.
Quartus consolator et nuntius.   The truth forsooth all[2]
    every deal[2]
  As you have told so shall I say.
  Go to your brother and cherish him well,
  For I walk forth straight in my way.
Martha. What cheer? good brother, tell me I pray.
  What will you eat? What will you drink?
  Look[3] what is pleasing to your pay:[3]
  You shall have what you will think.
Lazarus.   My wind is stopped, gone is my breath,
  And death is come to make my end.
  To God in heaven my soul I queath.[4]
  Farewell! sisteren, for hence I wend.
  Hic Lazarus moritur etc.[5]
Magdalen. Alas! for woe my hair I rend.
  My owen dear brother lieth here now dead.
  Now have we lost a trusty friend,
  The sibbest[6] blood of our kindred.
Martha.   Alas! alas! and welaway!
  Now are we twain both brotherless.
  For woe my heart is cold as clay.
  Ah! who shall comfort our carefulness?
  There had never woman more dolefulness.
  Ah! sister, Magdalen, what is your reed?[7]
  What wight may help our heaviness
  Now that our brother is gone and dead?
Magdalen.   Alas! dear sister, I cannot tell.
  The best comfort that I can say,
  But[8] some man do us slay and quell,
  Let us lie down by him and die.

---

[1] *Unless.*   [2] *in every detail.*   [3] *Consider what is pleasing to your taste.*
[4] *bequeath.*   [5] *Here Lazarus dies etc.*   [6] *closest.*   [7] *advice.*   [8] *Unless.*

Alas! why went he alone away?
If we had died with him, also,
Then had our care all turned to play,
There now all joy is turned to woe.
Primus consolator.   Be of good comfort and thank God of
    all!
For death is due to every man.
What time that death on us shall fall
No earthly wight the hour tell can.
Martha. We all shall die, that is certain.
But yet the[1] blood of kind nature,[1]
When death the brother away has tan,[2]
Must needes mourn that sepulture.[3]
Secundus consolator.   Good friendes, I pray you, hold
    your peace!
All your weeping may not amend it.
Of your sorrowing, therefore, now cease,
And help he[4] were[4] buried in a clay pit.
Magdalen. Alas! that word my heart does slit,
That he must now in clay be grave.
I would some man my throat would cut.
That I with him might lie in cave.
Tertius consolator.   Both head and foot now he is wound
In a sheet both fair and clean.
Let us bear him straight to that ground
Where that you think his grave shall been.
Martha. We are full loth that pit to seen,
But standing[5] it may no better be,
The corpse take up you three between,
With careful heart you follow shall we.
Hic portavit corpus ad sepelliendum.[6]
Magdalen.   Alas! comfort—I see no other,
But all of sorrow and care and woe.
We doleful women must bury our brother.

---

[1] *the kinsfolk through their natural relationship.*   [2] *taken.*   [3] *burying.*   [4] *that*
he may be.   [5] *understanding.*   [6] *Here they carry the body to be buried.*

Alas! that death me will not slay.
If I to pit with him might go,
Therein evermore with him to abide,
Then were my care all went me fro,
There[1] now great sorrow does wound me wide.

Primus consolator. This corpse we bury here in this pit.
Almighty God the soul may have.
And with this stone this grave we shut,
From ravenous beastes the body to save.

Magdalen. He is now brought into his cave.
My heart for woe this sight does kill.
Let us sit down here by the grave,
Ere we go hence weep all our fill.

Martha. Us for to weep no man may let,[2]
Before our face to see this sight.
Alas! why does death us not fet,[3]
Us for to bring to this same plight?

Secundus consolator. Arise! for shame! you do not right!
Straight from this grave you shall go hence.
Thus for to grudge against Godes might
Against high God you do offence.

Magdalen. Sith[4] I must needes with you hence gone,
My brotheres grave let me first kiss.
Alas! no wight may help my moan.
Farewell! my brother, farewell! my bliss.

Tertius consolator. Home to your place we shall you wisse.[5]
For Godes love, be of good cheer!
Indeed you do right sore amiss
So sore to weep as you do here.

Martha. Let us go home then to our place.
We pray you all with us to abide,
Us to comfort with some solace,
Till that our sorrow does slake and slide.

Primus consolator. You for to comfort at every tide[6]
We shall dwell here both night and day,

[1] *Where.* [2] *hinder.* [3] *fetch.* [4] *Since.* [5] *lead.* [6] *moment.*

And God, that made this world so wide,
Be your comfort, that best may.
Hic quartus consolator et nuntius loquitur Jesu.[1]

Quartus consolator.   Hail! holy prophet, Jesu by name,
Martha and Magdalen, those sisteren two,
Recommend them to your high fame,
And bade me say to you thus, lo!
How that Lazare, which that you loved so,
With great sickness is sore diseased.
To him they prayed you that you would go,
If that your Highness therewith were pleased.

Jesus.   Deadly sickness Lazare has none,
But for to show Godes great glory:
For that sickness is ordained alone
The Son of God to glorify.

Nuntius. They are in doubt[2] that he shall die:
Great sickness him sore does hold.
For fervent heat his blood does dry,
His colour changes as they me told.

Jesus.   Go home again and tell them thus,
I shall come to them when that I may.

Nuntius. At your commandment, oh! prophet Jesus,
I shall them tell as you do say.

Jesus. Come forth, bretheren, walk we our way!
Into Jewry go we anon!
I came not there full many a day,
Therefore thither now will I gon.

Omnes discipuli.[3]   The Jewes against thee were grim and
    grill,[4]
When thou wert there, they would thee have slain.
With stones they sought thee for to kill,
And wilt thou now go thither again?

Jesus. Twelve houres the day has in certain,
In them to walk both clear and bright.

---

[1] *Here the fourth mourner and messenger says to Jesus.*   [2] *fear.*   [3] *All the disciples.*   [4] *fierce.*

He shall not stumble against hill nor plain,
That goes the way while it is day-light.
    But if men walk when it is night,
Soon they offend[1] in that darkness;
Because they may have no clear sight
They hurt their feet oft in such mirkness.[2]
But as for this, yet, nevertheless,
The cause therefore I thither will wend
Is for to raise from bed express
Lazare that sleepeth, our[3] althere friend.[3]

Omnes discipuli.   Of his sickness he shall be save:
If that he sleep good sign it is.

Jesus. Lazare is dead and laid in grave:
Of his sleeping you deem amiss.
I was not there, you know well this.
To strength[4] your faith I am full glad,
Therefore I tell you the truth, iwis,[5]
Our friend is dead and under earth clad.[6]

Thomas.   Then go we all right[7] even[7] straight thither
Thereas our friend Lazare is dead,
And let us die with him together,
Thereas he lieth in the same stead.[8]

Jesus. Therefore to die have thou no dread.
The way straight thither in haste we take.
By the great might of my Godhead,
Out of his sleep he shall awake!

Nuntius.   All hail! Martha and Magdalen, eke,
To Jesu I have your message said.
I told him how that your brother was sick,
And with great pain in his bed laid.
He bade you should not be dismayed,
All his sickness he shall escape.
He will be here within a braid,[9]
As he me told, he cometh in rape.[10]

---

[1] *stumble.*   [2] *darkness.*   [3] *the friend of us all.*   [4] *strengthen.*   [5] *indeed.*
[6] *covered (in the grave).*   [7] *directly.*   [8] *place.*   [9] *moment.*   [10] *a hurry.*

Magdalen.   That holy prophet does come too late:
  Our brother is buried three days ere this.
  A great stone[1] stoppeth the pittes gate,
  Thereas our brother buried is.
Nuntius. Is Lazare dead? Now God his soul bless!
  Yet look you, take no heaviness!
  So long to weep you do amiss:
  It may not help your sorriness.
Martha.   Out of my heart all care to let,
  All sorrow and woe to cast away,
  I shall go forth in the street
  To meet with Jesu, if that I may.
Secundus consolator. God be your speed both ever and ay,
  For with your sister we will abide;
  Her to comfort we shall assay,
  And all her care to cast aside.
Tertius consolator.   Mary Magdalen, be of good heart!
  And well bethink you in your mind,
  Each creature hence must depart:
  There is no man but hence must wend.
  Death to no wight can be a friend:
  All thing to earth he will down cast.
  When that God will, all thing has end,
  Longer than him[2] list,[2] nothing may last.
Magdalen.   I thank you, friendes, for your good cheer.
  My head does ache as it should burst.
  I pray you, therefore, while you are here,
  A little while that I may rest.
Quartus consolator et nuntius. That Lord that made both east
      and west,
  Grant you good grace such rest to take
  That unto him should please most best,
  As he this world of nought did make.
Martha.   Ah! gracious Lord, had you been here,
  My brother Lazare this time had lived.

---

[1] *written above line in almost certainly different hand and ink.*   [2] *pleases him.*

But four days gone upon a bier,
We did him bury when he was dead.
Yet now I know withouten dread
What thing of God that thou do crave
Thou shalt speed[1] of[1] the high Godhead—
Whatso thou ask thou shalt it have.

Jesus.   Thy brother, Lazare, again shall rise,
A living man again to be.

Martha. I wot well that at the great last size[2]
He shall arise, and also we.

Jesus. Resurrection thou mayst me see,
And endless life I am also.
What man that dieth and liveth in me
From death to life he shall again go.
  Each man in me that faithful is,
And leadeth his life after my lore,
Of endless life may he never miss,
Ever he shall live and die nevermore.
The body and soul I shall restore
To endless joy—dost thou trow this?

Martha. I hope in thee, oh! Christ, full sore.
Thou art the son of God in bliss.
  Thy Father is God of life endless,
Thyself is Son of life and grace.
To cease this worldes wretchedness,
From heaven to earth thou took the pace.[3]

Jesus. Of heavenly might right great solace
To all this world men shall soon see.
Go call thy sister into this place,
Bid Mary Magdalen come hither to me.

Martha.   At thy bidding I shall her call,
In haste we were here you beforn.

Magdalen. Alas! my mouth is bitter as gall.
Great sorwin[4] my heart in twain has shorn.
Now that my brother from sight is lorn[5]

---

[1] *have success through.*   [2] *judgement.*   [3] *way.*   [4] *sorrow(s?).*   [5] *lost.*

There may no mirth my care relieve.
Alas! the time that I was born:
The sword of sorrow my heart does cleave.
Primus consolator.   For his dear love that all has wrought,
Cease some time of your weeping.
And put all thing out of thought
Into this care that you does bring.
Secundus consolator. You do yourself right great hindering,
And short your life ere you are ware.
For Godes love, cease of your sorrowing!
And with good wisdom refrain your care.
Martha.   Sister Magdalen, come out of hall,
Our master is come as I you say.
He sent me hither you for to call:
Come forth in haste, as I you pray.
Magdalen. Ha! where has he been many a long day!
Alas! why came he no sooner hither?
In haste I follow you anon the way,
Me thinketh long ere I come thither.
Tertius consolator.   Hark! good friendes, I you pray,
After this woman in haste we wend.
I am afraid right in good fay,[1]
Herself for sorrow that she will shend.[2]
Nuntius. Her brother so sore is in her mind
She may not eat, drink nor sleep.
Straight to his grave she goes on[3] end,[3]
As a mad woman there for to weep.
Magdalen.   Ah! sovereign Lord and master dear,
Had you with us been in presence,
Then had my brother alive been here,
Not dead but quick, that now is hence.
Against death is no resistance.
Alas! my heart is wonderly woe,
When that I think of his absence,
That you yourself in heart loved so.

[1] *faith.*   [2] *injure.*   [3] *incessantly.*

Primus consolator. When we have mind of his sore
    death,
  He was to us so gentle and good,
  That[1] mind of him our heartes slayth,[1]
  The loss of him does mar our mood.
Secundus consolator. By better neighbour never man stood:
  To every man he was right hend.[2]
  Us he did refresh with drink and food,
  Now he is gone, gone is our friend!
Jesus. Your great weeping does me constrain
  For my good friend to weep also.
  I cannot me for woe restrain,
  But I must weep like as you do.
  Hic Jesus fingit se lacrimari.[3]
Tertius consolator. Behold this prophet, how he does weep,
  lo!
  He loved Lazare right wonderly sore.
  He would not elles for him thus weep so.
  But if that his love on him were the more.
Nuntius. A straw for thy tale! What needeth him to
  weep?
  A man born blind did he not give sight?
  Might he not then his friend alive keep,
  By the virtue of that same high might?
Jesus. Where is he put?—tell me anon right.
  Bring me the way straight to his grave.
Martha. Lord, at your will we shall bring you tight,[4]
  Even to that place there he does lie in cave.
Magdalen. When that we had the messenger sent,
  Ere he had fully half a mile gone,
  Died my brother and up we him hent,[5]
  Here in this grave we buried him anon.
Jesus. The might of the Godhead shall glad[6] you everyone,[6]
  Such sight shall you see hence ere you wend.

---

[1] *That memory of him breaks our hearts.*   [2] *nice, pleasant.*   [3] *Here Jesus makes to be weeping.*   [4] *quickly.*   [5] *took.*   [6] *make you all rejoice.*

Set to your handes! Take off the stone!
A sight let me have of Lazare my friend.
Martha.　　He stinketh right foul long time ere this,
Four days gone, forsooth, he was dead.
Let him lie still right even as he is,
The stink of his carrion might hurt us I dread.
Jesus. As I have thee told, sight of the Godhead
Thyself shouldest have, faithful if thou be.
Take off the stone! Do after my rede![1]
The glory of the Godhead anon you shall see.
Primus consolator.　　Your bidding shall be done anon full
　　swift!
Set to your handes and help each one.
I pray you, sires, help me to lift,
I may not raise it myself alone.
Secundus consolator. In faith, it is an heavy stone,
Right sad of weight and heavy of[2] peise.[2]
Tertius consolator. Though it were twice so heavy as one,
Under us four we shall it raise.
Nuntius.　　Now is the stone take from the cave,
Here may men see a ruely[3] sight.
Of this dead body that lies here grave,[4]
Wrapped in a pitiful plight.
Jesus. (Elevatis ad caelum oculis.)[5] I thank thee, Father, of
　　thy high might,
That thou hast heard my prayer this day.
I know full well both day and night
Ever thou dost grant that I do say.
　　But for this people that standeth about,
And believe not the power of thee and me,
Them for to bring clean out of doubt
This day our might they all shall see.
Hic Jesus clamat voce magna.[6]
Lazare! Lazare! my friend so free[7]

---

[1] *advice.*　　[2] *in weight.*　　[3] *pitiful.*　　[4] *buried.*　　[5] *Lifting up his eyes to the heavens.*　　[6] *Here Jesus calls with a loud voice.*　　[7] *excellent.*

From that deep pit come out anon!
By the great might of the high majesty
Alive thou shalt on earth again gon.

Lazarus. At your commandment I rise up full right:
Heaven, hell and earth your bidding must obey.
For you are God and man and Lord of most might,
Of life and of death you have both lock and key.

*Hic resurget Lazarus ligatis manibus et pedibus ad modum
sepulti.*[1]

Jesus. Go forth! bretheren, and Lazare you untie,
And all his bondes looseth them asunder!
Let him walk home with you in the way:
Against[2] Godes might this miracle is no wonder.

Petrus. At your bidding his bondes we unbind.
All thing must lout[3] your majesty.
By this great miracle openly we find
Very God and man in truth that you be.

Johannes. That thou art very God every man may see,
By this miracle so great and so marvel.
All thing under heaven must needes obey thee,
When against thee though death be, he may not prevail.

Omnes consolatores. We all with one voice for God do
thee know,[4]
And for our saviour we do thee reverence.
All our whole love now in thee does grow,
Oh! sovereign Lord of most excellence.
Help us of your grace when that we go hence,
For against death us helpeth not to strive.
But against your might is no resistence,
Our death you may aslake[5] and keep[5] us still alive.

Jesus. Now I have showed in open sight
Of my Godhead the great glory,
Toward my passion I will me dight:[6]

---

[1] *Here Lazarus shall rise with his hands and feet bound after the fashion of a buried person.*   [2] *In view of.*   [3] *bow to.*   [4] *acknowledge.*   [5] *keep away and maintain.*   [6] *dispose .*

The time is near that I must die.
For all mankind his soul to buy,
A crown of thorn shall piercen my brain,
And on the Mount of Calvary
Upon a cross I shall be slain.

Passion I: Prologues[1]

Demon.   I am your lord, Lucifer, that out of hell came,
Prince of this world and great duke of hell.
Wherefore my name is cleped[2] Sir Satan,
Which appeareth among you a matter to spell.[3]
I am nourisher of sin to the confusion of man,
To bring him to my dungeon there in fire to dwell.
Whosoever serve me, so reward him I can
That he shall sing 'welaway' ever in paines fell.
    Lo! thus bounteous a lord then now am I.
To reward so sinners as my kind[4] is,
Whoso will follow my lore and serve me daily,
Of sorrow and pain enough he shall never miss.
    For I began in heaven sin for to sow
Among all the angeles that weren there so bright.
And therefore was I cast out into hell[5] full low,
Notwithstanding I was the fairest and bearer of light.
    Yet I drew in my tail of those angeles bright
With me into hell, taketh good heed what I say.
I left but twain against one to abide there in light,
But the third part came with me—this may not be said
    nay.
    Taketh heed to your prince, then, my people every one,

[1] n. 49. *Passion I examined by Prosser (chap vii) as 'work of a homiletic and dramatic genius', and by McNeir.*   [2] *called.*   [3] *tell.*   [4] *nature.*   [5] *nn. 1 and 21.*

And seeth[1] what masteries in heaven I gan there do play.[1]
To get a thousand soules in an hour me thinketh it but
scorn,
Sith[2] I won Adam and Eve on the first day!
But now marvellous mindes[3] runnen in my remem-
berance,
Of one, Christ, which is cleped[4] Joseph, and Maryes son.
Thries[5] I tempt him by right subtle instance[5]
After he fast forty days, against[6] sensual might or reason,[6]
For of the stones to have made bread—but soon I had
conclusion;
Then upon a pinnacle—but angeles were to him assistant,
His answeres were marvellous, I knew not his intention;
And at the last to vainglory—but never I had my intent.
And now has he twelve disciples to his attendance,
To each town and city he sendeth them as beadelles,[7]
In diverse place to make for him purveyance.[8]
The people of[9] his workes full greatly marveles:
To the crooked, blind and dumb his workes provailes;[10]
Lazare, that four days lay dead, his life recured;[11]
And where I purpose me to tempt, anon he me assailes;
Magdalen plain[12] remission[12] also he has ensured.
Godes Son he pretendeth,[13] and to be born of a maid,
And says he shall die for mannes salvation.
Then shall the truth be tried, and no further be delayed,
When the soul from the body shall make separation.
And as for them that are under my great domination,
He shall fail of his intent and purpose also
By this text of old remembered to my intention,[14]
'Quia in inferno nulla est redemptio.'[15]
But when the time shall nigh[16] of his persecution,

---

[1] *see what clever tricks I began to have played there in heaven* (?).   [2] *Since.*
[3] *thoughts.*   [4] *called.*   [5] *Thrice . . . by really cunning solicitation.*   [6] *contrary to
the strong cravings of his body and to reason.*   [7] *messenger officers.*   [8] *provision.*
[9] *at.*   [10] provailes, = prevailes (?) = *benefit(s).*   [11] *recovered.*   [12] *full remission (of her sins).*   [13] *pretends (to be); n. 50.*   [14] *purpose.*   [15] *Because there
is no redemption in Hell: Mr. Nellist points out is part of response to lesson seven of
Matins for the dead in* Sarum Breviary, *ii, 278.*   [16] *draw near.*

I shall arear[1] new engines of malicious conspiracy.
Plenty of reproofes I shall provide to his confusion.
Thus shall I false[2] the wordes that his people do testify.
His disciples shall forsake him and their master deny.
Innumerable shall his woundes be of woeful grievance.
A traitor shall contrive his death to fortify.[3]
The rebukes that he gives me shall turn to his displeasance.
    Some of his disciples[4] shall be chief[5] of this ordinance,[5]
That shall fortify[6] this term that, 'in trust is treason'.
Thus shall I venge by subtlety all my malicious grievance,
For nothing may exceed my prudence and discretion.
    Give me your love, grant me my affection,
And I will unclose the treasure of loves[7] alliance,[7]
And give you your desires[8] after your intention.
No[9] poverty shall approach you from plenteous abundance.[9]
    Behold the diversity of my disguised[10] variance:[10]
[*Indicates his own dress.*]
Each thing set of due natural disposition,
And each part according to his resemblance,
From the sole of the foot to the highest ascension.
    Of fine Cordovan,[11] a goodly pair of long peked[12] shon,[12]
Hosen enclosed of the most costious[13] cloth of crimson,
Thus a boy[14] to a gentleman to make comparition,[15]
With two dozen pointes[16] of cheverelle,[16] the aglottes[17] of silver fine.
    A shirt of fine Holland[18]—but care not for the payment!
A stomacher of clear[19] Reines,[19] the best may be bought.

---

[1] *raise up.*   [2] *make appear false.*   [3] *ensure.*   [4] *e.g. Judas, Peter.*   [5] *chief (executants) of this device (of mine).*   [6] *confirm; proverbial: Whiting, T492.*   [7] *the bond of love.*   [8] *n. 51.*   [9] *You won't suffer from poverty once you are rich (?).*   [10] *varied disguise.*   [11] *Cordovan leather.*   [12] *pointed (?) shoes.*   [13] *costly.*   [14] *man of low birth.*   [15] *comparison.*   [16] *laces of kid-leather.*   [17] *ornamental tags.*   [18] *Holland cloth.*   [19] *pure, bright linen from Rennes (?).*

Though poverty be chief, let pride there be present,
And all those that reprove pride, thou set them at nought!
    Cadace,[1] wool or flockes, where it may be sought,
To stuff withal thy doublet and make thee of proportion,
Two small legges and a great body, though it[2] rime not,[2]
Yet look that thou desire to have the new fashion.
    A gown of three yardes—look thou make comparison
Unto all degrees daily that pass[3] thy estate.[3]
A purse withouten money, a dagger for devotion,
And, there[4] reproof is of sin, look thou make debate![4]
    With side lockes I shrew[5] thy hair, to thy collar hanging down,
To harbour quick[6] beastes that tickle men at night.
An high small bonnet for curing[7] of the crown,
And[8] all beggares and poor people—have them in despite!
    Unto the great oathes and lechery give thy delight.
To maintain thy estate, let bribery be present,
And if the law reprove thee, say thou wilt fight,
And gather thee a fellowship[9] after thy intent.[9]
    Look thou set not by precept nor by commandment—
Both civil[10] and canon[10] set thou at nought.
Let no member[11] of God but with oathes be rent.
Lo! thus this world at this time to my intent is brought.
    I, Satan, with my fellowes this world have sought,
And now we have it at our pleasance,
For sin is not shamefast,[12] but boldness has bought[12]
That shall cause them in hell to have inheritance.
    A beggares daughter to make great purveyance,[13]
To counterfeit a gentlewoman, disguised as she can.
And if money lack, this is the new chevesance:[14]
With her privy[15] pleasance[15] to get it of some man.

---

[1] *Cotton wool.*   [2] *they don't go together.*   [3] *are superior to your position.*
[4] *if you're told off for doing wrong, make a fight of it.*   [5] *curse (?).*   [6] *lively.*
[7] *covering.*   [8] *And (with regard to).*   [9] *gang with a view to what you intend.*
[10] *i.e. law.*   [11] *limb (e.g. in oaths such as by 'God's blood').*   [12] *ashamed but has bought boldness.*   [13] *provision.*   [14] *means of getting it.*   [15] *private (i.e. sexual) pleasure-making.*

Her collar splayed and furred with ermine, Calabere[1]
    or satin,
A sign to sell lechery to them that will buy,
And they that will not buy it, yet enough shall they han,
And tell them it is for love, she may it not deny.
    I have brought you new names, and will you see
      why?—
For sin is so pleasant to each mannes intent!
You shall call pride, honesty, and natural kind,[2] lechery,
And covetise,[3] wisdom, there treasure is present,
    Wrath, manhood,[4] and envy called chastisement,[5]
Size[6] nor session,[6] let perjury be chief,
Gluttony, rest—let abstinence be absent—
And he that will exhort thee to virtue, put him to reproof.
    To rehearse all my servantes my matter is too brief,
But all these shall inherit the division eternal,
Though Christ by his subtlety many[7] matters move,[7]
In everlasting pain with me dwellen they shall.
    Remember[8] our servantes, whose soules are mortal,[8]
For I must remove for more matteres to provide.
I am with you at all times when you to counsel me call,
But for a short time myself I devoid.[9]

Johannes Baptista.   I, John Baptist, to you thus prophesy,
That one shall come after me and not tarry long,
In many fold more stronger than I,
Of whose shoes I am not worthy to loose the thong.
Wherefore I counsel thee you reform all wrong
In your conscience of the mortal[10] deedes seven,[10]
And for to do penance look that you fong,[11]
For now shall come the kingdom of heaven.
    The[12] ways of our Lord cast you to array,[12]

---

[1] *Calabrian fur.*   [2] *instinct.*   [3] *covetousness.*   [4] *being manly.*   [5] *i.e. of someone who is envied.*   [6] *Whether it be at the assizes or sessions.*   [7] *try on many expedients.*   [8] *You whose souls are mortal, remember our servants (of four lines before).*   [9] *take off.*   [10] *seven deadly sins: pride, concupiscence, anger, envy, sloth, covetousness, gluttony.*   [11] *undertake.*   [12] *Set yourself to make ready the ways, etc.*

And therein to walk, look you be applyand,[1]
And make his pathes as right as you may,
Keeping[2] right forth, and be not declinand[2]
Neither too fele[3] on right nor on left hand,
But in the middes purpose you to hold,
For that in all wise is most pleasand,
As you shall hear when I have told.
　　Of this way for to make moralisation:
By the right side you shall understand, mercy,[4]
And on the left side likened, desperation,[5]
And the path between bothen that may not wry[6]
Shall be hope and dread, to walk in perfectly,
Declining not too fele[3] for no[7] manner need.[7]
Great causes I shall show[8] you why
That you shall sue[9] the path of hope and dread:
　　On the mercy of God too much you shall not hold,
As in this wise, behold what I mean—
For to do sin be thou no more bold
In trust that God will merciful been;
And if by sensuality, as it is oft seen,
Sinnest deadly, thou shalt not therefore despair,
But therefore do penance and confess thee clean,
And of heaven thou mayst trust to be heir.
　　The path that lies to this blessed inheritance
Is hope and dread, coupled by conjunction.
Betwixt these twain may be no disseverance,
For hope withouten dread is manner of presumption,
And dread withouten hope is manner of desperation.
So these twain must be knit by[10] one accord[10]
How you shall array[11] the way I have made declaration,
Also the right pathes against the coming of our Lord.

---

[1] *endeavouring.*　　[2] *Keeping straight on without turning.*　　[3] *much.*　　[4] *i.e. of God.*　　[5] *despair.*　　[6] *go wrong.*　　[7] *any kind of reason.*　　[8] *MS* shove *or* sheve.　　[9] *follow.*　　[10] *in complete agreement.*　　[11] *prepare.*

Passion I: Council of Jews I[1]

Here shall Annas show himself in his stage,[2] besein[3] after[3] a bishop of the old[4] law, in a scarlet gown and over that a blue tabard, furred with white, and a mitre on his head after the old law, two doctors standing by him in furred hoods, and one before them with his staff of estate, and each of them on their heads a furred cap with a great knop in the crown, and one standing before as a Saracen,[5] the which shall be his messenger.

Annas.   As a prelate am I propered[6] to provide peace,
And of Jewes judge,[7] the law to fortify.[8]
I, Annas, by my power shall command doubtless:
The lawes of Moses no man shall deny.
Who[9] exceed my commandment anon you certify,[10]
If any heretic here reign, to me you complain,
For in me lies the power all truthes to try,
And principally our lawes, those must I sustain.

If I may espy the contrary, no while shall they reign,
But anon to me be brought and stand present
Before their judge, which shall not feign,
But after their trespass to give them judgement.
Now sires, for a prose[11]—heareth my intent:[11]
There is one, Jesus of Nazareth, that our lawes does exceed.
If he proceed thus, we shall us all repent,
For our lawes he destroys daily with his deed.

Therefore by your counsel we must take heed
What is best[12] to provide or do in this case,

---

[1] *MS continuous.*   [2] *scaffold, p. 41.*   [3] *dressed like.*   [4] *i.e. Jewish, Mosaic law (as contrasted new law of Christ). Jewish High Priests were commonly represented as mitred bishops: n. 52.*   [5] *Anderson (162) suggests Saracen may have worn scarf twisted round head and tied at back.*   [6] *empowered.*   [7] *(to be) judge.* [8] *uphold.*   [9] *(Those) who.*   [10] *officially notify.*   [11] *story–hear what's in my mind.* [12] *MS be.*

For, if we let him thus go and further proceed,
Against Caesar and our law we do trespass.
Primus doctor. Sir, this is my advice that you shall
do:
Send to Caiphas for counsel, know his intent,
For if Jesu proceed and thus forth go,
Our lawes shall be destroyed, this see[1] we present.[1]
Secundus doctor. Sir, remember the great charge that on
you is laid,
The law to keep which may not fail.
If any default proved of you be said,
The Jewes with truth will you assail.
Take heed what counsel may best provail.[2]
After Rewfin and Lyon I reed[3] that you send—
They are temporal[4] judges that knoweth the parail[4]—
With your cousin Caiphas this matter to amend.
Annas. Now surely this counsel revives my heart!
Your counsel is best as I can see.
Arfexe in haste look that thou start,
And pray Caiphas, my cousin, come speak with me.
To Rewfin and Lyon thou go, also,
And pray them they speak with me in haste,
For a principal matter that have to do,
Which must be known ere this day be past.
Arfexe. My sovereign at your intent I shall gon,
In all the haste that I can hie,
Unto Caiphas, Rewfin and Lyon,
And charge your intent that they shall ply.[5]
*Here goes the messenger forth, and in the meantime Caiphas
shows himself in his scaffold, arrayed like to Annas, saving
his tabard shall be red, furred with white. Two doctors with
him arrayed with pells[6] after the old guise and furred caps
on their heads.*

---

[1] *we see now.*   [2] = prevail (?).   [3] *counsel.*   [4] *secular judges (as opposed
to Annas and Caiphas who are 'ecclesiastical') . . . the ways and means.*   [5] *carry
out.*   [6] *skins.*

Caiphas. As a primate most prudent I present[1] here sensible[1]
Bishopes of the law with all the circumstance.
I, Caiphas, am judge with poweres possible
To destroy all errores that in our lawes make variance.
All thinges I convey by reason and temperance,
And all matteres possible to[2] me are palpable.[2]
Of the law of Moses I have a chief governance,
To[3] sever right and wrong in me is terminable.[3]

But there is one Christ, that[4] our lawes is variable,
He perverts the people with his preaching ill.[4]
We must seek a mean[5] onto him reproovable,[5]
For if he proceed our lawes he will spill.[6]

We must take good counsel in this case
Of the wisest of the law that can the truth tell,
Of the judges of Pharisee, and of my cousin Annas,
For if he proceed by process our lawes he will fell.

Primus doctor. My lord! pleaseth you to pardon me for to say
The blame in you is, as we find,
To let Christ continue thus, day by day,
With his false witchcraft the people to blind.
He worketh false miracles against all kind,[7]
And maketh our people to leve[8] them in.
It is your part to take him and do[9] him bind,[9]
And give him judgement for his great sin.

Secundus doctor. Forsooth sir, of truth this is the case,
Unto our law you do oppression
That you let Christ from you pass,
And will not do on him correction.
Let Annas know your intention,
With priestes and judges of the law,

---

[1] *represent (?) here before your eyes.* [2] *are within my scope (?).* [3] *I have the final say in distinguishing right and wrong.* [4] *He perverts ... by his false preaching that our laws can be varied (?).* [5] *way of reproving him.* [6] *destroy.* [7] *nature.* [8] *believe.* [9] *have him bound.*

And do Christ forsake his false opinion,
Or into a prison let him be throw.

Caiphas. Well! sires, you shall see within short while
I shall correct him for his trespass.
He shall no longer our people beguile—
Out of my danger[1] he shall not pass.

*Here comes the messenger to Caiphas and in the meantime
Rewfin and Lyon show them in the place in ray[2] tabards
furred and ray hoods about their necks furred.*

Messenger. My reverend sovereign, and[3] it do you please,
Sir Annas, my lord, has to you sent.
He prays you that you shall not cease
Till that you are with him present.

Caiphas. Sir! tell my cousin I shall not fail.
It was my purpose him for to see
For certain matteres that will provail,[4]
Though he had not have sent to me.

Messenger. I recommend me to your high degree.
On more messages I must wend.

Caiphas. Farewell! sir, and well you be!
Greet well my cousin and my friend.

Here the messenger meets with the judges.

Messenger. Hail! judges of Jewry, of reason most prudent,
Of my message to you I make relation.
My lord, Sir Annas, has for you sent,
To see his presence without delation.[5]

Rewfin. Sir, we are ready at his commandment,
To see Sir Annas in his place.
It was our purpose and our intent
To have been with him within short space.

Lyon. We are full glad his presence to see.
Sir, tell him we shall come in haste.
No[6] declaration therein shall be,[6]
But to his presence hie us fast.

---

[1] *power.* [2] *striped.* [3] *if.* [4] = prevail ? [5] *delay.* [6] *No announcement of our coming will be made (?).*

Messenger.   I shall tell my lord, sires, as you say,
    You will fulfil all his pleasance.
Rewfin. Sir, tell him we shall make no delay,
    But come in haste at his instance.
    Here the messenger comes to Annas.
Messenger.   My lord, and it please you to have intelli-
      gence,
    Sir Caiphas cometh to you in haste.
    Rewfin and Lyon will see your presence,
    And see you here ere this day be past.
Annas. Sir, I can[1] thee thank of[1] thy diligence.
    Now again[2] my cousin I will walk.
    Sires, followeth me unto his presence,
    For of these matteres we must talk.
    Here Annas goes down to meet with Caiphas.
Caiphas. (*In the meantime thus saying.*)   Now unto Annas
      let us wend,
    Each of us to know otheres intent.
    Many matteres I have in mind
    The which to him I shall present.
Primus doctor.   Sir, of all other thing remember this case:
    Look that Jesus be put to shame.
Secundus doctor. When we come present before Annas
    We shall rehearse all his great blame.
    Here the bishops with their clerks and the Pharisees meet at
    the mid-place and there shall be a little oratory with stools and
    cushions cleanly[3] besein like as[3] it were a council-house.
Annas.   Welcome! sir Caiphas, and you judges all.
    Now shall you know all my intent.
    A wonder case, sires, here is befall,
    On which we must give judgement,
    Lest that we after the case repent.
    Of one Christ, that Godes Son some do him call,
    He showeth miracles and says present[4]
    That he is Prince of Princes all.

---

[1] *thank you for.*   [2] *towards.*   [3] *nicely appointed as if.*   [4] *now.*

The people so fast to him do fall,
By privy meanes as we espy,
If he proceed soon see you shall
That our lawes he will destroy.
It is our part this to deny.
What is your counsel in this case?

Caiphas. By reason the truth here may we try:
I cannot deem him without trespass,
    Because he says in every a place
That he king of Jewes [is] in every degree,
Therefore he is false, know well the case—
Caesar is king and none but he!

Rewfin.   He is an heretic and a traitor bold
To Caesar and to our law certain,
Both in word and in work, and[1] you behold[1]—
He is worthy to die with mickle pain.

Lyon.   The cause that we are here present,
To fortify[2] the law and truth to say:
Jesus full near our lawes has shent,[3]
Therefore he is worthy for to die.

Primus doctor: Annas.[4] Sires, you that are ruleres of the law,
On Jesu you must give judgement.
Let him first be hangen and draw,
And then his body in fire be burnt.

Secundus doctor: Annas.   Now shall you hear the intent
    of me:
Take Jesu, that works us all great shame,
Put him to death, let him not flee,
For then the commones they will you blame.

Primus doctor: Caiphas.   He works with witchcraft in
    each place,
And draweth the people to his intent.
Beware, you judges, let him not pass,
Then by my troth you shall repent.

Secundus doctor: Caiphas. Sires, taketh heed unto this case,

---

[1] *if you consider.*   [2] *secure.*   [3] *destroyed.*   [4] *see stage direction p. 241.*

And in your judgement be not slow:
There was never man did so great trespass
As Jesu has done against our law.
Annas.   Now, bretheren, then will you hear my intent?
These nine days let us abide,
We may not give so hasty judgement:
But each man inquire on his side,
Send spies about the country wide,
To see and record and testimony,
And then his workes he shall not hide,
Nor have no power them to deny.
Caiphas.   This counsel accordeth to my reason.
Annas. And we all to the same.[1]

Passion I: Entry into Jerusalem[1]

Jesus.   Friendes, behold the time of mercy,
  The which is come now without doubt.
  Mannes soul in bliss now shall edify,[2]
  And the prince of the world is cast out.
    Go to yon castle that standeth you again—
  Some of my disciples go forth you, too—
  There shall you finden beastes twain,
  An ass tied and her foal, also.
  Unloosen that ass and bring it to me plain.[3]
  If any man ask why that you do so,
  Say that I have need to this beast certain,
  And he shall not let[4] you your ways for to go.
  That beast bring you to me.
Primus apostolus.[5] Holy prophet, we go our way:
  We will not your word delay.
  Also[6] soon as that we may,

---

[1] *n. 53.*   [2] *be exalted.*   [3] *openly (?).*   [4] *hinder.*   [5] *First apostle.* [6] *As.*

We shall it bring to thee.

Here they fetch the ass with the foal.

Burgensis.[1]   Hark you, men! Who gave you leave
Thus this beast for to take away?
But only[2] for poor men to relieve
This ass is ordained,[2] as I you say.

Philippus. Good sir, take[3] this at no grief.[3]
Our master us sent hither this day:
He has great need, without[4] reproof,[4]
Therefore not let[5] us I thee pray
This beast for to lead.

Burgensis. Sethin[6] that[6] it is so that he has you sent,
Worketh his will and his intent.
Take the beast as you are bent,
And ever[7] well may you speed![7]

Jacobus minor.   This beast is brought right now here, lo!
Holy prophet, at thy owen will,
And with this cloth anon, also,
This beastes back we shall soon hill.[8]

Philippus. Now mayst thou ride whither thou wilt go
Thy holy purpose to fulfil.
Thy beast full ready is dight[9] thee to—[9]
Both meek and tame, the beast is still—
And we are ready, also,
If it is pleasing to thy sight,
Thee to help anon forthright
Upon this beast that thou were dight,
Thy journey for to do.

Here Christ rides out of the place, and[10] *he will. And Peter and
John abide still. And at the last,*[11] *when they have done their
preaching, they meet with Jesu.*

Petrus.   Oh! you people despairing, be glad!

---

[1] *Burgess.*   [2] *this ass is assigned for the assistance of poor men only.*   [3] *don't
be upset about this.*   [4] *undoubtedly.*   [5] *hinder.*   [6] *Since.*   [7] *may things go
your way always.*   [8] *cover.*   [9] *prepared for you.*   [10] *if.*   [11] *i.e. at the end
of John's sermon on p. 250.*

A great cause you have, and[1] you can see.
The Lord, that all thing of nought made,
Is coming your comfort to be.
All your languores[2] salven[2] shall he,
Your health is more than you can wit.
He shall cause the blind that they shall see.
The deaf to hear, the dumb for to speak.

They that be crooked he shall cause them to go
In the way that John Baptist of prophesied.
Such a leech came you never none to:
Wherefore what he commandeth, look be[3] applied.
That some of you are blind it may not be denied,
For him that is your maker with your ghostly[4] eye you
shall not know.
Of his commandment in you great negligence is espied,
Wherefore,[5] deaf from ghostly hearing, clepe you I howe.[5]

And some of you may not go, you are so crooked,
For of good working in you is little abundance.
Twain feet every man should have, and[6] it were looked,[6]
Which should bear the body ghostly, most of substance:
First is to love God above all other pleasance,
The second is to love thy neighbour as thy owen person.
And if these twain be kept in perseverance,
Into the celestial habitation you are able to gone.

Many of you are dumb. Why?—for you will not
redress,
By mouth, your deedes mortal, but therein do perdure.[7]
Of the which, but[8] you have contrition and you confess,
You may not inherit heaven, this I you ensure.
And of all these maladies you may have ghostly cure,
For the heavenly leech is coming you for to visit.
And, as for payment, he will show you no redrure,[9]
For with the love of your heartes he will be acquit.

---

[1] *if.*   [2] *ills heal.*   [3] *MS ʒe.*   [4] *spiritual.*   [5] *Therefore it is in this way that (? : howe = how?) I call you deaf of spiritual hearing.*   [6] *if it were considered.*
[7] *persist.*   [8] *unless.*   [9] *= reddure (?), severity.*

Johannes Apostolus.   Unto my brotheres foresaid rehearsal
    That you should give the more very[1] confidence,
    I come with him as testimonial,[2]
    For to confirm and fortify[3] his sentence.[3]
    This Lord shall come without resistence!
    Unto the city-ward he is now coming.
    Wherefore dress you with all due diligence
    To honour him as your maker and king.

    And to fulfil the prophetes prophecy,
    Upon an ass he will hither ride,
    Showing you example of humility,
    Devoiding[4] the abominable sin of pride,
    Which has nigh conquered all the world wide,
    Greatest cause of all your tribulation,
    Use it whoso will, for it is the best guide
    That you may have to the place of damnation!

    Now brother in God, sith[5] we have intelligence
    That our Lord is nigh come to this city,
    To attend upon his precious presence
    It sitteth[6] to us,[6] as seemeth me,[7]
    Wherefore to meet with him now go we.
    I would for nothing we were too late!
    To the city-ward fast draweth he:
    Me seemeth he is nigh at the gate.
    Here speak the four citizens.

Primus cives de Jerusalem.   Neighboures, great joy in our
    heart we may make
    That this heavenly king will visit this city.
Secundus cives. If our earthly king such a journey should
    take,
    To do him honour and worship busy should we be.
Tertius cives. Much more then to the heavenly king bound
    are we
    For to do that should be to his person reverence.

---

[1] *true.*   [2] *witness.*   [3] *support his meaning.*   [4] *Driving out.*   [5] *since.*
[6] *is proper for us.*   [7] *(to) me.*

Quartus cives. Let us then welcome him with flowers and
    branches of the tree,
For he will take[1] that to pleasance because of redolence.[1]
*Here the four citizens make them ready for to meet with our
Lord, going bare-foot and bare-legged and in their shirts,
saving they shall have their gowns cast about them. And when
they see our Lord, they shall spread their clothes before him
and he shall light and go thereupon. And they shall fall down
upon their knees all at once.*
Primus cives.   Now blessed he be that in our Lordes name
  To us in any wise will resort!
And we believe, verily, that thou dost the same,
For by thy mercy shall spring mannes comfort.
*Here Christ passes forth. There meet with him a certain[2] of
children with flowers, and cast before him. And they sing:
'Gloria, laus.'*[3]
[*A child.*] Thou Son of David, thou be our support
  At our last day when we shall die.
Wherefore we all at ones to thee exhort,
Crying, 'Mercy, mercy, mercy!'
Jesu.   Friendes, behold the time of mercy,
  The which is come now, withouten doubt.
Mannes soul in bliss now shall edify,[4]
And the prince of the world is cast out.
As I have preached in places about,
And showed experience to man and wife,
Into this world Godes Son has sought
For very[5] love man to revife.[6]
    The truth of truthes shall now be tried,
And a perfect accord[7] betwixt God and man,
Which truth shall never be divide—
Confusion unto the fiend, Satan!
Primus pauper homo.[8]   Thou Son of David, on us have
  mercy,

---

[1] *take pleasure in that because of its fragrance.*   [2] *certain number.*   [3] *n. 54.*
[4] *be exalted.*   [5] *true.*   [6] *give back life (to).*   [7] *harmony; MS of corde.*   [8] *First
poor man.*

As we must steadfast believen in thee.
Thy goodness, Lord, let us be nigh,
Which[1] lie blind here and may not see.
Secundus pauper homo.   Lord, let thy mercy to us be sure,
And restore to us our bodily sight.
We know thou may us well recure[2]
With the least point of thy great might.
Jesu.   Your belief has made you for to see,
And delivered you from all mortal pain.
Blessed be all those that believe on me,
And see me not with their bodily eyn.[3]
Here Christ blesses their eyes and they may see.
Primus pauper homo.   Gramercy, Lord of thy great
grace!
I that was blind now may see.
Secundus pauper homo. Here I forsake all my trespass,
And steadfastly will believen on thee.

Passion I: Maundy I[4]

*Here Christ proceeds on foot, with his disciples after him,
Christ weeping upon the city.*
Jesu.   Oh! Jerusalem, woeful is the ordinance[5]
Of the day of thy great persecution!
Thou shalt be destroyed with woeful grievance,
And thy royalty brought to true confusion.
You that in the city have habitation,
They shall curse the time that they were born,
So great adversity and tribulation
Shall fall on them both even and morn.
They that have most childeren soonest shall wail,
And say, 'Alas! what may this mean?'

1 *Who.*   2 *recover.*   3 *eyes.*   4 *n. 55.*   5 *ordering, decree.*

Both meat and drink suddenly shall fail,
The vengeance of God there shall be seen.
The time is coming his woe shall been,
The day of trouble and great grievance,
Both temples and towers they shall down clean.
Oh! city, full woeful is thy ordinance!

Petrus. Lord, where wilt thou keep[1] thy maundy?[1]
I pray thee now let us have knowing,
That we may make ready for thee,
Thee to serve without letting.[2]

Johannes. To provide, Lord, for thy coming,
With all the obedience we can attend,
And make ready for thee in all thing,
Into what place thou wilt us send.

Jesu. Sires, go to Syon and you shall meet
A poor man in simple array,
Bearing water in the street.
Tell him I shall come that way,
Unto him meekly look that you say
That his house I will come till.[3]
He will not ones to you say nay,
But suffer to have all your will.

Petrus. At thy will, Lord, it shall be done,
To seek that place we shall us hie.

Johannes. In all the haste that we may go,
Thy commandment never to deny.
*Here Peter and John go forth, meeting with Simon Leprous
bearing a can with water.*

Petrus. Good man, the prophet, our Lord Jesus,
This night will rest within thy hall.
On message to thee he has sent us,
That for his supper ordain thou shall.

Johannes. Yea! for him and his disciples all
Ordain thou, for his maundy,

[1] *celebrate your last supper (referred to as if Jesus were observing what he is about
to institute).*   [2] *hindrance.*   [3] *to.*

A paschal lamb, whatso befall,
For he will keep his pasch[1] with thee.

Simon. What? will my Lord visit my place,
Blessed be the time of his coming!
I shall ordain within short space
For my good Lordes welcoming.
Sires, walketh in at the beginning,
And see what victuales that I shall take.
I am so glad of this tiding,
I wot never what joy that I may make!

Here the disciples go in with Simon to see the ordinance.[2]

Jesus. (Coming thitherward.) This path is Calsydon[3] by
ghostly[4] ordinance,[4]
Which shall convey us where we shall be.
I know full ready is the purveyance
Of my friendes that loven me.
Continuing[5] in peace now proceed we.
For mannes love this way I take,
With ghostly eye I verily see
That man for man an end must make.

Here the disciples come again to Christ.

Petrus. All ready, Lord, is our ordinance,
As I hope to you pleasing shall be.
Simon has done at your instance:
He is full glad your presence to see.

Johannes. All thing we have, Lord, at our pleasing,
That longeth[6] to your maundy, with full glad cheer.
When he heard tell of your coming,
Great joy in him then did appear.

Here comes Simon out of his house to welcome Christ.

Simon. Gracious Lord, welcome thou be!
Reverence be to thee, both God and man!
My poor house, that thou wilt see,
Which am thy servant as I can.

---

[1] *passover.*   [2] *arrangements.*   [3] *(?).*   [4] *spiritual ordering (?).*   [5] *MS* contewnyng.   [6] *relates.*

Jesu.   There joy of all joyes to thee is sure,
Simon, I know thy true intent.
The bliss of heaven thou shalt recure:[1]
This reward I shall thee grant present.[2]
Here Christ enters into the house with his disciples and eats the
paschal lamb. And in the meantime the council-house before-
said shall suddenly unclose showing the bishops, priests and
judges sitting in their estate like as it were a convocation.[3]

Passion I: Council of Jews II[4]

Annas.   Behold! it is nought, all that we do!
In all our matteres we profit nought!
Well you see which[5] puissance[5] of people draweth him to
For the marveles that he has wrought.
Some other subtlety[6] must be sought,
For in no wise we may not thus him leave:
Then to a shrewd[7] conclusion[7] we shall be brought,
For the Romanes then will us mischieve,[8]
    And take our estate[9] and put us to reproof,[10]
And convey[11] all the people at their owen request,
And thus all the people in him shall believe.
Therefore I pray you, cousin, say what is the best.
Caiphas.   Attend now, sires, to that I shall say:
Unto us all it is most expedient
That one man for the people should die
Than all the people should perish and be shent.[12]
Therefore let us work wisely that we us not repent.
We must needes put on him some false deed.

---

[1] *obtain.*   [2] *now.*   [3] *meeting, assembly (such as might be of clergy, etc.)*   [4] *Only*
suggestion of division in MS is larger capital at Behold.   [5] *what a mighty crowd.*
[6] *device.*   [7] *disastrous end.*   [8] *do injury.*   [9] *office, authority.*   [10] *shame.*
[11] *control.*   [12] *destroyed.*

I say for me I had liefer he were burnt
Than he should us all thus over lead.[1]
   Therefore every man, on[2] his party,[2] help at this need,
And counterfeit[3] all the subtleties[3] that you can.
Now let see who can give best rede[4]
To ordain some destruction for this man.

Gamaliel.   Let us no longer make delation[5]
But do[6] Jesu be[6] taken in handes fast,
And all their followeres to their confusion,
And into a prison do[7] him be[7] cast.
Lay on him iron that will last,
For he has wrought against the right,
And sithin[8] after we shall in haste
Judge him to death with great despite.

Rewfin.   For he has trespassed against our law
Me seemeth this were best judgement,
With wild horse let him be draw,
And after in fire he shall be burnt.

Lyon.   Sires, one thing myself heard him say,
That he was King of Jewes all:
That is enough to do[9] him die,
For treason to Caesar we must it call.
   He said also to persones that I know
That he should and might certain
The great Temple mightily overthrow,
And the third day raisen it again.
   Such matteres the people do constrain[10]
To give credence to his workes all.
In heaven he says shall be his reign,
Both God and man he does him call.

Rewfin.   And all this day we should contrive
What shameful death Jesu should have,
We may not do him too much mischief
The worship of our law to save.

---

[1] *rule, be superior (to).*   [2] *for his part.*   [3] *contrive . . . ruses.*   [4] *advice.*   [5] *delay.*
[6] *cause Jesus to be.*   [7] *cause him to be.*   [8] *then.*   [9] *have.*   [10] *compel; MS* conseyve.

Lyon.   Upon a gibbet let him hangen be!
   This judgement me seemeth it is reason,
   That all the country may him see
   And beware by his great treason.
Rewfin.   Yet one thing, sires, you must espy,
   And make a right subtle[1] ordinance,[1]
   By what meanes you may come him by,
   For he has many followeres at his instance.
Annas.   Sires, thereof we must have advisement,
   And be accorded[2] ere than[2] we go:
   How we shall have him at our intent
   Some way we shall find thereto.

Passion I: Maundy II[3]

Maria Magdalen.   As a cursed creature, closed all in care
   And as a wicked wretch, all wrapped in woe,
   Of bliss was never no bird[4] so bare
   As I myself that here now go.
   Alas! Alas! I shall forfare,[5]
   For those great sinnes that I have do,
   Less[6] than[6] my Lord God some-deal spare
   And his great mercy receive me to.
   Mary Magdalen is my name.
   Now will I go to Christ Jesu,
   For he is Lord of all virtue,
   And for some grace I think to sue,
   For of myself I have great shame.
      Ah! mercy, Lord, and salve my sin,
   Maidenes flower,[7] thou wash me free.
   There was never woman of mannes kin

---

[1] *clever arrangement.*   [2] *agreed before.*   [3] *n. 56. Prosser examines, chap. vii.*
[4] *lady, person.*   [5] *perish.*   [6] *Unless.*   [7] *= Jesus: n. 15.*

So full of sin in no country.
I have been fouled by[1] frith and fen,[1]
And sought sin in many a city:
But[2] thou me borrow,[3] Lord, I shall burn,
With black fiendes ay bound to be.
Wherefore, King of Grace,
With this ointment that is so sweet
Let me anoint thy holy foot,
And for my bales[4] thus win some boot,[5]
And mercy, Lord, for my trespass.

Jesus.   Woman for thy weeping[6] will[6]
Some succour God shall thee send.
Thee to save I have great[7] skill,[7]
For sorrowful heart may sin amend.
All thy prayer I shall fulfil,
To thy good heart I will attend,
And save thee from thy sin so ill,
And from seven deviles I shall thee fend.
Fiendes flee your way!
Wicked spirites, I you conjure,
Flee out of her bodily bower!
In my grace she shall ever flower,
Till death does[8] her to die!

Maria Magdalen.   I thank thee, Lord, of this great grace,
Now these seven fiendes are from me flit.
I shall never forfeit[9] nor do trespass
In word nor deed nor will nor wit.
Now I am brought from the fiendes brace,[10]
In thy great mercy closed and shut,
I shall never return to sinful trace,[11]
That should me damn to hell pit.
I worship thee on knees bare.
Blessed be the time that I hither sought,

---

[1] *up and down the land.*   [2] *Unless.*   [3] *redeem.*   [4] *ills.*   [5] *remedy.*
[6] *tearful intention, desire.*   [7] *good reason.*   [8] *causes.*   [9] *transgress.*   [10] *embrace.*
[11] *course.*

And this ointment that I hither brought,
For now my heart is cleansed from thought
That first was cumbered with care.
Judas.　　　Lord me thinketh thou dost right ill
To let this ointment so spill.
To sell it it were more skill,[1]
And buy meat[2] to[2] poor men.
The box was worth of good money
Three hundred pence, fair and free.
This might have bought meat plenty
To feed our poor kin.
Jesus.　　　Poor men shall abide—
Against the woman thou speakest wrong—
And I pass forth in a tide.[3]
Of mercy is her mourning song.
Here Christ rests and eats a little and says sitting to his
disciples and Mary Magdalen.
Jesus.　　　My heart is right sorry and no wonder is:
To death I shall go and never did trespass!
But yet most grieveth my heart ever of this—
One of my bretheren shall work[4] this menace,[4]
One of you here sitting my[5] treason shall trace,[5]
One of you is busy my death here to dight.[6]
And yet was I never in no sinful place,
Wherefore[7] my death should so shamefully be pight.[8]
Petrus.　　　My dear Lord, I pray thee the truth for to
　　　tell,
Which of us is he that treason shall do?
What traitor is he that his Lord that would sell?
Express his name, Lord, that shall work this woe.
Johannes. If that there be one that would sell so,
Good master, tell us now openly his name.
What traitor is him that from thee that would go,
And with false treason fulfil his great shame?

---

[1] *reasonable.*　　[2] *food for.*　　[3] *while.*　　[4] *execute this threat.*　　[5] *shall*
devise my betrayal.　　[6] *bring about.*　　[7] *on account of which.*　　[8] *fixed.*

Andreas. It is right dreadful such treason to think,
And well more dreadful to work that bad deed.
For that false treason to hell he shall sink,
In endless paines great mischief[1] to lead.[1]

Jacobus major. It is not I, Lord—for doubt[2] I have dread:
This sin to fulfil came never in my mind.
If that I sold thee thy blood for to bleed,
In doing that treason my soul should I shend.[3]

Matheus. Alas! my dear Lord, what man is so wood[4]
For gold or for silver himself so to spill?[5]
He that thee does sell for gold or for other good,
With his great covetise himself he does kill.

Bartholomeus. What man so ever he be of so wicked will,
Dear Lord, among us, tell us his name all out.
He that to[6] him tendeth this deed to fulfil,[6]
For his great treason his soul standeth in doubt.

Philippus. Gold, silver and treasure soon do pass away,
But withouten end ever does last thy grace.
Ah! Lord, who is that will chaffare[7] thee for money?
For he that selleth his Lord, too great is the trespass.

Jacobus minor. That traitor that does this horrible menace,
Both body and soul I hold he is lorn,[8]
Damned to hell pit, far from thy face,
Among all foul fiendes to be rent and torn.

Simon. Too bad a merchant that traitor he is,
And for that money he may mourning make.
Alas! what causes him to sell the King of Bliss?
For his false winning the devil him shall take.

Thomas. For his false treason the fiendes so black
Shall bear his soul deep down into hell pit.
Rest shall he none have but evermore wake,
Burning in hot fire, in prison ever shut.

Thadeus. I wonder right sore who that he should be,
Amongst us all bretheren, that should do this sin.

---

[1] *harm to bear.* [2] *fear.* [3] *destroy.* [4] *crazy.* [5] *kill.* [6] *intends to accomplish this act against him (viz. Jesus) (?).* [7] *trade.* [8] *lost.*

Alas! he is lorn! There may no grace be!
In deep hell dungeon his soul he does[1] pin.[1]
Jesus. In my dish he eateth this[2] treason shall begin.
Woe shall betiden him for his work of dread.
He may be right sorry such riches to win,
And wish himself unborn for that sinful deed.
Judas.   The truth would I know as lief as ye,
And therefore, good sir, the truth thou me tell:
Which of us all here that traitor may be—
Am I that person that thee now shall sell?
Jesus. So sayest thyself—take heed at thy spell.[3]
Thou askest me now here if thou shalt do that treason.
Remember thyself, advise thee right well:
Thou art of great age and wotest what is reason.

Passion I: Betrayal[4]

Here Judas rises privily and goes in the place.
Judas.   Now counterfeited[5] I have a privy treason,
My masteres power for to fell.
I, Judas, shall assay by some encheson[6]
Unto the Jewes him for to sell.
Some money for him yet would I tell.[7]
By privy meanes I shall assay,
My intent I shall fulfil.
No longer I will make delay.
    The princes of priestes now be present—
Unto them now my way I take.
I will go tellen them my intent.
I trow full merry I shall them make.

---

[1] *causes to languish.*   [2] *(who) this.*   [3] *words.*   [4] *n. 56.*   [5] *contrived.*
[6] *excuse.*   [7] *count.*

Money I will none forsake,
And they proffer to my pleasing:
For covetise[1] I will with them wake[1].
And unto my master I shall them bring.
   Hail! princes and priestes that are present,
New tidinges to you I come to tell!
If you will follow my intent,
My master, Jesu, I will you sell,
His intent and purpose for to fell,
For I will no longer followen his law.
Let see what money that I shall tell,
And let Jesu my master be hangen and draw.

Gamaliel.   Now welcome Judas, our owen friend!
Take him in, sires, by the hand!
We shall thee both give and lend,
And in every quarrel by thee stand.

Rewfin.   Judas, what shall we for thy master pay?
Thy silver is ready and[2] we accord.[2]
The payment shall have no delay,
But be laid down here at a word.

Judas.   Let the money here down be laid,
And I shall tell you as I can.
In old termes I have heard said
That money maketh chapman.[3]

Rewfin.   Here is thirty plates of silver bright,
Fast knit within this glove.
And we may have thy master this night,
This shalt thou have and all our love.

Judas.   You are reasonable chapmen to buy and sell:
This bargainy with you now shall I make.
Smite[4] up![4] You shall have all your will,
For money will I none forsake.

Lyon.   Now this bargainy is made, full and fast,
Neither part may it forsake.

[1] *love of money . . . watch.*   [2] *if we agree.*   [3] *the merchant: proverbial—*
Whiting, M629.   [4] *Shake hands.*

But, Judas, thou must tell us in haste
By what meanes we shall him take.

Rewfin.   Yea! there are many that him never saw
Which we will send to him in[1] fere,[1]
Therefore by a token we must him know,
That must be privy betwixt us here.

Lyon.   Yea! beware of that for anything,
For one disciple is like thy master in all[2] parail,[2]
And you go[3] like in all clothing,[3]
So might we of our purpose fail.

Judas.   As for that, sires, have you no doubt!
I shall ordain so you shall not miss.
When that you come him all about,
Take the man that I shall kiss.

I must go to my master again.
Doubt not, sires, this matter is sure enough.

Gamaliel. Farewell! Judas, our friend certain.
Thy labour we shall right well allow.

Judas.   Now will I subtly go seek my master again,
And make good face as[4] I nought knew.[4]
I have him sold to woe and pain:
I trow full sore he shall it rue.

Here Judas goes in subtly whereas he came from.

Annas.   Lo! sires, a part we have of our intent.
For to take Jesu now we must provide
A subtle[5] meinie[5] to be present,
That dare fight and well abide.

Gamaliel.   Ordain each man, on his party,
Cressetes, lanternes and torches light,
And this night to be there ready
With axes, glaives[6] and swordes bright.

Caiphas. No longer then make we tarrying,
But each man to his place him dight,

---

[1] *in a company.*   [2] *every respect.*   [3] *go about in the same clothes.*   [4] *as (if)*
I knew nothing.   [5] *clever company.*   [6] *lances.*

And ordain privily for this thing,
That it be done this same night.
Here the bishops part in the place and each of them takes their
leave by[1] countenance,[1]resorting each man to his place with
their meinie to make ready to take Christ. And then the place
there Christ is in shall suddenly unclose round about, showing
Christ sitting at the table and his disciples each in their degree.

Passion I: Maundy III[2]

Jesu.　　　Bretheren, this lamb[3] that was set us beforn,
That we all have eaten in this night,
It was commanded[3] by my Father to Moses and Aaron,
When they weren with the childeren of Israel in Egypt.
　　And as we with sweet[4] breades[4] have it eat,
And also with the bitter suckling,[5]
And as we take the head with the feet,
So did they in all manner thing.
　　And as we stooden so did they stand,
And their reines they girden verily,
With shoes on their feet and staves in their hand,
And, as we eat it, so did they hastily.
This figure[6] shall cease. Another shall follow thereby,
Which shall be of my body, that am your head,[7]
Which shall be showed to you by a mystery
Of my flesh and blood in form of bread.
　　And with fervent desire of heartes affection
I have entirely desired to keep my maundy
Among you ere[8] than[8] I suffer my passion,
For of this no more together sup shall we.

---

[1] *with gestures.*　　[2] *MS continuous: no gap or title.*　　[3] *Exodus xii, 3–14.*
[4] *unleavened (pieces of?) bread.*　　[5] *clover.*　　[6] *pp. 63–5.*　　[7] *Eph. i, 22–3.*
[8] *before.*

And as the paschal lamb eaten[1] have we[1]
In the old law was used for a sacrifice,
So the new lamb, that shall be sacred[2] by me,
Shall be used for a sacrifice most of[3] price.[3]
*Here shall Jesus take an obley[4] in his hand, looking upward
into heaven to the Father.*

    Wherefore to the Father of Heaven that art eternal
Thanking and honour I yield unto thee,
To whom by[5] the Godhead I am equal,
But by[5] my manhood I am of less degree.
Wherefore I as man worship the deity,
Thanking the Father that thou wilt show this mystery,
And thus through thy might, Father, and blessing of me,
Of this that was bread is made my body.
Here shall he speak again to his disciples.

    Bretheren, by the virtue of these wordes that rehearsed
      be,[6]
This that showeth as bread to[7] your appearance[7]
Is made the very flesh and blood of me,
To the which they that will be saved must give credence,
    And as in the old law[8] it was commanded and precept
To eat this lamb to the destruction of Pharaoh[9] unkind,[9]
So to destroy your ghostly[10] enemy this shall be kept
For your paschal lamb unto the worldes end.

    For this is the very lamb without spot of sin,
Of which John the Baptist did prophesy,
When this prophecy he did begin,
Saying, 'Ecce agnus dei.'[11]
    And how you shall eat this lamb I shall give information
In the same form as the old law does specify,
As I show by ghostly[12] interpretation,[12]
Therefore, to that I shall say, your willes look you reply.
With no bitter bread this bread eat shall be,

[1] *(that) we have eaten.*   [2] *consecrated.*   [3] *precious.*   [4] *mass bread.*   [5] *with
respect to.*   [6] *line omitted but written in margin and at foot of page.*   [7] *as it
appears to you.*   [8] *Exodus xii, 21-7.*   [9] *wicked Pharaoh.*   [10] *spiritual.*
[11] *John i, 29.*   [12] *giving it a spiritual interpretation: I Cor. v, 7-8.*

That is to say, with no bitterness of hate and envy,
But with the sweet bread of love and charity,
Which fortifieth the soul greatly.

 And it should be eaten with the bitter suckling,[1]
That is to mean, if a man be of sinful disposition,
Has led his life here with misliving,
Therefore in his heart he shall have bitter contrition.

 Also the head with the feet eat shall ye:
By the head you shall understand my Godhead,
And by the feet you shall take my humanity;
These twain you shall receive together indeed.

 This immaculate lamb that I shall you give
Is not only the Godhead alone
But both God and man, thus must you believe:
Thus the head with the feet you shall receive each one.

 Of this lamb uneat if ought be leaved, iwis,[2]
It should be cast in the clear fire and burnt:
Which is to mean, if thou understand not all this,
Put thy faith in God, and then thou shalt not be[3] shent.[3]

 The girdle that was commanded their[4] reines to spread[4]
Shall be the girdle of cleanness and chastity:
That is to say, to be continent in word, thought and deed,
And all lecherous living cast[5] you for to flee.[5]

 And the shoes that shall be your feet upon
Is not elles but example of virtuous living
Of your forefatheres you beforn:
With these shoes my steppes you shall be sueing.[6]

 And the staff that in your handes you shall hold
Is not elles but the examples to other men teach:[7]
Hold fast your staves in your handes and be bold
To every creature my preceptes for to preach.

 Also you must eat this paschal lamb hastily:
Of which sentence[8] this is the very intent—[9]

[1] clover. [2] indeed. [3] come to harm. [4] to put about their loins. [5] that you intend to eschew. [6] following. [7] (to) teach. [8] instruction. [9] intention.

At every hour and time you shall be ready
For to fulfil my commandment.
  For, though you live this day, you are not sure
Whether you shall live tomorrow or not;
Therefore hastily every hour do[1] your busy cure[1]
To keep my preceptes and then thar[2] you not doubt.[2]
  Now have I learned you how you shall eat
Your paschal lamb, that is my precious body.
Now I will feed you all with angeles meat:
Wherefore to receive it come forth seriatly.[3]
Petrus.   Lord, for to receive this ghostly sustenance,
  In due form it exceedeth my intelligence.
  For no man of himself may have substance
  To receive it with too much reverence.
    For with more delicious meat, Lord, thou mayst us not
        feed
  Than with thy owen precious body.
  Wherefore what I have trespassed in word, thought or
        deed,
    With bitter contrition, Lord, I ask thee mercy.
When our Lord gives his body to his disciples, he shall say to
each of them, except to Judas:
Jesus.   This is my body, flesh and blood,
  That for thee shall die upon the rood.[4]
When Judas comes last, our Lord shall say to him:
  Judas, art thou advised what thou shalt take?
Judas. Lord, thy body I will not forsake.
Jesu. My body to thee I will not deny.
  Sithin[5] thou wilt presume thereupon,
  It shall be thy damnation verily,
  I give thee warning now beforn.
And after that Judas has received he shall sit there he was,
Christ saying:
  One of you has betrayed me

---

[1] *take the utmost pains.*   [2] *you need have no fear.*   [3] *in order.*   [4] *cross.*
[5] *since.*

That at my board with me has eat.
Better it had him for to have be
Both unborn and unbegot.
Then each disciple shall look on other.
Petrus.　　　Lord, it is not I.
And so all shall say till they come at Judas.
Judas.　　　Is it ought I, Lord?
Jesu. Judas, thou sayst that word.
　　Me thou hast sold that was thy friend.
That thou hast begun, bring to an end.
*Then[1] Judas shall go again to the Jews and, if men will, shall
meet with him and say this speech following, or leave it whether
they will, the devil thus saying:[1]*
Demon.　　　Ah! Ah! Judas, darling mine,
　　Thou art the best to me that ever was bore.
Thou shalt be crowned in hell pain,
And thereof thou shalt be secure for evermore.
　　Thou hast sold thy master and eaten him also:
I would thou couldest bringen him to hell every deal.[2]
But yet I fear he should do there some sorrow and woe,
That all hell shall cry out on me that sel.[3]
　　Speed up thy matter that thou hast begun,
I shall to hell for thee to make ready.
Anon thou shalt come where thou shalt wone,[4]
In fire and stink thou shalt sit me by.
Jesu.　　　Now the Son of God clarified[5] is,
　　And God in him is clarified also.
I am sorry that Judas has lost his bliss.
Which shall turn him[6] to sorrow and woe.
　　But now in the memory of my passion,
To be partable[7] with me in my reign above,
You shall drink my blood with great devotion,
Which shall be shed for mannes love.

---

[1] *Presumably the implication is that it could be a matter of indifference whether
these devilish words are put in the mouth of the Jews or the devil.*　　[2] *bit.*　　[3] *occasion.*　　[4] *dwell.*　　[5] *glorified.*　　[6] *(for) him.*　　[7] *capable of participating.*

Taketh this chalice of the new testament,
And keepeth this ever in your mind.
As often as you do this with true intent
It shall defend you from the fiend.
Then shall the disciples come and take the blood.

This is my blood that for mannes sin
Out of my heart it shall run.
The disciples shall set [1]them again there[1] they were.

Taketh heed now bretheren what I have do:
With my flesh and blood I have you fed.
For mannes love I may do no mo[2]
Than for love of man to be dead.

Wherefore, Peter, and you everyone,
If you love me, feed my sheep.
That for fault[3] of teaching they go not wrong,
But ever to them taketh good keep.[4]

Giveth them my body as I have to you,
Which shall be sacred[5] by my word.
And ever I shall thus abide with you.
Unto the end of the werd.[6]

Whoso eateth my body and drinketh my blood,
Whole God and man he shall me take.
It shall him defend from the devil wood,[7]
And at his death I shall him not forsake.

And whoso not eat my body nor drink my blood,
Life in him is never a deal.
Keep well this in mind for your good,
And every man save himself well.
Here Jesus takes a basin with water, and towel girt about
him, and falls before Peter on his one knee.

Jesus.   Another example I shall you show
How you shall live in charity.
Sit here down at wordes few,
And what I do you suffer me.

---

[1] *sit down again where.*   [2] *more.*   [3] *default*   [4] *care.*   [5] *consecrated.*
[6] *world.*   [7] *mad.*

*Here he takes the basin and the towel and does as the rubric
says before.*

Petrus.   Lord what wilt thou with me do?
This service of thee I will forsake.[1]
To wash my feet thou shalt not so—
I am not worthy it of thee to take.

Jesu.   Peter, and[2] thou forsake my service all
The which to you that I shall do,
No part with me have thou shall,
And never come my bliss unto.

Petrus. That part, Lord, we will not forgo.
We shall obey his commandment.
Wash head and hand, we pray thee so—
We will do after thy intent.

*Here Jesus washes his disciples' feet by and by, and wipes them
and kisses them meekly, and sithin[3] sets him down.*

Jesu.   Friendes, this washing shall now prevail.
Your Lord and master you do me call,
And so I am withouten fail,
Yet I have washed you all.
A memory of this have you shall,
That each of you shall do to other:
With humble heart submit equal,
As each of you were otheres brother.
    Nothing, sires, so well pleaseth me,
Nor no life that man may lead,
As they that liven in charity:
In heaven I shall reward their meed.
The day is come I must proceed
For to fulfil the prophecy.
This night for me you shall have dread,
When number of people shall on me cry.
    For the prophetes spoke of me,
And saiden of death that I should take,

[1] *forego.*   [2] *if.*   [3] *after.*

From which death I will not flee,
But for mannes sin amendes make.
    This night from you be led I shall,
And you for fear from me shall flee;
Not ones[1] dare speak when I you call,
And some of you forsake me.
For you shall I die and rise again:
On the third day you shall me see,
Before you all walking plain,
In the land of Galilee.

Petrus.   Lord I will thee never forsake,
Nor for no periles from thee flee:
I will rather my death take
Than ones, Lord, forsake thee.

Jesu.   Peter, thou[2] [sayst] further than thou dost know.
As for that promise look thou not make,
For ere the cock has twies[3] crow
Thries thou shalt me forsake.
    But, all my friendes that are me[4] dear,
Let us go, the time draweth nigh:
We may no longer abiden here,
For I must walk to Bethany.
The time is come, the day draweth near,
Unto my death I must in haste.
Now, Peter, make all thy fellowes cheer,
My flesh for fear is quaking fast.

Passion I: Agony at Olivet[5]

*Here Jesus goes to Bethany-ward and his disciples following
with sad countenance.*
    Now, my dear friendes and bretheren each one,
Remember the wordes that I shall say:

[1] *once.*   [2] *MS may be read either* yn *or* þu.   [3] *twice.*   [4] *(to) me.*   [5] *n. 57.*

The time is come that I must gon
For to fulfil the prophecy,
That is said of me that I shall die,
The fiendes power from you to flem:[1]
Which death I will not deny,
Mannes soul, my spouse,[2] for to redeem.
    The oil[3] of mercy is granted plain
By this journey that I shall take:
By my Father I am sent certain
Betwixt God and man an end to make.
Man for my brother may I not forsake,
Nor show him unkindness by no way:
In paines for him my body shall shake,
And for love of man man shall die.

Here Jesus and his disciples go toward the Mount of Olivet.
And when he comes a little there beside in a place like to a park,
he bids his disciples abide him there, and says to Peter ere he
goes:

    Peter, with thy fellowes here shalt thou abide,
And watch till I come again.
I must make my prayer here you beside:
My flesh quaketh sore for fear and pain.
Petrus. Lord, thy request does me constrain:
In this place I shall abide still,
Not remove till that thou comest again,
In confirming Lord of thy will.

Here Jesus goes to Olivet and sets him down on his knees and
prays to his Father:

Jesu.   Oh! Father, Father, for my sake,
This great passion thou take from me,
Which[4] are[4] ordained that I shall take
If mannes soul saved may be.
And if it behove, Father, for me
To save mannes soul that should[5] spill,[5]

---

[1] *drive out.*   [2] *n. 58.*   [3] *n. 59.*   [4] *(?): passion treated as a plural (?).*
[5] *would be bound to die.*

I am ready in each degree
The will of thee for to fulfil.
Here Jesus goes to his disciples and finds them sleeping.
 Peter! Peter! thou sleepest fast.
Awake thy fellowes, and sleep no more!
Of my death you are not aghast,
You take your rest and I pain sore.
*Here Christ goes again the second time to Olivet and says
kneeling:*
 Father in Heaven, I beseech thee,
Remove my paines by thy great grace,
And let me from this death flee,
As I did never no trespass.
The water and blood out of my face
Distilleth for paines that I shall take;
My flesh quaketh in fearful case,
As though the jointes asunder should shake.
*Here Jesus goes again to his disciples and finds them asleep.
Jesus thus saying, letting them lie:*
 Father, the third time I come again,
Fully my errand for to speed:
Deliver me, Father, from this pain,
Which is reduced[1] with full great dread.
Unto thy Son, Father, take heed!
Thou wotest I did never deed but good.
It is not for me this pain I lead,
But for man I sweat both water and blood.
*Here an angel[2] descends to Jesus and brings to him a chalice
with a host therein.*
Angelus. Hail! both God and man indeed.
The Father has sent thee this present:
He bade that thou shouldest not dread,
But fulfil his intent,
As the Parliament of Heaven has meant
That mannes soul shall now redeemed be,

---

[1] *brought back.* [2] *n. 60.*

From heaven to earth, Lord, thou wert sent,
That[1] deed appendeth unto thee.[1]
   This chalice is thy blood, this bread is thy body,
For[2] mannes sin ever offered shall be
To the Father of Heaven that is almighty,
Thy disciples and all priesthood shall offer fore[3] thee.
Here the angel ascends again suddenly.

Jesu. Father, thy will fulfilled shall be,
It[4] is nought to say against the case.[4]
I shall fulfil the prophecy,
And suffer death for mannes trespass.
Here goes Christ again to his disciples and finds them sleeping still.
Awake! Peter, thy rest is full long.
Of sleep thou wilt make no delay.
Judas is ready with people strong,
And does his part me to betray.
Rise up! sires, I you pray.
Unclose your eyne[5] for my sake.
We shall walk into the way
And see them come that shall me take.
   Peter, when thou seest I am forsake
Among my friendes and stand alone,
All the cheer that thou canst make
Give to thy bretheren every one.

Passion I: Taking of Jesus[6]

Here Jesus with his disciples goes into the place. And there shall come in a ten persons, well beseen[7] in white harness and briganders,[7] and some disguised in other garments, with

---

[1] *i.e.: So that it is right for you to die (?).*   [2] *(Which) for.*   [3] *before (?), for (?).*
[4] *There is no point in disputing it.*   [5] *eyes.*   [6] *MS continuous without gap or title.*
[7] *equipped in white gear and body armour.*

swords, glaives,[1] and other strange weapons as cressetts with
fire and lanterns and torches light. And Judas, foremost of all,
conveying[2] them to Jesu by countenance.[3]

Jesu.   Sires, in your way you have great haste
To seek him that will not flee.
Of you I am right nought aghast.
Tell me, sires, whom seek ye?

Lyon.   Whom we seek here I tell thee now:
A traitor is[4] worthy to suffer death.
We know he is here among you—
His name is Jesus of Nazareth.

Jesu.   Sires, I am here that will not flee.
Do to me all that you can.
Forsooth I tell you I am he,
Jesus of Nazareth, that same man.

Here all the Jews fall suddenly to the earth when they hear
Christ speak, and when [he] bids them rise they rise.

    Arise! sires. Whom seek you? Fast have you gone!
Is ought your coming hither for me?
I stand before you here each one
That you may me both know and see.

Rewfin.   Jesus of Nazareth we seek,
And[5] we might him here espy.

Jesu. I told you now with wordes meek
Before you all that it was I.

Judas.   Welcome! Jesu, my master dear.
I have thee sought in many a place.
I am full glad I find thee here,
For I wist never where thou was.

Here Judas kisses Jesus. And anon all the Jews come about
him and lay hands on him and pull him as[6] they were wode,[6]
and make on him a great cry all at once.

Petrus.   I draw my sword now this sel.[7]
Shall I smite, master, fain would I wit?

---

[1] *lances.*   [2] *leading.*   [3] *gestures.*   [4] *(who) is.*   [5] *If.*   [6] *as (if) . . . demented.*
[7] *opportune moment.*

And forthwith he smites off Malcheus' ear. And he cries Help!
my ear, my ear! *And Christ blesses it and 'tis whole.*

Jesus. Put thy sword in thy sheath, fair and well,
    For he that smites with sword, with sword shall be smit.
      Ah! Judas, this treason counterfeited[1] hast thou,
    And that thou shalt full sore repent.
    Thou haddest been better have been unborn now,
    Thy body and soul thou hast shent.[2]

Gamaliel.   Lo! Jesus, thou mayst not the case refuse:
    Both treason and heresy in thee is found.
    Study now fast on thy excuse,
    Whiles[3] that thou gost in cordes bound.
    Thou callest thee King of this world round—
    Now let me see thy great power,
    And save thyself here, whole and sound,
    And bring thee out of this danger.

Lyon.   Bring forth this traitor, spare him not!
    Unto Caiphas thy judge we shall thee lead.
    In many a place we have thee sought,
    And to thy workes take good heed.

Rewfin.   Come on, Jesus, and follow me,
    I am full glad that I thee have.
    Thou shalt be hangen upon a tree—
    A million of gold shall thee not save!

Lyon.   Let me lay hand on him in[4] hie![4]
    Unto his death I shall him bring.
    Show forth thy witch-craft and necromancy—
    What helpeth thee now all thy false working?

Jesu.   Friendes, take heed—you do unright
    So unkindly with cordes to bind me here,
    And thus to fall on me by night,
    As though I were a[5] thiefes fere.[5]
    Many time before you I did appear:
    Within the Temple seen me you have,

---

[1] *contrived.*   [2] *destroyed.*   [3] *while.*   [4] *quickly.*   [5] *the accomplice of a thief.*

The lawes of God to teach and lere[1]
To them that will their soules save.
 Why did you not me disprove,[2]
And heard me preach both loud and low?
But now as woodmen[3] you gin to rave,
And do thing that you not know.
Gamaliel.   Sires, I charge you, not one word more this
   night,
But unto Caiphas in haste look you him lead.
Have him forth with great despite,[4]
And to his wordes take you no heed.
*Here the Jews lead Christ out of the place with great cry and
noise, some drawing Christ forward and some backward,
and so leading forth with their weapons aloft and lights
burning. And, in the meantime, Mary Magdalen shall run to
our Lady and tell her of our Lord's taking.*
Maria Magdalen.   Oh! immaculate Mother, of all women
   most meek,
Oh! devoutest, in holy meditation ever abiding,
The cause, Lady, that I to your person seek
Is to witen[5] if you hearen any tiding
 Of your sweet son and my reverend Lord, Jesu,
That was your daily solace, your ghostly consolation.
Maria Virgo.   I would you should tell me, Magdalen,
   and[6] you knew,
For to hear of him it is all my affection.
Maria Magdalen. I would fain tell, Lady, and I might for
   weeping.
Forsooth, Lady, to the Jewes he is sold.
With cordes they have him bound and have him in
   keeping;
They him beaty[7] spiteously[7] and have him fast in hold.
Maria Virgo. Ah! Ah! Ah! how my heart is cold!
Ah! heart hard as stone, how mayst thou last,

---

[1] *expound.*   [2] *refute.*   [3] *madmen.*   [4] *contempt, humiliation.*   [5] *know.*
[6] *if.*   [7] *beat scornfully.*

When these sorrowful tidinges are thee told?
So would to God, heart, that thou mightest burst.
　　Ah! Jesu, Jesu, Jesu, Jesu,
Why should you suffer this tribulation and adversity?
How may they find in their heartes you to pursue,
That never trespassed in no[1] manner degree?[1]
For never thing but that was good thought ye.
Wherefore then should you suffer this great pain?
I suppose verily it is for the trespass of me!
And[2] I wist that, my heart should cleave in twain.
　　For these languores[3] may I [not] sustain,
The sword of sorrow has so thirled[4] my mind.[4]
Alas! what may I do? Alas! what may I sayn?
These pronges my heart asunder they do rend.
　　Oh! Father of Heaven, where are all thy behestes[5]
That thou promisest me when a mother thou me made?
Thy blessed Son I bare betwixt twain beastes,
And now the bright colour of his face does fade.
　　Ah! good Father, why wouldest that thy owen dear
　　　Son shall suffer all this?
And did he never against thy precept, but ever was
　　obedient,
And to every creature most pitiful, most gentle and
　　benign, iwis,[6]
And now for all these kindnesses is now most shameful
　　shent.[7]
　　Why wilt thou, gracious Father, that it shall be so?
May man not elles be saved by no other kind?[8]
Yet, Lord Father, then that shall comfort my woe,
When man is saved by my child and brought to a good
　　end.
　　Now, dear son, since thou hast ever been so full of
　　　mercy,
That wilt not spare thyself for the love thou hast to man,

---

[1] *any kind of way.*　　[2] *If.*　　[3] *sorrows.*　　[4] *pierced my heart.*　　[5] *promises.*
[6] *indeed.*　　[7] *blamed.*　　[8] *mode.*

On all mankind now have thou pity,
And also think on thy mother, that heavy woman.

Procession of the Saints[1]
Omitted

Passion II: Prologue[2]

What time that procession is entered into the place, and the Herod taken his scaffold, and Pilate and Annas and Caiphas their scaffolds, also then come there an expositor in doctor's weed[3] thus saying:

Contemplatio. Sovereignes and friendes, you[4] may all be gret with good![4]

Grace, love and charity ever be you among!

The maidenes son preserve you, that for man died on rood,[5]

He that is one God in persones three defend you from your fon.[6]

By the leave and sufferance of almighty God

We intenden to proceed the matter that we left the last year,

Wherefore we beseech you that your willes be good,

To keep the Passion in your mind that shall be showed here.

The last year we showed here how our Lord for love of man

Came to the city of Jerusalem, meekly his death to take,

---

[1] *n. 61.*   [2] *n. 61.*   [3] *dress.*   [4] *may you all be greeted (? great, i.e. 'fat'?) with good things.*   [5] *cross.*   [6] *foes.*

And how he made his maundy, his body giving then
To his apostles ever with us to abiden for mannes sake.
    In that maundy he was betrayed of Judas that him sold
To the Jewes for thirty plates[1] to deliver him that night.
With swordes and glaives[2] to Jesu they came with the
    traitor bold,
And took him amongst his apostles about midnight.
    Now would we proceed how he was brought then
Before Annas and Caiphas, and sith[3] before Pilate.
And so forth in his Passion, how meekly he took it for man,
Beseeching you for meed[4] of your soules[4] to take good
    heed thereat.

Passion II: Jesus before Herod[5]

Here the Herod shall show himself and speak.
Rex Herodes.   Now cease of your talking and giveth lordly
    audience!
Not one word, I charge you, that are here present!
None so hardy to presume, in my high presence,
To unloose his lippes against my intent!
I am Herod, of Jewes King most reverend,
The lawes of Mahound[6] my power shall fortify.[6]
Reverence to that lord, of grace most excellent!
For by his power all thing does multiply.
    If any Christian is so hardy his faith to deny,
Or ones to err against his law,
On gibbetes with chaines I shall hangen him high,
And with wild horse those traitores shall I draw.
To kill a thousand Christian I give[7] not an haw![7]
To see them hangen or burnt to me is very pleasance,

---

[1] *pieces of silver or gold.*   [2] *lances.*   [3] *after.*   [4] *your souls' benefit.*   [5] *n. 62.*
[6] *(the false prophet) Mohammed . . . support.*   [7] *don't care a straw.*

To driven them into dungeones, dragones[1] to gnaw,
And to rend their flesh and bones unto their sustenance.
  John the Baptist christened Christ, and so he did many
    one.
Therefore myself did him[2] bring o daw.[2]
It is I that did him kill, I tell you every one,
For, and[3] he had gone forth, he should have destroyed
    our law.
Whereas[4] Christian appeareth to me is great grievance:[4]
It paineth my heart of those traitores to hear,
For the lawes of Mahound I have in governance,
The which I will keep—that lord has no peer!
  For he is god most prudent.
Now I charge you, my lordes that are here,
If any Christian dogges here do appear,
Bring those traitores to my high power,
And they shall have soon judgement.

Primus miles.[5]   My sovereign lord, highest of excellence,
  In[6] you all judgement is terminable.[6]
All Christian dogges that do not their diligence,
You put them to paines that are inportable.[7]

Secundus miles. Nothing in you may be more commendable
  As to destroy those traitores that err
Against our lawes, that are most profitable:
By righteousness, that law you must proffer.[8]

Rex Herodes.   Now by glorious Mahound, my sovereign
  saviour,
These promises I make as I am true knight.
Those that exceed his lawes, by any error,
To the most shamefullest death I shall them dight.
But one thing is sore in my great delight:
There is one, Jesus of Nazareth, as men me telleth—
Of that man I desire to have a sight,
For with many great wonderes our law he felleth.[9]

---

[1] (*for*) *dragons.*   [2] *deprive him of his life.*   [3] *if.*   [4] *It greatly troubles me wherever a Christian appears.*   [5] *First soldier.*   [6] *All judgement derives from you (?).*   [7] *unbearable.*   [8] ? = preffer ? = *promote, advance.*   [9] *overthrows.*

The Son of God himself he calleth,
And King of Jewes he says is he,
And many wonderes of him befalleth:
My heart desireth him for to see.
Sires, if that he come in this country,
With our jurisdiction look you espy,
And anon that he be brought unto me,
And the truth myself then shall try.

Primus miles.   Tomorrow my journey I shall begin
To seek Jesus with my due diligence.
If he come your province within
He shall not escape your high presence.

Secundus miles.   My sovereign, this my counsel, that you
shall take
A man that is both wise and strong
Through all Galilee a search to make
If Jesu be entered your people among,
Correct his deedes that are done wrong,
For his body is under your baily,[1]
As men talken them among
That he was born in Galilee.

Rex Herodes.   Then of these matteres, sires, take heed.
For a while I will me rest:
Appetite requireth me so indeed,
And physic telleth me it is the best.

Passion II: before Annas and Caiphas[2]

Here shall a messenger come into the place, running and crying, 'Tidings, tidings,' and so round about the place, 'Jesus of Nazareth is taken, Jesus of Nazareth is taken.' And forthwith hailing the princes:

Messenger.   All hail! my lordes, princes of priestes,

---

[1] *jurisdiction.*   [2] *MS continuous.*

Sir Caiphas and Sir Annas, lordes of the law,
Tidinges I bring you, receive them in your breastes:
Jesus of Nazareth is take, thereof you may be faw.[1]
    He shall be brought hither to you anon,
I tell you truly, with a great rout.[2]
When he was take I was them among,
And there was I near to catched[3] a clout!
    Malcus bore a lantern and put[4] him in press[4]—
Anon he had a touch and off went his ear!
Jesus bade his disciple put up his sword and cease,
And set Malcus ear again as whole as it was ere.[5]
    So[6] may I the![6] me thought it was a strange sight.
When we came first to him he came us[7] again,[7]
And asked whom we sought that time of night.
We said, 'Jesus of Nazareth, we would have him fain.'
    And he said, 'It is I that am here in your sight.'
With that word we over-thrown backward every one,
And some on their backes lying upright,[8]
But standing upon foot manly there was not one.
    Christ stood on his feet, as meek as a lamb,
And we lay still like dead men, till he bade us rise.
When we were up, fast handes we laid him upon,
But yet me thought I was not pleased with the new
    guise.[9]
    Therefore taketh now your counsel, and advise you
right well,
And be right[10] ware that he make you not amat,[10]
For by my thrift, I dare swearen at[11] this sell,[11]
You shall find him a strange wat![12]
Here bring they Jesus before Annas and Caiphas, and one
shall say thus:
    Lo! lo! lordes, here is the man
That you sent us for.

---

[1] *glad.*   [2] *crowd.*   [3] *(one who) received.*   [4] *joined the mob.*   [5] *before.*
[6] *So help me!*   [7] *towards us.*   [8] *face upwards.*   [9] *way of proceeding.*   [10] *on*
your guard that he doesn't overpower you.   [11] *on this occasion.*   [12] *chap.*

Annas. Therefore we can[1] you thank,[1] then,
    And reward you shall have the more.
        Jesus, thou art welcome hither to our presence.
    Full often-times we have thee[2] busily do sought.[2]
    We paid to thy disciple for thee thirty pence,
    And as an oxe or an horse we truly thee bought.
        Therefore now art ours, as thou standest us before.
    Say why thou hast troubled us and subverted our law.
    Thou hast oft concluded[3] us, and so thou hast done more:
    Wherefore it were full needful to bring[4] thee a daw.[4]
Caiphas.   What are thy disciples that followen thee
        about?
    And what is thy doctrine that thou dost preach?
    Tell me now somewhat, and bring us out of doubt,
    That we may to other men thy preaching forth teach.
Jesus.   All times that I have preached, open it was done,
    In the Synagogue or in the Temple, where that all Jewes
        come.
    Ask them what I have said and also what I have done:
    They can tell thee my wordes. Ask them everyone.
Primus judeus.[5]   What, thou fellow! To whom speakest
        thou?
    Shalt thou so speak to a bishop?
    Thou shalt have on the cheek—I make avow—
    And yet thereto a knock.
    Here he shall smite Jesus on the cheek.
Jesus.   If I have said amiss
    Thereof witness thou mayst bear,
    And if I have said but well in this
    Thou dost amiss me to dere.[6]
Annas.   Sires, taketh heed now to this man
    That he destroy not our law,
    And bring you witness against him that you can,
    So that he may be brought[7] of daw.[7]

---

[1] *thank you.*   [2] *had you thoroughly searched for.*   [3] *confuted.*   [4] *put an end to*
you.   [5] *First Jew.*   [6] *harm.*   [7] *put to death.*

Primus doctor.   Sir, this I heard him with his owen
    mouth sayn:
'Breaketh down this temple without delay,
And I shall setten it up again
As whole as it was by the third day.'
Secundus doctor.   Yea! sir, and I heard him say, also,
That he was the Son of God,
And yet many a fool weeneth[1] so,
I durst[2] lay thereon my hood.[2]
Tertius doctor.   Yea! yea! and I heard him preach much
    thing,
And against our law every deal,[3]
Of which it were long to make reckoning,
To tellen all at this seel.[4]
Caiphas.   What sayst now, Jesus, why answerest not?
Hearest not what is said against thee?
Speak! man, speak! Speak thou fop,
Hast thou scorn to speak to me?
Hearest[5] not in how many thinges they thee accuse?[5]
    Now I charge thee and conjure by the sun and the moon
That thou tell us and[6] thou be Godes Son.
Jesus.   Godes Son I am, I say not nay to thee,
And that you all shall see at Doomes-day
When the Son shall come in great power and majesty
And deem[7] the quick and dead, as I thee say.
Caiphas.   Ah! out! out! alas, what is this?
Heareth you not how he blasphemeth God?
What needeth us to have more witness?
Here you have heard all his owen word—
    Think you not he is worthy to die?
Et clamabunt omnes:[8]
Yes, yes, yes, all we say, he is worthy to die, yea, yea,
    yea!
Annas.   Taketh him to you and beateth him some-deal[9]

---

[1] *thinks.*   [2] *dare wager my hat on it.*   [3] *bit.*   [4] *time.*   [5] *extra-metrica*
line.   [6] *if.*   [7] *judge.*   [8] *And they shall all cry.*   [9] *somewhat.*

For his blaspheming at this seel.[1]
Here they shall beat Jesus about the head and the body, and spit in his face, and pull him down, and set him on a stool, and cast a cloth over his face.
Primus judeus.[2]   Ah! fellowes, beware what you do to this man,
For he prophesy well can.
Secundus judeus.   That shall be assayed by this bat![3]
What! thou Jesus, who gave thee that?
Et percutiet super caput.[4]
Tertius judeus.   Whar! whar!—now will I
Witen[5] how he can prophesy!
Who was that?
Quartus judeus.   Ah! and now will I a new game begin,
That we may play at, all that are herein:
'Wheel[6] and pill, wheel and pill,[6]
Cometh to halle[7] whoso will'—
Who was that?

Passion II: Peter's denial[8]

Here shall the woman come to Jews and say:
Prima ancilla.[9]   What! sires, how take you on with this man?
See you not one of his disciples, how he beholdeth you then?
Here shall the other woman say to Peter:
Secunda ancilla.   Ah! good man, me seemeth by thee
That thou one of his disciples should be.
Petrus.   Ah! woman, I saw[10] never ere this man,[10]

---

[1] *time.*   [2] *First Jew.*   [3] *blow.*   [4] *And he shall strike him on the head.*
[5] *Learn.*   [6] *Turn and tear off the hair (or skin).*   [7] *haul (?): n. 63.*   [8] *MS continuous.*   [9] *First maid servant.*   [10] *never saw this man before.*

Since that this world first began.
Et cantabit gallus.[1]
Prima ancilla.   What? Thou mayst not say nay! Thou
   art one of his men.
By thy face well we may thee ken.
Petrus.   Woman, thou sayst amiss of me:
I know him not, so[2] may I the.[2]
Primus judeus.   Ah! fellow mine, well met!
   For my cousines[3] ear thou off smit[3]
      When we thy master in the yard took,
   Then all thy fellowes him forsook.
      And now thou mayst not him forsake,
   For thou art of Galilee I undertake.
Petrus.   Sir, I know him not, by him that made me!
   And[4] you will me believe for an oath,
   I take record of all this company
   That I say to you is sooth.
Et cantabit gallus.
And then Jesus shall look on Peter, and Peter shall weep.
And then he shall go out and say:
   Ah! welaway! welaway! false heart, why wilt thou not
      burst,
Since thy master so cowardly thou hast forsake?
Alas! where shall I now on earth rest,
Till he of his mercy to grace will me take?
I have forsook my master and my Lord, Jesu,
Three times, as he told me that I should do the same.
Wherefore I may not have sorrow enough,
I, sinful creature, am so much to blame.
   When I heard the cock crowen, he cast on me a look,
As who says, 'Bethink thee what I said before!'
Alas! the time that I ever him forsook,
And so will I thinken from hence evermore.

---

[1] *And the cock shall crow.*   [2] *so help me.*   [3] *mate's . . . cut.*   [4] *If.*

Passion II: before Pilate[1]

Caiphas. Messenger! messenger!

Messenger. Here! lord, here!

Caiphas. Messenger, to Pilate in haste thou shalt gon,
  And say him[2] we commend us in word and in deed,
  And pray him that he be at the moot-hall[3] anon,
  For we have a great matter that he must needes speed.[4]
    In haste now go thy way,
    And look thou tarry not.

Messenger. It shall be done, lord, by this day.
  I am as wight[5] as thought!
Here Pilate sits in his scaffold and the messenger kneels to him.
    All hail! sir Pilate, that seemly is to see,
  Prince of all this jure,[6] and keeper of the law!
  My lord bishop, Caiphas, commended him to thee,
  And prayed thee to be at the moot-hall by the day daw.[7]

Pilate. Go thy way! pretty messenger, and commend
    me also.
  I shall be there in haste, and so thou mayst say.
  By the hour of prime[8] I shall comen them to:
  I tarry no longer, nor make no delay.
Here the messenger comes again and brings an answer.

Messenger.   All hail! my lordes and bishopes and princes
    of the law!
  Sir Pilate commendeth him to you and bade me to you say
  He will be at the moot-hall in haste, soon after the day
    daw,
  He would you should be there by prime without longer
    delay.

---

[1] *n. 64.* [2] *(to) him.* [3] *meeting-hall.* [4] *further.* [5] *swift.* [6] *Jewry (?),*
jurisdiction (?). [7] *dawn.* [8] *first division of the day and name of service at*
that time.

Caiphas.   Now well may thou fare, my good page!
Take thou this for thy message.
Here enters Judas unto the Jews.
Judas.   I, Judas, have sinned and treason have done,
For I have betrayed this rightful[1] blood.
Here is your money again, all and some,
For sorrow and thought I am wax[2] wood.[2]
Annas.   What is that to us? Advise thee, now!
Thou didest with us covenant make:
Thou soldest him us, as horse or cow—
Therefore thy owen deedes thou must take.
Then Judas casts down the money and goes and hangs himself.
Caiphas.   Now, sires, the night is passed, the day is come,
It were time this man had his judgement.
And Pilate abideth in the moot-hall alone,
Till we should this man present.
     And therefore go we now forth with him in haste.
Primus judeus.[3] It shall be done, and that in short space!
Secundus judeus. Yea! but look if he is bound right well and
     fast!
Tertius judeus. He is safe enough! Go we right a good pace!
Here they lead Jesu about the place till they come to the hall.
Caiphas.   Sir Pilate, taketh heed to this thing!
Jesus we have before thee brought
Which our law does down bring,
And mickle shame he has us wrought.
Annas.   From this city into the land of Galilee
He has brought our lawes near into confusion.
With his craftes, wrought by necromancy,
Showeth[4] to the people by false simulation.[4]
Primus doctor.   Yea! yet, sir, another, and worst of all—
Against Caesar, our Emperor, that is so free,[5]
'King of Jewes' he does him call,
So our Emperores power nought should be.

---

[1] *righteous.*   [2] *grown mad.*   [3] *First Jew.*   [4] *(He) shows (?) . . . by deceptive*
tricks.   [5] *excellent.*

CCP—T

289

Secundus doctor.   Sir Pilate, we cannot tell half the blame
  That Jesus in our country has wrought.
  Therefore we charge thee, in the Emperores name,
  That he to the death in haste be brought.
Pilate.   What sayst to these complaintes, Jesu?
  These people have thee sore accused,
  Because thou bringest up lawes new
  That in our days were not used.
Jesus.   Of[1] their accusing me rueth not,[1]
  So[2] that[2] they hurt not their soules nor none[3] mo.[3]
  I have not yet found that[4] I have sought:
  For my Fatheres will forth must I go.
Pilate. Jesus, by this then, I trow thou art a king,
  And the Son of God thou art, also,
  Lord of earth and of all thing—
  Tell me the truth, if it be so.
Jesus.   In heaven is knowen my Fatheres intent,
  And in this world I was born:
  By my Father I was hither sent
  For to seek that was forlorn.[5]
    All that me hearen and in me believen,
  And keepen their faith steadfastly,
  Though they weren dead I shall them recuren,[6]
  And shall them bring to bliss endlessly.
Pilate. Lo! sires, now you have heard this man, how think
    ye?
  Think you not all, by your reason,
  But as he says it may well be?
  And that should be by[7] this incheson:[7]
    I find in him none objection[8]
  Of error, nor treason, nor of no manner guilt.
  The[9] law will, in no conclusion,
  Without default he should be spilt.[9]

---

[1] *I am not concerned about their accusations.*   [2] *So long as.*   [3] *anyone else's (?).*
[4] *i.e. his crucifixion.*   [5] *utterly lost.*   [6] *recover.*   [7] *for this reason.*   [8] *impediment (?), obstacle (?).*   [9] *The law will not, on any reckoning, have him killed without an offence.*

Primus doctor.   Sir Pilate, the law resteth in thee,
  And we know verily his great trespass:
  To the Emperor this matter told shall be
  If thou let Jesus thus from thee pass.
Pilate.   Sires, then tell me one thing:
  What shall be his accusing?
Annas.   Sir, we tell thee all together,
  For his evil workes we brought him hither,
    And, if he had not an evil-doer be,
  We should not have brought him to thee.
Pilate.   Taketh him, then, after[1] your saw,[1]
  And deemeth[2] him after your law.
Caiphas.   It is not lawful to us, you seen,
  No[3] manner[3] man for to slayn:
    The cause why we bring him to thee,
  That he should not our king be.
    Well thou knowest king we have none,
  But our Emperor alone.
Pilate.   Jesu, thou art King of Jewry.
Jesus. So thou sayst now to me.
Pilate.   Tell me, then,
  Where is thy kingdom?
Jesus.   My kingdom is not in this world,
  I tell thee at one word.
    If my kingdom here had be
  I should not have been delivered to thee.
Pilate.   Sires, advise you as you can,
  I can find no default in this man.
Annas.   Sir, here is a great record, take heed thereto!
  And knowing great mischief in this man,
  And not only in one day or two—
  It is many yeares since he began!
  We can tell the time, where and when,
  That many a thousand turned has he,
  As all this people record well can,

---

[1] *according to, in compliance with, what you have said.*   [2] *judge.*   [3] *Any kind of.*

From hence into the land of Galilee.
Et clamabunt:[1] Yea! yea! yea!
Pilate.   Sires, of one thing, then, give me relation,
If Jesus were out[2] born in the land of Galilee,
For we have no power nor no jurisdiction
Of no man of that country.
Therefore the truth you tell me
And another way I shall provide:
If Jesus was born in that country
The judgement of Herod he must abide.
Caiphas.   Sir, as I am to the law truly sworn,
To tell the truth I have no fear.
In Galilee I know that he was born:
I can tell in what place and where.
Against this no man may answer,
For he was born in Bethlehem Judee,
And this you know now all, and have done here,
That it stands in the land of Galilee.
Pilate.   Well, sires, since that I know that it is so,
The truth of this I must needes see.
I understand right now what is to do:
The judgement of Jesu lies not to[3] me!
Herod is King of that country,
To judge that region in length and in bread:[4]
The jurisdiction of Jesu now have must he.
Therefore Jesu in haste to him you lead,
    In all the haste that you may speed,
Lead him to the Herod, anon[5] present[5],
And say, I commend me with word and deed,
And Jesu to him that I have sent.
Primus doctor.   This errand in haste sped shall be,
In all the haste that we can do.
We shall not tarry in no degree,
Till the Herodes presence we come to.

---

[1] *And they shall cry.*   [2] *ought (?) = at all (?) = perhaps (?).*   [3] *with.*
[4] *breadth.*   [5] *immediately.*

292

Passion II: before Herod II[1]

Here they take Jesu and lead him in great haste to the Herod.
And the Herodes scaffold shall unclose showing Herod in
estate, all the Jews kneeling except Annas and Caiphas. They
shall stand, etc.

Primus doctor.   Hail! Herod, most excellent King!
We are commanded to thy presence.
Pilate sendeth thee by us greeting,
And chargeth us, by our obedience—

Secundus doctor. —that we should do our diligence
To bring Jesus of Nazareth unto thee,
And chargeth us to make no resistence,
Because he was born in this country.

Annas.   We know he has wrought great folly[2]
Against the law, showed[3] present.[3]
Therefore Pilate sent him unto thee,
That thou shouldest give him judgement.

Herodes Rex.   Now, by Mahound! my god of grace!
Of Pilate this is a deed full kind.
I forgive him now his great trespass,
And shall be his friend withouten end,
Jesus to me that he will send.
I desired full sore him for to see!
Great ease in this Pilate shall find,
And, Jesus, thou art welcome to me.

Primus judeus.   My sovereign lord, this is the case:
The great falseness of Jesu is openly know.
There was never man did so great trespass,
For he has almost destroyed our law.

Secundus judeus.   Yea! by false craft of sorcery,

---

[1] *MS continuous.*   [2] *evil.*   [3] *it's immediately obvious (?).*

293

Wrought openly to the people all,
And by subtle pointes of necromancy,
Many thousandes from our law are fall.

Caiphas.   Most excellent King, you must take heed!
He will destroy all this country, both old and young,
If he ten monthes more proceed,
By his miracles and false preaching.
He bringeth the people in great fonning,[1]
And says daily among them all
That he is Lord, and of the Jewes King,
And the Son of God he does him call.

Rex Herodes.   Sires, all these matteres I have heard
said,
And much more than you me tell.
All together they shall be laid,
And I will take thereon counsel.
      Jesus, thou art welcome to me!
I can[2] Pilate great thank for his sending.
I have desired full long thee to see,
And of thy miracles to have knowing.
It is told me thou dost many a wonder thing,
Crooked to go and blind men to seen,
And they that are dead givest them living,
And makest lepers fair and whole to been.
      These are wonder workes wrought of thee:
By what way, I would know the true sentence.[3]
Now Jesu, I pray thee, let me see
One miracle wrought in my presence.
In haste, now, do thy diligence,
And peraventure I will show favour to thee,
For now thou art in my presence,
Thy life and death here lies in me.
And here Jesus shall not speak no word to the Herod.
      Jesus, why speakest not to thy King?
What is the cause thou standest so still?

[1] *error.*   [2] *give.*   [3] *significance.*

Thou knowest I may deem[1] all thing:[1]
Thy life and death lies at my will.
　　What! speak, Jesus, and tell me why
This people do thee so here accuse.
Spare not, but tell me now on[2] high[2]
How thou canst thyself excuse.

Caiphas.　　Lo! sires, this is of him a false[3] subtlety:[3]
He will not speak, but when he list.[4]
Thus he deceiveth the people in each degree.
He is full false, you verily trust!

Rex Herodes.　　What! thou unhanged harlot, why wilt
　　thou not speak?
Hast thou scorn to speak unto thy King?
Because thou dost our lawes break
I trow thou art afraid of our talking.

Annas.　　Nay! he[5] is not afraid, but of a false wile,
Because we should not him accuse.[5]
If that he answered you[6] until,[6]
He knoweth he cannot himself excuse.

Rex Herodes.　　What! speak I say, thou fouling, evil[7]
　　may thou fare![7]
Look up! The[8] devil may thee check![8]
Sires, beat his body with scourges bare,
And assay to make him for to speak.

Primus judeus.　　It shall be done withouten tarrying.
Come on, thou traitor, evil[7] may thou the![7]
Wilt thou not speak unto our King,
A new lesson we shall lere[9] thee.
Here they pull off Jesus' clothes and beat him with whips.

Secundus judeus.　　Jesus, thy bones we shall not break,
But we shall make thee to skip.
Thou hast lost thy tongue? Thou mayst not speak?
Thou shalt assay now of this whip!

[1] *come to any decision.*　[2] *speaking up (? at once ?).*　[3] *cunning trick.*　[4] *wants to.*　[5] *it's not out of fear (that he keeps his mouth shut) but by way of a deceitful strategem so that we shall not be able to accuse him.*　[6] *to you.*　[7] *curse you.*　[8] *May the devil take you.*　[9] *teach.*

Tertius judeus.   Sires, take these whippes in your hand,
  And spare not while they last,
  And beat this traitor that here does stand.
  I trow that he will speak in haste!
  And when they have beaten him till he is all bloody:
Herodes Rex.   Cease! sires, I command you, by name of
    the devil of hell!
  Jesus, thinkest this good game?
  Thou art strong to suffer shame!
  Thou haddest liefer be beaten lame
  Than thy defaultes for to tell.
    But I will not thy body all spill,[1]
  Nor put it here into more pain.
  Sires, taketh Jesus at your owen will,
  And lead him to Pilate home again.
  Greet him well and tell him certain
  All my good friendship shall he have—
  I give him power of Jesus, thus you him sayn,
  Whether he will him damn or save.
Primus doctor.   Sir, at your request it shall be do.
  We shall lead Jesus at your demand,
  And deliver him Pilate unto,
  And tell him all as you command.

Passion II: Dream of Pilate's Wife[2]

*Here enters Satan into the place in the most horrible wise, and
while that he plays they shall do[3] on Jesus clothes, and overest[4]
a white cloth, and lead him about the place, and then to Pilate
by the time that his wife has played.[5]*
Satan.   Thus I reign as a rochand[6] with a ringing rowth,[6]
  As a devil most doughty, dread is my dint.[7]

[1] *destroy.*   [2] *n. 65.*   [3] *put.*   [4] *on top.*   [5] *p. 299.*   [6] *(?).*   [7] *stroke.*

Many a thousand deviles to me do they lout,[1]
Burning in flames, as fire out of flint.

Whoso serves me, Satan, to sorrow is he sent,
With dragones in dungeones and deviles full dark,
In brass and in brimstone the brethelles[2] be burnt
That wone[3] in this world my will for to work.
With mischief[4] on mould[4] their members I mark
That japen[5] with Jesus that Judas sold.
Be he never so crafty nor cunning[6] clerk,[6]
I harry them to hell as traitor bold.

But there is one thing that grieveth me sore,
Of a prophet that Jesu men call.
He paineth me every day more and more,
With his holy miracles and workes all.

I had him ones[7] in a temptation,
With gluttony, with covetise, and vainglory.
I assayed him by all ways that I could don,[8]
And utterly he refused them and gan[9] me defy.[9]

That rebuke that he gave me shall not be unquit!
Somewhat I have begun, and more shall be do.
For all his barefoot-going, from me shall he not skip,
But my dark dungeon I shall bringen him to.

I have do[10] made ready his cross, that he shall die upon,
And three nailes to tack him with, that he shall not start.[11]
Be he never so holy, he shall not from me gon,
But with a sharp spear he shall be smit to the heart.

And sithin[12] he shall come to hell, be he never so stout!
And yet I am afraid, and[13] he come, he will do some wrake.[14]
Therefore I shall go warnen hell that they look about,
That they make ready chaines to bind him with in lake.[15]

Hell! hell! make ready, for here shall come a guest!
Hither shall come Jesus that is cleped[16] Godes Son!

---

[1] bow. [2] wretches. [3] are accustomed. [4] calamity on earth. [5] play games. [6] knowledgeable cleric. [7] p. 211. [8] do. [9] defied me. [10] had. [11] spring away. [12] after. [13] if. [14] mischief. [15] the pit (of hell). [16] called.

297

And he shall be here by the hour of noon,
And with thee here he shall wone,[1]
And have full shrewed[2] rest.
Here shall a devil speak in hell.
Demon. Out! upon thee, we conjure thee!
 That never in hell we may him see!
 For, and he ones in hell be,
 He shall our power burst.
Satan.　　Ah! Ah! then have I gone too far—
 But somewhile[3] help I have a shrewed turn.[3]
 My game is worse than I weened here.[4]
 I may say my game is lorn.[5]
　Lo! a[6] wile yet have I cast—[6]
 If I might Jesus life save,
 Hell gates shall be sparred fast,[7]
 And keep still all those I have.
　To Pilates wife I will now go,
 And she is asleep abed full fast,
 And bid her, withouten wordes mo,[8]
 To Pilate that she send in haste.
　I shall assay and[9] this will be,
 To bring Pilate in belief:
 Within a while you shall see
 How my craft I will go prove.
Here shall the devil go to Pilate's wife, the curtain drawn as
she lies in bed. And he shall no din make, but she shall, soon
after that he is come in, make a ruely[10] noise, coming and
running off the scaffold, and her shirt and her kirtle in her
hand. And she shall come before Pilate like a mad woman.
Uxor Pilati.　　Pilate, I charge thee that thou take heed!
 Deem not Jesu, but be his friend.
 If thou judge him to be dead,
 Thou art damned withouten end.

---

[1] *dwell.*　　[2] *wretched.*　　[3] *I have, incidentally, brought about a 'cursed' turn.*
of affairs (?).　　[4] *thought.*　　[5] *lost.*　　[6] *I've thought of a way out.*　　[7] *shut.*
[8] *more.*　　[9] *if.*　　[10] *pitiful.*

A fiend appeared me beforn,
As I lay in my bed sleeping fast.
Sethin[1] the time that I was born,
Was I never so sore aghast.
As wild fire and thunder blast,
He came crying unto me.
He said they that beat Jesu, or bound him fast,
Withouten end damned shall be.

    Therefore a way herein thou see,
And let Jesu from thee clear pass.
The Jewes, they will beguile thee,
And put on thee all the trespass.

Pilate.   Gramercy, my wife, for ever you be true!
Your counsel is good, and ever has be.
Now to your chamber you[2] do sue,[2]
And all shall be well, dame, as you shall see.

Passion II: before Pilate II[3]

Here the Jews bring Jesus again to Pilate.
Primus doctor. Sir Pilate, good tidinges thou[4] hear of[4] me!
Of Herod the King thou hast good will,
And Jesus he sendeth again to thee,
And biddeth thee choose him to save or spill.
Secundus doctor.   Yea! sir, all the power lies now in thee,
And thou knowest our faith he has near shent.[5]
Thou knowest what mischief thereof may be:
We charge thee to give him judgement.
Pilate.   Sires, truly you are to blame
Jesus thus to beat, despoil or bind,
Or put him to so great shame,
For no default in him I find.

---

[1] *Since.*   [2] *do you go.*   [3] *MS continuous.*   [4] *do thou hear from.*   [5] *destroyed.*

Nor Herod, neither, to whom I sent you,
Default in him could find right none,
But sent him again to me by you,
As you know well everyone.
    Therefore understand what I shall say:
You know the custom is in this land,
Of your Pasch-day, that is near-hand,
What thief or traitor is in bond,
Without any price,
For worship of that day shall go free away.
Now then me thinketh it were right
To let Jesus now go quite,[1]
And do to him no mo[2] despite.
Sires, this is my advice,
    I would wit what you say.
Here all they shall cry: Nay! nay! nay!
Primus doctor.   Deliver us the thief Barabbas,
That for manslaught prisoned was.
Pilate.   What shall I then with Jesu do?
Whether shall he abide or go?
Secundus doctor.   Jesus shall on the cross be done:
'Crucifigatur',[3] we cry each one.
Pilate.   Sires, what has Jesus done amiss?
Populus clamabit.[4] 'Crucifigatur', we say at ones.
Pilate.   Sires, since all[5] gates you willen so[5]
Putten Jesu to woe and pain,
Jesus a while with me shall go:
I will him examine betwixt us twain.
Here Pilate takes Jesu and leads him into the council-house.
    Jesus, what sayst, now let see.
This matter now thou understand:
In peace thou might be for me,
But for thy people of thy land.
Bishopes and priestes of the law,

---

[1] *free.*   [2] *more.*   [3] *'Let him be crucified.'*   [4] *The people shall cry aloud.*
[5] *whatever I say, you so wish (to).*

They love thee not, as thou mayst see,
And the common people against thee draw.
In peace thou might have been for me:
    This I tell thee plain.
What sayst, Jesus, why speakest not me to?
Knowest not I have power on the cross thee to do?
And also I have power to let thee forth go?
What canst thou hereto sayn?
Jesus.   On me power thou hast right none,
    But that my Father has granted beforn.
      I came my Fatheres will to fulfil,
    That mankind should not spill.[1]
      He that has betrayed me to thee at this time,
    His trespass is more than is thine.
Primus doctor.   You princes and masteres, taketh heed
    and see
How Pilate in this matter is favorable.
And thus our lawes destroyed might be,
And to us all unrecurable.[2]
Here Pilate lets Jesus alone and goes unto the Jews.
Pilate.   Sires, what will you now with Jesu do?
    I can find in him but good.
    It is my counsel you let him go:
    It is ruth to spill his blood.
Caiphas.   Pilate, me thinketh thou dost great wrong
    Against our law thus to fortify,[3]
    And the people here is so strong,
    Bringing thee lawful testimony.
Annas.   Yea! and[4] thou let Jesu from us pass,
    This we willen upholden all:
    Thou shalt answer for his trespass,
    And traitor to the Emperor we shall thee call!
Pilate.   Now then, since you willen[5] none other way,
    But in all wise that Jesus must die,
      Artise, bring me water I pray thee,

[1] *be destroyed.*   [2] *irrecoverable.*   [3] *uphold.*   [4] *if.*   [5] *MS* wolne.

And what I will do you shall see.
Hic unus afferet aquam.[1]
    As I wash with water my handes clean,
So guiltless of his death I may been.
Primus doctor.   The blood of him may be on us,
And on our children after us.
Et clamabunt:[2] Yea! yea! yea!
Then Pilate goes again to Jesu and brings him.
Pilate.   Lo! sires, I bring him here to your presence,
That you may know I find in him no offence.
Secundus doctor.   Deliver him! deliver him! and let us go,
On the cross that he were do.
Pilate.   Sires, would you your King I should on the cross done?
Tertius doctor. Sir, we say that we have no King but the Emperor alone.
Pilate.   Sires, since all[3] gates[3] it must be so,
We must sit and our office do.
    Bring forth to the bar that[4] are to be deemed,[4]
And they shall have their judgement.
Here they shall bring Barabbas to the bar, and Jesu, and two thieves in their shirts, bare-legged, and Jesus standing at the bar betwixt them. And Annas and Caiphas shall go into the council-house when Pilate sits.
    Barabbas, hold up thy hand!
And he holds up his hand.
For here at thy deliver[5] dost thou stand.
    Sires, what say you of Barabbas, thief and traitor bold?
Shall he go free? or he shall be kept in hold.
Primus doctor.   Sir, for the solemnity of our Pasch[6] day,
By our law he shall go free away.
Pilate.   Barabbas, then I dismiss thee,

---

[1] *Here one shall bring him water.*   [2] *And they shall cry out.*   [3] *at any rate.*
[4] *(those) that . . . judged.*   [5] *(delivery from prison for) trial.*   [6] *John xviii,*
39–40.

And give thee license to go free.
Et curret.[1]

Dismas and Jesmas, thereas you standes,
The law commandeth you to hold up your handes.
Sir, what say you of these thieves twain?
Secundus doctor. Sir, they are both guilty we sayn.
Pilate. And what say you of Jesu of Nazareth?
Primus doctor. Sir, we say he shall be put to death.
Pilate. And can you put against him no trespass?
Secundus doctor. Sir, we will all that he shall be put upon the
cross.
Et clamabunt omnes, voce magna dicentes:[2] Yea! yea! yea!
Pilate. Jesu, thine owen people have disproved[3]
All that I have for thee said or moved.
I charge you all at the beginning,
As you will answer me beforn,
That there be no man shall touch your King,
But if he be knight or gentleman born.
First his clothes you shall off don,
And maken him naked for to be.
Bind him to a pillar as sore[4] as you mon,[4]
Then scourge him with whippes that all men may see.
When he is beaten, crown him for your King,
And then to the cross you shall him bring.
And to the cross thou shalt be fast,
And on three nailes thy body shall rest:
One shall through thy right hand go,
Another through thy left hand, also,
The third shall be smit through both thy feet,
Which nail thereto be made full meet.
And yet thou shalt not hang alone,
But on either side of thee shall be one.
Dismas, now I deem[5] thee,
That on his right hand thou shalt be.

---

[1] *And he shall run.*   [2] *And they shall all cry, saying with a loud voice.*   [3] *re-
futed.*   [4] *tight as you will.*   [5] *judge.*

And Jesmas on the left hand hanged shall be,
On the Mount of Calvary that men may see.

Passion II: Way of the Cross[1]

*Here Pilate shall rise and go to his scaffold and the bishops
with him. And the Jews shall cry for joy with a great voice,
and arren[2] him, and pull off his clothes, and bind him to a
pillar, and scourge him.*

Primus judeus.   Does gladly our King?
For this is your first beginning.

*And when he is scourged they put upon him a cloth of silk,
and set him on a stool, and put a crown of thorns on his head
with forks,[3] and the Jews kneeling to Christ, taking him a
sceptre and scorning him. And then they shall pull off the
purple cloth and do on again his own clothes and lay the cross
on his neck to bear it, and draw him forth with ropes. And
then shall come two women weeping and with their hands
wringing.*

Prima mulier.[4]   Alas! Jesus, alas! Jesus, woe is me!
That thou art thus despoiled, alas!
And yet never default was found in thee,
But ever thou hast been full of grace.

Secunda mulier.   Ah! here is a rueful sight of Jesu so
good,
That he shall thus die against the right.
Ah! wicked men, you are more than wood[5]
To do that good Lord so great despite.

Here Jesus turns again to the women with his cross.

Jesus.   Daughteres of Jerusalem, for me weepeth not,
But for yourself weepeth, and for your children also.

---

[1] *n. 66.*   [2] *vex.*   [3] *n. 67*   [4] *First woman.*   [5] *insane.*

For the days shall come that they have after[1] sought[1],
Their[2] sin and their blindness shall turn them[3] to woe.
   Then shall be said, 'Blessed be the wombes that barren
     be!
And woe to the teates, those days, that do given sucking!'
And to their fatheres they shall say, 'Woe to the time that
   thou begat me!'
And to their motheres, 'Alas! where shall be our dwel-
   ling?'
   Then to the hilles and mountaines they shall cry and
     call,
'Open and hide us from the face of him sitting in throne,
Or elles over-throweth, and on us now come fall,
That we may be hid from our sorrowful moan.'
Here Jesus turns from the women and goes forth. And there
they meet with Simon in the place, the Jews saying to him:
Primus judeus.   Sir, to thee a word of good!
   A man is here, thou mayst see,
   Beareth[4] heavy of a rood,[4]
   Whereon he shall hanged be.
   Therefore we pray all thee
   Thou take the cross of the man,
   Bear it with us to Calvary,
   And right great thank thou shalt han.
Simon.   Sires, I may not in no degree:
   I have great errandes for to do.
   Therefore I pray you excuse me,
   And on my errand let me go.
Secundus judeus.   What! harlot, hast thou scorn
   To bear the tree when we thee pray?
   Thou shalt bearen it, haddest thou sworn,
   And it were ten times the way![5]
Simon.   Sires, I pray you, displease you not!
   I will help to bear the tree.

---

[1] *sought for.*   [2] *(When) their.*   [3] *(for?) them.*   [4] *Carries a heavy cross.*
[5] *distance.*

Into the place it shall be brought
Where you will command me.
Here Simon takes the cross of Jesus and bears it forth.
Veronica.   Ah! you sinful people, why fare thus?
For sweat and blood he may not see.
Alas! holy prophet, Christ Jesus,
Careful is my heart for thee.
And she wipes his face with her kerchief.[1]
Jesus.   Veronica, thy wiping does me ease.
My face is clean that was black to see.
I shall them keep from all mis-ease[2]
That looken on thy kerchief and remember me.

Passion II: Crucifixion[3]

Then shall they pull Jesu out of his clothes, and lay them[4]
together. And there they shall pull him down, and lay him
along on the cross, and after that nail him thereon.
Primus judeus.   Come on, now, here we shall assay
If the cross for thee be meet.[5]
Cast him down here, in the devil way!
How long shall he standen on his feet?
Secundus judeus.   Pull him down! evil[6] may he the![6]
And give me his arm in haste,
And anon we shall see.
His good days, they shall be past!
Tertius judeus.   Give his other arm to me!
Another take heed to his feet!
And anon we shall see
If the bores[7] be for him meet.[7]

---

[1] *Veronica episode in no other English cycle.*   [2] *distress.*   [3] *MS continuous, no title etc.*   [4] *the clothes.*   [5] *the right fit.*   [6] *curse him.*   [7] *bore-holes (for nails).*

Quartus judeus.   This is meet, take good heed.
  Pull out that arm to thee sore![1]
Primus judeus. This is short—the devil him speed!—
  By a large foot and more.
Secundus judeus.   Fast on a rope, and pull him long,
  And I shall draw[2] thee again.[2]
  Spare we not these ropes strong,
  Though we burst both flesh and vein.
Tertius judeus.   Drive in the nail anon, let see,
  And look and[3] the flesh and sinewes will last.
Quartus judeus. That I grant, so[4] may I the![4]
  Lo! this nail is drive right well and fast.
Primus judeus.   Fast a rope then to his feet,
  And draw[5] him down long enough.[5]
Secundus judeus. Here is a nail for both, good and great:
  I shall drive it through, I make avow.
  Here shall they leave off and dance about the cross shortly.
Tertius judeus. Lo! fellow, here a[6] lies, tacked on a tree!
Quartus judeus. Yea! and I trow thou art a worthy king!
Primus judeus. Ah! good sir, tell me now what helpeth thy
    prophecy thee?
Secundus judeus. Yea! or any of thy false preaching?
Tertius judeus.   Sires, set up the cross on the end,
  That we may look him in the face.
Quartus judeus. Yea! and we shall kneelen unto our king
    so kind,
  And pray him of his great grace.
  *Here when they have set him up they shall go before him say-
  ing each after other:*
Primus judeus.   Hail! King of Jewes, if thou be,
Secundus judeus. Yea! yea! sir, as thou hangest there, flesh
    and bones,
Tertius judeus. Come now down off that tree,
Quartus judeus. And we will worship thee all at ones.

---

[1] *Unscriptural stretching limbs general: n. 68.*   [2] *pull against thee.*   [3] *if.*
[4] *upon my life.*   [5] *give a good long pull down.*   [6] *one(?).*

Here shall poor commons stand and look upon the Jews, four or five, and the Jews shall come to them and do[1] them hang the thieves.

Primus judeus.   Come on! you knaves, and set up these
> two crosses right,
And hang up these two thieves anon.

Secundus judeus. Yea! and in the[2] worship[3] of this worthy
> knight,
On each side of him shall hangen one.

Here the simple men shall set up these two crossses, and hang up the thieves by the arms. And therewhiles shall the Jews cast dice for his clothes and fight and strive. And in the meantime shall our Lady come with three Marys[3] with her, and Saint John with them, setting them down aside before the cross, our Lady swooning and mourning and [by][4] leisure[4] saying:

Maria.   Ah! my good lord, my son so sweet,
What hast thou done? Why hangest now thus here?
Is there no other death to thee now meet
But the most shameful death among[5] these thieves fere?[5]
> Ah! out on, my heart, why burst thou not?
And thou art maiden and mother and seest thus thy child
> spill.[6]
How mayst thou abide this sorrow and this woeful
> thought?
Ah! death, death, death, why wilt thou not me kill?

Here our Lady shall swoon again.

Jesus.   Oh! Father almighty, maker of man,
Forgive these Jewes that do me woe,
Forgive them, Father, forgive them then,
For they wit not what they do.

Primus judeus.   Yea! what! what! now here is he,
That bade us destroy our Temple on a day,
And, within days three,
He should raisen it again in good array.

---

[1] *make.*   [2] *honour.*   [3] *n. 69.*   [4] *in course of time.*   [5] *in the company of these thieves.*   [6] *perish.*

Secundus judeus.   Now and[1] thou can do such a deed,
  Help now thyself, if that thou can,
  And we shall believe on thee withouten dread,[2]
  And say thou art a mighty man.
Tertius judeus.   Yea! if thou be Godes Son, as thou didest
    teach,
  From the cross come now down,
  Then of[3] mercy we shall thee beseech,
  And say thou art a lord of great renown.
Jesmas.[4]   If thou be Godes Son, as thou didest say,
  Help here now both thee and us.
  But I find[5] it not all in my fay[5]
  That thou shouldest be Christ, Godes Son, Jesus.
Dismas.   Do way! fool! why sayst thou so?
  He is the Son of God, I believe it well.
  And sin did he never, lo!
  That he should be put this[6] death till.[6]
    But we full much wrong have wrought:
  He did never thing amiss.
  Now mercy, good Lord, mercy, and forget me not
  When thou comest to thy kingdom and to thy bliss.
Jesus.   Amen! amen! thou art full wise.
  That thou hast asked I grant thee:
  This same day in paradise
  With me, thy God, thou shalt there be.
Maria.   Oh! my son, my son, my darling dear!
  What[7] have I defended[7] thee?
  Thou hast spoke to all those that are here,
  And not one word thou speakest to me.
    To the Jewes thou art full kind,
  Thou hast forgive all their misdeed;
  And the thief thou hast in mind:
  For ones asking mercy, heaven is his meed.
    Ah! my sovereign Lord, why wilt thou not speak

---

[1] *if.*   [2] *doubt.*   [3] *for.*   [4] *MS* jestes: *but cf. p.* 303.   [5] *cannot find it in me to believe.*   [6] *to this death.*   [7] *How have I offended* (?).

To me that am thy mother, in pain for thy wrong?
Ah! heart, heart, why wilt thou not break,
That I were out of this sorrow so strong?
Jesus. Ah! woman, woman, behold there thy son!
And thou, John, take her for thy mother!
I charge thee to keep her as busily as thou can:
Thou, a clean maid,[1] shall keep another.[1]
 And, woman, thou knowest that my Father of heaven
  me sent,
To take this manhood of thee, Adam his ransom to pay,
For this is the will, and my Fatheres intent,
That I shall thus die to deliver man from the deviles prey.
 Now, since it is the will of my Father it should thus be,
Why should it displease thee, Mother, now, my death
 so sore?
And for to suffer all this for man I was born of thee,
To the bliss that man had lost man again to restore.
Here our Lady shall rise and run and halse[2] the cross.
Maria Magdalen. Ah! good lady, why do you thus?
Your doleful cheer[3] now chieveth us sore,[3]
And for[4] the pain of my sweet Lord, Jesus—
That he seeth in you, it paineth him more.
Maria Virgo. I pray you all, let me be here,
And hang me up here on this tree;
By my friend and son that me is so dear,
For there he is, there would I be.
Johannes. Gentle Lady, now leave your mourning,
And go with us, now we you pray,
And comfort our Lord at his departing,
For he is almost ready to go his way.
*Here they shall take our Lady from the cross, and here shall
Pilate come down from his scaffold, with Caiphas and Annas
and all their meinie[5] and shall come and look on Christ.*
Caiphas. (*Scornfully.*) Lo! sires, lo! beholdeth and see!

---

[1] *i.e. John, a virgin, shall take care of another virgin.*   [2] *embrace.*   [3] *demeanour
gets us nowhere.*   [4] *(as) for.*   [5] *company.*

Here hangeth he that help many a man.
And now, if he Godes Son be,
Help now himself, if that he can!

Annas.   Yea! and if thou King of Israel be,
Come down off the cross among us all,
And let thy God now deliver thee,
And then our King we will thee call.

Here shall Pilate ask pen and ink, and a table[1] shall be take[1]
him, written[2] before, 'Hic est Jesus Nazarenus rex judeorum'.[2]
And he shall make[3] him[3] to write, and then go upon a ladder
and set the table above Christ's head. And then Caiphas shall
make him to read.

Caiphas.   Sir Pilate, we marveleth of this,
That you write him to be King of Jewes.
     Therefore we would that you should write thus,
That he named himself King of Jewes.

Pilate.   That I have written, written it is,
And so it shall be for[4] me, iwis![4]

And so forth all they shall go again to the scaffold.

Jesus.   Eloi, eloi,
Lamma sabacthani.
My Father in heaven on high,
Why dost thou me forsake?[5]
The frailty[6] of my mankind[6]
With strong pain it ginneth[7] to pind.[7]
Ah! dear Father, have me in mind,
And let death my sorrow slake.[8]

Secundus judeus.   Me thinketh he this does call—'Eli'.[9]
Let us go near and espy,
And look if he[9] come privily
From cross him down to reave.

Jesus. So great a thirst did never man take
As I have, man, now for thy sake,

---

[1] tablet . . . given.   [2] (on which is) written in advance, 'Here is Jesus, King of the Jews.'   [3] pretend.   [4] so far as I am concerned, for sure.   [5] n. 70.
[6] weakness of my human nature.   [7] torments.   [8] bring to an end.   [9] Elias.

311

For thirst asunder my lippes gin[1] crake,[1]
For dryness they do cleave.
Tertius judeus.   Your thirst, Sir Hoberd,[2] for to slake
Eisell[3] and gall here I thee take.[4]
What! me thinketh a mow[5] you make—
Is not this good drink?
To cry for drink you had great haste,
And now it seemeth it is but waste!
Is not this drink of good taste?
Now tell me how you think.
Quartus judeus.   Aloft, Sir Hoberd, now you are set,
We will no longer with you let.[6]
We greet you well on[7] the new jet,[7]
And make on you a mow.[8]
Primus judeus. We greet you well with a scorn,
And pray you, both even and morn,
Take good heed to our corn,
And chare[9] away the crow.
Jesus.   In manus tuas, Domine.[10]
Holy Father in heavenly see,
I commend my spirit to thee,
For here now endeth my fast.[11]
I shall go slay the fiend, that freke,[12]
For now my heart beginneth to break.
Wordes mo[13] shall I none speak,
Nunc consummatum est.[14]
Maria.   Alas! alas! I live too long,
To see my sweet son with paines strong,
As a thief on cross does hang,
And never yet did he sin.
Alas! my dear child to[15] death is dressed[15]—
Now is my care well more increased.

---

[1] *split.*   [2] *clown (?).*   [3] *vinegar.*   [4] *give.*   [5] *face.*   [6] *wait.*   [7] *in the new fashion.*   [8] *grimace.*   [9] *drive away.*   [10] *Into thy hands, O Lord.*   [11] *MS fest.*   [12] *creature.*   [13] *more.*   [14] *Now it is finished.*   [15] *for . . . ready.*

Ah! my heart with pain is pressed,[1]
For sorrow my heart does twin.[2]
Johannes.   Ah! blessed maid, change your thought,
For, though your son with sorrow is sought,[3]
Yet by his owen will this work is wrought,
And wilfully[4] his death to take.
You to keep he charged me here:
I am your servant, my Lady dear.
Wherefore I pray you, be of good cheer,
And mirthes that you make.
Maria.   Though he had never of me been born,
And[5] I saw his flesh thus all to-torn,
On back behinden, on breast beforn,
Rent with woundes wide,
Needes I must wonen[6] in woe,
To see my friend with many a foe
All to-rent from top to toe,
His flesh withouten hide.[7]
Johannes.   Ah! blessed Lady, as I you tell,
Had he not died we should to hell.
Amongst fiendes there ever to dwell,
In paines that are smart.[8]
He suffereth death for our trespass,
And through his death we shall have grace,
To dwell with him in heaven place.
Therefore be merry in heart!
Maria.   Ah! dear friend, well wot I this,
That he does buy us to his bliss.
But yet of mirth evermore I miss,
When I see this sight.
Johannes. Now, dear lady, therefore I you pray,
From this doleful dolour wend we our way.
For, when this sight you see not may,
Your care may wax more light.

---

[1] *oppressed.*   [2] *break in two.*   [3] *afflicted.*   [4] *voluntarily.*   [5] *If.*   [6] *live (lament?).*   [7] *skin.*   [8] *severe.*

313

Maria.   Now, sith[1] I must part him[2] fro,[2]
    Yet let me kiss, ere that I go,
    His blessed feet that sufferen woe,
    Nailed on this tree.
    So cruelly with great despite,[3]
    Thus shamefully was never man dight;[4]
    Therefore in pain my heart is pight,[5]
    All joy departeth from me.
    Hic quasi semi mortua cadat prona in terram.[6]

Johannes.   Now, blessed maid, come forth with me!
    No longer this sight that you see,
    I shall you guide in this country
    Where that it pleaseth you best.

Maria. Now, gentle John, my sonnes darling,
    To Godes Temple thou me bring,
    That I may pray God with sore weeping,
    And mourning that is prest.[7]

Johannes.   All your desire shall be wrought,
    With hearty will I work your thought.
    Now, blessed maid, tarryeth not
    In the Temple that you were.[8]
    For holy prayer may change your mood,
    And cause your cheer to be more good.
    When you see not your childes blood
    The less may be your care.
    Tunc transiet Maria ad Templum cum Johanne etc.[9]

Maria.   Here in this Temple my life I lead,
    And serve my Lord God with heartily[10] dread.[10]
    Now shall weeping me[11] food and feed[11]
    Some comfort till God send.
    Ah! my Lord God, I thee pray,
    When my child riseth the third day,

---

[1] *since.*   [2] *from him.*   [3] *malice.*   [4] *treated.*   [5] *pierced, placed.*   [6] *Here as if half-dead let her fall face-down to the earth; semi mortua, MS seminor tua.* [7] *urgent.*   [8] *might be.*   [9] *Then Mary will cross over to the Temple with John etc.*   [10] *heart-felt awe.*   [11] *be what I live on.*

Comfort then thy hand-may[1]
My care for to amend.

Passion II: Harrowing of Hell I[2]

Anima Christi.[3] Now all mankind in heart be glad,
With all mirthes that may be had!
For mannes soul, that was bestead[4]
In the lodge of hell,
Now shall I rise to live again,
From pain to plays[5] of paradise plain.[5]
Therefore, man, in heart be fain,
In mirth now shalt thou dwell.

I am the soul of Christ Jesu,
The which is King of all virtue.
My body is dead—the Jewes it slew—
That hangeth yet on the rood.[6]
Rent and torn, all bloody red,
For mannes sake my body is dead,
For mannes help my body is bread,[7]
And soul-drink my bodyes blood.[7]

Though my body be now slain,
The third day, this is certain,
I shall raise my body again
To live, as I you say.
Now will I go straight to hell,
And fetch from the fiendes fell
All my friendes that therein dwell,
To bliss that lasteth ay.
The soul goes to hell gates and says: Attollite portas prin-

---

[1] *hand-maiden.*   [2] *n. 71.*   [3] *Soul of Christ.*   [4] *beset.*   [5] *delights of perfect paradise (? of paradise entirely?).*   [6] *cross.*   [7] *John vi, 51-7, Mark xiv, 22-4.*

315

cipes vestras, et elevamini portae aeternales, et introibit
Rex gloriae.[1]

    Undo your gates of sorwatory![2]
On mannes soul I have memory.
Here cometh now the King of glory,
These gates for to break.
You deviles that are here within,
Hell gates you shall unpin.
I shall deliver mannes kin,
From woe I will them wreak.[3]

Belial.   Alas! alas! out! and harrow!
Unto thy bidding must we bow.
That thou art God now do we know,
Of thee had we great doubt.
Against thee may nothing stand,
All thing obeyth to thy hand,
Both heaven and hell, water and land,
All thing must to thee lout.[4]

Anima Christi.   Against me it were but waste
To holden or to standen fast.
Hell lodge may not last
Against the King of glory.
Thy dark door down I throw,
My fair friendes now will I know.[5]
I shall them bring, reckoned[6] by row,[6]
Out of their purgatory.

Passion II: Centurion[7]

Centurio.   In truth now I know with full open sight
That Godes dear Son is nailed on tree.

---

[1] *Psalm xxiv, 7 (A.V.): Lift up your heads, O ye gates, and be ye lift up, ye ever-lasting doors, and the King of glory shall come in.*   [2] *sorrowing (?).*   [3] *deliver.*
[4] *submit.*   [5] *acknowledge.*   [6] *all in due order.*   [7] *n. 72.*

These wonderful tokenes approven full right
Quod vere Filius Dei erat iste.[1]
Alius miles 2.[2] The very child of God I suppose that he be,
And so it seemeth well by his wonderful work.
The earth sore quaketh and that agreseth[3] me.
With mist and great[4] weather it is wonder dark.
Alius miles 3.   Such marveles show may no earthly man.
The air is right dark that first was right clear,
The earthquake is great, the cloudes wax[5] wan:[5]
Those tokenes prove him a lord without any peer.
Centurio. His Father is peerless King of most[6] empire,[6]
Both Lord of this world and King of heaven high.
Yet out of all sin to bring us out of danger
He suffereth his dear Son for us all to die.
Nicodemus.   Alas! alas! what sight is this
To see the Lord and King of bliss,
That never sinned nor did amiss,
Thus nailed upon a rood.
Alas! Jewes, what have you wrought?
Ah! you wicked wightes,[7] what was your thought?
Why have you bobbed[8] and thus beaten out
All his blessed blood?
Centurio.   Ah! now truly, tell well I can
That this was Godes owen Son.
I know he is both God and man
By this work that here is done.
      There was never man but God that could make this
         work!
That[9] ever was of woman born,
Were he never so great a clerk,
It passeth them all though they had sworn.[9]
      His law was true, I dare well say,
That he taught us here among,

---

[1] *That he was, truly, the Son of God.*   [2] *Another soldier 2.*   [3] *terrifies.*   [4] *low-ering.*   [5] *grow gloomy.*   [6] *greatest authority.*   [7] *men.*   [8] *struck in derision.*
[9] *Though they had sworn to do it, it is too much for anyone ever born of a woman, though he were never so learned.*

Therefore I rede[1] you, turn your fay,[1]
And amend that you have done wrong.

Passion II: Longeus and Burial[2]

Joseph of Aramathea.   Oh! good Lord Jesu, that diest
    now here on rood,
Have mercy on me and forgive me my miss![3]
I would thee worship here with my good,[4]
That I may come to thy bliss.
    To Pilate now will I goon,
And ask the body of my Lord Jesu.
To bury that now would I soon,
In my grave that is so new.
    Hail! Sir Pilate, that sitteth in seat,
Hail! Justice of Jewes, men do thee call,
Hail! with health I do thee greet,
I pray thee of a boon whatso befall.
    To bury Jesu[5] his body,[5] I will thee pray,
That he were out of mennes sight,
For tomorrow shall be our holiday[6]—
Then will no man him bury, I thee plight.
    And if we let him hang there still
Some would say thereof[7] enow,[7]
The people thereof would say full ill,
That[8] neither should be your worship nor prow.[8]

Pilate.   Sir Joseph of Aramathy, I grant thee:
With Jesu his body do thy intent.
But first I will wit that he dead be,
As it was his judgement.

---

[1] *advise you, be converted.*   [2] *MS continuous.*   [3] *misdeed.*   [4] *possessions.*
[5] *the body of Jesus.*   [6] *i.e. the Sabbath.*   [7] *plenty about it.*   [8] *So that neither would be to your honour or advantage.*

Sir knightes, I command you that you go
In haste with Joseph of Aramathy,
And look you take good heed thereto
That Jesu surely dead be.
　See that this commandment you fulfil
Without wordes any mo,[1]
And then let Joseph do his will,
What that he will with Jesu do.
Here come two knights before Pilate at once.
Primus miles.　Sir, we shall do our diligence,
With Joseph going to Calvary:
Be we out of thy presence,
Soon the truth we shall espy.
Joseph of Aramathea.　Gramercy! Pilate, of your gentleness,[2]
That you have granted me my list.[3]
Anything in my province
You shall have at your request.
Pilate.　Sir, all your list[3] you shall have!
With Jesu his body do your intent:
Whether you bury him in pit or grave,
The power I grant you here present.
The two knights go with Joseph to Jesus and stand and holden[4]
him in the face.
Secundus miles.　Me thinketh Jesu is sure enow.[5]
It is no need his bones to break.
He is dead, how thinketh you?
He shall never go nor speak!
Primus miles.　We will be sure ere[6] than[6] we go—
Of a thing I am bethought:
Yonder is a blind knight I shall go to,
And soon a wile[7] here shall be wrought.
Here the knight goes to blind Longeus.[8]
　Hail! Sir Longeus, thou gentle[9] knight,

---

[1] *more.*　　[2] *courtesy, nobility.*　　[3] *desire.*　　[4] *behold.*　　[5] *perfectly.*　　[6] *before.*
[7] *ruse.*　　[8] *cf.* Harrowing of Hell, *E.E.T.S. E.S. 100 (1907) lxviii f.*　　[9] *noble,*
excellent.

Thee I pray now right heartily
That thou wilt wend with me full wight[1]—
It shall be for[2] thy prow[2] verily.

Longeus. Sir, at your commandment with you will I wend,
In what place you will me have.
For I trust you are my friend:
Lead me forth, sir, our Sabbath you save.

Primus miles. Lo! Sir Longeus, here is a spear,
Both long and broad and sharp enough.
Heave it up, fast, that it were there.
For here is game—shove! man, shove!

*Here Longeus shoves the spear warily and the blood comes
running to his hand. And he adventurously[3] shall wipe his eyes.*

Longeus. Oh! good Lord, how may this be,
That I may see so bright now?
This thirty winter I might not see,
And now I may see, I wot never how.
But who is this that hangeth here now?
I trow it be the maidenes son:
And that he is, now I know well how!
The Jewes to him this villainy have done.

Here he falls down on his knees.

Now, good Lord, forgive me that,
That I to thee now done have,
For I did I wist not what:
The Jewes of[4] my ignorance did me rave.[4]

Mercy, mercy, mercy, I cry![5]

*Then Joseph does set up the ladders, and Nicodemus comes
to help him.*

Nicodemus. Joseph of Aramathy, blessed thou be!
For thou dost a full good deed.
I pray thee, let me help thee,
That I may be partner[6] of thy meed.[6]

---

[1] *quickly.* [2] *to your advantage.* [3] *by chance.* [4] *in my ignorance, caused
me to act like a madman.* [5] *extrametrical line (?), written on right where tail-rime
lines usually are.* [6] *sharer in your reward.*

Joseph. Nicodemus, welcome indeed!
  I pray you you will help thereto.
  He[1] will acquit[1] us right well our meed,
  And I have licence[2] for to do.
  Here Joseph and Nicodemus take Christ off the cross, one on
  one ladder and the other on another ladder. And when [he]
  is had down, Joseph lays him in our Lady's lap, seying[3] the
  knightes turning heme.[3]
Joseph.   Lo! Mary, Mother good and true,
  Here is thy son, bloody and blue.[4]
  For him my heart full sore does rue.
  Kiss him now, ones,[5] ere he go.
Maria Virgo.   Ah! mercy, mercy, my owen son so dear!
  Thy bloody face now I must kiss.
  Thy face is pale, withouten cheer.
  Of much joy now shall I miss.
  There was never mother that saw this,
  So her son despoiled with so great woe.
  And my dear child never did amiss!
  Ah! mercy, Father of Heaven, it should be so.
Joseph.   Mary, your son you[6] take[6] to me,
  Into his grave it shall be brought.
Maria. Joseph, blessed ever may thou be
  For the good deed that you have wrought.
  Here they shall lay Christ in his grave.
Joseph. I give thee this sindony[7] that I have bought,
  To wind thee in while it is new.
Nicodemus. Here is an ointment that I have brought
  To anoint withal my Lord Jesu.
Joseph.   Now Jesu is within his grave,
  Which I ordain[8] some time for me.[8]
  On the Lord I vouch[9] it save[9]—
  I know my meed full great shall be.

---

[1] *i.e. Christ will pay.*   [2] *permission (from Pilate).*   [3] *seeing (saying?) the*
knights (i.e. Joseph and Nicodemus are) turning him (towards Mary for her kiss? or
turning themselves away?): n. 73.   [4] *discoloured.*   [5] *once.*   [6] *do you give.*
[7] *shroud: n. 74.*   [8] *provided at one time for myself.*   [9] *bestow it.*

Nicodemus.   Now let us lay on this stone again,
And Jesu in this tomb still shall be.
And we will walk home full[1] plain[1]—
The day passeth fast I see.
Farewell! Joseph, and well you be!
No longer tarrying here we make.
Joseph. Sir, almighty God be with thee!
Into his bliss he[2] may[2] you take!
Maria. Farewell! you gentle princes kind.
In joy ever may you be!
The bliss of heaven, withouten end,
I know verily that you shall see.
Here the princes shall do reverence to our Lady, and go their way, and leave the Marys at the sepulchre. Caiphas goes to Pilate.

Passion II: Setting of Watch[3]

Caiphas. Hark! Sir Pilate, list to me.
I shall thee tell tidinges new.
Of one thing we must ware be,
Or elles hereafter we might it rue.
    Thou wotest well that Jesu,
He said to us with wordes plain,
He said we should find it true
The third day he would rise again.
If that his disciples come certain,
And out of his grave steal him away,
They will go preach and plain sayn
That he is risen the third day.
    This is the counsel that I give here:
Take men and give them charge thereto

---

[1] *quite openly* (?).   [2] *may he.*   [3] *n. 74a.*

To watch the grave with great power,
Till the third day be go.
Pilate. Sir Caiphas, it shall be do!
For, as you say, there is peril in.
And it happened that it were so,
It might make our lawes for to blin.[1]

You shall see, sir, ere that you go,
How I shall this matter save,
And what I shall say thereto,
And what charge they shall have.

Come forth you, Sir Amoraunt,
And Sir Arfaxat, come near also,
Sir Cosdram, and Sir Affraunt,
And hear the charge that you must do.
Sires, to Jesu his grave you shall go,
Till that the third day is gone,
And let neither friend nor foe
In no way to touch the stone.

If any of his disciples come there,
To fetch the body from you away,
Beat him down—have you no fear!
With shameful death do[2] him die.

On pain of your goodes and your lives
That you let him not scape you[3] fro,[3]
And of your childeren and your wives,
For all you lose and[4] you do so!
Primus miles.   Sir Pilate, we shall not cease:
We shall keep it strong enow.[5]
Secundus miles. Yea! and[6] an hundred put them in press,[6]
They shall die, I make avow!
Tertius miles.   And an hundred? Fie! on an hundred,
and[7] an hundred, thereto![7]
There is none of them shall us withstand!

---

[1] *cease.*   [2] *have.*   [3] *from you.*   [4] *if.*   [5] *exceedingly.*   [6] *if . . . come*
as a mob.   [7] *and a second hundred as well!*

323

Quartus miles. Yea! and there come an hundred thousand
    and mo[1]
    I shall them kill with my hand.
Pilate. Well, sires, then your part you do,
    And to your charge look you take heed.
    Withouten wordes any mo.[1]
    Wisely now that you proceed.
    Here the knights go out of the place.
      Lo! Sir Caiphas, how thinketh you?
    Is not this well brought about?
Caiphas. In faith, sir, it is sure enow:[2]
    Hardily,[3] have you no doubt!
Arfaxat.   Let see, Sir Amoraunt, where will you be?
    Will you keep the feet or the head?
Amoraunt. At the head, so[4] may I the,[4]
    And whoso comes here, he is but dead!
Arfaxat.   And I will keep the feet this tide,[5]
    Though there come both Jack and Jill!
Cosdram. And I shall keep the right side,
    And whoso comes I shall him kill!
Affraunt.   And I will on the left hand been,
    And whoso comes here he shall never then![6]
    Full[7] securely[7] his bane shall I been,
    With dintes[8] of doubt.[8]
    Sir Pilate, have good day!
    We shall keepen the body in clay
    And we shall waken[9] well the way,
    And waiten[10] all about.
Pilatus.   Now, gentle sires, will you vouchsafe
    To go with me and seal the grave?
    That he not arise out of the grave,
    That is now dead?
Caiphas. We grant well—let us now go!
    When it is sealed and kept also,

---

[1] *more.*   [2] *exceedingly.*   [3] *It is indeed.*   [4] *upon my life.*   [5] *time.*   [6] *succeed.*
[7] *Most certainly.*   [8] *fearful blows.*   [9] *guard.*   [10] *watch.*

Then are we secure, withouten woe,
And have of him no dread.
Tunc ibunt ad sepulcrum Pilatus, Caiphas, Annas et omnes milites.[1]

Annas. Lo! here is wax full ready dight![2]
Set on your seal anon, full right,
Then are you secure, I you plight,
He shall not risen again!

Pilatus. On this corner my seal shall sit,
And with this wax I seal this pit.
Now dare I lay he shall never flit
Out of this grave, certain.

Annas. Here is more wax full ready, lo!
All the corneres you seal, also,
And with a lock lock it, too.
Then let us go our way,
And let these knightes abiden thereby,
And if his disciples come privily,
To steal away this dead body,
To us they them bring without delay.

Pilatus. On every corner now is set my seal,
Now is my heart in wealth and weal,
This may no briber away now steal,
This body from under stone.
Now, Sir Bishop, I pray to thee,
And Annas, also, come on with me:
Even together, all we three,
Homeward the way we gone.
 As[3] wind wroth,
Knightes, now goth,
Clapped in cloth,
And keepeth him well.[3]
Look you be bold

---

[1] *Then shall go to the tomb Pilate, Caiphas, Annas and all the soldiers.* [2] *prepared.*
[3] *Knights, now be fierce as the wind, and guard him well who is bound in grave-clothes (?).*

With me for to hold:
You shall have gold,
And helm of steel.
Pilate, Annas and Caiphas go to their scaffolds.
Affraunt.   Now in this ground
He lieth bound,
That tholed[1] wound
For he was false.
This left corner
I will keep here,
Armed clear
Both head and hals.[2]
Cosdram.   I will have this side,
Whatso betide.
If any man ride
To steal the corse
I shall him chide
With woundes wide,
Among them glide
With fine force.
Amoraunt.   The head I take
Here by to wake.[3]
A steal stake
I hold in hand
Masteries[4] to make:[4]
Crownes I crack
Shaftes to shake
And shapen[5] shond.[5]
Arfaxat.   I shall not let[6]
To[7] keep[7] the feet.
They are full wet[8]
Weltered in blood,
He that will stalk[9]

---

1 *suffered.*   2 *neck.*   3 *watch.*   4 *To exercise my skill.*   5 *cause shame.*
6 *leave.*   7 *Guarding.*   8 (?) wete, *MS all but* w *obliterated by alteration to*
white (?).   9 *walk (stealthily).*

By[1] brook or balk,[1]
Hither to walk—
Those wretches are wood![2]
Primus miles.[3]   My head dulleth,
My heart filleth
Of sleep.
Saint[4] Mahound,[4]
This burying ground
Thou keep.
Secundus miles.   I say the same!
For[5] any[5] blame
I fall,
Mahound-whelp
After thy help
I call.
Tertius miles.   I am heavy as lead!
For[5] any[5] dread,
I sleep.
Mahound of might,
This stone tonight
Thou keep.
Quartus miles.   I have no foot
To stand on[6] root
By brink.[6]
Here I ask
To go to task
A wink.

[1] *By . . . ridge (i.e. anywhere).*   [2] *crazy.*   [3] *First soldier.*   [4] *The 'false prophet', Mohammed, addressed as a Christian saint.*   [5] *Whatever the.*   [6] *rooted on the brink (of the tomb).*

Harrowing of Hell II[1]

Tunc dormient milites, et veniet Anima Christi de inferno
cum Adam et Eva, Abraham, Johan Baptista et aliis.[2]
Anima Christi.   Come forth Adam and Eve with thee,
     And all my friendes that here-in be,
     To paradise come forth with me,
     In bliss for to dwell.
     The fiend of hell, that is your foe,
     He shall be wrapped and wounden in woe:
     From woe to wealth now shall you go,
     With mirth evermore to mell.[3]
Adam.   I thank thee, Lord, of[4] thy great grace,
     That now is forgiven my great trespass:
     Now shall we dwellen in blissful place,
     In joy and endless mirth.
     Through my sin man was forlorn,
     And man to save thou wert all torn,
     And of a maid in Bethlehem born,
     That ever-blessed be thy birth!
Eva.   Blessed be thou, Lord of life!
     I am Eve, Adam his wife.
     Thou hast suffered stroke and strife
     For workes that we wrought.
     Thy mild mercy has all forgiven,
     Deathes[5] dentes[5] on thee were driven,
     Now with thee, Lord, we shall liven—
     Thy bright blood has us bought!
Johannes Baptista.   I am thy cousin: my name is John.
     Thy woundes have beaten thee to the bone.

---

[1] n. 75.   [2] *Then the soldiers shall sleep, and the soul of Christ shall come from*
hell with Adam . . . and others.   [3] *mix.*   [4] *for.*   [5] *The blows of death.*

I baptized thee in Flom[1] Jordan,
And gave thy body baptize.
With thy grace now shall we gone
From our enemies every one,
And finden mirthes many one
In play of paradise.

Abraham.   I am Abraham, father true,
That reigned after Noes flow.[2]
A sorry sin Adam gan[3] sow,[3]
That clad us all in care.
A Son, that maidenes milk has sucken,
And with his blood our bond has broken—
Hell lodge lies unlocken,
From filth with friend we fare.

Anima Christi.   Fair friendes, now are you won,
On you shineth the soothfast sun.
The ghost[4] that all grievance has[5] gun[5]
Full hard I shall him bind!
As wicked worm thou gun[6] appear,[6]
To tray[7] my childeren that were so dear—
Therefore, traitor, evermore here
New paines thou shalt ever find!
       Through blood I took of mannes kind,
False devil, I here thee bind,
In endless sorrow I thee wind,
Therein evermore to dwell.
Now thou art bound thou mayst not flee,
For thy envious cruelty
In endless damnation shalt thou be,
And never comen out of hell!

Belial.   Alas! harrow! now am I bound,
In hell gong[8] to lie on ground.
In endless sorrow now am I wound,
In care evermore to dwell.

---

[1] *River.*   [2] *flood.*   [3] *sowed.*   [4] *spirit (i.e. Satan).*   [5] *began.*   [6] *didst*
appear.   [7] *betray.*   [8] *privy.*

In hell lodge I lie alone,
Now is my joy away all gone,
For all fiendes shall be my fone,[1]
I shall never come from hell.
Anima Christi.　　Now is your foe bounden in hell
That ever was busy you for to quell.
Now will I risen,[2] flesh and fell,
That rent was for your sake,
My owen body that hung on rood;
And, be the Jewes never so wood,[3]
It shall arise, both flesh and blood—
My body now will I take.

Resurrection and Appearance to Mother[4]

Tunc transiet Anima Christi ad resuscitandum corpus.[5]
Jesus.　　Hard gates[6] have I gone,
And paines suffered many one,
Stumbled at stake and at stone,
Nigh three and thirty year.
I light out of my Fatheres throne,
For to amend mannes moan:
My flesh was beaten to the bone,
My blood I bled clear.
　　For mannes love I tholed[7] dead,
And for mannes love I am risen up red,[8]
For man I have made my body in[9] bread,
His soul for to feed.
Man, and[10] thou let me thus gone,[10]
And wilt not followen me anon,

---

[1] *foes.*　　[2] *raise.*　　[3] *distraught.*　　[4] *MS continuous.*　　[5] *Then the Spirit of Christ shall cross to resurrect the body.*　　[6] *ways.*　　[7] *suffered.*　　[8] *i.e. stained with blood.*　　[9] *into.*　　[10] *if . . . go.*

Such a friend findest thou never none,
To help thee at thy need.
   Salve! sancta parens,[1] my mother dear,
All hail! mother, with glad cheer,
For now is arisen with body clear
Thy son that was delve[2] deep[2].
This is the third day that I you told
I should arisen out of the clay so cold:
Now am I here with breast full bold—
Therefore, no more you weep!

Maria.   Welcome! my Lord, welcome! my grace,
Welcome! my son and my solace.
I shall thee worship in every place.
Welcome! Lord God of might.
Mickle sorrow in heart I led,[3]
When thou wert laid in deathes bed,
But now my bliss is newly bred—
All men may joy[4] this sight.

Jesus.   All this world that was forlorn
Shall worship you both even and morn,
For, had I not of you been born,
Man had been lost in hell.
I was dead and life I have,
And through my death man do I save,
For now I am risen out of my grave,
In heaven man shall now dwell.

Maria.   Ah! dear son, these wordes are good,
Thou hast well comforted my mourning mood.
Blessed be thy precious blood,
That mankind thus does save!

Jesus. Now, dear mother, my leave I take,
Joy in heart and mirth you[5] make,
For death is dead and life does wake,
Now I am risen from my grave.

---

[1] *Greetings! holy parent: n. 76.*   [2] *dug deep (in grave).*   [3] *endured.*   [4] *enjoy.*
[5] *(do) you.*

Maria.　　　Farewell! my son, farewell! my child,
Farewell! my Lord, my God so mild.
My heart is well that first was wild.
Farewell! my owen dear love.
Now all mankind be glad with glee,
For death is dead, as you may see,
And life is raised endless to be,
In heaven dwelling above.

　　When my son was nailed on tree,
All women might rue with me,
For greater sorrow might never none be
Than I did suffer, iwis.[1]
But this joy now passes all sorrow
That my child suffered in that hard morrow,
For now he is our[2] alderers borrow,[2]
To bring us all to bliss.

Story of the Watch[3]

Tunc evigilabunt milites sepulchri.[4]
Primus miles.[5]　　　Awake! awake!
Hilles gin[6] quake,
And trees are shake
Full near in two!
Stones cleaved,
Wittes are reaved,[7]
Eares are deafed—
I am served so!
Secundus miles.　　　He is arisen, this is no nay!
That was dead and cold in clay

---

[1] *for sure.*　　[2] *the security, sponsor of us all.*　　[3] *MS continuous.*　　[4] *Then the soldiers of the tomb shall wake up.*　　[5] *First soldier.*　　[6] *do.*　　[7] *deprived.*

Now is risen belive[1] this day.
Great wonder it is to me!
He is risen by his owen might,
And forth he goes his way full right.
How shall we now us[2] quit[2]
When Pilate does us see?

Tertius miles.   Let us now go
Pilate unto,
And right even so
As we have seen
The truth we say,
That out of clay
He is risen this day
That Jewes have slain.

Quartus miles.   I hold it best
Let us never rest,
But go we prest[3]
That it were done.
All hail! Pilate,
In thy estate—
He is risen up late
That thou gast[4] doom.[4]

Pilatus.   What! what! what! what!
Out upon thee! Why sayst thou that?
Fie upon thee, harlot![5]
How darst thou so say?
Thou dost[6] my heart right great grief!
Thou liest upon him, false thief!
How should he risen again to life,
That lay dead in clay?

Primus miles.   Yea! though thou be never so wroth,
And of[7] these tidinges never so loth,[7]
Yet, goodly on ground, alive he goth,
Quick and living man.

---

[1] *suddenly.*   [2] *clear ourselves.*   [3] *quickly.*   [4] *sentenced.*   [5] *rascal.*
[6] *causest.*   [7] *to this news never so averse.*

If thou haddest have been there we were,
In heart thou shouldest have had great care,
And of bliss have been right bare,
Of colour both pale and wan.

Pilatus.   Ere you came there
You did all swear
To fight in[1] fere,[1]
And beat and bind.
All this was train:[2]
Your wordes were vain.[3]
This is certain,
You false I find.

Secundus miles.   By the death the devil died!
We were of[4] him so sore atried[5]
That for fear we us down laid,
Right even upon our side.
When we were laid upon the ground
Still we lay as we had been bound,
We durst not rise for a thousand pound,
Nor not for all this world so wide.

Pilatus.   Now, fie upon your great boast!
All your worship[6] is now lost.
In field, in town, and in every coast,[7]
Men may you disproven.[8]
Now all your worship is it lorn,
And every man may you well scorn,
And bid you go sitten in the corn
And chare[9] away the raven!

Tertius miles.   Yea! it was high time to lain[10] our boast,[10]
For when the body took again the ghost
He would have fraid[11] many an host,
King, knight and knave![12]
Yea! when he did rise out of his lake,[13]

---

[1] *together.*   [2] *deceit.*   [3] *empty.*   [4] *by.*   [5] *upset.*   [6] *honour.*   [7] *region.*
[8] *say ill of you, refute your boast (?).*   [9] *drive.*   [10] *cast down our pride.*
[11] *frightened.*   [12] *boy.*   [13] *grave.*

334

Then was there such an earth-quake
That all the world it gan to shake,
That made us for to rave.

Quartus miles.   Yea! yea! hark! fellowes, what I shall
     say,
Let us not cease, by night nor day,
But tell the truth, right as it lay,
In country where we go,
And then, I dare lay[1] my head,
That they that Christes lawes lead
They will never cease till they be dead,
His[2] death that brought him to.[2]

Primus miles.   By Belial! this was now well meant.
To this counsel let us consent!
Let us go tellen with one assent
He is risen up this day.

Secundus miles. I grant thereto and that forthright,
That he is risen by his owen might,
For there came none, by day nor night,
To help him out of clay.

Pilatus.   Now, gentle sires, I pray you all
Abide still a little thrall,[3]
While that I my council call,
And hear of their counsel.

Primus miles. Sir, at your prayer we will abide
Here in this place a little tide,[3]
But tarry not too long, for we must ride,
We may not long dwell.

Pilatus.   Now, gentle sires, I pray you here
Some good counsel me to lere,[4]
For, certes,[5] sires, without dwere,[5]
We stand in right great doubt.[6]

Caiphas. Now truly, sir, I you tell,
This matter is both fierce and fell:

---

[1] *wager.*   [2] *Who brought him to his death.*   [3] *while.*   [4] *teach.*   [5] *certainly
. . . doubt.*   [6] *danger.*

Cumbrous it is therewith to mell,[1]
And evil[2] to be brought about.[2]
Annas.   Sir Pilate, thou great Justice,
Though thou be of wittes wise,
Yet hark! full[3] sadly, with good device,[3]
What that thou shalt do.
I counsel thee, by my reed,[4]
This wonderful tale pray them to heed,
And upon this give them good meed,
Both gold and silver also.
    And, sir, I shall tell you why
In your eares privily,
Between us three certainly—
Now hark! sires, in your eares.
Hic faciant Pilatus, Caiphas et Annas privatim inter se consilium.[5]

Annas. For meed[6] does most in every quest,
And meed is master both east and west,
Now truly, sires, I hold this best—
With meed men may bind beares.
Caiphas.   Secure,[7] sir, this counsel is good!
Pray these knightes to change their mood![8]
Give them gold, feast, and food,
And that may change their wit.[9]
Pilatus. Sires, your good counsel I shall fulfil.
Now, gentle knightes, come hither me[10] till![10]
I pray you, sires, of your good will,
No further that you flit.
    Gentle knightes, I you pray,
A better saw[11] that you say.
Say there he was caught away
With his disciples by night!
Say he was with[12] his disciples fet![13]

---

[1] *have to do.*   [2] *difficult to effect.*   [3] *absolutely seriously, with good intent.*
[4] *advice.*   [5] *Here let Pilate etc. take counsel apart.*   [6] *bribe, reward: n. 77.*
[7] *For sure.*   [8] *attitude.*   [9] *mind.*   [10] *to me.*   [11] *report.*   [12] *by.*   [13] *fetched.*

I would you were in your saddles set,
And have here gold in a purse knit,[1]
And to Rome rideth right.

Quartus miles.   Now, Sir Pilate,
We go our gate:[2]
We will not prate,[3]
No longer now.
Now we have gold,
No tales shall be told
To wightes[4] on wold,[4]
We make thee a vow.

Pilatus.   Now, you men of might,
As you have hight,[5]
Even so forthright
Your[6] wordes not fall.[6]
And you shall gon
With me anon,
All everyone,
Into my hall.

Primus miles.   Now hence we go,
As light as roe,
And right even so
As we have said.
We shall keep counsel
Wheresoever we dwell,
We shall no tales tell—
Be not dismayed!

---

[1] *fastened.*   [2] *way.*   [3] *chatter, blab.*   [4] *people anywhere.*   [5] *promised.*
[6] *Do not let your words fall (?).*

Three Marys at the Tomb[1]

Hic venient ad sepulcrum Maria Magdalen, Maria Jacobi et Maria Salome.[2]

Magdalen.   Sweet sisteren, I you beseech,
Heareth now my special speech.
Go we with salves for to leech[3]
Christ that tholed[4] wound.
He has us wonnen out of wretch.[5]
The right way God will us teach
For to seek my Lord, my leech:
His blood has me unbound.

　　Seven deviles in me were pight.[6]
My love, my Lord, my God almight,
Away he wered[7] those fiendes wight[8]
With his wise word.
He drove from me the fiendes lease,[9]
In my sweet soul his chamber he[10] chose,
In me beliveth the Lord of peace—
I go to his burying[11] board.[11]

Maria Jacobi.   My sisteres son I wot he was.
He lies in her as sun[12] in glass.
The child was born by oxe and ass,
Up in a beastes stall.
Though his body be graved under grass,
The great Godhead is[13] nevertheless.
The Lord shall risen and go his pace,[14]
And comforten his friendes all.

Maria Salome.   My name is Mary Salome!

[1] *n. 78.*   [2] *Here shall come to the tomb, etc.*   [3] *heal.*   [4] *suffered.*   [5] *wretchedness.*   [6] *set.*   [7] *repelled.*   [8] *strong (?), quickly (?).*   [9] *deceit.*   [10] *MS* I.
[11] *funeral feast.*   [12] *traditional image of incarnation: M.E.L. p. 377.*   [13] *(he?) is, exists (?).*   [14] *way.*

His mother and I sisteres we be,
Annes daughteres we are all three.
Jesu, we are thy aunties.
The nailes gun[1] his limbes fein[1]
And the spear gan[2] punch and pain,[2]
On those woundes we would[3] have eyn[3]—
That grace now God grant us.

Maria Magdalen.   Now go we still
With good will
There he is laid.
He died on crutch.[4]
We would him touch
As we have said.

Tunc respicit Maria Magdalene in sepulcro.[5]
   Where is my Lord that was here?
That for me bled, bounden in brier.[6]
His body was buried right by this mere,[7]
That for me gan[8] die.
The Jewes, fickle and false found,
Where have they done[9] the body with wound?
He lies not upon this ground—
The body is done away!

Maria Jacobi.   To[10] my Lord, my love, my friend,
Fain would I salve have spent,
And[11] I might aught amend
His woundes deep and wide.
To my Lord I owe lowlity,[12]
Both homage and fealty:
I would, with my duty,
Have softed[13] hand and side.

Maria Salome.   To mightful God omnipotent
I bear a box of ointment.
I would have softed his sore dent,[14]

[1] fein (?), *emend* frein (? M.E.D. s.v. fraien v. (2)): *bruised his limbs.*   [2] *pierced and hurt.*   [3] *want to look.*   [4] *cross.*   [5] *Then M. M. looks into the tomb.* [6] *a crown of thorns.*   [7] *path (?), boundary (?).*   [8] *did.*   [9] *put.*   [10] *On.*   [11] *If.* [12] (?) *humility (?), emend* loyilte (?) = *loyalty.*   [13] *eased the pain of.*   [14] *wound(s).*

His sides all about.
Lamb of love, without loth,[1]
I find thee not, my heart is wroth.[2]
In the sepulchre there lies a cloth,
And gentle Jesu is out.

Angelus.　　Wendeth forth, you women three,
Into the street of Galilee!
Your saviour there shall you see,
Walking in the way.
Your fleshly Lord now has life
That died on tree with stroke and strife.
Wend forth, thou weeping wife,[3]
And seek him, I thee say.

　Now go forth fast, all three,
To his disciples fair and free,[4]
And to Peter the truth tell ye—
Thereof have you no dread!
Spare you not the sooth to say:
He that was dead and closed in clay,
He is risen, this same day,
And liveth with woundes red.

Maria Magdalen.　　Ah! mirth and joy in heart we have,
For now is risen out of his grave,
He liveth now our life to save,
That dead lay in the clay.

Maria Jacobi. In heart I was right sore dismayed,
The angel to us when that he said
That Christ is risen—I was afraid
The angel when I saw.

Maria Salome.　　Now let us all three fulfil
The angeles word and Godes will.
Let us say with voice[5] well shrill[5]—
Christ that Jewes did slay,
Our Lord, that nailed was on the rood,
And beaten out was his bodyes blood,

---

[1] *evil, spot.*　　[2] *grieved.*　　[3] *women.*　　[4] *excellent.*　　[5] *the loudest voice.*

He is arisen, though they are wood.[1]
Ah! Lord, yet well thou be!

The Apostles at the Tomb[2]

Maria Magdalen. (*Petro et ceteris apostolis.*[3])
    Bretheren all, in heart be glad,
Both blithe and joyful, in heart full fain,
For right good tidinges have we had
That our Lord is risen again!
An angel us bade right thus certain
To thee, Peter, that we should tell,
How Christ is risen, the which was slain,
A living man evermore to dwell.
Maria Jacobi.   To live is risen again that Lord,
The which Judas to Jewes sold.
Of this I bear right true record
By wordes that the angel told.
Now mirth and joy to man on mould![4]
Everyman now mirth may have!
He that was closed in clay full cold
This day is risen out of his grave.
Petrus.   Say me, sisteren, with wordes blithe,
May I trust to that you say?
Is Christ risen again to live,
That was dead and cold in clay?
Maria Salome. Yea! trusteth us, truly, it is no nay!
He is arisen, it is no lease![5]
And so an angel us told this day,
With open voice and speech express.
Johannes.   Yea! these are tidinges of right great bliss,

---

[1] *distraught, mad.*   [2] *MS continuous.*   [3] *To Peter and the other apostles.*
[4] *earth.*   [5] *lie.*

That our master risen should be.
I will go run in haste, iwis,[1]
And look my Lord if I may see.
Petrus. For joy also I run with thee,
My brother, John, as I thee say.
In haste anon even forth go we,
To his grave we run our way.
*Hic currunt Johannes et Petrus simul ad sepulcrum, et
Johannes prius venit ad monumentum sed non intrat.*[2]
Johannes. The same sheet here I see
That Christes body was in wound,
But he is gone wheresoever he be—
He lies not here upon this ground.
Petrus intrat monumentum.[3]
Petrus. In this corner the sheet is found,
And here we find the sudary[4]
In the which his head was wound,
When he was take from Calvary.
Hic intrat Johannes monumentum.[5]
Johannes. The same sudary and the same sheet,
Here with my sight I see both twain.
Now may I well know and wit
That he is risen to live again.
Unto our bretheren let us go sayn
The truth right even as it is,
Our master liveth, the which was slain,
Almighty Lord and King of bliss.
Petrus. No longer here will we dwell:
To our bretheren the way we take.
The truth to them when that we tell,
Great joy in heart then will they make.
Hic Petrus loquitur omnibus apostolis simul collectis.[6]
Be merry, bretheren, for Christes sake!

---

[1] *for sure.* [2] *Here J. and P. run together to the tomb and J. comes to it first but
does not enter.* [3] *Peter goes in.* [4] *cloth, napkin.* [5] *Here J. goes in.* [6] *Here
Peter speaks to all the apostles gathered together.*

That man that is our master so good,
From death to live he is awake,
That sore was rent upon the rood.
Johannes.   As women said, so have we found,
Removed away we saw the stone.
He lies no longer under the ground:
Out of his grave our master is gone.
Thomas. (*Omnibus congregatis.*)[1] We have great wonder every
    one
Of these wordes that you do speak:
A stone full heavy lay him upon—
From under that stone how should he break?
Petrus.   The truth to tellen it passeth our wit,
Whether he is risen through his owen might,
Or elles stolen out of his pit
By some man, privily by night.
That he is gone we saw with sight,
For in his grave he is not.
We cannot tellen in what plight
Out of his grave that he is brought.

Appearance to Mary Magdalen[2]

Maria Magdalen goes to the grave and weeps.
Maria Magdalen.   For heartily sorrow my heart does
    break,
With weeping teares I wash my face.
Alas! for sorrow I may not speak,
My Lord is gone that herein was.
My owen dear Lord and King of grace,
That seven deviles from me did take,

---

[1] (*Speaking*) *for them all gathered together.*   [2] *n. 79.*

I cannot see him, alas! alas!
He is stolen away out of this lake.[1]

Angelus. Woman, that standest here alone,
Why dost thou weep, and mourn, and weep so sore?
What cause hast thou to make such moan?
Why makest thou such sorrow, and wherefore?

Maria Magdalen. I have great cause to weep evermore—
My Lord is take out of his grave,
Stolen away and from me lore:[2]
I[3] cannot wit where him to have.[3]

Hic parum deambulet a sepulcro.[4]

Alas! alas! what shall I do?
My Lord away is from me take.
Ah! woeful wretch, whither shall I go?
My joy is gone out of this lake![5]

Jesus. Woman, such mourning why dost thou make?
Why is thy cheer so heavy and bad?
Why dost thou sigh so sore and quake?
Why dost thou weep so sore and sad?

Maria Magdalen. A greater cause had never woman
For to weep both night and day
Than I myself have in certain
For to sorrowen ever and ay.
Alas! for sorrow my heart does bleed,
My Lord is take from me away.
I must needes sore weep and greet,[6]
Where he is put I cannot say.
But, gentle gardener, I pray to thee,
If thou him took out of his grave,
Tell me where I may him see,
That I may go my Lord to have.

Jesus. (*Spectans.*[7]) M.A.R.I.A.

Maria Magdalen. Ah! master and Lord, to thee I crave,
As thou art Lord and King of bliss,

---

[1] *grave.* [2] *lost.* [3] *I do not know where to find him.* [4] *Here let her walk a little away from the tomb.* [5] *grave.* [6] *wail.* [7] *Looking at her; this line is extrametrical.*

Grant me, Lord, and[1] thou vouchsave,
Thy holy feet that I may kiss.
Jesus.   Touch me not as yet, Mary,
For to my Father I have not ascend.
But to my bretheren in haste thee hie,
With these good wordes their care amend.
Say to my bretheren that I intend
To stey[2] to my Father and to your,
To our Lord, both God and friend,
I will ascend to heaven tower.[3]

In heaven to ordain you a place
To my Father now will I go,
To mirth and joy and great solace
And endless bliss to bring you to.
For man I suffered both shame and woe—
More spiteful death never man did take:
Yet will I ordain for all this, lo!
In heaven an hall[4] for mannes sake.
Maria Magdalen.   Gracious Lord, at your bidding,
To all my bretheren I shall go tell
How that you are man living,
Quick[5] and queathing of flesh and fell.[5]
Now all heaviness I may expel
And mirth and joy now take to me:
My Lord, that I have loved so well,
With open sight I did him see.

When I sought my Lord in grave
I was full sorry and right sad,
For sight of him I might none have:
For mourning sore I was near mad.
Greater sorrow yet never wight[6] had
When my Lord away was gone,
But now in heart I am so glad,
So great a joy never wife had none.

---

[1] *if.*   [2] *ascend.*   [3] *n. 3.*   [4] *n. 3.*   [5] *Alive and speaking in flesh and blood (skin).*   [6] *person.*

How might I more greater joy have
Than see that Lord with open sight,
The which my soul from sin to save
From deviles seven he made me quight.[1]
  There can no tongue my joy express,
Now I have seen my Lord alive,
To my bretheren I will me dress
And tell to them anon right belive.[2]
With open speech I shall me shrive,[3]
And tell to them, with wordes plain,
How that Christ from death to live
To endless bliss is risen again.
  Bretheren all, blithe you be!
For joyful tidinges tellen I can:
I saw our Lord Christ, list well to me,
Of flesh and bone, quick, living man.
Be glad and joyful, as[4] for than,[4]
For, trust me truly, it is right thus:
Mouth to mouth, this certain,
I spoke right now with Christ Jesus.
Petrus.   A wonderful tale forsooth is this!
Ever honoured our Lord may be!
We pray thee, Lord and King of bliss,
Ones[5] thy presence that we may see
Ere thou ascend to thy majesty.
Gracious God, if that you please,
Let us have some sight of thee,
Our careful heartes to set in ease.   Amen.
Explicit apparitio Mariae Magdalenae.[6]

---

[1] *free.*   [2] *quickly*   [3] *confess.*   [4] *therefore.*   [5] *Once.*   [6] *Here ends*
‘ The appearance to M.M.’

Appearance to Cleopas and Luke[1]

Hic incipit apparitio Cleophae et Lucae.[2]

Cleophas.　　My brother, Lukas, I you pray,
　Pleasing to you if that it be,
　To the castle of Emmaus a little way
　That you vouchsafe to go with me.
Lucas. All ready, brother, I walk with thee,
　To yon castle with right good cheer.
　Even together anon go we,
　Brother Cleopas, we two in[3] fere.[3]
Cleophas.　　Ah! brother Lukas, I am sore moved
　When Christ our master cometh in my mind,
　When that I think how he was grieved,[4]
　Joy in my heart can I none find.
　He was so lowly, so good, so kind,
　Holy of life, and meek of mood.
　Alas! the Jewes, they were too blind
　Him for to kill that was so good.
Lucas.　　Brother Cleopas, you say full sooth!
　They were too cursed and too cruel,
　And Judas, that traitor, he was too loth[5]
　For gold and silver his master to sell.
　The Jewes were ready him for to quell,[6]
　With scourges beat out all his blood.
　Alas! they were too fierce and fell:
　Shamefully they hung him on a rood.[7]
Cleophas.　　Yea! between two thieves, alas! for shame,
　They hung him up with body rent.
　Alas! alas! they were to blame,

---

[1] *n. 80.*　　[2] *Here begins 'The appearance to C. and L.'*　　[3] *together.*　　[4] *made to suffer.*　　[5] *loathsome.*　　[6] *kill.*　　[7] *cross.*

Too cursed and cruel was their intent.
When for thirst he was near shent,[1]
Eisell and gall they gaven him to drink.
Alas! for ruth, his death they bent,[2]
In a foul place of horrible stink.

Lucas.   Yea! and cause in him could they none find.
Alas! for sorrow, what was their thought?
And he did help both lame and blind,
And all sick men that were him brought.
Against vice always he wrought.
Sinful deed would he never do,
Yet him to kill they spared not.
Alas! alas! why did they so?

Jesus.   Well[3] over-take you, sires, in same![3]
To walk in fellowship with you I pray.

Lucas. Welcome, sir,[4] in Godes name!
Of good fellowship we say not nay.

Jesus. What[5] is your language, to me you say,
That you have together, you two?[5]
Sorry and heavysome you are alway,
Your mirth is gone—why is it so?

Cleophas.   Sir, me thinketh thou art a poor pilgrim
Here walking by thyself alone,
And in the city of Jerusalem
Thou knowest right little what there is done.
For[6] pilgrimes comen and go right soon,
Right little while pilgrimes do dwell.
In all Jerusalem, as thou hast gone,
I trow no tidinges that thou canst tell.

Jesus.   Why? In Jerusalem what thing is wrought?
What tidinges from thence bring ye?

Lucas. Ah! there have they slain a man for nought!
Guiltless he was, as we tell thee.
An holy prophet with God was he,

---

[1] *overcome.*   [2] *brought about.*   [3] *Gentlemen, you are well-overtaken together.*
[4] MS serys.   [5] *Do tell me what you two are talking about together.*   [6] *Because.*

348

Mightily in word and eke[1] in deed.
Of God he had right great poosty:[2]
Among the people his name gan[3] spread.
  He hight[4] Jesu of Nazareth.
A man he was of right great fame.
The Jewes him killed with cruel death,
Without trespass or any blame.
Him to scorn they had great game,
And nailed him straight until a tree.
Alas! alas! me thinketh great shame
Without cause that this should be.

Cleophas.   Yea! sir, and right great trust in him we had
All Israel country that he should save.
The third day is this that he was clad
In cold clay and laid in grave,
Yet wonderful tidinges of him we have
Of women that sought him before day-light.
Whether they say truth or elles do rave,
We cannot tell the true verdict.
  When Christ in grave they could not see
They camen to us and even thus told,
How that an angel said to them three
That he should live, with breast full bold.
Yet Peter and John prove this would—
To Christes grave they ran, they twain,
And when they came to the grave so cold
They found the women full true certain.

Jesus.   Ah! you fonnes[5] and slow of heart
For to believe in Holy Scripture,
Have not prophetes, with wordes smart,[6]
Spoke by tokenes[7] in signifure[7]
That Christ should die for[8] your valure,[8]
And sith[9] enter his joy and bliss.

---

[1] *also.*   [2] *might.*   [3] *did.*   [4] *was called.*   [5] *fools.*   [6] *sharp.*   [7] *signs
to signify.*   [8] *(in satisfaction) for your value (p. 212, ll. 4–6, pp. 115 ff.).*
[9] *afterwards.*

Why are you of heart so dure,[1]
And trust not in God that mightful is?
Both Moses and Aaron and other[2] mo[2]—
In Holy Scripture you may read it—
Of Christes death they spoke also,
And how he should rise out of his pit.
Out of faith then why do you flit
When holy prophetes you teach so plain?
Turn your thought and change your wit,
And trust well that Christ does live again.

Lucas.   Live again, man? Be[3] in peace![3]
How should a dead man ever arise?
I counsel thee such wordes to cease
For doubt[4] of Pilate that high Justice.
He was slain at the great assize
By counsel of Lordes, many one.
Of such language take better advice
In every company there thou dost gone.

Christus.   Truth did never his master shame.
Why should I cease then truth to say?
By Jonas, the prophet, I prove the same,
That was in a whales body three nightes and three day,
So long Christ in his grave lay
As Jonas was within the sea.
His grave is broken that was of clay:
To life risen again now is he.

Cleophas.   Say not so, man, it may not be!
Though thy example be some-deal[5] good.
For Jonas alive evermore was he,
And Christ was slain upon a rood.[6]
The Jewes on[7] him they were so wood[7]
That to his heart a spear they pight:[8]
He bled out all his heart blood—
How should he then rise with might?

---

[1] *hard.*   [2] *many others.*   [3] *Don't talk so!*   [4] *fear.*   [5] *somewhat.*   [6] *cross.*
[7] *were so mad at him.*   [8] *stabbed.*

Christus.   Take heed at Aaron and his dead stick,[1]
  Which was dead of his[2] nature,
  And yet he[2] flourished with flowers full thick,
  And bore almondes of great valure.[3]
  The dead stick was signifure[4]
  How Christ, that shamefully was dead and slain,
  As that dead stick bore fruit full pure,
  So Christ should rise to live again.

Lucas.   That a dead stick fruit should bear
  I marvel sore thereof, iwis.[5]
  But yet himself from death to rear
  And live again more wonder it is!
  That he does live—I trust not this,
  For he has bled his blood so red.
  But yet of[6] mirth evermore I miss[6]
  When I have mind that he is dead.

Christus.   Why are you so hard of trust?
  Did not Christ raise through his owen might
  Lazare that dead lay under the dust,
  And stinked right foul, as I you plight?
  To life Christ raised him again full right
  Out of his grave, this is certain.
  Why may not Christ himself thus quight,[7]
  And rise from death to live again?

Cleophas.   Now truly, sir, your wordes are good!
  I have in you right great delight.
  I pray you, sir, with mild mood
  To dwell with us all this night.

Christus. I must go hence anon full right
  For great messages I have to do.
  I would abide if that I might,
  But at this time I must hence go.

Lucas.   You shall not go from us this night!
  It waxeth all dark, gone is the day,

[1] *Num. xvii, 8.*   [2] *it(s).*   [3] *worth.*   [4] *a prefiguration: pp. 63–4.*
[5] *indeed.*   [6] *I am for ever without joy.*   [7] *redeem.*

The sun is down, lorn[1] is the light—
You shall not go from us away!
Christus. I may not dwell, as I you say.
    I must this night go to my friend.
    Therefore, good bretheren, I you pray,
    Let[2] me not my way to wend.
Cleophas.   Truly from us you shall not go!
    You shall abide with us here still.
    Your goodly dalliance[3] pleaseth us so
    We may never have of you our fill.
    We pray you, sir, with hearty will,
    All night with us abide and dwell,
    More goodly language to talken us till,
    And of your good dalliance more for to tell.
Lucas.   Yea! brother Cleopas, by my assent,
    Let us him keep with strength and might.
    Set on your hand with good intent,
    And pull him with us the way well right.
    The day is done, sir, and now it is night—
    Why will you hence now from us go?
    You shall abide, as I you plight,
    You shall not walk this night us fro.
Cleophas.   This night from us you go not away!
    We shall you keep between us twain.
    To us therefore you say not nay,
    But walk with us, the way is plain.
Christus. Sithen[4] you keep me with might and main,
    With hearty will I shall abide.
Lucas. Of your abiding we are full fain,
    No man more welcome in this world wide.
Cleophas.   Of our master, Christ Jesu,
    For you do speak so much good,
    I love you heartily, trust me true!
    He was both meek and mild of mood.
    Of him to speak is to me food.

[1] *lost.*   [2] *Hinder.*   [3] *conversation.*   [4] *Since.*

If you had known him, I dare well say,
And in what plight with him it stood,
You would have thought on him many a day.

Lucas.   Many a day, yea! yea! iwis.[1]
He was a man of holy living.
Though he had been the child of God in bliss,
Both wise and wonderful was his working.
But after your labour and far walking,
Taketh this loaf and eateth some bread,
And then will we have more talking
Of Christ our master, that is now dead.

Christus.   Be merry and glad, with heart full free,
For of Christ Jesu, that was your friend,
You shall have tidinges of game and glee
Within a while, ere you hence wend.
    With my hand this bread I bless,
And break it here as you do see.
I give you part also of this,
This bread to eat and blithe to be.
Hic subito discedat Christus ab oculis eorum.[2]

[*Cleophas.*]   Ah! mercy, God, what[3] was our hap![3]
Was not our heart with love burning,
When Christ, our master, so[4] near our lap,[4]
Did sit and speak such sweet talking?
He is now quick and man living,
That first was slain and put in grave.
Now may we change all our mourning,
For our Lord is risen his servantes to save.

Lucas.   Alas! for sorrow, what hap was this?
When he did walk with us in way
He proved by Scripture, right well, iwis,[5]
That he was risen from under clay.
We trusted him not, but ever said nay.
Alas! for shame, why said we so?

---

[1] *indeed.*   [2] *Here let Christ disappear from their eyes suddenly.*   [3] *what fortune was ours!*   [4] *so intimate with us.*   [5] *indeed.*

He is risen to live this day,
Out of his grave our Lord is go.

Appearance to Thomas[1]

Cleophas.   Let us here no longer dwell,
But to our bretheren the way we wend.
With tales true to them we tell
That Christ does live our master and friend.
Lucas. I grant thereto with heart full[2] hend.[2]
Let us go walk forth in our way.
I am full joyful in heart and mind
That our Lord liveth that first dead lay.
Cleophas.   Now was it not goodly done
Of Christ Jesu, our master dear?
He has with us a large way gone.
And of his uprising he did us lere.[3]
When he walked with us in[4] fere,[4]
And we supposed him both dead and cold,
That he was arisen from under bere[5]
By Holy Scripture the truth he told.
Lucas.   Right lovingly done, forsooth, this was!
What might our master till[6] us do more
Than us to cheer, that forth did pass,
And for his death we mourned full sore?
For love of him our mirth was lore.[7]
We were for him right heavy in heart,
But now our mirth he does restore,
For he is risen, both hale and quart.[8]
Cleophas.   That he is thus risen I have great wonder.
An heavy stone over him there lay.

---

[1] *MS continuous.*   [2] *most happy.*   [3] *teach.*   [4] *together.*   [5] *burying.*   [6] *for.*
[7] *lost.*   [8] *well.*

How should he break the stone asunder,
That was dead and cold in clay?
Every man this[1] marvel may,[1]
And dread that Lord of mickle might.
But yet of this no man say nay,
For we have seen him with open sight.

Lucas.   That he does live I wot well this:
He is arisen with flesh and blood.
A living man, forsooth, he is,
That ruely[2] was rent upon a rood.[3]
All hail! dear brother, and change your mood!
For Christ does liven and has his heal.[4]
We walked in way with Christ so good,
And spoke with him wordes fele.[5]

Cleophas.   Even till[6] Emmaus, the great castell,
From Jerusalem with him we went,
Sixty furlong, as we you tell,
We went with him even[7] passent.[7]
He spoke with us with good intent:
That Christ should live he told till[6] us,
And proved it by Scripture, verament.[8]
Trust me true, it is right thus!

Lucas.   Yea, and when he had long spoken us till,[6]
He would from us have gone his way.
With strength and might we kepten him still,
And bread we tooken[9] him to eaten, in[10] fay.[10]
He broke the loaf as even[11] in tway[11]
As any sharp knife should cut bread.
Thereby we knew the truth that day
That Christ did live and was not dead.

Petrus.   Now truly, sires, I have great wonder
Of these great marveles that you us tell.
In breaking of bread full even asunder
Our master you knew and Lord right well.

---

[1] *may wonder (at) this.*   [2] *pitifully.*   [3] *cross.*   [4] *health.*   [5] *many.*   [6] *to.*
[7] *steadily travelling.*   [8] *truly.*   [9] *gave.*   [10] *believe us.*   [11] *exactly in two.*

You say Christ liveth that Jewes did quell[1]—
Till[2] us glad tidinges, this is certain,
And that our master with you so long did dwell
It does well prove that he liveth again.
    Ah! brother Thomas we may be right glad
Of these good novel[3] that we now have.
The grace of our Lord God is over us all spread!
Our Lord is risen his servantes to save!

Thomas. Be in peace, Peter, thou ginnest[4] to rave![4]
Thy wordes are wanton and right unwise.
How should a dead man that dead lay in grave
With quick flesh and blood to live again rise?

Petrus.   Yes, Thomas, doubt thee not our master is alive!
Record of Magdalen and of her sisteres two;
Cleopas and Lukas, the truth for to contrive,[5]
From Jerusalem to Emmaus with him did they go.

Thomas. I may never in heart trust that it is so.
He was dead on cross and cold put in pit,
Kept with knightes four, his grave sealed also:
How should he liven again that[6] so straight was shut?[6]

Petrus.   When Magdalen did tell us that Christ was arisen,
I ran to his grave and John ran with me.
In truth there we found he lay not in prison,
Gone out of his grave and alive then was he.
Therefore, dear brother Thomas, I will rede[7] thee,
Steadfastly thou trust that Christ is not dead,
Faithfully believe a quick man that he be,
Arisen from his death by might of his Godhead.

Thomas.   I may never believe these wonder marveles,
Till that I have sight of every great wound,
And put in my finger in place of the nailes,
I shall never believe it, elles, for no man on ground,
And till that my hand the speares pit has found,

---

[1] *kill.*   [2] *To.*   [3] *news.*   [4] *art talking nonsense.*   [5] *establish (?), tell (?).*
[6] *who was so narrowly confined.*   [7] *advise.*

Which did cleave his heart and made him spread his
    blood,
I shall never believe that he is quick and sound,
In truth, while I know that he was dead on rood.[1]

Petrus.   Christ be thy comfort and change thy bad wit[2]—
For faith but[3] thou have, thy soul is but lorn![4]
With steadfast belief God[5] inform[5] thee yet,
Of a meek maid as he was for us born.

Christus. Peace be among you! Behold how I am torn!
Take heed of my handes, my dear brother Thomas.

Thomas. My God and my Lord! Night and every morn
I ask mercy, Lord, for my great trespass.

Christus.   Behold well, Thomas, my woundes so wide,
Which I have suffered for all mankind.
Put thy whole hand into my right side,
And in my heart blood thy hand that thou wind.
So faithful a friend where mayst thou find?
Be steadfast in faith, believe well in me!
Be thou not doubtful of me in thy mind,
But trust that I live that dead was on a tree.

Thomas.   My Lord and my God, with sight do I see
That thou art now quick which hung dead on rood.
More faithful than I there may no man be,
For my hand have I washed in thy precious blood.

Christus. For thou hast me seen, therefore thy faith is good.
But blessed be those of this that have no sight
And believe in me! They, for their meek mood,
Shall come into heaven my bliss that is so bright.

Thomas.   As a ravished man whose wit is all gone
Great mourning I make for my dreadful doubt.
Alas! I was doubtful that Christ from under stone
By his owen great might no wise might go out.
Alas! what moved me thus in my thought?
My doubtful belief right sore me[6] avexit.[6]

---

[1] *cross.*   [2] *understanding.*   [3] *unless.*   [4] *lost.*   [5] *(may) God instruct (inspire ?).*   [6] *carried me away.*

The truth do I know that God so has wrought
Quod mortuus et sepultus nunc resurrexit.[1]
   He that was both dead and cold put in grave
To live is arisen by his owen might.
In his dear heart blood my hand washed I have,
Where that the spear point was painfully pight.[2]
I take[3] me[3] to faith, forsaking all unright,[4]
The doubt that I had full sore me avexit,
For now I have seen with full open sight
Quod mortuus et sepultus nunc resurrexit.[1]
   I trusted no tales that were me told
Till that my hand did in his heart blood wade.
My doubt does approven[5] Christ living full bold,
And is a great argument in faith us to glad.[6]
Thou man, that seest this, from faith never thou fade.[7]
My doubt shall ever cheer thee, that sore me avexit.
Trust well in Christ that such miracle has made,
Quod mortuus et sepultus nunc resurrexit.
   The preaching of Peter might not convert me
Till I felt the wound that the spear did cleave.
I trusted never he lived, that dead was on a tree,
Till that his heart blood did run in my sleeve.
Thus, by my great doubt, our faith may we prove.
Behold my bloody hand, to faith that me avexit.
By[8] sight of this mirror from faith not remove,[8]
Quod mortuus et sepultus nunc resurrexit.
   Though that Mary Magdalen in Christ did soon
     believe,
And I was long doubtful, yet put me in no blame,
For by my great doubt our faith we may prove
Against all the heretickes that speak of Christ shame.
Trust well Jesu Christ, the Jewes killed the same.
The fiend has he feared,[9] our faith that ever avexit.

---

[1] *That, dead and buried, now he is risen.*   [2] *thrust.*   [3] *give myself.*   [4] *wrong.*
[5] *prove.*   [6] *gladden.*   [7] *weaken, grow dim.*   [8] *By looking at my example,*
stick to your faith.   [9] *scared.*

To heaven you bring, and save you all in [1] same,[1]
That mortuus[2] et sepultus iterum resurrexit.[2]   Amen.

Ascension[3]

*Hic incipit Ascensio Domini nostri, cum Maria et undecim
discipulis et duobus angelis sedentibus in albis.*[4]
Jesus.   Pax vobis! Among you peace!
Both love and rest and charity,
Among all virtues let it not cease,
For among all virtues principal is he.
    You are to blame, I may well prove,
For I will use to you wordes plain,
That you are so hard of heart to believe
That from death to live I am risen again.
Notwithstanding, as you know certain,
To you eight sithes[5] appeared have I
By sundry times the truth to sayn,
And this is the ninth time, soothly,
Even and no mo.[6]
But now some meat
Anon[7] do get,[7]
For I will eat
With you and go.
    My disciples, hear what I say,
And to my wordes giveth attention.
From Jerusalem look you go not away,
But meekly abideth my Fatheres promiscion,[8]
Of which, by my mouth, you have had information,
While bodily with you I was dwelling.
For John, soothly, for mannes salvation,

---

[1] *together.*   [2] *dead and buried is risen again.*   [3] *n. 81.*   [4] *Here begins*
'The Ascension of our Lord' with M. and eleven disciples and two angels sitting in
albs.   [5] *times.*   [6] *more.*   [7] *have brought immediately.*   [8] *promise.*

Only in water was me baptizing.
But I you behete,[1]
Within few days, that ye
In the Holy Ghost shall baptized be.
Therefore riseth up, and followeth me
Unto the Mount of Olivet.

Jacobus major. Oh! Lord, vouchsafe us for to tell
If thou wilt now without more delay
Restoren the Kingdom of Israel,
And give us the joy, Lord, that lasteth ay?

Jesus. Sires, the times and the monthes know[2] you ne
    may[2]
Which my Father has put in his owen power.
But you shall take, within short day,
Of the Holy Ghost the virtue clear,
Through which shall ye
In Jerusalem and in Jewry,
And, moreover, also in Samary,
And to the worldes end utterly,
My witness only be.
    Loveth no wrath nor no wrong,
But liveth in charity with[3] mild steven.[3]
With mirth and melody and angel song,
Now I stey[4] straight from you to heaven.
Hic ascendit ab oculis eorum et in caelo cantent etc.[5]

Angelus. Returneth again to your lodging,
To Jerusalem, for he will[6] thus,[6]
His promise meekly there abiding.
For doubtless this foresaid Jesus,
Which from you is take
In a cloud, as you him seen,
Steying[4] up, so shall comen again.
Of all mankind, this is certain,
Judgement shall he make.

---

[1] *promise.*   [2] *you may not know.*   [3] *gently spoken.*   [4] *ascend(ing).*   [5] *Here he ascends from their eyes, and in heaven let them sing etc.: n. 82.*   [6] *wishes it.*

Matthias[1]

[*Peter*].   Oh! you bretheren, attendeth to me,
And taketh good heed what I shall sayn.
It behoveth the Scripture fulfilled to be
That of[2] David[2] was said with wordes plain,
Of Judas, which was the guide certain
Of them that Christ slew cruelly,
Which after from death rose up again,
And has abiden in earth full days fourty.
And after all this
Before our eye
In a bright sky
He did up sty[3]
To heaven bliss.
    This said Judas was amongst us,
Numbered apostle and had like dignity.
But when he betrayed our Lord Jesus,
He hung himself upon a tree.
In whose stead must needes ordained be
Another our number for to restore,
One of those which as well know we
Have been conversant here long before
In our company,
Which shall witness
Bearen[4] express[4]
To more and less
Of Christes resurrection steadfastly.
Hic statuent duos Joseph Justum et Matthiam etc.[5]
    Oh! sovereign Lord, which of every man

---

[1] *n. 82a.*   [2] *by David: Psalms xli, 9; lxix, 25; cix, 8.*   [3] *ascend.*   [4] *Bear
plainly, certainly.*   [5] *Here they shall set up two, J. J. and M. etc.*

The heartes dost know most inwardly,
With all the lowliness we may or can
To thee we pray full[1] benignly[1]
That thou vouchsafe, through thy mercy,
Us him to show which, in this case,
Thou likest to choosen effectuously[2]
To occupy the lot of Judas place.
Hic dabunt sortes et cadet super Matthiam etc.[3]
Now gramercy, Lord!
And to fulfil
Thy holy will,
As it is skill,[4]
We all accord.[5]

Pentecost[6]

Modo de die Pentecostes. Apostoli dicant genuflectentes.
Spiritus Sanctus descendat super eos etc.[7]

Petrus.[8] Honour	*Andreas.* Worship	*Jacobus major.* and Reverence
Johannes. Glory	*Philippus.* Grace	*Jacobus minor.* and Goodness
Thomas. Dignity	*Bartholomeus.* Virtue	*Simon.* and Excellence
Matheus. Beauty	*Judas.* Blessing	*Matheas.* and Brightness

[1] *with all humility (?).* [2] *effectively.* [3] *Here they will give the lots, and it will fall on M. etc.* [4] *right.* [5] *agree.* [6] *n. 83.* [7] *Now about the Day of Pentecost. Let the apostles speak genuflecting. Let the Holy Spirit descend upon them etc.* [8] *The names of the apostles, each of whom says one word of the first four lines of the stanza, are written in red in rather larger letters.*

Petrus. Be to that Lord high worthiness!
Andreas. Which has performed that[1] he us hight,[1]
Jacobus major. And us embalmed with such sweetness,
Johannes. Which to descry[2] far passeth our might.
Philippus. This we all well ken.
Jacobus minor. Now, gracious Lord Jesu,
Thomas. Confirm us in thy virtue,
Bartholomeus. And grant us grace ever it to sue,[3]
Simon. Say we all together—Amen! Amen!

    Et omnes osculant terram.[4]

Primus judeus.[5]   Now, fellowes, take heed for, by my troth,
    Yonder sitteth a drunken fellowship.
Secundus judeus. To do them good it were great ruth.
Tertius judeus. Yea, I pray God give them all shenship.[6]
Primus judeus. Must[7] in their brain so slyly does creep
    That they chatteren and chatteren as they jays were.
Secundus judeus. Yea, were[8] they any well brought asleep,[8]
    It[9] were almes to the river them to bear,[9]
    There them to baptize!
Primus judeus. That were, as thinketh[10] me,[10]
    A gentle sport to see!
    A better game to be
    Could no man devise.
Petrus.   Sires, alas! what do you mean?
    Why scorn you now thus Godes grace?
    It is nothing as you do ween.
    There is no drunk man in this place,
    Wherefore right great is your trespass.
    But, sires, list what it does signify:
    Fulfilled is now to mannes solace
    Of Joel[11] the pregnant prophecy,
    In which that he

---

[1] *what he promised us.*   [2] *describe.*   [3] *follow.*   [4] *And they all kiss the ground.*   [5] *First Jew.*   [6] *disgrace.*   [7] *New wine.*   [8] *were any of them to fall into a good sleep (?).*   [9] *It would be charitable to carry them to the river.*   [10] *it seems to me.*   [11] *Joel ii, 28.*

That[1] you have seen,
In wordes plain,
Declareth certain.
Now blessed God be!   Amen.

Assumption[2]

[*Doctor introduces* The Assumption of the Glorious
Mother Mary *to* right worshipful sovereignes, *saying she
was sixty when she was assumed into Heaven* as Scripture
does specify *and* Legenda Sanctorum authorizeth.]
. . . blessed may she be! We ought to be saying
How she was assumpt, here men shall be playing,
Praying you of audience, now cease and take heed! . . .
[*The Jewish rulers are shown planning to burn Mary's body
when she dies and to kill the disciples who are preaching that
Jesus lives. Divine Wisdom sends an angel to Mary, who
asks his name.*]
Angelus. What needeth you, Lady, my name be desiring?
Maria. Ah! yes, gracious angel, I beseech you requiring.
Angelus.   My name is great and marvellous, truly you
     telling,
The high God, your son, abideth you in bliss.
The third day hence you shall be expiring,
And ascend to the presence, there my God, your son, is.
Maria. Mercy and gramercy, God, now may I be saying,
Thanking you, sweet angel, for this message, iwis.[3]
Angelus. In tokening whereof, Lady, I am here presenting
A branch of a palm—out of paradise came this.
Before your bier God biddeth it be bore.
Maria. Now thank be to that Lord of his mercy evermore.

---

[1] *That (which).*   [2] *n. 84.*   [3] *indeed.*

Angelus.   Your meekness, your lowness and your high
    lore[1]
Is most acceptable in the Trinity sight.
Your seat royal in heaven apparelled[2] is there:
Now dispose you to die, your son wills thus right.
Maria. I obey the commandment of my God here before.
    But one thing I beseech that Lord, of his might,
    That my brothers, the apostles, might me be before,
    To see me and I them ere I pass to that light.
    But they are so desevered[3] me thinketh it nil[4] be.
Angelus. Ah! yes, Lady, impossible to God nothing trow ye!

. . . .

[*The angel ascends.*]

. . . .

*Hic subito apparet Sanctus Johannes Evangelista ante
portam Mariae.*[5]
Johannes.   Ah! mirable[6] God, much is thy might!
Many wonderes thou workest even as thy will is.
In Pheso I was preaching, a far country right,
And by a white cloud I was rapt to these hilles.
Here dwelleth Christes Mother I see well in sight.
Some marvellous message is comen that maid till.[7]
I will go saluse[8] that bird[8] that in virtue is most bright,
And of my sudden coming wit[9] what is the skill.[9]
Hic pulsabit super portam intrante domum Mariae.[10]
Hail! Mother Mary, maiden perpetual!
Maria.   Ah! welcome maid[11] John, with all my heart in
    special!
For joy of your presence my heart ginneth[12] sweme.[12]
Think you not, John, how my child eternal,
When he hung on cross, said[13] us this theme:[13]
Lo! here thy son, woman, so bade he me you call,

---

[1] *teaching* (? *of her son* ?), *story* (?), *doctrine* (?).   [2] *prepared.*   [3] *separated.*
[4] *will not.*   [5] *Here S. J. E. suddenly appears before M.'s door.*   [6] *wondrous.*
[7] *to.*   [8] *greet that lady.*   [9] *learn . . . reason.*   [10] *Here he shall knock on the door
as he enters the house of M.*   [11] *virgin.*   [12] *is overcome.*   [13] *spoke in these
words to us.*

365

And you me mother, each other to queme.[1]

He betook[2] you the governail[2] there of my body terrestrial:

One maid to another as convenience[3] would seem.[3]

. . . .

[*Mary continues: Now an angel says I shall die. Please carry this palm which he gave me before my bier and see that I am buried, for I hear the Jews intend to burn my body since Jesus was born of me. The other apostles promise assistance and Mary dies. Miracles prevent the Jewish rulers interrupting the burial.* Hic ponent corpus in sepulcrum incensantes et cantantes.[4]]

. . . .

Dominus.[5]   Now angel, and all this court celestial,

Into earth now descendeth with me,

To raise the body of my mother terrestrial,

And bring we it to the bliss of my deity.

Assent you hereto now the[6] unity.[6]

Angeli. Yea, for your high mercy, Lord, all heaven maketh melody.

Dominus. (*Hic descendit et venit ad apostolos.*[7])

Peace be to you all, my postles so dear.

Lo! me here, your Lord and your God now right is.

Petrus. Ah! welcome Christ, our comfort, in thy manhood[8] clear.

Great, marvellous God, mickle now thy might is!

Dominus. What[9] worship and grace seemeth you now here,[9]

That I do to this body, Mary[10] that hight is?[10]

Johannes. Lord, as thou rose from death and reignest in thy empire,

So raise thou this body to thy bliss that light is—

Us seemeth this right is.

---

[1] *gratify.*   [2] *committed to you the direction.*   [3] *would seem suitable.*   [4] *Here they shall place the body in the tomb, incensing it and singing.*   [5] *The Lord.* [6] *everyone of you* (?).   [7] *Here he descends and comes to the Apostles.*   [8] *human (as distinct from divine) nature.*   [9] *What honour and favour do you now here think fit.*   [10] *Mary by name.*

Michael. Yea, glorious God, lo! the soul[1] here, prest now,
    To this blessed body liketh it you to fast[1] now,
    Heaven and earth would think this the best now,
    In as much as she bore you, God, in your mightes.
    Hic vadit anima in corpus Mariae.[2]
Dominus.   Go, then, blessed soul, to that body again!
    Arise now, my dove, my neighbour, and my sweet friend!
    Tabernacle of joy, vessel of life, heavenly temple to reign,
    You shall have the bliss with me, Mother, that has no end.
    For as you were clean in earth of[3] all sinnes grain,[3]
    So shall you reign in heaven, cleannest[4] in mind.[4]
Maria. Ah! endless worship be to you, Jesu, releaser of
    pain.
    I and all earth may bless you, come of our kind.[5]
    Lo! me ready with you for to wend.
Dominus. Aboven heavenes, Mother, ascend then we,
    In endless bliss for to be.
Michael. Heaven and earth now enjoy may ye,
    For God through Mary is made mannes friend.
    Et hic ascendent in caelum cantantibus organis.[6]
    Assumpta es, Maria, in caelum.[7]
Dominus.   You to worship, Mother, it liketh[8] the whole
    Trinity,
    Wherefore I crown you here in this kingdom of glory.
    Of all my chosen, thus shall you cleped[9] be,
    Queen of Heaven[10] and Mother of Mercy.
Michael. Now blessed be your names, we cry!
    For this holy Assumption all heaven maketh melody.

---

[1] *(if) it pleases you to fasten the soul to this body speedily.*   [2] *Here the spirit goes into the body of M.*   [3] *of the colour of all sins.*   [4] *purest in heart.*   [5] *nature.* [6] *And here they shall ascend into the heavens with instruments playing.* (*Hildburgh,* 64–8).   [7] *Mary, thou art taken up into the heavens.*   [8] *pleases.*   [9] *called.* [10] *Coronation: n. 85.*

Doomsday[1]

Hic incipit Dies Iudicii et Jesu descendente cum Michaele et Gabriele Archangelis.[2]

Michael.   Surgite! All men arise!
    Venite ad judicium![3]
    For now is set the high Justice,
    And has assigned the Day of Doom.
    Rape[4] you readily[4] to this great assize,
    Both great and small, all and some,
    And of your answer you now advise,
    What he shall say when that you come
    Your answer for to tell.
    For when that God shall you appose[5]
    There[6] is no help of no gloss.[6]
    The truth full truly he will tose,[7]
    And send you to heaven or hell.

Gabriell.   Both Pope, Prince and Priest with crown,
    King and Caesar and Knightes keen,
    Rapely[8] you run your reasones to rown,[8]
    For this shall be the day of teen.[9]
    Neither poor nor rich of great renown,
    Nor all the deviles in hell that been,
    From this day you hide not mown,[10]
    For all your deedes here shall be seen
    Openly in sight.
    Who that is founden in deadly guilt,
    He were better to been hilt.[11]

---

[1] n. 86.   [2] *Here begins the Day of Judgement and Jesus descending with the archangels M. and G.: n. 87.*   [3] *Come to the Judgement.*   [4] *Hasten quickly.*
[5] *examine.*   [6] *Explanations won't be of any help.*   [7] *search out.*   [8] *Run quickly to tell your reasons.*   [9] *wrath.*   [10] *may.*   [11] *hidden away.*

In endless hell he shall be spilt:[1]
His deedes his death shall dight.[2]
Omnes resurgentes subtus terram clamaverunt:[3] Ha! aa! ha!
    aa! ha! aa! *Deinde surgentes dicant:*[4]
    Ha! aa! cleave asunder, you clodes of clay,
Asunder you break and let us pass!
Now may our song be 'welaway',
That ever we sinned in deadly trespass.
Omnes daemones clamant:[5] Harrow and out! What shall we
    say?
    Harrow! we cry, out! and alas!
Alas! harrow! is this that day
To endless pain that us must pass?
Alas! harrow! and out! we cry.
Omnes animae resurgentes dicant:[6]
    Ah! mercy, Lord, for our misdeed,
And let thy mercy spring and spread!
But, alas! we biden[7] in dread:
It is too late to ask mercy.
Deus.   Venite! benedicti,[8] my bretheren all,
Patris[9] mei[9] you childeren dear,
Come hither to me to my high hall,
All those my[10] suitores[10] and servantes were.[11]
All those foul wormes from you fall.
With my right hand I bless you here,
My blessing burnisheth you as bright as beryl,
As crystal clean it cleanseth you clear,
All filth from you fade.
Peter to heaven gates thou wend and go,
The lockes thou loosen and them undo.
My blessed childeren thou bring me to,
Their heartes for to glad.
Petrus.   The gates of heaven I open this tide.[12]

---

[1] *destroyed.*   [2] *bring about.*   [3] *All rising from under the ground, they cry.*
[4] *Then rising, let them say.*   [5] *All the demons cry out.*   [6] *All the souls rising
shall say.*   [7] *wait.*   [8] *Come, blessed ones.*   [9] *Of my father.*   [10] *(who) my
followers.*   [11] *MS be.*   [12] *moment.*

Now welcome, dear bretheren, to heaven, iwis![1]
Come on and sit on Godes right side,
Where mirth and melody never may miss.
Omnes salvati.[2] On knee we creep, we go, we glide,
 To worship our Lord that merciful is,
 For through his woundes that are so wide
 He has brought us to his bliss.
 Holy Lord, we worship thee.
Deus. Welcome you are in heaven to sit!
 Welcome! from me shall you never flit.
 So secure of bliss you shall be yet,
 To mirth and joy welcome you be!
Animae damnandum.[3] Ah! Ah! mercy! mercy! we cry
  and crave,
 Ah! mercy! Lord, for our misdeed,
 Ah! mercy! mercy! we rub,[4] we rave,[4]
 Ah! help us, good Lord, in this need!
Deus. How would you wretches any mercy have?
 Why ask you mercy now in this need?
 What have you wrought your soul to save?
 To whom have you done any merciful deed,
 Mercy for to win?
Primus diabolus.[5] Mercy?—nay! nay! they shall have
  wrake![6]
 And that on their forehead witness I take:
 For there is written with letteres black
 Openly all their sin.
Deus. To hungry and thirsty[7] that asked in my name
 Meat and drink would you give none.
 Of naked men had you no shame.
 You would not visit men in no prison.
 You had no pity on sick nor lame.
 Deed of mercy would you never done.

---

[1] *indeed.*   [2] *All the redeemed.*   [3] *The souls of the damned.*   [4] *fret* (?), *wring* (*hands*) (?), *we go frantic.*   [5] *First devil.*   [6] *retribution.*   [7] *Corporal works of mercy follow.*

Unharboured[1] men you served the same.
To bury the dead poor man would you not gone.
These deedes do you spill.[2]
For your love was I rent on rood,[3]
And for your sake I shed my blood:
When I was so merciful and so good,
Why have you wrought against my will?
Secundus diabolus.　　I find here written on thy forehead
Thou were so stout and set in pride[4]
Thou wouldest not give a poor man bread,
But from thy door thou wouldest him chide.
Tertius diabolus. And in thy face here do I read
That if a thirsty man came any[5] tide,[5]
For thirst though he should be dead,
Drink from him thou wouldest ever hide—
On covetise[6] was all thy thought.
Primus diabolus. In wrath thy neighbour to backbite,
Them for to anger was thy delight.
Thou were ever ready them to indict.
On the sick man ruest[7] thou not.[7]
Secundus diabolus.　　Evermore on envy was all thy mind:
Thou wouldest never visit no prisoner.
To all thy neighboures thou wert unkind:
Thou wouldest never help man in danger.
Tertius diabolus. The sin of sloth thy soul shall shend:[8]
Mass nor matines wouldest thou none hear;
To bury the dead man thou wouldest not wend.
Therefore thou shalt to endless fire:
To[9] sloth thou were full prest.[9]
Primus diabolus. Thou haddest rejoice in gluttony,
In drunkeship and in ribaldry;[10]
Unharboured[11], with villainy[11]
Thou puttest from their rest.

[1] *Homeless.*　　[2] *destroy, ruin.*　　[3] *cross.*　　[4] *Seven deadly sins follow.*　　[5] *(at)
any time.*　　[6] *covetousness.*　　[7] *thou haddest no compassion.*　　[8] *destroy.*　　[9] *You
were always ready to neglect your duties.*　　[10] *debauchery.*　　[11] *The homeless
shamefully.*

Secundus diabolus. Sibyl Slut, thou[1] salte sewe.[1]
All your life was lecherous lay.[2]
To all your neighboures you were a shrew,
All your pleasance was lecherous play.
Godes men you loved but few.
Naked men and feeble of array
You would not succour with a little drew,[3]
Not with a[4] thread,[4] the sooth to say,
When they asked in Godes name.

Omnes damnandi.[5] Ah! mercy! Lord, mickle of might,
We ask thy mercy and not thy right.[6]
Not after our deed so us quight:[7]
We have sinned—we are to blame.

Deus.[8] [When time of grace was enduring
To seek it you had no liking.
Therefore must I for anything
Do righteousness today.
And though my sweet Mother dear
And all the saintes that ever were
Prayed for you right now here,
All it were [now] too late.
No grace may go through their prayer:
Then Righteousness had no power.
Therefore go to the fire in[9] feere[9]—
There gaines none other grace.

Tunc daemones exportabunt eos.[10]
Now is fulfilled all my forethought,
For ended is all earthly thing:
All worldly wightes[11] that I have wrought
After their workes have now woning,[12]
They that would sin and ceased not

---

[1] *you shall follow (? into hell), (you sexy sow ?).* [2] *conduct (?).* [3] *morsel.* [4] *(so much as) a thread (? i.e. the meanest amount ?).* [5] *All the damned.* [6] *justice.* [7] *requite.* [8] Deus, *the catchword, is the last word on the last page—the rest of the play is missing. I have provided a composite conclusion borrowed from Chester and York (n.* [88]*).* [9] *all together.* [10] *Then the demons shall carry them off.* [11] *persons.* [12] *their dwelling.*

Of sorrowes sere[1] now shall they sing,
And they that mended them whilst they might
Shall build[2] and bide in my blessing.
*Et sic facit finem cum melodia angelorum transiens a loco
ad locum.*[3]]

---

[1] *divers.*   [2] *flourish.*   [3] *And so it makes an end with the music of angels
crossing over from place to place.*

PART TWO

Abraham and Isaac Plays

BROME[1]

Abraham.　　　Father of heaven omnipotent,
　With all my heart to thee I call.
　Thou hast give me both land and rent,[2]
　And my livelod[3] thou hast me sent:
　I thank thee highly evermore of all.
　　First of the earth thou madest Adam,
　And Eve also to be his wife:
　All other creatures of them two came.
　And now thou hast grant to me, Abraham,
　Here in this land to lead my life.
　　In my age thou hast granted me this,
　That this young child with me shall wone.[4]
　I love nothing so much, iwisse,[5]
　Except thy owen self, dear Father of bliss,
　As Isaac here, my owen sweet son.
　　I have divers children mo[6]
　The which I love not half so well:
　This fair sweet child he cheeres me so,
　In every place where that I go,
　That no disease[7] here may I feel.
　　And therefore, Father of heaven, I thee pray
　For his health and also for his grace:
　Now, Lord, keep him both night and day,
　That never disease[8] nor no fray[9]
　Come to my child in no place.
　　Now come on, Isaac, my owen sweet child!
　Go we home and take our rest.
Isaac. Abraham! my owen father so mild,

---

[1] *n. 89.*　　[2] *income.*　　[3] *livelihood.*　　[4] *dwell.*　　[5] *for sure.*　　[6] *more.*　　[7] *disquiet.*　　[8] *harm.*　　[9] *fear.*

To follow you I am full glad
Both early and late.

Abraham. Come on, sweet child! I love thee best
Of all the children that ever I begat.

Deus. My angel, fast hie thee thy way,
And unto middle-earth anon thou go:
Abrams heart now will I assay,
Whether that he be steadfast or no.

Say I commanded him for to take
Isaac his young son, that he loves so well,
And with his blood[1] sacrifice he make,
If any of my friendship he[2] will feel.

Show him the way unto the hill
Where that his sacrifice shall be:
I shall assay now his good will,
Whether he loveth better his child or me.

All men shall take example by him
My commandmentes how they shall keep.

Abraham. Now, Father of heaven, that formed all thing,
My prayeres I make to thee again,
For this day my tender offering
Here must I give to thee, certain.

Ah! Lord God, almighty King,
What[3] manner beast will make thee most fain?[3]
If I had thereof very[4] knowing[4]
It should be done with all my main
Full soon anon.
To do thy pleasing on a hill
Verily it is my will,
Dear Father, God in Trinity.

The Angel. Abraham, Abraham, wilt thou rest!
Our Lord commandeth thee for to take
Isaac, thy young son that thou lovest best,
And with his blood sacrifice that thou make.

---

[1] *kinsman. [2] MS yf he. [3] What kind of animal will most please you (by way of sacrifice)? [4] true knowledge.*

378

Into the land of Vision[1] thou go,
And offer thy child unto thy Lord.
I shall thee lead and show also.
Unto[2] Godes hest, Abraham, accord,[2]
And follow me upon this gren.[3]
Abraham. Welcome to me be my Lordes sand![4]
And his hest I will not withstand.
Yet Isaac, my young son in land,
A full dear child to me has been.

 I had liefer,[5] if God had been pleased,
For to have forborne[6] all the good that I have
Than Isaac my son should have been diseased,[7]
So God in heaven my soul may save!

 I loved never thing so much in earth,
And now I must the child go kill.
Ah! Lord God, my conscience[8] is strongly stirred,
And yet, my dear Lord, I am sore afraid
To grutch[9] anything against your will.

 I love my child as my life,
But yet I love my God much more.
For though my heart would make any strife,
Yet will I not spare for child nor wife
But do after my Lordes lore.[10]

 Though I love my son never so well,
Yet smite off his head soon I shall.
Ah! Father of heaven, to thee I kneel:
A hard death my son shall feel,
For to honour thee, Lord, withal.
The Angel.   Abraham, Abraham, this is well said!
And all these commandmentes look that thou keep,
But in thy heart be nothing dismayed.[11]
Abraham. Nay! nay! forsooth, I hold me well pleased
To please[12] my God with the best that I have,

[1] *Gen. xxii, 14:* MS Vsyon.   [2] *Abraham, comply with God's bidding.*   [3] gren,
MS *unclear:* = green = *grassy area, playing place* (?) (*p. 392, n. 1*).   [4] *message.*
[5] *rather.*   [6] *gone without.*   [7] *made to suffer.*   [8] *heart, (conscience ?).*   [9] *complain.*
[10] *instruction.*   [11] (dysmayd) *so Holthausen,* MS dysmasyd.   [12] MS *pels(s?)e.*

For though my heart be heavily[1] set,[1]
To see the blood of my owen dear son,
Yet, for all this, I will not let,[2]
But Isaac, my son, I will go fet,[3]
And come as fast as ever we can.
    Now, Isaac, my owen son dear,
Where art thou, child? Speak to me!

Isaac. My fair, sweet father, I am here,
And make my prayeres to the Trinity.

Abraham.   Rise up, my child, and fast come hither!
My gentle bairn, that art so wise,
For we two, child, must go together,
And unto my Lord make sacrifice.

Isaac.   I am full ready, my Father, lo!
Even[4] at your handes I stand right here,
And whatsoever you bid me do
It shall be done with glad cheer,
    Full well and fine.

Abraham. Ah! Isaac, my owen son so dear,
Godes blessing I give thee, and mine!
    Hold this fagot upon thy back,
And here myself fire shall bring.

Isaac. Father, all this here will I pack,
I am full fain to do your bidding.

Abraham. Ah! Lord of heaven, my handes I wring—
This childes wordes all to-wound my heart.
    Now Isaac, son, go we our way
Unto yon mount with all our main.

Isaac. Go we, my dear father, as fast as I may,
To follow you I am full fain,
    Although I am slender.

Abraham. Ah! Lord, my heart breaketh in twain,[5]
This childes wordes they are so tender.
    Ah! Isaac, son, anon lay it down,

---

[1] *stricken with grief.*   [2] *hold back.*   [3] *fetch.*   [4] *MS* ʒovyn (?).   [5] *MS* tewyn.

No longer upon thy back it bear,
For I must make me ready[1] boun[1]
To honour my Lord God as I should.

Isaac.   Lo! my dear father, where it is!
To cheer you always I draw me near.
But, father, I marvel sore of this,
Why[2] that you make this heavy cheer?[2]
    And also, father, evermore dread I,
Where is your quick[3] beast that you should kill?
Both fire and wood we have ready,
But quick beast have we none on this hill.
    A[4] quick beast I wot well must be dead
Your sacrifice for to make.[4]

Abraham. Dread thee nought,[5] my child, I thee red![6]
Our Lord will send me, unto this stead,[7]
Some manner[8] a beast for to take
Through his sweet sand.[9]

Isaac. Yea! father, but my heart beginneth to quake
To see that sharp sword in your hand.
    Why bear you your sword drawen so?
Of your countenance[10] I have much wonder.

Abraham. Ah! Father of heaven, so[11] I am woe![11]
This child here breaketh my heart in two.

Isaac.   Tell me, my dear father, ere that you cease,
Bear you your sword drawn for me?

Abraham. Ah! Isaac, sweet son, peace! peace!
For, iwis,[12] thou breakst my heart in three.

Isaac.   Now truly somewhat, father, you think,
That you mourn thus more and more?

Abraham. Ah! Lord of heaven thy grace let sink,
For my heart was never half so sore.

Isaac.   I pray you, father, that you will let me it wit,
Whether shall I have any harm or no?

---

[1] *all prepared.*   [2] *Why you are so downcast.*   [3] *live.*   [4] *MS reverses order of these lines.*   [5] *MS* no(?)wgth.   [6] *counsel.*   [7] *place.*   [8] *kind of.*   [9] *dispensation.*   [10] *MS* conwnauns.   [11] so, *MS* os; *how grieved I am.*   [12] *indeed.*

Abraham. Iwis,[1] sweet son, I may not tell thee yet,
My heart is now so full of woe.

Isaac.   Dear father, I pray you, hide[2] it[2] not from me,
But some of your thought that you tell me.

Abraham. Ah! Isaac, Isaac, I must kill thee.

Isaac. Kill me, father? Alas! what have I done?
If I have trespassed against you ought
With a yard[3] you may make me full mild,
And with your sharp sword kill me not.
For, iwis, father, I am but a child.

Abraham.   I am full sorry, son, thy blood for to spill,
But, truly, my child, I may not choose.

Isaac. Now I would to God my mother were here on this
hill!
She would kneel for me on both her knees
To save my life.
And, sithin[4] that[4] my mother is not here,
I pray you, father, change your cheer,[5]
And kill me not with your knife.

Abraham.   Forsooth, son, but[6] if[6] I thee kill,
I should grieve God right sore, I dread.
It is his commandment, and also his will,
That I should do this same deed.
He commanded me, son, for certain,
To make my sacrifice with thy blood.

Isaac. And is it Godes will that I should be slain?

Abraham. Yea, truly, Isaac, my son so good,
And therefore my handes I wring.

Isaac. Now, father, against my Lordes will
I will never grutch[7] loud nor still:
He might have sent me a better destiny
If it had have been his pleasure.

Abraham.   Forsooth! son, but[8] if[8] I did this deed,
Grievously displeased our Lord will be.

---

[1] *indeed.*   [2] *MS* hydygth.   [3] *stick.*   [4] *since.*   [5] *mind.*   [6] *unless.*
[7] *complain.*   [8] *unless.*

Isaac. Nay! nay! father, God forbid,
  That ever you should grieve him for me.
    You have other children one or two,
  The which you should love well by kind.[1]
  I pray you, father, make you no woe,
  For, be I ones dead and from you go,
  I shall be soon out of your mind.
    Therefore do our Lordes bidding,
  And, when I am dead, then pray for me.
  But, good father, tell you my mother nothing:
  Say that I am in another country dwelling.[2]
Abraham. Ah! Isaac, Isaac, blessed may thou be!
    My heart beginneth strongly to rise[3]
  To see the blood of thy blessed body.
Isaac. Father, since it may be no other wise,
  Let it pass over as[4] well as I[4].
    But, father, ere I go unto my death,
  I pray you bless me with your hand.
Abraham. Now, Isaac, with all my breath
  My blessing I give thee upon this land,
  And Godes, also, thereto, iwis.
  Isaac! Isaac! son up thou stand,
  Thy fair sweet mouth that I may kiss.
Isaac.   Now farewell! my owen father so fine,
  And greet well my mother in earth.
  But I pray you, father, to hide my eyne,
  That I see not the stroke of your sharp sword,
  That my flesh shall defile.
Abraham. Son, thy wordes make me to weep full sore!
  Now, my dear son, Isaac, speak no more.
Isaac. Ah! my owen dear father, wherefore?
  We shall speak together here but a while.
    And, sithin[5] that[5] I must needes be dead,
  Yet, my dear father, to you I pray,
  Smite but few[6] strokes at my head,

---

[1] *nature.*   [2] *MS* dewllyng.   [3] *revolt.*   [4] *as readily as I do.*   [5] *since.*   [6] *MS* feve (?).

And make an end as soon as you may,
And tarry not too long.
Abraham. Thy meek wordes, child, make me afraid,
So 'welawey' may be my song,
Except all only Godes will.
Ah! Isaac, my owen sweet child,
Yet kiss me again upon this hill—
In all this world is none so mild.
Isaac.   Now truly, father, all this tarrying,
It does my heart but harm.
I pray you, father, make an ending.
Abraham. Come up, sweet son, unto my arm:
I must bind thy hands two,
Although thou be never so mild.
Isaac. Ah! mercy, father why should you do so?
Abraham. That thou shouldest not let[1] [me], my child.
Isaac.   Nay, iwis, father, I will not let you!
Do[2] on for me your will,[2]
And on the purpose that you have set you,
For Godes love, keep it forth still.
I am full sorry this day to die,
But yet I keep[3] not my God to grieve.
Do[4] on your list for me hardly,[4]
My fair sweet father, I give you leave.
But, father, I pray you evermore,
Tell you my mother no[5] deal:[5]
If she wost[6] it she would weep full sore,
For, iwis, father, she loveth me full well.
Godes blessing may she have!
Now farewell! my mother so sweet,
We two are like no more to meet.
Abraham. Ah! Isaac, Isaac, son, thou makest me to greet,[7]
And with thy wordes thou distempurst[8] me.

---

[1] *prevent.*   [2] *Where I am concerned, do what you want.*   [3] *wish.*   [4] *Where
I am concerned by all means do what pleases you.*   [5] *nothing.*   [6] *should know.*
[7] *weep.*   [8] *dost distress.*

Isaac. Iwis, sweet father, I am sorry to grieve you.
   I cry you mercy of that I have done,
   And of all trespass that ever I did move[1] you.
   Now, dear father, forgive me that I have done.
   God of heaven be with me!
Abraham. Ah! dear child, leave off thy moanes!
   In all thy life thou grieved me never ones.
   Now blessed be thou, body and bones,
   That ever thou were bred and born:
      Thou hast been to me child full good.
   But, iwis, child, though I mourn never so fast
   Yet must I needes here, at the last,
   In this place shed all thy blood.
   Therefore, my dear son, here shalt thou lie.
   Unto my work I must me[2] stead.[2]
   Iwis, I had as lief myself to die—
   If God will be pleased with my deed—
      And my owen body for to offer.
Isaac. Ah! mercy, father, mourn you no more!
   Your weeping makes my heart sore.
   As my owen death that I shall suffer,
   Your kerchief, father, about my eyes you[3] wind.
Abraham. So I shall, my sweetest child in earth.
Isaac. Now yet, good father, have this in mind,
   And smite me not often with your sharp sword,
      But hastily, that it be sped.
Here Abraham laid a cloth over Isaac's face.
Abraham. Now, farewell! my child so full of grace.
Isaac. Ah! father, father, turn downward my face,
   For of your sharp sword I am ever adread.
Abraham. To do this deed I am full sorry,
   But, Lord, thy hest I will not withstand.
Isaac. Ah! Father of heaven, to thee I cry,
   Lord, receive me into thy hand.
Abraham. Lo! now is the time come, certain,

[1] *cause.*   [2] *apply myself.*   [3] *do you.*

That my sword in his neck shall sink.
Ah! Lord, my heart raiseth[1] there again,[1]
I may not find[2] it[2] in my heart to smite.
My heart will not now thereto,
Yet fain I would work my Lordes will,
But this young innocent lies so still
I may not find[2] it[2] in my heart him to kill.
Oh! Father of heaven, what shall I do?

Isaac. Ah! mercy, father, why tarry you so,
And let me lie thus long on this heath?
Now I would to God the stroke were do.
Father, I pray you heartily, short me of my woe,
And let me not look[3] thus after[3] my death.

Abraham. Now, heart, why wouldest not thou break in
  three?
Yet shalt thou not make me to my God unmild.
I will no longer let[4] for thee,
For that my God agrieved would be.
Now hold that[5] stroke, my owen dear child!
Here Abraham drew[6] his stroke and the angel took the sword
in his hand suddenly.

The Angel. I am an angel, thou mayest be blithe,
That from heaven to thee is sent.
Our Lord thanks thee an hundred sithe[7]
For the keeping of his commandment,
  He knoweth thy will and also thy heart,
That thou dreadest him above all thing,
And, some of thy heaviness for to depart,[8]
A fair ram yonder I gan[9] bring[9]—
  He standeth tied, lo! among the brieres.
Now, Abraham, amend[10] thy mood![10]
For Isaac, thy young son that here is,
This day shall not shed his blood.

---

[1] *rebels against it.* [2] *MS* fyndygth. [3] *wait thus anxiously for.* [4] *delay.*
[5] *MS* tha. [6] *MS* draw (?). [7] *times.* [8] *remove.* [9] *have brought.*
[10] *cheer up.*

Go! make thy sacrifice with yon ram.
Now,[1] farewell! blessed Abraham!
For unto heaven I go now home.[1]
The way is full gain,[2] [there I have come.]
Take up thy son so free.[3]

Abraham. Ah! Lord, I thank thee of thy great grace,
Now am I yethed[4] in divers wise.
Arise up, Isaac, my dear son, arise.
Arise up, sweet child, and come to me.

Isaac. Ah! mercy, father, why smite you not yet?
Ah! smite on, father, ones[5] with your knife.

Abraham. Peace! my sweet son, and take no thought,
For our Lord of heaven has grant thy life
By his angel now,
That thou shalt not die this day, son, truly.

Isaac. Ah! father, full glad then were I,
Iwis, father, I say, iwis,
If this tale were true.

Abraham. An hundred times, my son, fair of hue,
For joy thy mouth now will I kiss.

Isaac. Ah! my dear father, Abraham,
Will not God be wroth that we do thus?

Abraham. No! no! harly,[6] my sweet son,
For yon same ram he has us sent,
Hither down to us.
Yon beast shall die here in thy stead,
In the worship of our Lord alone.
Go! fet[7] him hither, my child, indeed.

Isaac. Father, I will go hent[8] him by the head,
And bring yon beast with me anon.
Ah! sheep, sheep, blessed may thou be!
That ever thou were sent down hither,
Thou shalt this day die for me,
In the worship of the Holy Trinity.

---

[1] MS *reverses order of these lines.*   [2] *straight.*   [3] *excellent.*   [4] *eased: MS*
yeyed.   [5] *once.*   [6] *for certain.*   [7] *fetch.*   [8] *catch.*

Now, come fast, and goowe[1] together,
To my Father of heaven.
Though thou be never so gentle and good,
Yet had I liefer thou sheddest thy blood,
Iwis, sheep, than I!
   Lo! father, I have brought here full smart
This[2] gentle sheep, and him to you I give.[2]
But, Lord God, I thank thee with all my heart,
For I am glad that I shall live,
And kiss ones[3] my dear mother.
Abraham. Now be right merry, my sweet child,
For this quick beast, that is so mild,
Here I shall present before all other.
Isaac.   And I will fast begin to blow—
This fire shall burn a full good speed.
But, father, while I stoop down low,
You will not kill me with your sword, I trow?
Abraham. No! harly,[4] sweet son, have no dread!
My mourning is past.
Isaac. Yea, but I would that sword were in a gled![5]
For, iwis, father, it makes me full ill aghast.
Here Abraham made his offering, kneeling.
Abraham.   Now, Lord God of Heaven in Trinity,
Almighty God omnipotent,
My offering I make in the worship of thee,
And with this quick beast I thee present.
Lord, receive thou my intent,
As [thou] art God and ground of our grace.
Deus.   Abraham, Abraham, well may thou speed!
And Isaac, thy young son thee by!
Truly, Abraham, for this deed,
I shall multiply youres[6] botheres seed,[6]
As thick as starres are in the sky,
Both more and less.

---

[1] *let us go.*   [2] *MS has as two lines divided after* sheep.   [3] *once.*   [4] *for sure.*
[5] *fire.*   [6] *the progeny of you both.*

And as thick as gravel in the sea,
So thick multiplied your seed shall be.
This grant I you for your goodness.
    Of you shall come fruit great,
And ever be in bliss without end,
For you dread me as God alone,
And keep my commandmentes every one,
My blessing I give wheresoever you go.
Abraham. Lo! Isaac, my son, how think ye,
By this work that we have wrought?
Full glad and blithe we may be
Against the will of God that we grutched[1] not
Upon this fair heath.
Isaac. Ah! father, I thank our Lord every[2] deal[2]
That my wit served me so well
For to dread God more than my death.
Abraham.   Why! dearworthy[3] son, wert thou adread?
Hardily,[4] child, tell me thy lore.[5]
Isaac. Yea, by my faith, father, now have[6] I red,[6]
I was never so afraid before
As I have been at yon hill.
But, by my faith, father, I swear
I will nevermore come there,
But[7] it be against my will!
Abraham.   Yea,[8] come on with me, my owen sweet
    son,
And homeward fast now let us goon.
Isaac. By my faith, father, thereto I grant—
I had never so good will to go home,
And to speak with my dear mother!
Abraham. Ah! Lord of heaven, I thank thee,
For now may I lead home with me
Isaac, my young son so free,[9]

---

[1] *complained: MS* grutthed (?).   [2] *in every respect.*   [3] *precious.*   [4] *Boldly,*
Quickly.   [5] *story.*   [6] *so help me* (?); have, *MS* hath.   [7] *Unless.*   [8] *I cannot*
make out the original stanzas in the following lines.   [9] *excellent.*

The gentlest child above all earth,
 This may I well avow.
Now go we forth, my blessed son!
Isaac. I grant, father, and let us gon,
 For, by my troth, were I at home,
 I would never go out under[1] that form.[1]
 I pray God give us grace evermo,[2]
 And all those that we are holding[3] to.
Doctor. Lo! sovereigns and sires, now have we showed
 This solemn story[4] to[4] great and small.
 It is good learning to[5] learned and lewed,[5]
 And the wisest of us all,
 Withouten any barring.[6]
 For this story showeth you
 How we should keep, to[7] our power,[7]
 Godes commandmentes without grutching.[8]
  Trow[9] you, sires, and God[9] sent an angel,
 And commanded you to smite off your childes head,
 By your troth, is there any of you
 That either would grutch or strive there[10] again?[10]
 How think you now, sires, thereby?
 I trow there are three or a four or mo![11]
 And these women that weep so sorrowfully
 When that their children die[12] them fro,[12]
 As nature will[13] and kind[14]—
 It is but folly, I may well avow,
 To grutch against God or to grieve you,
 For you shall never see him mischieved, well I know,
 By land nor water, have this in mind.
  And grutch not against our Lord God,
 In wealth[15] or woe, whether that[15] he you send,
 Though you are never so hard bestead,

---

[1] *in that manner.* [2] *evermore.* [3] *under an obligation.* [4] *MS* story hath schowyd to. [5] *for the educated and the uneducated.* [6] *reservation.* [7] *so far as we can.* [8] *complaining.* [9] *Do you believe, gentlemen, if God.* [10] *against it.* [11] *more.* [12] *are lost to them in death.* [13] *MS repeats word.* [14] *family.* [15] *prosperity or misfortune, whichever.*

For when he will he may it amend.
His commandmentes truly if you keep with good heart,
As this story has now showed you before,
And faithfully serve him, while you are quart,[1]
That you may please God both even and morn.
Now, Jesu, that weareth the crown of thorn,
Bring us all to heaven bliss!
Finis.

CHESTER

Pagina quarta de Abrahamo et Melchisedech et Lot:[2]
The Barbers

Qualiter Abraham reversus est de cæde 4 regum, et occurret ei Melchisedech equitando, et erit Lot cum Abrahamo et dicat Preco:[3]

Nuntius.[4] All peace, lordinges, that are present,
And harken now with good intent,
How Noah away from us is went
And all his company;
And Abraham, through Gods grace,
He is comen into this place,
And[5] you will give him room and space
[To tell you of story.[6]]
    This play, forsooth, begin shall he,
In the worship of the Trinity,
That we may all with eye see
That shall be done today.

[1] *alive and well.* [2] *The fourth pageant of Abraham and Melchizedek and Lot (performed by the Guild of Barbers): pp.63 f. and n. 90.* [3] *How Abraham came back from the killing of the four kings, and Melchizedek shall meet him on horse-back, and Lot shall be with Abraham, and let Preco say.* [4] *Announcer.* [5] *If.* [6] *MS omits this line (supplied, from other mss.) and leaves a space for one line after* 'That shall be', *etc.*

My name is Gobet-on-the-Green,[1]
With you no longer I may been.
Farewell! lordinges, all[2] bideen,
For letting of[2] your play.
Et exit.

Abraham.　　Thou high God, and granter[3] of grace,
That ending nor beginning has,
I thank thee, Lord, that to me has
Today given victory.
Lot, my brother, that taken was,
I have restored in this case,
And brought him home into this place,
Through thy might and thy mastery.

　　To worship thee I will not wond,[4]
That four kinges of uncouth[5] land
Today hast sent into my hand,
And of riches great array.
Therefore of all that I can[6] win[6]
To give thee tithe I will begin,
The[7] city soon when I come in,[7]
And part[8] with thee my prey.[8]

　　Melchizedek, that here[9] king is,[9]
And Gods priest, also, iwis,[10]
The tithe I will give him of this,
As skill[11] is that I do.
God that has sent me victory
Of four kinges graciously,
With him my prey depart[12] will I,
The city when I come to.

Lot.　　Abraham, brother, I thank it thee,
That this day hast delivered me
Of enemies handes and their posty,[13]
And saved me from woe.

---

[1] *grassy spot, playing-place* (?): *cf. Southern, 28–33.*　　[2] *straightway, so as not to hold up.*　　[3] MS *graunt.*　　[4] *hesitate.*　　[5] *foreign.*　　[6] *have won.*　　[7] *Immediately I enter the city.*　　[8] *share . . . booty.*　　[9] MS *here is kinge is.*　　[10] *indeed.*　　[11] *right.*　　[12] *divide.*　　[13] *power.*

Therefore I will give tithing
Of my good, while I am living,
And now also of his sending
Tithe I will give also.

Tunc venit armiger ad Melchisedech.[1]

Armiger.   My lord, the King, tidinges aright,
Your heart for to glad and light!
Abraham has slain in fight
Four kinges, sith[2] I went.
Here he will be this ilke[3] night,
And riches with him enough[4] dight.[4]
I heard him thank God almight
Of[5] grace he had him sent.

Melchisedech. (*Extendens manus ad caelum.*[6])   Ah! blessed
be God that is but one!
Against[7] Abraham I will gone,
Worshipfully, and that anon,
My office to fulfil,
And present him with bread and wine,
For the grace of God is him within.
Speedes[8] fast, for love mine[8]!
For this is Godes will.

Armiger. (*Cum*[9] *cuppa.*[9])   Sir, here is wine, without[10] were,[10]
And tharf[11] bread, both white and clear,
To present him in good manner
That so us helpen has.

Melchisedech. To God, I wot, he is full dear,
For of all thinges his prayer
He has, without[12] danger,[12]
And specially great grace.

*Equitabit versus Abraham offerens calicem cum vino et panem
super patinam.*[13]

[1] *Then the squire comes to Melchizedek.*   [2] *since.*   [3] *same.*   [4] *plentifully
provided.*   [5] *For.*   [6] *Stretching out his hands towards heaven.*   [7] *Towards.*
[8] *Let us make haste, for love of me.*   [9] *With a cup.*   [10] *for sure.*   [11] *there is
need of; other mss.* (t)*hereto.*   [12] *readily.*   [13] *He shall ride towards Abraham
offering a chalice* (or) *cup of wine and bread on a paten* (or) *dish.*

Abraham, welcome must thou be,
Gods grace is fully in thee,
Blessed ever must thou be
That enemies so can meek.
I have brought, as you may see,
Bread and wine for[1] thy degree.[1]
Receive this present now at[2] me,
And that I thee beseech.

Abraham.   Sir King, welcome, in good fay![3]
Thy present is welcome to my pay.[4]
God has helpen me today,
Unworthy though I were.
He shall have part of my prey
That I won, sith[5] I went away.
Therefore to thee—thou take it may—
The tenth I offer here.

Tunc tradet equum oneratum sibi.[6]

Melchisedech.   And your present, sir, take I,
And honour it devoutly,
For much good it may signify
In time that is coming.

Abraham. Therefore horse, harness,[7] and pery,[7]
As falles[8] for your dignity,[8]
The tithe of it take at[9] me,
And receive my offering.

*Tunc Abraham recipiet panem et vinum, et Melchisedech
equum oneratum nomine decimae.*[10]

Lot.   And I will offer with good intent
Of such good God has me sent
To Melchizedek here present,
As Christ will so it be.
Abraham, my brother, offered has,
And so will I through Gods grace:

---

[1] *as befits your rank.*   [2] *from.*   [3] *faith.*   [4] *pleasure.*   [5] *since.*   [6] *Then
he shall hand over the laden horse to him.*   [7] *equipment and precious stones.*
[8] *befits your rank.*   [9] *from.*   [10] *Then Abraham shall receive the bread and the
wine, and Melchizedek the laden horse by way of a tithe (or) tenth.*

This royal cup before your face,[1]
Receive it at me.

Tunc Lot offeret cuppam cum vino et panem et recipiet
Melchisedech.[2]

Melchisedech.   Sir, your offering welcome is,
And well I wot forsooth, iwis,[3]
That fully Gods will it is
That is done today.
Go we together to my city,
And now God heartily thank we,
That helps us ay through his posty,[4]
For so we full well may.

Expositor.[5]   Lordes, what this may signify,
I will expound apertly,[6]
That[7] lewd,[7] standing hereby,
May know what this may be.
This[8] offering, I say, verament,[9]
Signifieth the new testament,
That now is used with good intent
Throughout all Christianity.

In the old law, without leasing,[10]
When these two good men were living,
Of beastes was all their offering
And their sacrament.
But sith[11] Christ died on the rood[12] tree,[12]
With bread and wine him worship we,
And on Sher[13] Thursday in his maundy
Was his commandment.

---

[1] *On p. 393 Lot intended to give a tithe. It is not clear why he here gives bread and*
wine.   [2] *Then Lot shall offer a cup of wine and bread and Melchizedek shall re-*
ceive it; panem, MS pane.   [3] *indeed.*   [4] *power.*   [5] *Other mss. include*
equitando *after* Expositor.   [6] *plainly.*   [7] *So that those who lack learning.*
[8] *The exposition in the next twenty-eight lines is not entirely clear but is helped when*
it is understood that Abraham is said to have a double significance: he is, historically,
the first man to give a tithe of his goods to God (ll. 17–18), but he is also, allegorically,
God the Father himself (ll. 21–2) to whom the sacrifice of the Mass is offered in the
form of consecrated bread and wine by all Christian priests, here signified by Melchi-
zedek (ll. 23–8). Most of the exposition is about this and not about tithing (n. 91).
[9] *truly.*   [10] *lying.*   [11] *since.*   [12] *cross.*   [13] *Maundy.*

But for this thing used should be
Afterward as now do we,
In signification, leve[1] you me,
Melchizedek did so;
And tithes-making, as you see here,
Of Abraham begunnen were.
Therefore he was to God full dear,
And so were they both two.

By Abraham understand I may
The Father of heaven, in good fay,[2]
Melchizedek a priest to his pay,[3]
To minister that sacrament
That Christ ordained on Sher[4] Thursday,
In bread and wine, to honour him ay—
This[5] signifieth, the sooth to say,[5]
Melchizedeks present.

Deus.   Abraham, my servant, I say to thee,
Thy help and succour I will be,
For thy good deed much pleaseth me,
I tell thee witterly.[6]

Abraham. Lord, in one thing that thou wilt see,
That I pray after with heart free,
Grant me, Lord, through thy posty,[7]
Some fruit of my body.

I have no child, foul nor fair,
Save my nurry,[8] to be my heir,
That makes me greatly to apaire.[9]
On me, Lord, have mercy!

Deus. My friend, Abraham, leve[10] thou me,
Thy nurry thine heir shall not be,
But one son I shall send thee,
Gotten of thy body.
Abraham, do as I thee say:

---

[1] *believe.*   [2] *faith.*   [3] *liking.*   [4] *Maundy.*   [5] *MS omits this line (supplied
from other mss.) and leaves a one-line space after 'Melchizedeks present'.*   [6] *certainly.*
[7] *power.*   [8] *foster-child.*   [9] *get worse.*   [10] *believe.*

Look up and tell[1] me, if thou may,
Starres standing on the stray[2]—
That impossible were;
No more shalt thou, for thy meed,
Number of thy body the seed
That thou shalt have for thy good deed,
Thou art to me so dear.

    Wherefore, Abraham, servant free,[3]
Look that thou be true to me,
And forward[4] here I make with thee
Thy seed to multiply.
So[5] much more, further, shalt thou be,
Kinges of thy seed men shall see,[5]
And one child, great of degree,
All mankind shall forby.[6]

    I will that from henceforth, alway,
Each knave[7]-child, the eighth day,
Be circumcised, as you say,
And thou thyself full soon.
And who circumcised ne is
Forsaken[8] with[8] shall be, iwis,[9]
For disobedient that man is—
Therefore, look that this be done.

Abraham.   Lord, already, in good fay,[10]
Blessed be thou, ever and ay!
For[11] that men very[11] know may
Thy folk from other men,
Circumcised they shall be all,
Anon, for ought that may befall,
I thank[12] thee,[12] Lord, thy own thrall,
Kneeling on my kneen.

[1] *count for.*   [2] stray, *astray (? a filler to rime ?): so other mss. but this MS* shaye:
= ?   [3] *noble, good.*   [4] *agreement.*   [5] *So much more (even than in this increase
of your family) . . . (that) kings shall be among your progeny (and they are conspicuous
in the Jesse play): MS omits both lines (supplied from MS Add. 10305), and writes,
'Be circumcised . . . shall be, iwis' as two lines to restore 4-line groupings.*   [6] *redeem.*
[7] *MS* knaves: *male.*   [8] *utterly condemned;* with = ?.   [9] *indeed.*   [10] *faith.*   [11] *In
order that men truly.*   [13] *So other mss: this MS* thrall thou.

Expositor.   Lordinges all, take good intent[1]
What betokens this commandment:
This was sometime a sacrament
In th' old law truly tane.[2]
As[3] followeth is now, verament,[3]
So was this in th' old Testament,
But when Christ died, away it went,
And Baptism then began.
    Also God behetes[4] here
To Abraham, his servant dear,
So much seed that in no manner
Numbered might not be;
And seed, mankind to forby[5]—
That was Jesus Christ, witterly,[6]
For of his[7] kind[7] was our Lady,
And so also was he.
Deus.   Abraham, my servant Abraham!
Abraham. Lo! here already, here I am.
Deus. Take Isaac, thy son by name,
That thou lovest most of all,
And in sacrifice offer him to me
Upon that hill, beside thee.
Abraham, I will that it so be,
For ought that may befall.
Abraham.   My Lord, to thee is my intent
Ever to be obedient.
That son that thou to me hast sent,
Offer I will to thee,
And fulfil thy commandment
With hearty will, as I am kent.[8]
High God, Lord omnipotent,
Thy bidding done shall be.
    My[9] meinie and my children each one[9]

---

[1] *heed.*   [2] *understood.*   [3] *Other mss. omit* is: *As (what) follows is now, truly (?).*
[4] *promises.*   [5] *redeem.*   [6] *certainly.*   [7] *Abraham's family.*   [8] *directed.*
[9] *My household and everyone of my children.*

Lenges[1] at home, both all and one,
Save Isaac[1] shall with me gone
To an hill here beside.
Make thee ready, my darling,
For we must do a little thing.
This wood upon thy back thou bring,
We must not long abide.
　　A sword and fire I will take,
For sacrifice I must make:
His bidding will I not forsake,
But ay obedient be.
Isaac. Father, I am all ready
To do your bidding meekly:
To bear this wood bowne[2] am I,
As you command me.
Abraham. 　　Ah! Isaac, Isaac, my darling dear,
My blessing I give thee here.
Take up this fagot with good cheer,
And on thy back it bring,
And fire with me I will take.
Isaac. Your bidding I will not forsake,
Father, I will never slake[3]
To fulfil[3] your bidding.
*Tunc Isaac accipiet lignum super tergum et ad montem pariter
ibunt.*[4]
Abraham. 　　Now Isaac, son, go we our way
To yonder mountain, if that we may.
Isaac. My dear father, I will assay
To follow you full fain.
Abraham. Oh! my heart will break in three,
To hear thy wordes I have pity.
As thou wilt, Lord, so must it be:
To thee I will be bain.[5]
　　Lay down thy fagot, my son dear!

[1] *remain at home without exception, save Isaac (who).* 　　[2] *ready.* 　　[3] *fall off in fulfilling.* 　　[4] *Then Isaac shall take the firewood on his back and they shall go together to the mountain.* 　　[5] *obedient.*

Isaac. All ready, father, lo! it is here.
　But why make[1] you so heavy cheer?[1]
　Are you anything adread?
　Father, if it be your will,
　Where is the beast that we shall kill?
Abraham. Thereof, son, is none upon this hill
　That I see here in this stead.[2]
Isaac.　　Father, I am full sore afraid
　To see you bear this drawn sword.
　I hope for all middle-yorde[3]
　You will not slay your child.
Abraham. Dread not thou, my child, I red![4]
　Our Lord will send, of his Godhead,
　Some manner[5] beast into this stead,
　Either tame or wild.
Isaac.　　Father, tell me, ere I go,
　Whether I shall have harm or no.
Abraham. Ah! dear God, that[6] me is woe![6]
　Thou burstest my heart in sunder.
Isaac. Father, tell me of this case,
　Why you your sword drawn has,
　And bear it naked in this place?
　Thereof I have great wonder.
Abraham.　　Isaac, son, peace! I pray thee,
　Thou breakest my heart even in three.
Isaac. I pray you, father, lean[7] nothing from me,
　But tell me what you think.
Abraham. Oh! Isaac, Isaac, I must thee kill.
Isaac. Alas! father, is that your will,
　Your own child for to spill,[8]
　Upon this hill brink?
　　If I have trespassed in any degree,
　With a yard[9] you might beat me.

---

[1] *are you so downcast.*　　[2] *place.*　　[3] *all the world (middle-earth).*　　[4] *counsel.*
[5] *kind of.*　　[6] *how it grieves me.*　　[7] *conceal.*　　[8] *destroy.*　　[9] *stick.*

Put up your sword if your will be,
For I am but a child.
Abraham. Oh! my son, I am sorry
To do this great annoy:[1]
Gods commandment do must I,
His workes are ay full mild.
Isaac. Would God my mother were here with me!
She would kneel upon her knee,
Praying you, father, if it might be,
For to save my life.
Abraham. Oh! comely creature, but[2] I thee kill,
I grieve my God, and that full ill.
I may not work against his will,
But ever obedient be.
Oh! Isaac, son, to thee I say,
God has commanded me, this day,
Sacrifice—this[3] is no nay[3]—
To make of thy body.[4]
Isaac. Is it Gods will I should be slain?
Abraham. Yea, son, it is[5] not to laine.[5]
To his bidding I will be baine,[6]
Ever to his pleasing.
But[7] I do this doleful deed,
My Lord will not quite[8] me my meed.[8]
Isaac. Mary! father, God forbid
But you do your offering.
Father, at home your sons you shall find,
That you must love by course of kind.[9]
Be I out once of your mind,
Your sorrow may soon cease.
But you must do Gods bidding.
Father, tell my mother for nothing.
Abraham. For sorrow I may my handes wring,
Thy mother I cannot please.

---

[1] *harm.*   [2] *unless.*   [3] *this is the truth.*   [4] *so other mss, this* MS *bloode.*
[5] *can't be disguised.*   [6] *obedient.*   [7] *Unless.*   [8] *give me my reward.*   [9] *nature.*

Oh! Isaac, Isaac, blessed may thou be!
Almost my wit I lose for thee.
The blood of thy body free[1]
Me think full loth to shed.

Isaac. Father, sith[2] you must needs do so,
Let it pass lightly and overgo;
Kneeling on my knees two,
Your blessing on me spread!

Abraham. My blessing, dear son, give I thee,
And thy mothers with heart free.
The blessing of the Trinity,
My dear son, on thee light!

Isaac. Father, I pray you, hide mine eyne
That I see not your sword so keen;
Your stroke would I not seen,
Lest I against[3] it grill.[3]

Abraham. My dear, son Isaac, speak no more,
Thy wordes make my heart full sore.

Isaac. Oh! dear father, wherefore? wherefore?
Sith[2] I must needes be dead,
Of one thing I would you pray,
Since I must die the death this day,
As few strokes as you may,
When you smite off my head.

Abraham. Thy meekness, child, makes me afray.[4]
My song may be 'Welaway'.

Isaac. Oh! dear father, do[5] away
Your making so mickle moan![5]
Now, truly, father, this talking
Does but make long tarrying.
I pray you, come, and make ending,
And let me hence gone!

Abraham. Come hither, my child, that art so sweet!

---

[1] *fair.* [2] *since.* [3] *shudder from it.* [4] *fear (?).* [5] *give over making such a great complaint.*

Thou must be bounden, hand and feet.
Tunc colliget eum et ligabit.[1]

Isaac. Ah! father, we must no more meet
By ought that I can see,
But do with me right as you will,
I must obey, and that is skill,[2]
Gods commandment to fulfil,
For[3] needes so must it be.[3]

   Upon the purpose that you have set you,
Forsooth, father, I will not let[4] you,
But evermore unto you bow,
While that I may.
Father, greet well my brethren young,
And pray my mother of her blessing,
I come no more under her wing.
Farewell for ever and ay!
But, father, I cry you mercy:
Of that I have trespassed to thee,
Forgiven that it may be
Unto Doomesday.

Abraham.   My dear son, let be thy moanes!
My child, thou grieved me but ones.[5]
Blessed be thou, body and bones,
And I forgive thee here.
Lo! my dear son, here shalt thou lie;
Unto my work now must I hie,
I had as lief myself to die
As thou, my darling dear.

Isaac.   Father, if you be to me kind,
About my head a kerchief bind,
And let me lightly out of your mind,
And soon that I were sped.[6]

Abraham. Farewell, my sweet son of grace!
Isaac. I pray you, father, turn down my face

---

[1] *Then he shall pick him up and bind him;* ligabit, MS ligavit.   [2] *right.*   [3] *So other mss., this MS* and let me hence gone.   [4] *hinder.*   [5] *once.*   [6] *despatched.*

403

A little while, while you have space,
For I am full sore adread.

Abraham.   To do this deed I am sorry.

Isaac. Yea, Lord, to thee I call and cry,
On my soul thou have mercy,
Heartily I thee pray.

Abraham. Lord, I would fain work thy will.
This young innocent that lies so still,
Full loth me were him to kill
By any manner of way.

Isaac.   My dear father, I you pray,
Let me take my clothes away,
For¹ shedding blood on them today
At my last ending.

Abraham.   Heart, if thou would break in three,
Thou shalt never master me.
I will no longer let² for thee,
My God I may not grieve.

Isaac. Ah! mercy, father, why tarry you so?
Smite off my head, and let me go!
I pray God rid me of my woe,
For now I take my leave.

Abraham.   Ah! son, my heart will break in three
To hear thee speak such wordes to me.
Jesu, on me thou have pity,
That I have most in mind!

Isaac. Now, father, I see that I shall die,
Almighty God in majesty,
My soul I offer unto thee—
Lord, to it be kind.

*Tunc accipiet gladium, faciens occidendi signum, et angelus
veniens capiet punctum gladii illius.*³

Angelus.   Abraham, my servant dear!

Abraham. Lo! Lord, I am already here.

---

¹ *For fear of.*   ² *delay.*   ³ *Then he shall take the sword, making a gesture as
if to kill, and an angel coming shall seize the point of that sword.*

Angelus 1. Lay not thy sword in no manner
  On Isaac, thy dear darling!
  Nay! do thou him no annoy!
  For thou dreadest God, well see I,
  That of thy son hast no mercy
  To fulfil his bidding.
Angelus 2.　　And for his bidding thou doest ay,
  And sparest neither for fear nor fray[1]
  To do thy son to death today,
  Isaac, to thee full dear,
  Therefore God has sent by me, in fay,[2]
  A lamb that is both good and gay
  Into this place, as thou see may.
  Lo! it is right here.
Abraham.　　Ah! Lord of heaven and King of bliss,
  Thy bidding I shall do, iwis.[3]
  Sacrifice here to me sent is,
  And all, Lord, through thy grace.
  A horned wether here I see,
  Among the brieres tied is he:
  To thee offered it shall be,
  Anon, right in this place.
  Tunc Abraham mactabit arietem.[4]
Deus.　　Abraham, by myself I swear
  For thou hast been obedient ever,
  And spared not thy son so dear,
  To fulfil my bidding,
  Thou shalt be blessed—thou art worthy!
  Thy seed I shall multiply,
  As stars and sand, so many het[5] I
  Of thy body coming.
　　Of enemies thou shalt have power,
  And thy[6] blood also, in fear,[6]
  For thou hast been meek and boneer[7]

---

[1] *terror.*　　[2] *faith.*　　[3] *indeed.*　　[4] *Then Abraham shall sacrifice the ram.*
[5] *promise.*　　[6] *so shall your descendants, also.*　　[7] *obedient.*

To do as I thee bade.
And all nations, leve[1] thou me,
Blessed evermore shall be,
The fruit that shall come of thee,
And saved through thy seed.

Expositor.   Lordinges, this signification
Of this deed of devotion,
And[2] you will you wit mon,[2]
May turn you to much good.
This deed that you see done in this place,
In example of Jesu done it was,
That, for to win mankind grace,
Was sacrificed on the rood.[3]

    By Abraham I may understand
The father of heaven, that[4] can fand,[4]
With his[5] blood,[5] to break that bond
The Devil had brought us to.
By Isaac understand I may
Jesu that was obedient ay,
His fathers will to work alway,
His death to underfong.[6]

                 Finis paginæ quartæ.[7]

DUBLIN[8]

Deus.   Of all thing there ever was I am the beginner,
Both heavenly and earthly, and of them that are in hell.
At my bidding was wrought both good man and sinner,
All in joy to have dwelled, till Adam to sin fell.
His unkindness has displeased me, truth for to tell,

---

[1] *believe.*   [2] *If you will you must know.*   [3] rood (rode), *so other mss, this MS*
tree.   [4] *who undertook.*   [5] *i.e. Jesu's blood (or) God's relation, son.*   [6] *undergo.*
[7] *End of the fourth pageant.*   [8] *n. 92.*

For many a thing made I for his joy and dalliance.[1]
Why should he displease me that I loved so well?
And commanded him but one thing, and yet he forfeited
    my pleasance.[2]
But yet, sith[3] he has displeased me, I have made purvey-
    ance[4]
That another of his kind shall please me again,
The which has ever been my servant in all manner[5]
    observance:
Abraham is his name, my man that cannot feign,
But ever has been true.
Herebefore[6] he required me high[6]
To have a child of his body,
And I granted him, and has one readily—
Isaac, full fair of hue.
    Of all thing earthly, I wot well, he loveth him best.
Now he should love me most, as reason would and
    skill:[7]
And so, I wot well, he does—I did it never mistrust.
But yet, for to prove him, the truth will I feel.
My angel, go to Abraham, that I love right well,
And say that I commanded and charged him, above all
    thing,
The first deed that he does, either[8] meat or meal,
To make sacrifice unto me of Isaac his son young.
Angelus. Oh! blessed Lord, I am ready at thy bidding
    To do that shall please thee in heaven, earth and hell,
    For all these owen to thee obedience above all thing.
    This message unto Abraham thy servant I will go tell.
Deus. Then hie[9] thee that thou were on ground![9]
    I[10] do not but to assay him,[10]
    And, if he do it, I will not dismay him.
    Of his sorrow I shall delay[11] him,

---

[1] *pleasure.*   [2] *pleasure.*   [3] *since.*   [4] *provision.*   [5] *kinds of.*   [6] *In time past he begged me earnestly.*   [7] *right.*   [8] *(before taking) either.*   [9] *speed to the earth.*   [10] *I am only testing him.*   [11] *relieve.*

And for one child increase him a thousand.
Et vadit angelus ad terram et expectat usque.[1]
Abraham.   Oh! great God on high, that all the world madest,
And lendest[2] us our living here to do thy pleasance,
With sweet comfort of the earth all our heartes gladest,
To thee be honour, to thee be joy and all due obeisance;
And highly, Lord, I thank thee that so makest my purveyance,[3]
To provide, ere I die, a child of my own body.
To[4] rejoice that thou gave me in earth to my dalliance,
And to please thee, sovereign Lord, I shall charge him perfectly,
Isaac, my son so dear[4],
I have been out all day:
Now shall I go home and to my wife I[5] say.
There shall I find both tway,
Sara and Isaac in[6] fere.[6]
Et vadit et in eundo obruat ei angelus.[7]
Angelus.   Abraham! Abraham!
Abraham.   All ready! Who calleth? Lo! here I am.
Who is there, in the high Lordes name,
That all thing shope[8] of nought?
Angelus. I am here, a messenger
Of that sovereign Lord entire.[9]
Therefore harken now and hear
What message I have brought.
   The good Lord of all heavenes high
Commandeth thee to take and sacrify
Isaac, thy son, that thou lovest so heartly,
To his sovereignty and pleasance blive.[10]
Farewell! for my message I have thee said.
Abraham. Angel, as God will, I am right[11] well paid,[11]

---

[1] *And the angel goes to the earth and keeps looking about.*   [2] *givest.*   [3] *provision (for the future).*   [4] *I shall charge him . . . Isaac . . . to rejoice . . . and to please.*   [5] *MS and.*   [6] *together.*   [7] *And he goes and, as he goes, let the angel rush up to him.*   [8] *made.*   [9] *perfect.*   [10] *at once.*   [11] *thoroughly satisfied.*

For of[1] me his will shall never be withnaid,[2]
While I am alive.
    And hardly,[3] angel, trust thereto,
For doubtless it shall be do.
Angelus. Farewell, then, for I will go
To bring our Lord relation.[4]
Abraham. Now, good Lord, grant me heart theretill,
That I may do that is thy will,
And, by my troth, I shall it fulfil
Without fraud either cavelation.
    Et vadit angelus.[5]
    Ah! good Lord, what is now best to do?
Home to my wife I must needes go,
For there is Isaac, and I trow she will be full woe,
If she knew the case—
For she has him and no mo[6]—
And if I tell her that it is so,
That God will have him to death ido,[7]
She[8] faileth not of sorrowes trace.[8]
    No[9] force[9]! I have liefer that she displeased be
Than that God be wroth with me.
Now doubtless[10] I shall go and see
How privily[11] that I can it do.
Undo these gates! Hey! who is here?
Sara. None but I and my son dear.
Welcome! my lord, welcome! my fere,[12]
Welcome! my comfort, also.
    Ah! you have walked far about—
How have you fared while you have been out?
Without fail, I have had great doubt[13]
Lest anything did you grievance.
Abraham. Nay! I thank the good Lord,
    All[14] thing and I do well accord,[14]

---

[1] *by.*   [2] *denied.*   [3] *certainly.*   [4] *report.*   [5] *And the angel goes.*   [6] *more.*
[7] *done,* MS I do.   [8] *She will have to go the way of sorrow.*   [9] *No matter.*
[10] *fearless, unquestioning.*   [11] *secretly, privately.*   [12] *companion.*   [13] *fear.*
[14] *Everything in my life is harmonious.*

Saving this, my good Lord has sent me word
That I must needes go do his pleasance:
   I must do sacrifice upon that hill on[1] high.[1]
[*To servants.*] And, therefore, sirs, maketh mine ass ready,
And Isaac, son, thou never yet me saw
Do no such observance,
Therefore array thee and go with me,
And learn how God should pleased be:
For, son, and[2] ever thou think to thee,[2]
Put[3] ever God to honourance.[3]

Isaac.   So shall I, father, and ever have do,
   As you have taught me, and my mother, also.
   Look, whenever that you will go,
   I shall not be behind.

Sara. Yea! but I pray you, gentle fere,[4]
   As ever you have loved me dear,
   Let Isaac abide at home here,
   For I kept[5] not he went[5] in the wind.

Abraham.   Peace, dame, let be! do way!
   Thou wost[6] well I wax[7] right grey,
   And this child never yet saw
   How God should be pleased.
   And, therefore, now he shall go with me,
   And there he shall both know and see
   How that God shall pleased be,
   And my heart i-eased.

Sara.   Then, sith[8] you will have forth my child,
   Good,[9] look that his horse be not too wild,
   [*To servants.*] And, sirs, wait on him that he be not
     defiled,
   With neither clay nor fen,
   And look well that his horse go round,
   And that he stumble not for[10] no pound.[10]

---

[1] *quickly.*   [2] *if ever thou dost intend to prosper.*   [3] *Always honour God.*
[4] *mate.*   [5] *I don't like him going.*   [6] *dost know.*   [7] *grow.*   [8] *since.*   [9] *Good*
(husband).   [10] *on any account.*

[*To Isaac.*] Now, good heart, God send thee home sound,
  Thy father and all his men.
Abraham.   Get hither our horses and let us go hen,[1]
  Both I and Isaac and these two men!
  And look we have fire and stickes to burn!
  Leapeth up! have[2] ido, anon![2]
Sara. All thing is ready, I you say,
  But, gentle heart, I you pray,
  Tarry as little while out as you may,
  Because of Isaac, my son.
Abraham. (*Et equitat et equitando dicit*[3] [*to the servants*]).
    Now, sirs, abide here, you two,
  Taketh here my horse and Isaac[4] also,
  For he and I must a little farther go
  To do this sacrifice.
  And I charge you that you abide here indeed,
  And that you remove not from this stead[5]
  While Isaac and I go do this deed
  To God in our best wise.
    Come hither, Isaac, my son good!
  Take up this fire and this wood!
  Spare not thy clothes! Give me thy hood!
  I shall not cumber thee sore.
Isaac. Now gawe,[6] father, that this deed were hied,[7]
  For this wood on my back is well tied.
  But where is that quick beast that shall be sacrified?
  Behind us or before?
Abraham.   Son, care[8] not therefore on never a side,[8]
  But let[9] God alone therewith this tide,[9]
  And for our way he shall provide,
  And defend us from fear.
  Ah! son, I have espied the place
  That God has provided us of his grace.

---

[1] *hence.*   [2] *get it done, straightway.*   [3] *And he rides and says as he does.*
[4] *Isaac('s horse).*   [5] *place.*   [6] *let us go.*   [7] *quickly done.*   [8] *don't be worried
about that in any way.*   [9] *now leave it entirely to God.*

Come on, son, a right good pace,
And hie us that we were there!
   Now, Isaac, son, I may no longer refrain,
But I must tell the truth, certain,
And, therefore, look thou be not thereagain,[1]
But do it with all thy will.
The high God, that all has wrought,
Commanded me that hither thou shouldest be brought,
And here thy body shall be brought to nought
Unto sacrifice on this hill.
   Lay down that wood on that altar there,
And fast deliver[2] thee, and do off thy gear![2]

Isaac.   Alas! gentle father, why put you me in this fear?
Have I displeased you anything?
If I have trespassed, I cry you mercy!
And, gentle father, let me not die!
Alas! is there no other beast but I
That may please that high King?

Abraham.   Nay! son, to me thou hast done no trespass,
But thou hast my blessing in every place.
But I may not forfeit that Lordes grace,
That all thing has me sent.
For, and[3] it should be after me,[3]
I had liefer have slain all my beastes than thee,
But his will needes fulfilled must be,
And, truly, so[4] is my intent.[4]

Isaac.   Alas! what[5] have I displeased this Lord of
    bliss,
That I shall be martyred in[6] this miss?[6]
But, gentle father, wot[7] my mother[7] of this,
That I shall be dead?

Abraham. She? Mary![8] son, Christ forbid!
Nay! to tell her it is no need,

---

[1] *opposed, resistant.*   [2] *give thyself up and take off thy things.*   [3] *if it were for me to decide.*   [4] *that is what I intend.*   [5] *(in?) what.*   [6] *so unjustly (? for this misdeed ?).*   [7] *does my mother know.*   [8] *(By) Mary!*

For when that ever she knoweth this deed,
    She will eat after but little bread.
Isaac.   In faith, for my mother I dare well say,
    And[1] she had wist of this array,[1]
    I had not ridden out from her this day,
    But she had ridden, also.
Abraham.   Yea! son, God must be served ay.
    Thy mother may not have her will alway.
    I love thee as well as she does, in[2] fay,[2]
    And yet this deed must be do.
Isaac.   Ah! father, then do off my gown!
    Ungird me, and take them with you to town!
    For I may not—I fall in swoon,
    Death has embraced my heart.
    But one thing, father, I pray you thus,
    Let never my mother see my clothus,
    For, and[3] she does—withouten othus—[3]
    It will grieve her too smart.[4]
Abraham.   Ah! dear heart, what shall I do by thee?
    Woe is me, that shall slay thee!
    With all my goodes I would buy thee,
    And[5] God would assent thereto.
Isaac. Ah! father, do now whatever you list,[6]
    For of[7] my mother, I wot well, I shall be missed.
    Many a time has she me clipped[8] and kissed,
    But, farewell! now, for that is do.
        She was wont to call me her treasure and her store,[9]
    But, farewell! now, she shall no more.
    Here I shall be dead and wot never wherefore,
    Save that God must have his will.
    Father, shall my head off also?
Abraham. Yea! forsooth, son, that must needes be do.
    Alas! good heart, that[10] me is woe,[10]
    That ever I should thee thus spill.[11]

[1] *If . . . known . . . arrangement.*   [2] *believe me.*   [3] *if she does—there's no need to swear to this; and, MS a;.*   [4] *painfully.*   [5] *If.*   [6] *wish.*   [7] *by.*   [8] *embraced.*   [9] *rich possession.*   [10] *how wretched I am.*   [11] *destroy.*

Isaac.　　　Then, father, bind my handes and my legges fast,
　　And give me a great stroke that my paines were past,
　　For lest I shrink I am right sore aghast,
　　And then you will smite me in another place—
　　Then is my pain so much the more.
　　Ah! soft, gentle father, you bind me sore.
Abraham. Ah! dear heart, woe is me therefore,
　　My mind[1] is worse than ever it was.
Isaac.　　　Ah! father, lay me down soft and fair,
　　And have ido now, and slay your heir.
　　For I am hampered[2] and in despair,
　　And almost at my lifes end.
Abraham. Ah! fair heart-root,[3] leave thy cry!
　　Thy[4] sore language[4] goes my heart full nigh.
　　There is no man therefore so woe as I,
　　For here shall I slay my friend.
　　　　The high Lord bade me to do this deed,
　　But my heart grutcheth,[5] so God me speed.[5]
　　My blood abhorreth to see my son bleed,
　　For all[6] one blood it is.[6]
　　Alas! that my heart is wonder sore,
　　For I am now right old and hore,
　　But God has chose thee for his own store,[7]
　　In[8] comfort of all my miss,[8]
　　　　And to be offered to him that is Lord on high.
　　And, therefore, son, take it patiently!
　　Peraventure in battle or other mischief thou mightest die,
　　Or elles in another ungoodly[9] vengeance.[9]
Isaac. Now, father, then, sith[10] it is so,
　　With all my heart I assent thereto.
　　Stretch out my neck, anon, have do!
　　And put me out of penance.[11]
Abraham. Now kiss me first, heart-root!

---

[1] *(state of) mind.*　　[2] *distressed.*　　[3] *dear one.*　　[4] *Thy pitiful words.*　　[5] *is reluctant, as God is my helper.*　　[6] *i.e. we are relations.*　　[7] *treasure.*　　[8] *As a cure for all my misdeeds.*　　[9] *evil act of vengeance.*　　[10] *since.*　　[11] *suffering.*

414

Now lie down—stretch out thy throat!
This[1] taketh me full nigh, God wot![1]
Good Lord, to do thy pleasance.
Et extendit manum ut immolaret eum.[2]

Angelus.   Abraham, leave off and do not smite!
Withdraw thy hand, it is Godes will.
Take up Isaac, thy son so white,
For God will not that thou him spill.[3]
He seeth that thou art ready for to fulfil
His commandment in weal and woe,
And therefore now he sent me thee[4] till[4]
And bade that Isaac should not be sacrificed so.
And as for thy sacrifice,
Turn thee and take that wether there,
And sacrifice him on that altar,
And look that Isaac have no dere,[5]
I charge thee in all wise.

Abraham.   Ah! sovereign Lord, thy will be fulfilled
In heaven, in earth, in water and clay.
And, Lord, I thank thee that Isaac is not killed.
Now, Lord, I know well thou didest but assay
What I would say thereto, either yea or nay.
Thou knowest my heart now, and so thou didest afore:
Haddest not sent thine angel, Isaac had died this day,
But, good Lord, save[6] thy pleasance, this proof[6] was right
    sore.
But yet I thank thee high[7]
That I have my sonnes life.
Gawe![8] son—do on thy clothes blife,[8]
And let not thy mother wit of this strife,[9]
I pray thee, son, heartly.

Deus.   Abraham, look up and harken to me.
Sithe[10] thou wouldest have done that I charged thee,

---

[1] *God knows, this touches me nearly.*   [2] *And he stretches out his hand to sacrifice him.*   [3] *kill.*   [4] *to thee.*   [5] *hurt.*   [6] *saving your pleasure, this trial.*   [7] *heartily.*   [8] *Let us go, son—put on . . . quickly.*   [9] *trouble.*   [10] *Since.*

4I5

And sparedest not to slay Isaac, thy son so free,[1]
The chief treasure that thou hast,
By my own self I swear, certain,
Thy good will I shall quite[2] again,[2]
That shall be worship[3] unto you twain
While the world shall last.
    For thou sparedest not thy son for me,
Go and number the gravel in the sea,
Either motes in the sun, and[4] it will be,
By any estimation,
And as thick as gravel in the sea does lie,
As thick thy seed shall multiply,
And one shall be born of thy progeny
That to all shall cause salvation.

Abraham.   Ah! Lord, ithanked ever be thy might,
By[5] time, by tide, by day and night.[5]
Now, Isaac, son, let us hence dight[6]
To our horses and our men.
Gawe![7] they are here fast by.
Hey! sirs, bring thence our horses in[8] high,[8]
And let us leap up here lightly,
Fast that we were hen.[9]
    Leap up, son, and fast have ido.

Isaac. All ready, father, I am here, lo!
You shall not be let[10] whenever you go.
My mother I would fain see.
And yet, that hour I saw this day,
I weened I should have gone my way.

Abraham. Yea! blessed be that Lord that so can assay
His servant in every degree!
    Et equitat versus Saram.[11]

Sara.   Ah! welcome sovereign, withouten doubt!
How have you fared whilst you have been out?

---

[1] *goodly.*   [2] *requite in return.*   [3] *honour.*   [4] *if.*   [5] *Every moment always.*
[6] *go.*   [7] *Let us go.*   [8] *speedily.*   [9] *hence.*   [10] *delayed.*   [11] *And he rides towards Sara.*

And, Isaac, son in all this rout,[1]
Heartly welcome home be ye!
Abraham. Gramercy! wife, fair[2] may you befall![2]
Come thence, wife, out of your hall,
And let us go walk, and I will tell you all
How God has sped this day with me.
     Wife, I went for to sacrify—
But how[3], trow you?[3] Tell me verily.
Sara. Forsooth, sovereign, I wot not I.
Peraventure some quick[4] beast?
Abraham. Quick? Yea! forsooth, quick it was!
As well—I may tell you all the case—
As another that was in the same place,
For I wot well it will be wist.[5]
     Almighty God, that sitteth on high,
Bade me take Isaac, thy son, thereby,
And smite off his head and burn him, verily,
Above upon yonder hill.
And when I had made fire and smoke,
And drew my knife to give him a stroke,
An angel came and my[6] will broke,[6]
And said our Lord allowed[7] my will.
Sara.   Alas! all then had gone[8] to wrake,
Would you have[8] slain my son Isaac.
Nay! then all my joy had me forsook.
Alas! where[9] was your mind?[9]
Abraham. My mind?—upon the good Lord on high!
Nay! and[10] he bid me—trust it verily—
Though it had been thyself and I,[11]
It should not have been left behind.[12]
     God gave him betwixt us twain,
And now he asked him of us again.
Should I say nay?—nay! in certain,

---

[1] *company.*   [2] *may yours be good fortune.*   [3] *in what way do you think?*   [4] *live.*
[5] *known.*   [6] *prevented my intention.*   [7] *commended.*   [8] *turned into disaster, if
you had.*   [9] *what were you thinking of?*   [10] *if.*   [11] *i.e. who were to die.*
[12] *undone.*

Not for all the world wide.
Now he knoweth my heart, verily.
Isaac has his blessing, and also I,
And has blessed also all our progeny,
For ever to abide.
Sara.   Now blessed be that Lord sovereign,
That[1] so liketh[1] to say to you twain.
And what that ever he lust,[2] I say[2] not there again,
But his will be fulfilled!
[*Abraham.*] Isaac[3] has no harm, but in manner I was sorry.[3]
And yet I have won his love, truly,
And evermore, good Lord, gramercy,
That my child is not killed!
   Now you that have seen this array,[4]
I warn you all, both night and day,
What God commandeth, say not nay,
For you shall not lose thereby.

TOWNELEY

Sequitur Abraham.[5]
Abraham.   Adonai, thou God veray,[6]
Thou[7] hear us when we to thee call!
As thou art he that best may,
Thou art most succour and help of all.
Mightful Lord, to thee I pray,
Let ones[8] the oil[8] of mercy fall.
Shall I never abide[9] that day?
Truly yet I hope I shall.
   Mercy, Lord omnipotent!

---

[1] *Who so pleases.*   [2] *desires, I speak.*   [3] *i.e. though in the outcome Isaac did not suffer, in the event he did (?).*   [4] *event, performance (?).*   [5] *Here follows* 'Abraham': n. 93.   [6] *true.*   [7] *(Do) thou.*   [8] *once; oil, n. 59.*   [9] *live to see.*

Long since he this world has wrought.
Whither are all our elders went?[1]—
This[2] muses mickle in my thought.[2]
From[3] Adam unto Eve assent—
Eat of that apple spared he not[3]—
For all the wisdom[4] that he meant,
Full dear that bargain has he bought.

From Paradise they bade him gang:[5]
He went mourning with simple[6] cheer,[6]
And after lived he here full long,
More than three hundred year,
In sorrow and in[7] travail strong,[7]
And every day he was in were.[8]
His children angered him among:[9]
Cain slew Abel, was[10] him full dear.[10]

Sithen[11] Noah, that was true and good,
His and his children three
Were saved when all was flood:
That was a wonder thing to see.
And Lot from Sodom when he yede,[12]
Three cities burnt, yet escaped he.
Thus, for[13] they menged my Lordes mode,[13]
He venged[14] sin through his pousty.[14]

When I think of our elders all,
And of the marvels that have been,
No gladness in my heart may fall,
My comfort goes away full clean.
Lord, when shall Death make me his thrall?
An hundred yeares, certes, have I seen:
My[15] fay![15] soon I hope he shall,
For it were right high time I ween.

---

[1] *gone; a traditional question: n. 94.*   [2] *I reflect much on this in my mind.*
[3] *From (the time when) Adam assented to Eve—he did not refrain from eating that apple—.*   [4] *p. 80.*   [5] *go.*   [6] *humble demeanour.*   [7] *with strenuous labour.*
[8] *trouble, difficulty.*   [9] *as well, from time to time.*   [10] *(who) was most dear to him.*
[11] *Afterwards.*   [12] *went.*   [13] *because they upset my Lord's mind.*   [14] *avenged . . .*
power.   [15] *Honestly.*

Yet Adam is to hell gone,
And there has ligen[1] many a day;
And all our elders, everyone,
They are gone the same way
Unto[2] God will hear their moan.
Now help, Lord, Adonai!
For certes, I can[3] no better wone,[3]
And there is none that[4] better may.[4]

Deus.   I will help Adam and his kind,
Might I love and lewty[5] find,
Would they to me be true, and blin[6]
Of their pride and of their sin.
    My servant I will found[7] and frast,[7]
Abraham, if he be trust.[8]
    In certain wise I will him prove
If he to me be true of love.
    Abraham! Abraham!

Abraham. Who is that? Ware! let me see!
I heard one neven[9] my name.

Deus. It is I, take[10] tent[10] to me,
That formed thy father, Adam,
And everything in its degree.

Abraham. To hear thy will, ready I am,
And to fulfil whatever it be.

Deus.   Of[11] mercy have I heard thy cry,
Thy devout prayers have me bun.[12]
If thou me love, look that thou hie
Unto the land of Vision,[13]
And the third day be there, bid I,
And take with thee Isaac, thy son,
As a beast to sacrify.
To slay him look thou not shun,
    And burn him there to[14] thy offerand.[14]

---

1 *lain.*   2 *Until.*   3 *know no better resource.*   4 *who may be of more help.*
loyalty.   6 *cease.*   7 *try and test.*   8 *trusty.*   9 *utter.*   10 *pay attention.*
1 *For.*   12 *overcome.*   13 *n. 1 on p. 379.*   14 *as thy offering.*
420

Abraham. Ah! loved be thou, Lord in throne!
Hold over me, Lord, thy holy hand,
For certes, thy bidding shall be done,
Blessed be that Lord in every land
Would visit his servant thus so soon.
Fain would I this thing ordand,[1]
For it[2] profittes nought to hone:[2]
    This commandment must I needes fulfil.
If that my heart wax heavy as lead,
Should I offend my Lordes will?
Nay!—yet were I liefer my child were dead!
Whatso he biddes me, good or ill,
That shall be done in every stead,[3]
Both wife and child, if he bid spill,[4]
I will not do against his rede.[5]
    Wist[6] Isaac,[6] whereso he were,
He would be abast,[7] now,
How that he is in danger.
Isaac, son, where art thou?
Isaac. All ready, father, lo! me here.
Now was I coming unto you:
I love you mickle, father dear.
Abraham. And dost thou so? I would wit how.
    Lovest thou me, son, as thou hast said?
Isaac. Yea! father, with all my heart—
More than all that ever was made:
God[8] hold me long your life in quart.[8]
Abraham. Now, who would not be glad that had
A child so loving as thou art?
Thy lovely[9] cheer[9] makes my heart glad,
And many a time so has it gart.[10]
    Go home, son, come soon again,
And tell thy mother I come full fast.

Hic transiet Isaac a patre.[1]
So now God thee save and sain![2]
Now[3] well is me that he is past.[3]
Alone right here in this plain
Might I speak to[4] my heart burst.
I would that all were well, full fain.
But it must needes be done at last,
 And it is good that I be ware,[5]
To[6] be advised[6] full good it were.
The land of Vision is full far:
The third day end must I be there.
My ass shall with us, if it[7] thar,[7]
To bear our harness, less and more.
For my son may be slain no nar,[8]
A sword must with us yet therefore.
 And I shall found[9] to make me yare:[9]
This night will I begin my way,
Though Isaac be never so fair,
And my own son, the sooth to say,
And though he be my right heir,
And all should wield[10] after my day,
 Godes bidding shall I not spare—[11]
Should I that gainstand?[12] We! nay, my fay![12]
 Isaac!

Isaac.   Sir!
Abraham.   Look[13] thou be bowne,[13]
 For certain, son, thyself and I,
We two must now wend forth of[14] town,
In far country to sacrify,
For certain skilles[15] and encheson.[15]
Take wood and fire with thee, in[16] hie.[16]

---

[1] *Here Isaac shall go across from his father.*   [2] *bless.*   [3] *Now it is good for me that he has gone.*   [4] *until.*   [5] *prudent.*   [6] *To think things out.*   [7] *there is need.* [8] *(?).*   [9] *seek . . . ready.*   [10] *command, enjoy.*   [11] *refrain from.*   [12] *oppose? Heavens! no, upon my word!*   [13] *See to it thou art ready.*   [14] *from.*   [15] *reasons and cause.*   [16] *quickly.*

By hilles and dales, both up and down,
Son, thou shalt ride and I will go by.
    Look thou miss[1] nought that thou should need:
Do make thee ready, my darling!
Isaac. I am ready to do this deed,
    And ever to fulfil your bidding.
Abraham. My dear son, look thou have no dread,
    We shall come home with great loving.
Both to and fro I shall us lead.
Come now, son, in my blessing.
    [*To servants.*] You two here with this ass abide,
For Isaac and I will to yond hill:
It is so high we may not ride,
Therefore you two shall abide here still.
Primus puer.[2] Sir, you ought not to be denied:
We are ready your bidding to fulfil.
Secundus puer. Whatsoever to us betide,[3]
    To do your bidding ay we will.
Abraham.   Godes blessing have you both in[4] fere![4]
    I shall not tarry long you[5] fro.[5]
Primus puer. Sir, we shall abide you here,
    Out of this stead[6] shall we not go.
Abraham. Children, you are ay to me full dear:
    I pray God keep [you] ever from woe.
Secundus puer. We will do, sir, as you us lere.[7]
Abraham. Isaac, now are we but we two.
    We must go a full good pace,
For it is farther than I weened:
We shall make mirth and great solace[8]
By[9] this thing be brought to end.
Lo! my son, here is the place.
Isaac. Wood and fire are in my hand,
    Tell me now, if you have space,
    Where is the beast that should be burned?

---

[1] *lack.*   [2] *First boy.*   [3] *may happen.*   [4] *together.*   [5] *from you.*   [6] *place.*
[7] *instruct.*   [8] *rejoicing.*   [9] *By (the time).*

Abraham. Now, son, I may no longer lain,[1]
Such[2] will is into my heart went.[2]
Thou wast ever to me full bain,[3]
Ever to fulfil my intent,
But certainly thou must be slain,
And[4] it may be[4] as I have meant.
Isaac. I am heavy and nothing fain,
Thus hastily that shall be shent.[5]
Abraham. Isaac!
Isaac. Sir?
Abraham. Come hither! bid I.
Thou shalt be dead whatsoever betide!
Isaac. Ah! father, mercy! mercy!
Abraham. That I say may not be denied:
Take thy death therefore meekly.
Isaac. Ah! good sir, abide.
Father!
Abraham. What son?
Isaac. To do your will I am ready,
Wheresoever you go or ride—
If I may ought[6] overtake[6] your will,
Since I have trespassed I would be beat.
Abraham. Isaac!
Isaac. What sir?
Abraham. Good son, be still!
Isaac. Father!
Abraham. What, son?
Isaac. Think on thy get![7]
What have I done?
Abraham. Truly, no ill.
Isaac. And shall be slain?
Abraham. So have I het.[8]
Isaac. Sir! what may help?
Abraham. Certes,[9] no skill.[9]

[1] *be silent.* [2] *Such a purpose has entered my mind.* [3] *obedient.* [4] *If it is to be.* [5] *destroyed.* [6] *in any way accomplish.* [7] *offspring.* [8] *promised.* [9] *For sure, there's nothing.*

Isaac. I ask mercy.

Abraham.   That may not let.[1]

Isaac.   When I am dead, and closed in clay.
  Who shall then be your son?

Abraham. Ah! Lord, that I should abide this day!

Isaac. Sir! who shall do that[2] I was won?[2]

Abraham. Speak no such wordes, son, I thee pray.

Isaac. Shall you me slay?

Abraham.   I trow I mon.[3]
  Lie still! I smite!

Isaac.   Sir! let me say.

Abraham. Now, my dear child, thou may not shun.[4]

Isaac.   The shining of your bright blade,
  It gars[5] me quake for[6] fearde to die.[6]

Abraham. Therefore grovlinges[7] thou shalt be laid,
  Then, when I strike, thou shalt not see.

Isaac. What have I done, Father, what have I said?

Abraham. Truly, no kins[8] ill to me.

Isaac. And thus, guiltless, shall be arrayed?[9]

Abraham. Now, good son, let such wordes be!

Isaac.   I love you ay.

Abraham.   So do I thee.

Isaac. Father!

Abraham.   What son?

Isaac.   Let now be seen,
  For my mother love.

Abraham.   Let be! let be!
  It[10] will not help that thou would mean,[10]
  But lie still till I come to thee—
  I[11] miss a little thing,[11] I ween.
  [*To himself apart.*] He speakes so ruefully to me
  That water shootes in both my eein.
    I were liefer than all wordly[12] win[12]

---

[1] *prevent (my intention).*   [2] *what I was used (to do).*   [3] *must.*   [4] *escape.*
[5] *makes.*   [6] *for fear to die (?), terribly afraid to die (?).*   [7] *face-down.*   [8] *kind of.*   [9] *afflicted.*   [10] *What you have in mind is of no avail.*   [11] *One little thing is missing.*   [12] *joys in the world.*

That I had found him ones[1] unkind.[1]
But no default I found him in.
I would be dead for him, or pind.[2]
To slay him, thus, I think great sin,
So rueful wordes I with him find.
I[3] am full woe that we should twin,[3]
For he will never out of my mind.

What shall I to his mother say?
For, 'Where is he?' tite[4] will she spir.[4]
If I tell her, 'Run away!'
Her answer bese,[5] belife,[5] 'Nay, sir!'
And I am feared her for to slay.
I ne[6] wot what I shall say till[6] her.
He lies full still thereas he lay,
For, to[7] I come, dare he not stir.

Deus.   Angel, hie with all thy main!
To Abraham thou shalt be sent.
Say, Isaac shall not be slain—
He shall live and not be burnt.
My[8] bidding standes he not again.[8]
Go, put him out of his intent!
Bid him go home again,
I know well how he meant.

Angelus.   Gladly, Lord, I am ready!
Thy bidding shall be magnified.[9]
I shall me speed full hastily,
Thee to obey at[10] every tide.[10]
Thy will, thy name, to glorify,
Over all this world so wide.
And to thy servant now in hie,
Good, true Abraham, will I glide.

Abraham.   But might I yet of weeping cease,
Till I had done this sacrifice!

---

[1] *once undutiful.*   [2] *made to suffer.*   [3] *I'm deeply grieved that we have to part.*   [4] *soon . . . ask.*   [5] *will be, straightway.*   [6] *know not . . . say to.*   [7] *until.*   [8] *He does not resist my command.*   [9] *extolled.*   [10] *on every occasion.*

It must needes be, withouten[1] lease,[1]
Though[2] all I carp on this kin wise[2]
The more my sorrow it will increase.
When I look to him, I grise.[3]
I[4] will run on a rese,[4]
And slay him here, right as he lies.

Angelus.   Abraham! Abraham!

Abraham.   Who is there now?
Ware![5] Let thee go![5]

[*He falls down before the angel.*]

Angelus.   Stand up, now, stand!
Thy good will[6] come I to allow,[6]
Therefore I bid thee hold thy hand.

Abraham. Say who bade so?—any but thou?

Angelus. Yea! God—and sendes this beast to[7] thine
offerand.[7]

Abraham. I[8] speke with God latter I trow,
And doing he me command.[8]

Angelus.   He has perceived thy meekness,
And thy good will,[9] also, iwis.[9]
He will[10] thou do thy son no distress,
For he has grant to thee his bliss.

Abraham. But wot thou well that it is
As thou hast said?

Angelus.   I say thee, yes!

Abraham. I thank thee, Lord, well of goodness,
That all thus has released me this.[11]

    To speak with thee have I no space
With my dear son till I have spoken.
My good son, thou shalt have grace,
On thee now will I not be[12] wroken.[12]
Rise up, now, with thy frely[13] face!

---

[1] *of a truth.*   [2] *However I talk in this kind of way.*   [3] *tremble.*   [4] *I shall make one rush at him.*   [5] *Look out! Please go away!: explained p. 67.*   [6] *intention . . . commend.*   [7] *for your offering.*   [8] *?: I believe I spoke with God later (than you did), and (I am) doing (what) he ordered me to (?).*   [9] *intention, also, for certain.*   [10] *wishes.*   [11] *from this.*   [12] *inflict punishment.*   [13] *noble.*

Isaac. Sir! shall I live?
Abraham.   Yea!—this to[1] token.
   Et osculatur eum.[2]
   Son thou hast scaped a full[3] hard grace[3]—
   Thou should have been both burnt and broken.
Isaac.   But, father, shall I not be slain?
Abraham. No, certes, son!
Isaac.   Then am I glad!
   Good sir, put up your sword again.
Abraham. Nay, hardily,[4] son, be thou not adread.
Isaac. Is all forgein?[5]
Abraham.   Yea! son, certain.
Isaac. For feard, sir, was I nearhand mad.[6]

   . . . .

YORK
Abraham[7]

[*Abraham.*]   Great God, that all this world has wrought,
   And wisely wote[8] both good and ill,
   I thank him thraly[9] in my thought
   Of[10] all his loan he lends me till.[10]
   That thus from bairnhood[11] has me brought
   A hundred winter to fulfil,
   Thou grant me might so that I might
   Ordain[12] my workes after[12] thy will:
   For in this earthly life
   Are none to God more bound[13]
   Than is I and my wife
   For friendship we have found.

   [1] *as.*   [2] *And he kisses him.*   [3] *fate most hard.*   [4] *by all means.*   [5] *forgiven.*
   [6] *these are the last words at the bottom of a folio: the next two folios are missing—the*
   play presumably continued onto them.   [7] *So entitled in MS: n. 95.*   [8] *knows.*
   [9] *eagerly.*   [10] *For the whole grant he makes to me.*   [11] *childhood.*   [12] *Order my*
   doings according to.   [13] *obedient.*

Unto me told God on[1] a tide,[1]
Where I was telde[2] under a tree—
He said my seed should multiply
Like to the gravel of the sea,
And as the starres were strewed wide
So said he that my seed should be,
And bade I should be circumcised
To fulfil the law—thus learninde[3] he me.[3]
In world whereso[4] we wonne[4]
He sendes us riches rife:[5]
As far as shines the sun
He is stinter of strife.

Abram[6] first named was I,
And sithen[7] he set a sylipp ma;[7]
And my wife hight[8] Sarae,
And sithen[9] was she named Sara.
But Sara was uncertain then
That[10] ever our seed should sagates yield,[10]
Because herself she was barren,
And we were both gone in great eld.[11]
But she wrought as a wise woman
To have a bairn[12] us for to bield:[12]
Her servant privily she won
Unto my bed my will[13] to wield.[13]
Soon after[14] then befell,[14]
When God our deed[15] would dight,[15]
She brought forth Ishmael,
A son seemly to sight.
Then afterward, when we waxed old,
My wife she fell in fear for[16] same:[16]
Our God needes[17] tidinges till us told,[17]

---

[1] on one occasion.   [2] encamped.   [3] (was ?) he teaching me.   [4] wheresoever
we dwell.   [5] abundant (ly).   [6] MS Abraham.   [7] then he added another
syllable.   [8] was called.   [9] then.   [10] That we should ever have children in this
way (i.e. as promised).   [11] age.   [12] child to look after us.   [13] to have my will of
her.   [14] afterwards it happened.   [15] (?).   [16] on account of our age (?).   [17] had
to give us the news.

Where we were in our house at home,
Till[1] have a son we should be bold,[2]
And Isaac should be his name,
And his seed should spring manifold.
If I were blithe, who would me blame?
And, for I trowed[3] this tiding
That God told to me then,
The ground and the beginning
Of Truth[4] that time began.

   Now ought I greatly God to yield,[5]
That so would tell me his intent,
And, not gainstanding our great eld,
A seemly son he has us sent.
Now is[6] he wight himself to wield,[6]
And from me is[7] all wightness went,[7]
Therefore shall he be my bield:[8]
I lowe[9] him that this loan has lent.[9]
For he may stint[10] our strife,[10]
And fend[11] us from all ill,
I love him as my life
With all my heart and will.

Angelus.   Abraham! Abraham!
Abraham.   Lo! I am here.
Angelus. Now bodeword[12] unto thee I bring:
God will assay thy will and cheer,[13]
If thou wilt bow till[14] his bidding.
Isaac, thy son, that is thee[15] dear,
Whom thou lovest o'er all thing,
To the land of Vision wend in[16] feere,[16]
And there of him thou make offering.
I shall thee show full soon

---

[1] *To.*   [2] *certain.*   [3] *believed.*   [4] *Faith: Rom. iv, 16–25; Gal. iii, 6–9;* Abraham *is the type of Faith in* Piers Plowman *Bxvi.*   [5] *repay.*   [6] *he has himself strength to be ruler.*   [7] *all strength is gone out.*   [8] *succour.*   [9] *praise him who this gift has granted.*   [10] *put an end to our troubles.*   [11] *defend.*   [12] *a command.*   [13] *mind, disposition.*   [14] *to.*   [15] *to thee.*   [16] *together.*

The stead[1] of sacrifice:
God wills this deed be done,
And therefore thee[2] advise.[2]

Abraham.   Lord God, that lends[3] ay lasting light,
This is a ferly[4] fare to feel,[4]
Till[5] have a son seemly to sight,[5]
Isaac, that I love full well,
He is of eld,[6] to reckon right,
Thirty year and more some deal,
And unto death him[7] buse be dight.[7]
God has said me so for my seele,[8]
And biddes me wend on[9] all wise[9]
To the land of Vision,
There to make sacrifice
Of Isaac, that is my son.

And that is hithen[10] three dayes journey,
The gainest[11] gate that [I] gan go,[11]
And, certes,[12] I shall not say him nay,
If God command myself to slo.[13]
But, to my son, I will nought say,
But take him and my servantes two,
And with our ass wend forth our way:
As God has said, it shall be so!
Isaac, son, I understand
To wilderness now wend will we,
Therefore to make our offerand,
For so has God commanded me.

Isaac.   Father, I am ever at your will,
As[14] worthy is, withouten train:[14]
Godes commandment to fulfil
Ought all folk for to be fain.

Abraham. Son, thou sayst me full[15] good skill,[15]

---

[1] *place.*   [2] *make thy plans.*   [3] *grants.*   [4] *terrible state of affairs to experience.*   [5] *To . . . good to look at.*   [6] *age.*   [7] *he has to be put.*   [8] *happiness (?).*   [9] *at all costs.*   [10] *away.*   [11] *most direct way that I went.*   [12] *for sure.*   [13] *slay.*   [14] *Truly as is fitting.*   [15] *what is perfectly right.*

But all[1] the sooth is not to sayn.[1]
Go we, since we shall[2] theretill,[2]
I pray God send us well again.
Isaac. [*To servants.*] Children, lead forth our ass
With wood that we shall burn:
Even as God ordained has
To work we will begin.
Primus famulus.[3]   At your bidding we will be bown,[4]
What way in world that you will wend.
Secundus famulus. Why[5] shall we truss ought forth a-town[5]
In any uncouth[6] land to lend?[7]
Primus famulus. I hope then have[8] in this season[8]
From God of heaven some solace send.[9]
Secundus famulus. To fulfil it[10] is good reason,
And kindly[11] keep that he has kend.[11]
Primus famulus. But what they mean, certain,
Have I no knowledge clear.
Secundus famulus. It may not greatly gain
To move[12] of swilke matter.[12]
Abraham.   No! Noy[13] you not in no degree,[13]
So for to deem[14] here of our deed,
For, as God commanded, so work will we—
Until[15] his tales us bus take heed.[15]
Primus famulus. All those that will his servantes be
Full specially he will them speed.
Isaac. Children, with all the might in me,
I lowe[16] that Lord of ilke[17] a lede,[17]
And worship[18] him, certain,
My will is ever unto.
Secundus famulus. God give you might and main
Right here so for to do.

---

[1] *the whole truth cannot be said (?).*   [2] *have to go there.*   [3] *First servant.*
[4] *obedient.*   [5] *Why must we take ourselves off at all from our homes.*   [6] *strange.*
[7] *go.*   [8] *to have at this time.*   [9] *sent.*   [10] *i.e. God's bidding.*   [11] *dutifully abide by what he has taught us.*   [12] *consider such matters.*   [13] *Do not trouble yourself in any way.*   [14] *judge.*   [15] *To what he says we ought to pay heed.*   [16] *Humble (myself to?), love (?).*   [17] *of every nation.*   [18] *to worship.*

Abraham.   Son, if our Lord God almighty
  Of[1] myself would have his offerand[1]
  I would be glad for him to die,
  For all our heal[2] hanges in[2] his hand.
Isaac. Father, forsooth, right so would I,
  Liefer than long to live in land.[3]
Abraham. Ah! son, thou sayst full well, forthi—[4]
  God give thee grace grathely[5] to stand!
  Children, bide you here still,
  No farther shall you go,
  For yonder I see the hill
  That we shall wend unto.
Isaac.   Keep well our ass and all our gear
  To[6] time we come again you[7] till.[7]
Abraham. My son this wood behoves[8] thee bear,[8]
  Till thou come high upon yon hill.
Isaac. Father, that may do no dere,[9]
  Godes commandment to fulfil,
  For from all wathes[10] he will us were,[10]
  Whereso we wend to work his will.
Abraham. Ah! son, that was well said!
  Lay down that wood even here,
  Till our altar be graithed,[11]
  And, my son, make good cheer.
Isaac.   Father, I see here wood and fire,
  But whereof shall our offering be?
Abraham. Certes, son, good God, our sovereign Sire,
  Shall ordain it in good degree.
  For, son, and[12] we do his desire,
  Full good reward therefore get we:
  In heaven there mon[13] we have our hire,[14]
  For unto us so hight[15] has he.
  Therefore, son, let us pray,

---

[1] *Would have myself for his offering.*   [2] *welfare depends on.*   [3] *the world.*
[4] *therefore.*   [5] *properly, well.*   [6] *Until the.*   [7] *to you.*   [8] *(it) behoves thee to*
carry.   [9] *harm.*   [10] *dangers . . . defend.*   [11] *made ready.*   [12] *if.*   [13] *shall.*
[14] *reward.*   [15] *promised.*

To God, both thou and I,
That we may make this day
Our offering here duly.
    Great God! that all this world has wrought,
And grathely[1] governes good and ill,
Thou grant me might so that I mought[2]
Thy commandmentes to fulfil.
And, if my flesh grutch[3] or grieve ought,
Or, certes,[4] my soul assent theretill,[4]
To burn all that I hither brought,
I shall not spare if[5] I should spill.[5]

Isaac. Lord God! of great pousty,[6]
To whom all people prayes,
Grant both my father and me
To work thy will always.
    But, father, now would[7] I frayne full fain[7]
Whereof our offering should be graithed?[8]

Abraham. Certes, son, I may no longer lain——[9]
Thyself[10] should bide that bitter brayde.[10]

Isaac. Why, father? Will God that I be slain?

Abraham. Yea! soothly, son, so has he said.

Isaac. And I shall not grutch[3] there-again:
To work his will I am well paid![11]
Since it is his desire,
I shall be bain[12] to be
Brittened[13] and burnt in fire,
And, therefore, mourn not for me.

Abraham.   Nay! son, these gates[14] must needes be
    gone,
My Lord God will I not gain-say.
Nor never make mournes[15] nor moan
To make offering of thee this day.

---

1 *well.*   2 *may be able.*   3 *resist, complain.*   4 *for sure, before my soul assents to it (i.e. the reluctant complaint of the flesh).*   5 *(even) if I were to die (doing so).*   6 *power.*   7 *I would dearly like to ask.*   8 *furnished.*   9 *keep silent.*   10 *It is you who must undergo that bitter torment.*   11 *pleased.*   12 *willing.*   13 *Butchered.*   14 *paths.*   15 *lamentations.*

Isaac. Father, since God, our Lord alone,
   Vouchsafed to send, when you go[1] pray,[1]
A son to you, when you had none,
And now wills that he wend[2] his way,[2]
Therefore fained[3] me to fell
Till offering[3] in this place.
But first I shall you tell
My counsel in this case:
   I know myself, by[4] course of kind,[4]
My flesh for death will be dreadand——[5]
I am feared that you shall find
My force[6] your forward to withstand——[6]
Therefore is best that you me bind
In bandes fast, both foot and hand,
Now, whiles I am in might and mind.
So shall you safely make offerand,
For, father, when I am bound,
My might may not avail:
Here shall no fault be found
To make your forward[7] fail.
   For you are old and all unwield,[8]
And I am wight and wild of thought.[8]
Abraham. To bind him that should be my beld![9]
Outtane[10] Godes will,[10] that would I not.
[*Binds Isaac.*] But lo! here shall no force be feld,[11]
So shall God have that he has sought.
Farewell! my son, I shall thee yield
Till[12] him that all this world has wrought.
   Now kiss me heartily, I thee pray,
Isaac, I take my leave for ay.
Me[13] bus thee miss.[13]
My blessing have thou entirely!

---

[1] *prayed.*   [2] *i.e. die.*   [3] *I was glad to act as offering (?).*   [4] *as a natural consequence.*   [5] *terrified.*   [6] *strength resist your agreement.*   [7] *agreement.*   [8] *feeble. . . strong and have violent feelings.*   [9] *protector, comfort.*   [10] *God's will excepted.*   [11] *felt.*   [12] *To.*   [13] *I'm bound to lose you.*

[*Isaac.*¹] And I beseech God almighty
  He give thee his!²
[*Abraham.*¹]   Thus aren we samen³ assent,
  After³ thy wordes wise.
  Lord God! to this take tent—⁴
  Receive thy sacrifice!
    This is to me a peerless⁵ pine,⁵
  To see my own dear child thus boun:⁶
  Me⁷ had well liefer my life to tine⁷
  Than see this sight thus of my son.
  It is Godes will—it shall be mine!
  Against his sand⁸ shall I never shun.
  To Godes commandment I shall incline,
  That in me fault none be foun.
  Therefore my son so dear,
  If thou wilt anything say,
  Thy death it drawes near:
  Farewell! for ones and ay.
Isaac.   Now, my dear father, I would you pray,
  Hear me three wordes—grant me my boon!
  Since I from this shall pass for ay,
  I see my hour is com full soon.
  In word, in work, or any way,
  That I have trespassed or ought misdone,
  Forgive me, father, ere I die this day,
  For his love that made both sun and moon.
  Here, since we two shall twine,⁹
  First God I ask mercy,
  And you, in more¹⁰ and mine,¹⁰
  This day ere ever I die.
Abraham. Now, my great God, Adonai,
  That all this world has worthily wrought,

---

¹ *Speech continuous in MS with no character headings.* ² *his (blessing).* ³ *two of one mind, according to.* ⁴ *heed.* ⁵ *torment unequalled.* ⁶ *bound.* ⁷ *I would much rather lose my life.* ⁸ *dispensation.* ⁹ *part.* ¹⁰ *absolutely everything.*

Forgive thee, son, for his mercy,
In word, in work, in deed and thought.
   Now, son, as we are lered,[1]
Our time may not miscarry.
Isaac. Now, farewell! all middle-earth,
My flesh waxes faint for fearde!
Now, father, take your sword—
Me think full long you tarry.
Abraham.   Nay! nay! son, nay! I thee behet—[2]
That do I not, withouten[3] were.[3]
Thy wordes make me my wanges[4] to wet,
And change, child, full often my cheer.[5]
Therefore, lie down hand and feet,
Now may thou wit thine hour is near.
Isaac. Ah! dear father, life is full sweet!
The dread of death does[6] all my dere.[6]
As I am here your son,
To God I take[7] me till.[7]
Now am I laid here bone,[8]
Do with me what you will,
   For, father, I ask no more respite,
But hear a word what[9] I would mean:[9]
I beseech you, ere that you smite,
Lay down this kerchief on my een,[10]
Then may your offering be perfect,
If you will work thus, as I ween.
And here to God my soul I wite,[11]
And all my body to burn, bideen.[12]
Now, father, be not missing,
But smite fast as you may.
Abraham. Farewell! in Godes dear blessing,
And mine, for ever and ay.
   That peerless prince, I pray,

---

[1] *taught.*   [2] *promise.*   [3] *certainly.*   [4] *cheeks (with tears).*   [5] *mind.*
[6] *causes . . . trouble.*   [7] *give myself.*   [8] *ready.*   [9] *of what is in my mind.*
[10] *eyes.*   [11] *bequeath.*   [12] *indeed.*

My offering here till[1] have it.
My sacrifice this day,
I pray thee, Lord, receive it.

Angelus.   Abraham! Abraham!

Abraham.   Lo! here, iwis.[2]

Angelus. Abraham, abide and hold thee still!
Slay not thy son—do him no miss.[3]
Take here a sheep, thy offering till,[4]
Is[5] sent thee from the King of bliss.
That[6] faithful ay to thee is fone,
He biddes[6] thee make offering of this
Here at this time, and save thy son.

Abraham.   I lowe[7] that Lord with heart entire,
That of his love this[8] loan me lent,[8]
To save my son, my darling dear,
And sent this sheep to this intent
That we shall offer it to thee here,
So shall it be as thou hast meant.
My son, be glad and make good cheer!
God has till[9] us good comfort sent.
He will not thou be dead,
But till[9] his lawes take keep,[10]
And see, son, in thy stead,
God has sent us a sheep.

Isaac.   To make our offering at his will
All for our sake he has it sent.
To lowe[11] that Lord I hold great[12] skill[12]
That till[13] his meinie thus has meant.[13]
This deed I would have tane[14] me till,[14]
Full gladly, Lord, to thy intent.

Abraham. Ah! son, thy blood would he not spill,
Forthy[15] this sheep thus has he sent.
And, son, I am full fain[16]

[1] to.   [2] for sure.   [3] harm.   [4] for.   [5] (Which) is.   [6] He who is found ever true to thee bids.   [7] praise.   [8] made me this grant.   [9] to.   [10] heed. [11] praise.   [12] most right.   [13] to his own people has shown that this is what is his purpose.   [14] given myself to.   [15] Therefore.   [16] happy.

Of[1] our speed[1] in this place,
But go we home again
And lowe[2] God of[3] his grace.

Angelus.   Abraham! Abraham!

Abraham.   Lo! here indeed!
Hark! son, some salving[4] of our sore.[4]

Angelus. God says thou shalt have mickle meed
For this good will[5] that thou in were.
Since thou for him would do this deed,
To spill thy son, and not to spare,
He meanes to multiply your seed
On[6] sides seere,[6] as he said ere.[7]
And yet he hight[8] you this,
That of your seed shall rise,
Through help of him and his,
Over-hand of all enemies.

    Look you him love, this is his list,[9]
And lelly[10] live after his lay,[10]
For in your seed all mon[11] be blessed,
That there are born by night or day.
If you will in him trow or trust,
He will be with you ever and ay.

Abraham. Full well were us, and[12] we it wist[12]
How we should work his will alway.

Isaac. Father, that shall we frain[13]
At[13] wiser men than we,
And fulfil it full fain
Indeed, after our degree.

Abraham.   Now, son, since we thus well have sped,
That God has granted me thy life,
It is my will that thou be wed,
And wield[14] a woman to thy[14] wife.
So shall thy seed spring and be spread,

---

[1] *for our success.*   [2] *praise.*   [3] *for.*   [4] *healing for our pain.*   [5] *disposition.*
[6] *Everywhere.*   [7] *before.*   [8] *promised.*   [9] *desire.*   [10] *live loyally according to his law.*   [11] *shall.*   [12] *if we knew.*   [13] *inquire of.*   [14] *enjoy . . . as thy.*

In the lawes of God, by[1] reason rife.[1]
I wot in[2] what stead she is stead
That thou shalt wed, withouten strife.[2]
Rebek, that damsel,
Her[3] fairer is none fon,[3]
The daughter of Batwell,
That was my brother son.

Isaac. Father, as thou likest my life to spend,
I shall assent unto the same.

Abraham. One of my servantes, son, shall I send
Unto that bird[4] to bring her home.
The gainest[5] gates[5] now will we wend.
[*Returning to servants.*] My bairnes, you are not to blame
If you think long that we here lend![6]
Gather same[7] our gear, in Godes name!
And go we home again,
Even unto Barsaby.
God[8] that is most of main,
Us wisse,[8] and with you be!

---

[1] *as is abundantly reasonable.* [2] *I know where she is to be found whom you shall undoubtedly marry.* [3] *Fairer than her is found no one.* [4] *maiden.* [5] *shortest way.* [6] *go.* [7] *together.* [8] *May God, who is the most mighty, guide us.*

LIST OF WORKS MENTIONED AND FURTHER READING

Le mystère d'Adam, ed. P. Studer (Manchester and London, 1918). See also *Medieval French plays*.

Anderson, M. D., *Drama and imagery in English medieval churches* (Cambridge, 1963).

Auerbach, E., 'Adam and Eve' in *Mimesis* (Berne, 1946), trans. W. Trask (Princeton, 1953; N. York, 1957).

Block, K. S., ed. *Ludus Coventriae*, E.E.T.S. E.S. 120 (1922 for 1917, repr. 1960).

Brown, A., 'Folk-lore elements in the medieval drama', *Folk-lore*, lxiii (1952), 65–78.

Brown, A., 'The study of English medieval drama' in *Medieval and linguistic studies in honor of Francis Peabody Magoun, Jr.*, ed. J. B. Bessinger, Jr., and R. P. Creed (London, 1965).

Chambers: Chambers, E. K., *The mediaeval stage* (Oxford, 1903), 2 vols.

Chambers, E. K., 'Medieval drama' in *English literature at the close of the middle ages* (Oxford, 1945).

Chambers, E. K., *The English folk-play* (Oxford, 1933, repr. 1969).

The Chester plays, Part I, ed. H. Deimling, E.E.T.S. E.S. 62 (1892, etc., 1968) and Part II ed. Matthews, E.S. 115 (1916 for 1914, etc., 1968).

The ancient Cornish drama, ed. and trans. E. Norris (Oxford, (1859), 2 vols. See also *The Cornish ordinalia* on p. 444.

Two Coventry Corpus Christi plays, ed. H. Craig, E.E.T.S. E.S. 87 (1902, 2nd edn. 1957).

Craddock, L. G., 'Franciscan influences on early English drama', *Franciscan Studies* (1950), 383–417.

Craig, H., *English religious drama of the middle ages* (Oxford, 1955).

Curtius, E. R., *European literature and the Latin middle ages* (Berne, 1948), trans. R. Trask (London, 1953).

The Digby plays, ed. F. J. Furnivall, E.E.T.S. E.S. 70 (1896, 1967).

Everyman and medieval miracle plays, ed. A. C. Cawley (London, 1956, etc.).

Frank, G., *The medieval French drama* (Oxford 1954, 1967).

Fry, T., 'The unity of the *Ludus Coventriae*', *St. in Phil.*, xlviii (1951), 527–70.

Gardiner, H. C., *Mysteries' end: an investigation of the last days of the medieval religious stage* (New Haven and London, 1946, 1967).

Greg, W. W., 'Bibliographical and textual problems of the English miracle plays', *The Library*, 3rd series, V (1914), 1 ff., 168 ff., 280 ff., 365 ff.

Gwynn, A. 'The end of medieval drama in England', *Studies* (Dublin), xxxvi (1947), 283–95.

Harbage, A., *Annals of English drama, 975–1700* (Philadelphia and London, 1940), rev. S. Schoenbaum (1964), supplement S. Schoenbaum (1966).

Hardison, O. B., *Christian rite and Christian drama in the middle ages* (Baltimore Md., 1965).

Hildburgh, W. L., *English alabaster carvings as records of the medieval religious drama* (Oxford, 1949).

The Holkham Bible picture-book, ed. W. O. Hassall (London, 1954).

James, M. R., trans., *The apocryphal New Testament* (Oxford, 1924).

Kahrl, S. J. and Cameron, K., 'The N-town plays at Lincoln', *Theatre Note-book*, xx (1965–6), 61–9.

Kolve, V. A., *The play called Corpus Christi* (London, 1966).

Loomis, R. S., 'Lincoln as a dramatic centre' in *Mélanges offerts à Gustave Cohen* (Paris, 1950), 241–7.

McNeir, W. F., 'The Corpus Christi passion plays as dramatic art', *St. in Phil.* xlviii (1951), 601–28.

The Macro plays: The castle of perseverance; Wisdom; Mankind, ed. M. Eccles, E.E.T.S. 262 (1969).

Marshall, M. H., 'Aesthetic values of the liturgical drama' in *English Institute Essays: 1950,* ed. A. S. Downer (N. York, 1951), 89–115.

Medieval French plays, trans. R. Axton and J. Stevens, (Oxford, 1971). Includes *Mystère d'Adam* and *La Seinte Resureccion.*

M.E.D.: Middle English dictionary, ed. H. Kurath and S. M. Kuhn.

M.E.L.: Medieval English lyrics, ed. R. T. Davies (London, 1963, 1966).

Mill, A. J., *Mediaeval plays in Scotland* (Edinburgh and London, 1927).

Mirk, J., *Festial: a collection of homilies,* ed. T. Erbe, E.E.T.S. 96 (1905).

Non-cycle plays and fragments, ed. N. Davis, E.E.T.S. S.S. 1 (1970).

Owst, G. R., *Literature and pulpit in medieval England* (London, 1933; 2nd edn., Oxford, 1961).

Pächt, O. E., *The rise of pictorial narrative in twelfth-century England* (Oxford, 1962).

Prosser, E., *Drama and religion in the English mystery plays* (Stanford, 1961).

Salter, F. M., *Medieval drama in Chester* (Toronto and London, 1955).

Sarum breviary: Breviarium ad usum insignis ecclesiae Sarum, ed. F. Procter and C. Wordsworth (Cambridge, 1879–86), 3 vols.

The Sarum missal, ed. J. W. Legg (Oxford, 1916).

Shergold, N. D., *A history of the Spanish stage from medieval times until the end of the seventeenth century* (Oxford, 1967).

Smoldon, W. L., 'Liturgical drama' in *Early medieval music up to 1300* (*New Oxford history of music,* ii), ed. Dom A. Hughes (Oxford, 1954).

Southern. R., *The medieval theatre in the round* (London, 1957).

Stratman, C. J., *Bibliography of medieval drama* (Berkeley and London, 1954).

The Towneley plays, ed. G. England, E.E.T.S. E.S. 71 (1897, 1952).

The Wakefield pageants in the Towneley cycle, ed. A. C. Cawley (Manchester, 1958, 1963).

Wells, J. E., *A manual of the writings in middle English 1050-1400,* with nine supplements (New Haven, 1916–51).

Whiting, B. J., *Proverbs etc. before 1500* (London, 1968).

Wickham, G., *Early English stages 1300 to 1600:* i, 1300-1576 (London, 1959).

Williams, A. L., *The characterization of Pilate in the Towneley plays* (East Lansing, 1950).

Wilson, R. M., *The lost literature of medieval England* (London, 1952, 2nd edn. 1970).

Woolf, R. 'The effect of typology on the English mediaeval plays of Abraham and Isaac', *Speculum,* xxxii (1957), 805–25.

York plays, ed. L. T. Smith (1885, reissued N. York, 1963).

Young, K., *The drama of the medieval Church* (Oxford, 1933), 2 vols.

The Cornish ordinalia: a medieval dramatic trilogy, trans. M. Harris (Washington, 1969).

EPISODE[1]	YORK[2]	TOWNELEY[2]	CHESTER[2]	BEVERLEY[3]	CORNISH[4]
Creation and fall of Lucifer	I	I	I	I	1–48
Creation and fall of man	II–VI	Gap	II	II–V	49–416
Cain and Abel	VII	II	II	VI	417–633
Noah and the flood	VIII–IX	III	III	VIII	917–1258
Abraham and Isaac	X	IV	IV	IX	1259–1394
Moses and laws (and Exodus)	XI	VII VIII	V		1395–1898
Jesse/(Prophets)	XII	VII	V		
Annunciation	XII	X	VI	X	
Joseph	XIII	X	VI	?	
Salutation of Elizabeth	XII	XI	VI	?	
Nativity	XIV	XII, XIII	VI	XI	
Shepherds	XV	XII, XIII	VII	XII	
Herod and Three Kings	XVI, XVII	XIV	VIII, IX	XIII	
Presentation and Purification		XVII	XI	XIV	
Slaughter of Innocents	XVIII, XIX	XV, XVI	X	XV, XVI	
Jesus and Doctors	XX	XVIII	XI	XVII	
Baptism	XXI	XIX		XVIII	
Temptation	XXII		XII	XIX	
Woman taken in adultery	XXIV		XII		
Raising of Lazarus	XXIV	XXXI	XIII	XX	

[1] All are in *Ludus Coventriae*, and in this order, except those in brackets.
[2] Numbers are those of plays in editions listed on pp. 441 ff.
[3] See Chambers, ii, 340–1: a list only, of about 1520.
[4] Line numbers in edition listed on p. 441.

Episodes before the Passion

No mention of Lucifer in Cornish text except once only in stage direction after fifth day of Creation: *hic ludit Lucifer de caelo.*

Beverley (VII) and Cornish include 'Adam and Seth' (cf. n. 59).

Lud. Cov. includes 'Lamech' in 'Noah'.

Chester includes 'Abraham and Melchizedek' in 'A. and I.'

Towneley includes V 'Isaac' (blessing Jacob), VI 'Jacob' (renamed Israel).

Cornish includes 'three rods of grace'; Towneley calls VIII 'Pharaoh'.

Cornish includes episodes of which the theme, though not emphasized or exclusive, is that David and Solomon are transmitters of the Wood of the Cross.

Chester V includes 'Balaam and ass'.

Lud. Cov. includes 'Mother of Mercy' plays.

Beverley X is 'Salutation of our Lady', XI is 'Bedleem'.

Towneley includes IX 'Caesar Augustus'; *Lud. Cov.* includes 'Trial of Joseph and Mary'.

Chester VI includes 'Prophecy of Sybil' and 'Conversion of Emperor'.

Lud. Cov. and Chester X include 'Death of Herod'; York XVIII, Towneley XV and Beverley XV are separate 'Flight into Egypt'.

York includes XXIII 'Transfiguration'.

Chester XIII includes 'Healing of blind Chelidonius'.

NOTES

1. There is no title in MS for this section, nor any suggestion for one. *1* is written in right margin (p. 58). Jerome (c. 342–420), maker of the Latin bible, translated as 'Lucifer' (Latin: 'morning star') the metaphorical reference to the fall of the king of Babylon in Isa. xiv, 12 (Hebrew: 'bright morning star'). The Church Fathers interpreted as a reference to this passage Jesus's words in Luke x, 18 (A.V.), 'I beheld Satan as lightning fall from heaven,' and Lucifer seems thus to have come to be seen as the name of Satan before his fall. See also II Pet. ii, 4, Rev. xx, 1–2 etc. and Craig, 183. **2.** *2* is written in right margin and, in the left, a mark such as usually begins a new stanza. But these indications of a new section are not conclusive. There is no title and 'In . . . dight' is at the bottom of a page: no space is left, *Deus* being written there but not at the top of the new page, suggesting continuity. Though Chester and York both begin a new pageant at approximately this point, Towneley does not (p. 446). The Proclamation describes a second pageant beginning here, its subject being the creation of the world and fall of man. **3.** Heaven: *Piers Plowman* B. Prol. 14, 'a tower on a tofte'; *M.E.L.* no. 36, l. 24, 'When may I see thy tower? . . . Me longes to thy hall' (Richard Rolle). In pictorial representations of such episodes as occur in these plays, when God, e.g., is seated in heaven, heaven is often shown like a battlemented gallery at the back (Hildburgh and Anderson). **4.** Various representations of such a creature (a good one in Anderson, pl. 15b), sometimes also winged, sometimes with the head of a woman, sometimes looking like a dragon, can be found in art from late 13 c. J. K. Bonnell concludes that they were copied from stage representations and not vice versa (*Amer. Journ. Archaeology*, xxi (1917), 255–91). Cf. Chester cycle where, in this play, Demon says, 'A manner of an adder is in this place / That winges like a bird she has, / Feet as an adder, a maidens face— / Her kind I will take . . . / My adders coat I will put on.' **5.** The text in MS is continuous without any gap or title. The first letter of Abel's speech is rather more elaborate and touched with red. *3* is written in right margin and the pageant of Cain and Abel is the third in the Proclamation. It is a separate pageant in York and Towneley cycles but it is continuous with the Creation and Fall of Man in the second pageant of Chester (p. 446). **6.** There is no mark in MS to indicate a new stanza and it is doubtful whether there should be. The preceding stanzas in Cain and Abel are all varied and, in particular, the stanza immediately preceding this (p. 87, l. 22–p. 88, l. 5) comprises seventeen lines while the first eight lines of the first stanza (p. 86, ll. 6–13) comprise two unconnected quatrains. **7.** Jaw-bone: common but unscriptural. Apparently an English addition found in 9 c. in Old English literature and in ms illustrations from 11 c. See e.g. *Holkham*, fol. 5v and p. 67, and M. Schapiro, *Art Bulletin*, xxiv (1942). Covering up: less common and also unscriptural. See e.g. *Holkham*, fol. 5v and p. 68. **8.** *Introitus Noë* is written in the right margin opposite p. 92, l. 8, *Introitus* being underlined in red and *Noe* being in bigger letters touched with red, indicating, in my opinion, not so much the character himself as the pageant called 'Noah' (cf. explicits of 'Moses' and 'Jesse', p. 115 and also p. 119). **9.** Continuity of some kind between Cain and Abel and

NOTES

Noah is suggested by the place of the stage direction discussed in n. 8. But this new section begins on a new page in MS after a space at the end of the last page, has *Noe* written in bigger letters, touched with red, has a large red capital for *God* (and has *4* in the margin and constitutes a separate pageant in The Proclamation). **10.** The episode of Lamech killing Cain is widely found in European art, e.g. *Holkham*, fol. 6v and pp. 70–1; Craig, 65, 257–8. It attempts to explain the mysterious Gen. iv, 23–4. In *Holkham* the extreme wickedness of Lamech in capping his parricide (Gen. iv, 17–19) with a second murder is represented in the same scene as that in which God warns Noah of the punishment to come and Noah begins boat-building. Presumably the Lamech of this story was confused with Lamech, father of Noah (Gen. v, 28–9), as it appears that he was also, for example, in 'Of the life of Adam' in Caxton's *Golden Legend*. But the dramatist has used this episode, so related in tradition, to bring home Man's ripeness for destruction and to cover the time that passes while Noah is off stage ostensibly making his ark (p. 60). The York cycle has two separate plays, one for the warning and making of the ark, the other for the flood, but Towneley and Chester present both episodes in one (p. 446). **11.** Illustrated in *Holkham*, fol. 8 and pp. 74–6. The raven pecks at the head of a dead horse floating on the flood, and is painted black, which could signify evil. The dove is white, which could signify virtue. The question is how much meaning the illustrator or the dramatist understood these conventional representations to have. Certainly the dramatist does not explicitly draw out the potential meaning in these figures, viz. eating carrion, which is unnatural, the olive branch, symbol of peace and reconciliation, or Noah and his ark, symbols of Christ and his Church (pp. 63–4). **12.** The stage direction is written continuously from *Et* to *etc.* and underlined in red. Presumably *Abraham etc.* here is not so much the title of the pageant as the name of the character and what goes with him (cf. n. 8). The text is continuous, without gap; the same stanza is used in the Noah and Abraham sections. All other English cycles have a separate Abraham pageant (p. 446), but the only indication that a new section may begin with Abraham's speech, apart from *5* in the right margin, is that *Most* begins with a big red capital. **13.** MS clearly intends new section to begin here: a gap of one and a third pages follows Abraham. *Introitus Moyses* is underlined in red and centred at the top of the new page, *6* written in margin. **14.** The bush burning but unburnt prefigures Mary's bearing Christ while remaining a virgin (pp. 63–4 and cf. *M.E.L.* no. 34, l. 19). **15.** *7* in margin, gap of three quarters of a page and new start at the top here with a big red capital 'I' (l. 16). This pageant not found in other English cycles and should not be confused with the Prophets play which they include. This tries to dramatize the 'Tree of Jesse' motif, popular in European art from at least 11 c., wherein is represented the royal part of the family tree of Christ (Matt. i, 6–16, and p. 116, ll. 6–13) shown as physically growing out of Jesse who lies at the foot. The prophets are among the branches or at the sides, pointing to Christ, the 'flower' in whom the whole tree culminates. Not all the prophecies can be identified in the Scriptures so that it has been suggested that the play is derived from visual art (which represented the prophets but not their words). See J. K. Bonnell in *Pub. Mdn. Lang. Ass.*, xxix (1914), 327–40, Anderson, 36–7, and *Holkham*, fol. 10 and 10v and pp. 78–80. Play was made on *virga* and *virgo* and in some versions of the motif it is Mary in whom the 'tree' culminates so that in the Proclamation the seventh pageant (Of Jesse rote) is said to prophesy of Mary. In 16 c., the Aldermen of Lincoln each year provided gowns for the Kings in such an episode (Loomis, 247, Craig, 274). **16.** The priesthood of Christ is traditionally said to be 'after the Order of Melchisedec' who had no parents (Heb. vii, 3), for Jesse's line were not priests (Heb. vii, 14–22). This is,

449

therefore, an odd reference. Can it be to a belief mentioned by Hone in his *Apocryphal New Testament* (London, 1820, 17) citing an apocryphal gospel according to which Mary was of the tribe of Levi, her father being a priest called Joachim?   **17.** Jeremiah: cf. Jer. iii; xxiii, 5–8; xxxi, 31–40; xxxii, 37–42. Fairford church ('Prophets windows': p. 21, n. 2) has, on Jeremiah's scroll, parts of iii, 19, and xxxii, 17. Micah: cf. *Gospel of Nicodemus?* (James, 140); Fairford scroll quotes Zeph. iii, 9. Daniel: Fairford scroll quotes Ezek. xxxvii, 12. Habbakuk: cf. *Gospel Nicodemus?* (James, 140). Hosea: Fairford scroll quotes Hos. xiii, 14. Zephaniah: ditto Mal. iii, 5. **18.** see pp. 55–61. A new page is begun, leaving a third of the last empty, and beside *Christ* in the left margin is a more elaborate double sign. *8* is written on the right. **19.** At *Contemplatio says* on p. 121 there is no break in the text and no big capital for *Sovereignes*, but *9* in right margin. The next section of the action, however, begins on new page with speech of Joachim in the Temple. This has large red capital: space left empty for two lines at bottom of last page. The Presentation comprises some two hundred and seventy-five lines in the two stanza forms riming, a, b, a, b, b, c, b, c, and a, b, a, b. At *After this, Contemplatio continues* on p. 121, he does so without any sign of discontinuity though *10* is written on the right, part way down his speech. The action of Mary's Marriage, however, begins at top of new page with big red capital (and *10* repeated), after a gap of one and a half pages, but, on the other hand, continuity is suggested by the use in Contemplatio's speech and in the action apparently separated from it of the same long stanza with its two short lines.   **20.** Contemplatio begins speaking on a new page, after a four-line space at the end of the last, without any big red capital but with *11* in the margin. The subject of this new section is not found in other English cycles (p. 446) but is found in the morality play, the *Castle of Perseverance* (p. 20). There: 'The four daughters shall be clad in mantles, Mercy in white, Righteousness in red altogether, Truth in sad [dark] green, and Peace all in black' (*Macro plays*, 1, and cf. n. 3129, p. 200). The scene is a dramatization of a very old motif which developed under many influences, not least of Jewish and Christian commentaries on the Scriptures, particularly on Psalm lxxxv, 10–11, (A.V.), and of apocalyptic literature, e.g., IV Esdras (Vulgate), from at least 5 c. but especially in 12 c. (H. Traver, *Pub. Mdn. Lang. Ass.*, xl (1925), 44–92; alabaster representation in Anderson, pl. 6a; see S. C. Chew, *The virtues reconciled: an iconographic study* (1947).) Allegorical figures uncommon in English cycles (but cf. Mors, p. 198 and see p. 56). Centred at the top of this section and in red is written '1ᵘˢ'. *2* is written in red in left margin opposite l. 17, p. 123. Can it be the rubricator intended Contemplatio's speech to be divided in two, and, perhaps, spoken by two other characters? Did he think l. 11, p. 124, referred to these, viz. *Patriarchs and Prophets?* Greg proposed that the two characters were the *Angels and Archangels* of l. 13, but these stanzas are obviously spoken by earthly creatures, not by angels.   **21.** Nine orders of angels in medieval lore. Though all are, apparently, scriptural, pseudo-Dionysius the Areopagite (5 c. A.D.) first arranged them in three ranks, thus: 1, Seraphim, Cherubim, Thrones; 2. Dominations, Virtues, Powers; 3. Principalities, Archangels, Angels. The Virtues were placed by some in the lowest rank (e.g. Bartholomaeus Anglicus, *De proprietatibus rerum*, II). All nine orders take part in the Chester Fall of Lucifer play, one ms of which refers to ten orders: Lucifer and his kind were sometimes regarded as constituting the tenth.   **22.** I suggest two interpretations and prefer the second. 1. Rays: for this mode of representation see, e.g., Simone Martini's Annunciation in the San Marco, Florence, or Carlo Crivelli's in the National Gallery, London. The beams would, presumably, be represented by beams of wood and the business on stage would be difficult to manage convincingly. Anderson (132) proposes that small dolls were slid down three gilded wires. 2. Lights: however these were managed, they seem to be the only explanation of an item listed in an inventory of the Lincoln Cordwainers' Company, quoted H. Craig, *Pub. Mdn. Lang. Ass.*, xxxii (1917), 606: a 'great head gilded set with seven beams and seven glasses for the same, and one long beam for the mouth of the said head. Three great stars for the same with three glasses and a cord for the same stars.'   **23.** See *M.E.L.*, p. 373—(turtle) dove, cf. Song of Songs vi, 9, p. 371—chamber, cf. Psalm xix, 5. Play on the paradoxes of the Incarnation was conventional (cf. *M.E.L.*, no. 62).   **24.** This section begins on a new page after a gap of one and two-thirds pages. *Joseph* is written on the right where the name of the character is to be expected but a little more to the left than the names below and in larger and different letters with a big red capital. I suspect that this name is meant to serve also, therefore, as the title of this section, and I have so used it. The germ of this play may be found in both Matt. i, 19, 20, and Protevangelium xiii, xiv (James, 44), but this play differs from both in that Joseph is not dreaming when he meets the angel (nor is he in *Holkham*, fol. 12).   **25.** Proverbial, see Whiting. Literally, *to bend a bow* is to draw back its string, thus, figuratively, 'to set things going, to experience'. Though there need be none it is likely there is a sexual connotation, fetched out in p. 153, l. 4. Thus the French style is that of lechery, cf. *Handlyng Synne* (E.E.T.S. O.S. 119 (1901)), ll. 4151–2: 'French men sin in lechery / And English men in envye.'   **26.** Section begins at top of page with big red capital for *But, 13* in margin, and after leaving half of last page empty. **27.** An MS puzzle. Block transcribes *I cast (?)* and notes, correctly, 'a small stroke between the *j* and *cast* as if the scribe had begun to write *jn*'. (Cf. l. 4 *in hast* (?).)   **28.** Cf. Caxton's *Golden Legend* (Of the Nativity of Saint John Baptist): John moved 'in his mother's womb in making to our Lord reverence'. **29.** Cf. *M.E.L.*, pp. 377 and 378, and no. 144, ll. 27–8: 'high throne regal / Of Godes celsitude', and no. 104, l. 33: 'true tabernacle of virginity'.   **30.** These three lines written in MS at foot of page with mark for insertion as alternative (*si placet*) to twenty-eight lines here omitted because they concern Mary and Joseph's leaving which is inconsistent with lines beginning 'Mary with Elizabeth' below. **31.** Contemplatio introduced the Mother of Mercy sequence on p. 120 and there mentioned this *conclusion* (p. 146, beginning of speech) which he is now speaking and which was to follow the *meeting with Elizabeth, in few wordes talked that it should not be tedious*. This *conclusion* began with reference to the *Ave, Maria* and now ends with the singing of another of the Church's psalms to Mary, *Ave, Regina caelorum*.   **32.** Last section ends at very bottom of preceding page and this begins at top without big red capital for *Avoid* but with more elaborate sign in margin and *Den* in larger letters of different kind on right. It is, however, at *Hic intrabit pagetum* on p. 148 that a new section is begun unmistakably, at top of new page with big red capital and *14* in margin, and after a space of some three or four lines at the end of last page. For these reasons and because the metre is different, it has been suggested that these opening words of the summoner (referred to as his 'prologue') were separately conceived and, moreover, copied into MS after the pageant beginning on p. 148 (J. A. Bryant, *Journal Eng. and Germ. Philol.*, lii (1953), 340–5). But their tone and content is the same as that of ll. 19–30, p. 152, which are also addressed to 'sirs': these latter lines are in the metre of the pageant and it is not argued that they are a later addition. In both, it could be that the summoner speaks to other actors, but, bearing in mind the number of people referred to in his prologue, it is more likely that he speaks to the audience, pretending that particular people are John Jordan and Malkin Milk-duck. He may have moved between a raised stage (scaffold or wagon, and where Episcopus is seated) and the playing space around, and gone among the audience itself. Among them he could create a great and diverting stir as Herod did at Coventry (pp. 38–9). Whether he actually collected money for the players at l. 19, p. 148, and l. 27 p. 152, as has been suggested, seems to me possible but uncertain (p. 35). I take it that *Den* is the name of the summoner, which is odd, for he is called *Sim Summoner* on p. 152. A summoner was an officer of the ecclesiastical court of Bishop or Archdeacon. For other examples of this conventionally detestable type see Chaucer's *Canterbury Tales*. (See also L. A. Haselmayer, *Speculum*, xii (1937), 43–57.)   **33.** Begins new page with big red capital after half-page space, *15* in margin, and *Joseph* in bigger letters of different kind.   **34.** The unscriptural and common episode of the midwives derives ultimately from *Protevangelium* (James, 46–7) where Zelomy is unnamed. (In Mirk's version of the story she is Zebel (p. 23).)   **35.** For the possibility that the damaged hand was represented in the play artificially and slipped onto the actor's hand (and not only mimed) see Anderson, 139, and *Holkham*, fol. 12v and pp. 88–9.   **36.** Some two lines of the last written page and the whole of next folio are left blank. This section begins with big red capital and *16* in margin. There is much evidence of revision by another hand up to the stage direction on p. 173. (a) In MS, l. 23, p. 172, to l. 3, p. 173, succeeds l. 4, p. 173, to l. 19 on p. 173, but they are re-ordered as I have printed them by 'A' written in the margin against the first, 'B' against the second, and 'C' against l. 20, p. 173. A speech for a third shepherd is wanting in the section lettered 'B'. It probably comprised a stanza to precede that beginning this section in MS because the last stanza of the section leads into a 'song' (that could be the Latin hymn 'Stella caeli extirpavit' or, possibly, 'Hail! flower of flowers' at l. 20, p. 173, or possibly some other), and the first refers to Boosdras (and is, therefore, presumably not spoken by Boosdras) as does the speech of the second shepherd at l. 15, p. 171, where it is preceded by the speech of Boosdras who is 'Primus pastor'. Moreover l. 4, p. 173, would make best sense if it referred to a prophecy just made. It is Block's opinion that section 'A' was intended to replace this stanza since its character is different, and, in that it uses the same kind of devices as a much longer comic dialogue in the Chester 'Shepherds' play, may be a borrowed interpolation. But there is no other reason to think it was derived from Chester for there are no exact verbal similarities. (b) At the beginning of The Shepherds before l. 21, p. 170, is written 'Angelus ad pastores dicit Gloria in excelsis deo,' and 'Gloria . . . deo' is crossed out in what Block thinks is a different ink, but that it is different is not clear to me. It may be revision by a later hand but it could be a change of mind by the original scribe when he found himself writing the English equivalent of the Latin in l. 21. (c) Ll. 23–27, p. 171, are altered to: 'thow I make lytyl noyse of this / I am an herde man that hattyht sayyng Amys / I herde spekyng of a chyld of blys / of Moyses in his lawe / Of a mayd a child xuld be borne.' Presumably the reviser wishes to avoid the unfruitful repetition of *Mo(y)se* which one might have suspected had crept in by some earlier mistake of a scribe were it not that, as the name of the shepherd, *Mo(y)se* rimes twice. (d) Some words are altered, e.g. *sheen* l. 8, p. 171, is crossed out and *bryght* written above etc.   **37.** Christ as a knight defeating the devil in battle is a common motif—sometimes he rides the horse of the cross as he does: e.g. the Old English *Dream of the Rood* and *Piers Plowman*, B xviii and xix, and R. Woolf, *Rev. Eng. st.*, xiii (1962).   **38.** Begins at top of new page with big red capital, *18* in margin, and after one-third of last page left empty. *Herod*, however, is written normally. Matt. ii, 1–16, refers to nameless wise men, but within five centuries there developed a tradition of three Kings with such names and provenance as these: cf. Psalm lxxi, 10, (A.V. lxxii, 10), 'Reges Tharsis et insulae munera offerent; reges Arabum et Saba dona adducent.' Mirk, 48–9, mentions no names but explains, 'These three kings were of the lineage of Balaam that prophesied how that a star should spring of Jacob [cf. p. 177, l. 2; p. 181, ll. 1–4; and Num. xxiv, 17]; and though they were no Jews of kind [by nature] nevertheless they had heard by ancestry of the star. . . . . Then upon Christmas night, the same time that Christ was born, as they were ifere [together] disputing of that star, a star came to them brighter than any sun and in the star a fair child . . . and said thus to them: "[Offer to the king of the Jews] and I will be your guide." [They offered] gold and incense and myrrh, acknowledging by the gold that he was king of all kings, and by incense that he was very God, and by myrrh that he was very man that should be dead and laid in grave without rotting.' **39.** I note here all the instances in which I incorporate revisions. Otherwise my text restores the erasures as far as possible, and I indicate them as such only when they are difficult to read: p. 178, l. 7: *lik a* written over erasure; p. 178, l. 14: *leveris* erased: may read *loveris* (?); p. 178, l. 25: *bedde* (?); p. 180, l. 7: *ginny* altered to *wonyt*. **40.** Cf. *Harley lyrics*, ed. G. L. Brook (Manchester, 1948), 49, l. 41. **41.** Begins top new page, after quarter page empty, with big red capital, *Simeon Justus* in larger and different letters, and *19* in margin. **42.** Begins top new page, after quarter page left empty, with big red capital and *20* in margin. But *Senescallus* is not distinguished. A reviser has made many alterations (which I disregard) on pp. 193, 194. **43.** Death, so personified, is conspicuous in the European motif of the Dance of Death, increasingly common from later 14 c. through a period intensely absorbed with mortality. The motif was embodied in semi-dramatic performances in continental churches and variously in pictorial art. Death's part is that of unpredictable, indiscriminate and unavoidable arrester of all men without exception. He had appeared earlier in one known play in English, *The Pride of Life* (mid-14 c.? see *Non-cycle plays*), and appears contemporaneously in the *Castle of Perseverance* (Craig, 343–8; my pp. 20, 56), not to mention homiletic literature (Owst, 531). **44.** New section begins at top of page, after two and a quarter empty, with more elaborate red double sign but no big red capital and no special treatment of the first actor's name. *21* is written in margin. **45.** Both omitted pageants begin on new pages after gaps and the second has *23* in the margin. The first begins in a hand other than that of the principal scribe and on an interpolated folio, which doubtless explains the absence of *22*. The stanza throughout both, however, is a, b, a, b, a, b, a, b, c, d, d, d, c. **46.** Begins on new page after two and one-third pages empty, with big red capital, *Jesus* normal, *24* in margin. L. 1 is written in larger letters continuous and uniform with the title (*Hic . . . deprehensa*) from which it is separated only by a large version of the red sign that usually begins stanzas. P. Meredith has brilliantly maintained it is with the latin text in the first line that the playwright begins a sermon, and that this is how the play should be understood throughout (*Medium Aevum*, xxxviii (1969), 38–54). **47.** A kind of sermon-ending (p. 45) in which Jesus not only steps outside the illusion or 'game' of the play and addresses the audience (pp. 48–9), but also, very oddly, steps outside himself, for he refers to God who died in l. 27 as if it were someone other than himself. For this reason, presumably, another hand has altered *Jesus* to *Doctor*. **48.** Begins top new page, after two-page space, with big red capital and *25* in margin. **49.** Begins top new page, after space of one or two lines at end of last, *26* in margin, but no big red capital, and *Demon* normal. Dividing stanzas in this section is not straightforward. There are some obvious forms such as the quatrain, a, b, a, b, p. 235, ll. 14–17, or the octave, a, b, a, b, b, c, b, c, p. 236, ll. 4–11, and these the scribe has so indicated. But he has also indicated two stanzas in ll. 6–13, p. 235, whereas the ear is aware of one, and three stanzas in l. 18, p. 235, to l. 3, p. 236, whereas the ear is aware that all three are linked, though in different ways. Equally, what may be eight-line stanzas in ll.

28, p. 236 to l. 7, p. 237, and line 8, p. 237, to l. 15, p. 237 (following pattern of twenty-four lines before), are manifestly linked, and are, perhaps, better understood as a series of linked quatrains. This is how the scribe has seen the last of these eight lines, as a pair of quatrains, but the first eight he has treated as one stanza! **50.** It was sometimes said that the object of the wedding of Joseph and Mary was to deceive the devil into thinking Jesus was an ordinary human being and not, being God, conceived by the Holy Ghost (e.g. Mirk, 46). **51.** Demon's promises are all sins deplored time and again in similar concrete detail by sermons and homiletic literature (Owst, chap. vii). **52.** *Holkham*, fol. 30; Mirk, p. 81; Hildburgh, pl. xvid. **53.** There is no clue to why the pages of thin palaver in 'Council of Jews I' end here suddenly with two abrupt, extra-metrical lines spoken by Caiphas and Annas. Although I do not see how, the reason may be connected with the fact that, immediately after, there continues for the rest of page in MS the same matter as in the first six lines of Peter's speech on pp. 248–49; but preceded by *here entereth the apostle Peter and John the Evangelist with him*, all of which is cancelled and a folio interpolated on which is written (by the same hand as the main part of MS but writing better than in the immediate context) from Jesus's speech, 'Friendes, behold' to the last of these six lines of Peter's. 'He shall cause the blind, etc.' starts a new page again. **54.** The hymn sung in the Palm Sunday procession (*Thesaurus hymnologicus*, ed. H. A. Daniel (1855), i, 215–16); an English translation by William Herbert of early 14 c. in *M.E.L.*, no. 29. **55.** Opposite speech of Jesus beginning 'Oh! Jerusalem' is written 27, but the only other indication of division here is that *O* at its beginning is a little larger and more elaborate than usual. **56.** Several signs in MS of a scribe's changing his mind about what to include next, and, in all likelihood, therefore, evidence of the compiler himself changing his mind in shaping his work. (Further evidence lies in Demon's reference on p. 236, to the Magdalen episode as having already happened.) At bottom of page below 'Some way we shall find thereto', is stage-direction *here Judas cometh into the place*, followed by *Jesus* as the name of next speaker. Both are crossed out. Beneath are alternative catchwords (i.e. indications of what is to be found on next page): *now counterfeited* (crossed out: cf. Judas's speech on p. 261); *mine heart is right* (crossed out: cf. Jesus's speech on p. 259); *as a cursed*, and with this the text does continue. It does so on a separate group of pages (quire O) which are of different paper and in a hand with slightly different features from that in the pages on either side. The last fifteen lines or so on this group of pages are spaced wider than usual as if the scribe were hoping to fill the pages out, and one and a quarter pages are left empty. The conclusion is that the compiler here later included a section he had not originally intended and which he wrote out for this purpose. **57.** Opposite next few lines *28* is written: no other signs of division. **58.** Figure characteristic of tradition of medieval affective piety in which, e.g., Song of Songs was interpreted as the love-song of Christ for the soul. (*M.E.L.*, p. 22, and no. 45, ll. 95–8; p. 46 above.) **59.** According to the apocryphal *Acts of Pilate* (James, 126–8) the dying Adam sent his son Seth to the gates of paradise to secure oil from the tree of mercy for his anointing in sickness, but he was told he could not have it until the Son of God came on earth when he would anoint with it all believers. **60.** Luke xxii, 42–3, represents Jesus praying the Father 'to remove this [metaphorical] cup from me' (Vulgate: *calicem*) and an angel appearing 'unto him from heaven, strengthening him'. According to Pächt (57–8) the artist of the St. Albans Psalter (12c) was the first in England, in representing the agony in the garden, to show the angel coming down to comfort Jesus, and the first in Europe to show a chalice (or is it a lidded ciborium?) standing on a rock between Jesus and the angel. The dramatist's unscriptural interpretation of the chalice is quite consistent with this motif. For the angel's descent see p. 41 above.   **61.** After 'And also think' etc., p. 279, a couple of inches are left empty and all next page. On next two pages of MS are written ten quatrains spoken alternately by two 'doctors' to accompany a procession of saints. It is conceivable that this quite unrelated episode was intended to be an epilogue to the performance so far, but I think it unlikely, despite the reference to 'procession' at its beginning, that it was meant to be a prologue to the next section. This section, to which I have given the title, 'Passion II', begins at top of new page, *29* being written above. Two pages, originally empty, precede the text: they comprise the first of a new group of folios (quire S). The outer of these two pages has on it stains which correspond with those on the outer and last page of quire O (n. 56), so that, at some stage, these two quires must have been side by side. Block considers this stained leaf of quire S may, at some time, have been an outside leaf suggesting the separate use of the next section.   **62.** Indication of new section here in that *herodes Rex* is written, centred, in larger letters between stage-direction and 'Now cease of' etc., on p. 280, preceded by a paragraph sign, the character heading being *herowdys*.   **63.** Presumably the Jews turn Jesus round several times, singing out these lines as in a children's game, and then one tugs at him, when they cry, 'Who was that?' This episode is a development of Luke xxii, 64, and there are variants in other cycles and in sermons. (Cf. J. Strutt, *Sports and pastimes of the people of England* (1833), 393–4, for a comparable game called 'Hot Cockles'.)   **64.** Opposite first four lines is written *30*: no more signs of division.   **65.** Opposite first lines Satan's speech, pp. 296–7, is written *31*; no more signs of division.   **66.** Opposite lines beginning 'For this is your' etc, p. 304, is written *32*: no more signs of division.   **67.** Forks are also used in an alabaster representation (Hildburgh, pl. xviic) to force the crown down, and in *Holkham*, fol. 29v.   **68.** Occurs all English cycles and Cornish (pp. 46, 51). See also, e.g., *Northern Passion*, E.E.T.S. O.S. 145 (1913 for 1912), 188–9, *Holkham*, fol. 31v. Hildburgh pp. 83–4 suggests that the binding of Christ to the cross in his pl. xviid records the way in which the crucifixion was managed in these plays. Anderson's pl. 19b shows Christ's hand grasping the nail as well as being loosely bound to the cross with rope.   **69.** Three Marys (who are named, p. 338) commonly attend at the cross and/or at the resurrection (*Holkham*, f. 36 and p. 141).   **70.** Block says (xiv–xv) that a change in colour of ink here and the fact that the writing becomes smaller suggest that the scribe paused. From here until p. 346 there are indications of a compiler at work with disparate materials (e.g. pp. 323–7). As a consequence, the second Passion play modulates into Resurrection Appearances without break (cf. p. 328 and n. 75).   **71.** Here *33* in margin: no more signs of division. Cf. *Stanzaic life of Christ* (E.E.T.S. 166 (1926), ll. 7805 ff.: 'Although no gospel speak of it / As Austin [Augustine] says now tell will I / And als how Nicodemus wit / Writes in his evangeley [gospel] / Austin says that Christ anon / As he had yolden the ghost on rood / His soul and godhead both alone / He went to hell for mannes good.' One of the exciting dramatic opportunities afforded by simultaneous staging (pp. 37 ff.) is seen at this point where Christ's soul, represented by another actor, goes down to hell while his body remains hanging dead on the cross at a different spot in the playing-space.   **72.** *34* in margin at lines beginning, 'The very child of God', p. 317: no more signs of division.   **73.** This 'pieta' episode occurs in no other English cycle and is a motif that seems to have come to England from France in early 15c.: J. Evans, *English art: 1307– 1461* (Oxford, 1949), 88. The descent or deposition from the cross, however, is a motif first found in England in 12 c. in the St. Albans Psalter (Pächt, 21–32) and the action of Nicodemus in this miniature, 'presenting Christ's body and holding it in a position which affords to the mourners the best opportunity of showing their affection and grief', supports the interpretation of the stage direction here as 'turning him'. **74.** *Harrowing of hell*, E.E.T.S. E.S. 100 (1907, 1961), lix, quotes a story, in an edition by Wynkyn de Worde of the *Gospel of Nicodemus*, about Syndonia, the girl who made the cloth bought by Joseph for the shroud and after whom he named it. **74a.** MS continuous but first *Caiphas* in paler ink, and in left margin in another hand and blacker ink than those of text *nota* and *Incipit hic*. **75.** Opposite lines beginning, 'Come forth Adam,' etc., *35* written in margin: no other signs of division. The Passion play has been extended by the compiler imperceptibly into these later episodes (cf. nn. 70 & 78). The Harrowing of Hell is a separate pageant in all other English cycles. Only in this cycle is it in two parts (for which there are parallels in non-English plays: Craig, 39). It derives principally from the second part of the apocryphal *Gospel of Nicodemus* (*Harrowing of hell*, E.E.T.S. E.S. 100 (1907, 1961), lx–lxviii) and is one of the most popular of Old English and medieval beliefs. For a splendid version see *Piers Plowman* B xviii. **76.** Cf. *Stanzaic life of Christ*, E.E.T.S. 166 (1926), ll. 7777 ff.: And if this well ne levet [believed] were / That Christ appeared first to Mary / It would seem he came not near / There she was that time witerly [certainly] / And that may no way levet be / That Christ did so unkindly [unnaturally] / Although man may not find nor see / Written in none evangely [gospel]. **77.** Both *meed* . . . *quest* and 'binding bears' are regarded as proverbial by Whiting, the latter indicating strength and courage, the former found also in the form 'gold and silver overcome all the world' (cf. five lines above). **78.** Three Marys, n. 69. Here is written *36*, and the only other evidence of an intended division is a slightly larger double sign to begin the stanza. But in the left margin has been added, by the hand responsible for some of the alterations elsewhere (nn. 36, 39), *finem prima die Nota* ('note the end on the first day'), which suggests not only that there was on one occasion a division here but, moreover, a major one. **79.** Title supplied from *explicit* at end, p. 346. Opposite speech is written *37*: no other signs of division. **80.** A new play begins at top of new page, after a gap of nearly two whole pages, with big red capital and *38* in margin. Title from Latin following. **81.** New play begins at top of page after one and a half left empty, with big red capital and *39* in margin. **82.** Perhaps an effigy was substituted for the actor and made to ascend (Hildburgh, 64–5). That hoisting machinery might be used is known from records: *Coventry Plays*, 93, 95, 99; G. Cohen, *Histoire de la mise-en-scène dans le théâtre religieux français du moyen âge* (Paris, 1926, rev. 1951), 152 ff. **82a.** Speech beginning 'Oh! you bretheren' obviously not said by angel. I have given it to Peter (Acts i). More space than usual is left between last line and this speech, and stanza sign at its beginning is rather more elaborate. **83.** New play begins at top of new page after half a page left empty, *40* in margin. Title from Latin following. **84.** The Assumption starts at top of new page with *41* in margin. It is written in a hand different from the rest of MS on an interpolated quire (pp. 57–8), of which the first folio is left empty before this play begins on the second. **85.** 'I believe that a combination of the Coronation with the Assumption was rare in medieval art, excepting that of England.' (Hildburgh 68.) **86.** New play begins at top of new page, with big red capital, after the first page of this new quire left empty, the usual hand beginning again, and *42* in margin. Title from Latin following. **87.** Christ was expected on Doomsday to come in the clouds (Mark xiii, 26–7) but how was this descent achieved here? Hoisting apparatus was certainly known (n. 82). On the other hand, on p. 369, God the Son is throned in judgement, presumably on a raised platform (p. 42 and n. 3), and presumably in Heaven, since Peter is instructed to open the gates of Heaven and bring the righteous to him. Perhaps when Peter opens the gates he discloses God and Heaven, hidden until then. The gates may have been like those of a battlemented castle (Anderson, 126–7). At Coventry in 16 c. the Doomsday pageant included angels dressed in gold with wings, God dressed in a (white?) leather coat and three yards of red sendal and gloves, the good and bad souls in white and black, respectively, the bad souls with blackened faces, and a 'hell-mouth' or 'hell-head', at which fire was kept burning, doubtless the traditional gaping jaw of a sea-monster, cavern-like, leading into the bowels of the earth. (*Coventry plays*, 99–102.) At Lincoln in 1564 among properties mentioned is a 'Hell-mouth, with a nether chap' (Chambers, ii, 379). (Hell-mouth, see e.g. W. front Lincoln Cathedral, and Jonah ii, 2, Job xli; Christ in judgement, see e.g. S. porch Lincoln Cathedral.) **88.** Since the Ascension and Pentecost pageants are brief and the Doomsday pageant, up to this point, is spare and unelaborate (and has no comic devilish by-play in it as has Towneley), I have concluded that only some twenty or thirty lines are missing. I have supplied them from Chester (in the E.E.T.S. edition, ll. 609–20 and the stage-direction which follows l. 676) and York (the last stanza and stage direction). **89.** This is the only play in a commonplace book of the last half of 15 c. and earlier 16 c., commonly known as the 'Book of Brome' because its home was once Brome Hall in Suffolk. It is now in the Library of Yale University. At least two different writers have recorded in it, for example, assorted verses, which are chiefly didactic, financial accounts, a saint's life, a recipe and various legal documents as well as this play. 'Abraham and Isaac' is written with some care and the exceptional irregularity of its verse forms suggests that what the writer was recording had already been grossly distorted in transmission (pp. 62–3). Previous editors, much more knowledgeable than I, especially Holthausen, Manly and, most recently, N. Davis, have proposed numerous emendations, particularly where lines have been lost, but I have felt it best for me to be more generally conservative. We do not know where the play was performed. (See *Non-cycle plays*.) **90.** This play is from the cycle performed at Chester on pageant-wagons (pp. 38–41). For its place in the cycle see p. 63 and for manuscripts see pp. 47 and 53. For theories about authorship and sources see Craig and Salter: that there are detailed resemblances between this as well as other Chester plays and the French *Le Mistère du Viel Testament* is certain. (See *Chester plays*.) **91.** For the point that Expositor is making see the much wider exposition in Heb. vii–x. Under the old law, in Old Testament times (l. 5), when Melchizedek and Abraham actually lived (l. 6), it was beasts that had to be sacrificed (and their blood spilt) as an offering to God (ll. 7–8). But at the Last Supper on the first Maundy Thursday (ll. 11–12) Christ commanded that henceforth in New Testament (= covenant) times (l. 2), following man's redemption by Christ's shedding his blood on the cross (l. 9), it should be bread and wine that were offered in God's honour (ll. 23–8), as they are in the Sacrament of the Mass. Offering the sacrifice after the Consecration of bread and wine, the celebrant begs God 'to accept them as thou wast pleased to accept the offerings of thy good servant Abel, and the sacrifice of our father Abraham, and that which thy great priest Melchisedech sacrificed to thee'. (*Sarum missal*, 223.) **92.** Although the manuscript containing this play is now in the Library of Trinity College, Dublin, there is nothing about the play, though there may be one feature of the manuscript, to connect it with Ireland. On the other hand, the manuscript is a commonplace book containing, among other entries, various verses, some political, and one about the battle of Northampton, as well as lists of officials of that town, and it is the conclusion of Professor N. Davis, after a study of its language, that 'it is likely enough that the play was composed in or near Northampton itself' (lvii). The handwriting is mid-15 c. and it is the only play in the manuscript. (See pp. 55, 66 and *Non-cycle plays*.) **93.** This play is from the cycle recorded in a manuscript that once had Towneley Hall in Lancashire for its home and is now in the Huntington Library in California (p. 53). There is little doubt that the cycle was performed at Wakefield and probably on pageant-wagons (pp. 38–41). For its place in the cycle see p. 446 and for sources and analogues see Craig. There are several gaps in the manuscript, one of which, comprising the loss of two folios, means that the end of this play is missing, as is the beginning of the next. (See *Towneley plays* and *Wakefield pageants*.) **94.** A traditional question frequently asked in medieval literature of the kind called 'in contempt of the world', which was haunted by a sense of life's mutability. For this specific convention, 'ubi sunt', cf. the Latin 'Cur mundus militat', probably of 11 c. or 12 c. (*M.E.L.*, n. 83, p. 339) and, ultimately, Baruch, iii, 16–19. See J. E. Cross, *Rev. Eng. St.*, ix (1958), 1–7; *M.E.L.*, n. 8, p. 311. **95.** This play is from the cycle performed at York on pageant-wagons (pp. 38–41). For its place in the cycle see p. 446, and for the manuscript see pp. 52–3 and 65. For sources and analogues see Craig. (See *York plays*.) The name of the guild performing this play (that of the makers or sellers of parchment and the bookbinders) forms, in MS, a running title throughout, but the only title at the beginning is made by displacing the name of the first character from the usual position on the right to the middle, and there underlining it.